ASA Special Series No. 44

10 Years of Swiss Rules of International Arbitration

Nathalie Voser

Editor

Association Suisse de l'Arbitrage
Schweiz. Vereinigung für Schiedsgerichtsbarkeit
Associazione Svizzera per l'Arbitrato
Swiss Arbitration Association

JURIS

Questions About This Publication

For assistance with shipments, billing or other customer service matters, please call our Customer Services Department at:

1-631-350-2100

To obtain a copy of this book, call our Sales Department:

1-631-351-5430
Fax: 1-631-351-5712

Toll Free Order Line:

1-800-887-4064 (United States and Canada)

See our web page about this book:
www.arbitrationlaw.com

Printed in the United States of America
ISBN 978-1-937518-49-3

JurisNet, LLC
71 New Street
Huntington, New York 11743
USA
www.arbitrationlaw.com

TABLE OF CONTENTS

Panel 4: Swiss Rules in Practice: The Insiders' View

Panel 5: Perspectives from Users, Arbitrators and Counsel, and the Way Forward

Appendices

FOREWORD

On the occasion of the 10th anniversary of the Swiss Rules of International Arbitration, the ASA decided to devote its annual conference in January 2014 to this topic. I would also like to thank the ASA for having chosen this topic and having entrusted me as its Conference Chair and for its support in the organization of the conference.

This volume of the ASA Special Series contains the written versions of all the presentations given during this conference. Most of the contributions were based on the verbatim protocol which was prepared on the conference day and thus retain their informal speaking style.

In their 10 years of existence, the Swiss Rules have established themselves as modern arbitration rules, offering a user efficient and transparent arbitral proceedings. Probably the most distinguishing feature of the Swiss Rules with regard to the administration of the cases is their "light touch" as applied by the Swiss Chambers' Arbitration Institution, reserving however a supervisory function for its Court.

This present volume of the ASA Special Series is structured along the panels of the conference. The first panel addressed the history and the background of the Rules as well as their main characteristics. The second and the third panels explore the key features of the revised Swiss Rules, namely the consolidation and joinder provisions, the set-off and counter-claim provisions, the expedited procedure, provisional measures and the emergency arbitrator as well as provisions on confidentiality and settlement facilitation. While the fourth panel provided the insiders' view into how the Institution administers its cases, the fifth and last panel discussed the perspectives of the users, the arbitrators and counsel as well as their experiences with the Swiss Rules.

The contributors are all outstanding and experienced arbitration practitioners or administrators whose insights, experiences and perceptions were of great value for the conference. This volume containing their written contributions will be a welcome additional reference book for Swiss Rules arbitration in general and I would like to thank them all for their effort and for having adhered to a strict time line, which was necessary to publish this volume still during the 10th anniversary of the Swiss Rules.

My thanks also go to the Session Chairs: without their guidance and supervision of the panelists, the high quality of the present contributions would not have been possible.

Finally, a special thank you goes the Schellenberg Wittmer team consisting of Benjamin Gottlieb (*Associate*), and Dimitrij Euler (*Trainee*), who helped me with the organization of the conference, and, in particular, Julia Donchi (*Research Assistant*), who was in charge of editing the manuscripts and organizing the timely publication of this volume.

Zurich, October, 2014
Prof. Dr. Nathalie Voser
Member of the ASA Board and Conference Chair

ABOUT THE EDITOR

Nathalie Voser is a Partner in Schellenberg Wittmer's Dispute Resolution Group in Zurich and co-heads the firm's arbitration team. She often acts as arbitrator or counsel in arbitration and advises clients involved in complex multi-jurisdictional disputes. Her areas of specialization include general contract law, private international law (conflicts of laws), and international procedural law such as (pre-trial) attachment and recognition of foreign judgments and arbitral awards. Her practice focuses on construction and civil engineering projects, research and development, distribution and license agreements, joint ventures as well as mergers and acquisitions. She has particular expertise in the automotive, pharmaceutical and power production industries.

In 1988, Nathalie Voser graduated *summa cum laude* from the University of Basel and was admitted to the bar in Switzerland in 1990. In 1992, she became a *juris* doctor with *summa cum laude* and earned an LL.M. from Columbia University (New York) in 1994 with honors. In 2005, she received the *venia docendi* for private law, conflicts of laws, and comparative law and, in spring 2014, she was awarded the title of Professor in private law, arbitration law, private international law, and comparative law (*Titularprofessur*) by the University of Basel, where she regularly teaches courses in commercial arbitration and other areas of Swiss private law. Nathalie Voser is the author of many publications on general commercial law and international arbitration and currently also serves as Board member of the Swiss Arbitration Association and the Arbitration Institute of the Stockholm Chamber of Commerce.

ABOUT THE ASA PRESIDENT

Elliott Geisinger is a Partner in Schellenberg Wittmer's International Arbitration Group in Geneva. Since 1994, his practice has focused on international arbitration. He has acted as counsel and arbitrator in complex commercial disputes involving international construction contracts, consortia and joint venture agreements, sponsorship contracts, sales and distribution contracts, and consultancy contracts.

In addition, Elliott Geisinger has regularly represented clients in arbitration-related court proceedings, and several of his cases have been reported on in the official collection of Swiss Supreme Court cases and in arbitration journals. Contract management in large-scale construction projects is a further specialization of his. He has also advised Swiss corporations in investment disputes.

Elliott Geisinger has authored and co-authored several publications in the fields of international arbitration and private international law. He sat on the Arbitration Committee of the Geneva Chamber of Commerce and Industry from 1999 to 2003 and was elected to the executive board of the Swiss Arbitration Association in 2007, becoming Vice-President in 2010, and President effective 2014.

After graduating from the School of Law of the University of Geneva in 1986, where he also obtained a Master of Laws in 1990, Elliott Geisinger served as a teaching and research assistant in private international law from 1986 to 1992. He was a trainee and then an associate with another business law firm in Geneva before joining Schellenberg Wittmer in 1996 and becoming a partner in 2002.

ABOUT THE SESSION CHAIRS AND PANELISTS

Bennar Balkaya is a Lawyer based in Turkey and a member of the Board of Management of the Chartered Institute of Arbitrators (CIArb). She is also an Approved Faculty Member of the CIArb, tutor on international arbitration and a member of the CIArb Practice and Standards Committee. She holds LLB, LLM and postgraduate degrees from Marmara University, The Hague Academy of International Law, Istanbul Commerce University and the College of Law of England and Wales. She acts both as counsel and arbitrator, is specialized in international arbitration, international trade and sales transactions (focusing on CISG), and has represented her clients in numerous cases before and under the rules of the Swiss Chambers, ICC, LCIA, LMAA, HKIAC and *ad hoc* arbitrations, particularly in commodity trading and international sales of goods with particular focus on iron and steel industry, transportation, maritime and banking disputes. Bennar is the immediate past chairman of the CIArb European Branch, has served as the regional coordinating committee member of the ICC YAF Turkey, Middle East and Africa Section and global advisory board member of the ICDR Y&I.

Christopher Boog is a Partner in Schellenberg Wittmer's International Arbitration Practice based in Singapore and Zurich. He specializes in international arbitration, with a particular focus on construction and engineering disputes and disputes in the pharmaceutical industry. He has acted as counsel and arbitrator in a wide array of disputes relating to construction and civil engineering projects, oil & gas, telecommunication, post-M&A and joint venture disputes, consultancy and license agreements, research and development projects, the energy sector and the pharmaceutical, automotive and mining industries in *ad hoc* arbitrations and arbitrations involving a variety of institutional arbitration rules, including ICC, Swiss, LCIA, SCC, VIAC, WIPO, DIS and the Rules of the German Maritime Arbitration Association. Christopher Boog graduated with honors from the law schools of the Universities of Fribourg and Amsterdam, was a Visiting Scholar at Columbia Law School in New York and completed his PhD thesis in the field of international arbitration and arbitration-related civil procedure (*summa cum laude*; Professor Walther Hug Prize) at the University of Zurich. He regularly speaks and publishes in the fields of international arbitration, civil procedure law and sales and construction law and teaches international arbitration at the EBS Law School in Wiesbaden, Germany.

Ignacio de Castro is the Deputy Director of the WIPO Arbitration and Mediation Center in Geneva. Ignacio is a Spanish Lawyer and an English Solicitor. Ignacio holds an LL.M. degree in commercial and corporate law from King's College London. Before joining WIPO in 2002, he was on the legal staff at the United Nations Compensation Commission in Geneva and, prior to that, practiced in London in the areas of international arbitration and litigation with the law firms Baker & McKenzie and Freshfields Bruckhaus Deringer.

Daniele Favalli is a Partner in the Dispute Resolution Team of VISCHER. He represents Swiss and international clients in commercial disputes before Swiss and international courts and arbitral tribunals (Swiss Rules, ICC, AAA, etc.). He also serves occasionally as arbitrator. Moreover, he regularly represents insurance companies and its' insured in general insurance matters, court proceedings, and on issues of coverage. Daniele Favalli advises clients as well as general procedural and organizational issues of legal proceedings abroad, in particular, with respect to proceedings in the U.S. and Latin America (having worked as a practitioner in these regions). In addition to German and English, his working languages are Italian, Spanish, and French. He is a founding member and a member of the Academic Council of the Swiss Arbitration Academy, and has a teaching assignment as head coach of the VIS Moot Team of the University of Lucerne. He publishes and regularly lectures on arbitration, procedural law, and international private law. In 1994, Daniele Favalli graduated and in 1997, he was admitted to the Zurich bar. In 2000, he earned an LL.M. from the University of Texas at Austin.

Rudolf Fiebinger is a Partner of Fiebinger Polak Leon Attorneys-At-Law in Vienna, Austria, and head of the firm's litigation and international arbitration group. His practice is focused on international dispute resolution. He has significant experience as an arbitrator (co-arbitrator and chairman) and as counsel before arbitral tribunals in disputes covering all areas of substantive law. In 1979 Rudolf Fiebinger graduated from the University of Vienna and in 1978, after gaining admission to the bar, established his own legal practice in Vienna. Three years later, he co-founded Fiebinger Polak Leon Attorneys-At-Law in Vienna. Mr. Fiebinger served as a member of the Board of the Austrian Arbitration Association from 2001 through 2009, being its Chairman in 2008 and 2009. He is currently a Member of the ICC Court of Arbitration.

Michael Fischer is Legal Counsel at the Zurich Chamber of Commerce where his main responsibility is the case administration for the Zurich Secretariat of the Swiss Chambers' Arbitration Institution (The Swiss Chambers of Commerce Association for Arbitration and Mediation). In this function, he assists the Arbitration Court, which shall render decisions as provided under the Swiss Rules of International Arbitration. In 2012, Michael Fischer graduated magna cum laude from the University of Zurich. Before joining the Zurich Chamber of Commerce, he worked for three years in the legal and compliance departments of a leading international Swiss bank and for two years as an associate for a mid-sized law firm in Switzerland.

Philipp Habegger is a Partner at LALIVE in Zurich. He has acted in more than one hundred fifty international arbitrations under a variety of applicable arbitration rules and substantive laws both as counsel and arbitrator. His areas of expertise include agency and distribution, joint ventures, consortia, shareholder agreements, M&A, food and drugs, engineering and construction. Philipp Habegger has the distinct honour of being a Court Member of the ICC International Court of Arbitration. He serves as President of the Arbitration Court of the Swiss Chambers' Arbitration Institution (Swiss Rules) and is a former Vice-Chair of the Arbitration Committee of the International Bar Association. Philipp Habegger was educated at Zurich University (lic. Iur. 1989, Dr. iur. 1996) and the University of Chicago Law School (LL.M. 1994). He has working experience as a District Court law clerk and as attorney at Zurich and New York law firms. Philipp Habegger teaches international arbitration and international sales at the University of Zurich Law School and acts as a course director of the Swiss Arbitration Academy. Mr. Habegger is the author of many publications on international arbitration.

Christoph Hauser is an Associate of Fiebinger Polak Leon Attorneys-At-Law in Vienna, Austria. His practice is focused on international commercial arbitration and litigation. Mr. Hauser graduated from the University of Vienna in 2010 and joined Fiebinger Polak Leon Attorneys-At-Law at the beginning of 2012. He holds significant international experience and regularly handles cases based in an intercultural setting.

Pascal Hollander is a member of the Brussels bar since 1984 and a Founding Partner of Hanotiau & van den Berg in 2001. He represents clients in complex arbitration and litigation, and has acted in more as arbitrator (chairman of tribunals, sole arbitrator or co-arbitrator) in more than 80 mostly international disputes, in areas such as commercial distribution, corporate disputes, intellectual property, industrial projects & energy disputes, under the aegis of ICC, LCIA, SCC, Swiss Chambers, WIPO, CEPANI (Belgian Arbitration Center) or in UNCITRAL and ad hoc proceedings. Pascal Hollander regularly writes articles and gives lectures on these topics. He teaches arbitration law at the Professional School of the Brussels Bar. He received in 1984 his JD degree, magna cum laude, from the University of Brussels (ULB) and in 1986 a LL.M. from the University of Pennsylvania Law School. He is fluent in English, French and Dutch.

Christoph Müller is an Ordinary Professor at the University of Neuchâtel, Switzerland where he teaches contracts, torts, drafting and negotiating international commercial contracts as well as European and comparative private law. His practice is focused on international commercial arbitration. He regularly acts as arbitrator (mainly as chairman) and legal expert in international commercial arbitrations (ICC, Swiss Rules, LCIA, SCC, UNCITRAL, TAS, ad hoc). He has special expertise in disputes relating to international commodity sales, agency, distribution, transport, corporate law, finance and banking, joint ventures, intellectual property and private international law. He is a member of the ASA Board and a member of the Arbitration Court and the Court Special Committee under the Swiss Rules. In 1995, Christoph Müller graduated summa cum laude and two years later was admitted to the bar in Switzerland. In 2002, he became a juris doctor with summa cum laude and earned an LL.M. from Columbia University (New York) in 2000 with honours. From 2001 to 2006, Christoph Müller was an attorney-at-law in the arbitration team of two major commercial law firms in Zurich and Berne. Christoph Müller is also the author of many publications in his fields of research and in international commercial arbitration.

Francois Naef is Chairman of the Board of Merck Seron S.A. and Group General Counsel, Head of Legal and Compliance of Merck. Mr. Naef was previously Chief Administration Officer and Head of Human Resources, Legal and Communications of Merck Serono S.A after the acquisition of Serono by Merck in 2007. Francois Naef joined Serono in 1988 and held several positions within this company prior to its integration within the Merck Group, including Head of Human Resources, Legal and Communications and General Manager of Serono International S.A. Prior to joining Serono, Mr. Naef practiced as an attorney within the law firm Combes de Senarclens and the law firm Rossetti. Mr. Naef was the Chairman of the Geneva Chamber of Commerce Industry and Services from 2008 to 2012. He holds a qualification as an attorney-at-law from the State of Geneva, a law degree and a Master in European Law from the Geneva University.

Vladimir Pavić is an Associate Professor at the Faculty of Law, University of Belgrade, where he teaches private international law, arbitration, competition law and international business law. He is a recurrent Visiting Professor at University of Graz and Central European University and has taught courses at University of Pittsburgh and Pace University, New York. He currently serves as Vice-President of the Belgrade Arbitration Center and is a member of the State Council of the Republic of Serbia for Private International Law. He acted as arbitrator, counsel and expert witness in a number of ad hoc arbitrations and arbitrations organized under various institutional rules, and is listed in 2013 and 2014 Global Arbitration Review *The International Who's Who Legal* for Arbitration, as well as on the lists of arbitrators of institutional arbitrations attached to chambers of commerce in Serbia, Croatia, Montenegro and Macedonia. He has advised and acted in a number of cross-border litigations in both civil and common law jurisdictions. He holds his LL.B from the University of Belgrade, Faculty of Law (1994), and his LL.M. (1996) and S.J.D. (1998) from the Central European University, Budapest. He was a FCO Chevening/Soros Visiting Student at the Lincoln College, Oxford University (1996-7) and a researcher at the T.M.C. Asser Instituut, Den Haag (1996).

Wolfgang Peter is a Founding Partner of Python & Peter, where he heads a team specializing in international arbitration. He has acted as counsel or arbitrator in more than 220 international arbitrations under all major arbitral institutions and ad hoc. Cases involved disputes in the following industry sectors: energy (including supply price adjustments), telecom, pharmaceutical, heavy industry and automotive, banking and finance, subcontractor disputes, defense and military contracts. Moreover, he has been retained as counsel in numerous cross-border M&A deals. Wolfgang was engaged in corporate management for 15 years. In particular he served as CEO of the Breguet Watch Manufacturing Group. He published various articles on business law and international arbitration. His study on "Arbitration and Renegotiation of International Investment Agreements" was published by Kluwer. Wolfgang studied business administration, law and political sciences at the Universities of Lausanne, Geneva, Harvard and Frankfurt and is fluent in English, French and German.

Joya Raha was Legal Counsel in the Arbitration and Mediation Department of the Geneva Chamber of Commerce, Industry and Services from 2010-2014. In this role, she was in charge of the legal service of the Arbitration and Mediation Department, responsible for managing the administration of cases under the Swiss Rules of International Arbitration and Commercial Mediation. Ms. Raha also contributed to the promotion of arbitration and mediation as forms of dispute resolution in various fields—such as commodity trading—and frequently spoke at seminars and conferences. Ms. Raha previously worked for the Faculty of Law at the University of Geneva (2009-2010), as well as for one of the most prominent legal publishers in the United States (2007-2012) and a leading financial services law firm in Washington, D.C. (2007). Ms. Raha graduated from Tufts University with a Bachelor of Arts in Philosophy (2004) and earned her Juris Doctor from California Western School of Law (2008), where she was Editor-in-Chief of the Recent Developments section of the Journal of BioLaw and Business and was awarded the E. Donald Shapiro prize for outstanding paper in law and medicine (2008). Ms. Raha is admitted to the New York bar.

Thomas Rohner is a Partner and member in the litigation/arbitration group of Pestalozzi in Zurich, Switzerland. He has represented multinational corporations and individuals in numerous complex both national and international litigation and arbitration matters involving various industries. Thomas Rohner further regularly sits as an Arbitrator in proceedings under various rules and is a lecturer on international arbitration at the University of Administrative Sciences at Speyer/Germany. He is the author of various publications on international arbitration and on litigation topics. Thomas Rohner is a graduate of the University of St. Gall (lic.iur., 1998; Dr.iur., 2002, with a doctoral thesis on insolvency law). In 2003, he graduated from the University of Chicago Law School (LL.M.). Thomas Rohner served as a law clerk at a Swiss district court. In 2000, he was admitted to the bar. From 1997 until 2005, Thomas Rohner served as a part-time judge at a Swiss district court. In addition, he was a temporary vice-president of this court on a full-time basis in 2001. Prior to joining Pestalozzi, Thomas Rohner worked as an international associate for a major law firm in Washington DC.

Frank Spoorenberg is a Partner with Tavernier Tschanz in Geneva, where he is the co-head of the arbitration and commercial litigation group. He acts as Counsel before arbitral tribunals and as co-arbitrator, sole arbitrator and chairman. His cases are related among others to M&A, joint ventures, distribution, agency, service agreements and to international sales. His industry experience includes among others telecommunications, trading, machine industry, construction, oil and gas, pharma, sport industry and real estate. He has published in the area of contract and arbitration law. Before focusing on international arbitration and commercial litigation, Mr. Spoorenberg developed a strong expertise in M&A, financing, general corporate and commercial contracts. In 1993, he received an LLM Degree from the College of Europe in Bruges (Belgium). He graduated from the University of Fribourg (Switzerland) in 1991. He is a member of the Board of the Swiss Arbitration Association and vice-chairperson of the Arbitration Court of the Swiss Chambers' Arbitration Institution.

Ruth Stackpool-Moore is an Australian and UK qualified lawyer working as Managing Counsel of the Hong Kong International Arbitration Centre (HKIAC). She oversees the administration of arbitrations by Counsel at the HKIAC and works to promote the use of Hong Kong arbitration and other forms of dispute resolution worldwide. She is a frequent speaker on arbitration-related issues as well as the benefits of resolving disputes in Hong Kong and has published a variety of articles on the same topics. Prior to joining the HKIAC in 2013, Ruth had six years' experience in private practice working in the international arbitration and dispute resolution practice groups for law firms in London, Paris and Sydney, advising clients on a wide range of proceedings conducted under many of the most recognised sets of institutional rules of arbitration as well as associated national court proceedings in civil and common law jurisdictions. She also provided advice regarding the formulation and drafting of arbitration and dispute resolution clauses in commercial contracts, including multi-party and multi-contract situations.

Bertrand Stoffel is a Trainee at the law firm Schellenberg Wittmer in Zurich and a PhD candidate at the University of Zurich. He studied at the University of Zurich and the University of Copenhagen and was a graduate research trainee at McGill University, Montreal. He has worked as a research and teaching assistant in private, European and commercial law at the University of Zurich, with a focus on contract law. He has also participated in a major Swiss National Science

Foundation research project. The research team worked on a new draft for the General Part of the Swiss Code of Obligations (CO 2020) and has recently published its results. Bertrand Stoffel publishes and speaks in the fields of contract law and civil procedure and teaches law at the FFHS College in Basel, Switzerland.

Rolf Trittmann has been a Partner in Freshfields Bruckhaus Deringer since 1993 and works in their Frankfurt office. He is a member of the dispute resolution practice group and specialises in litigation, arbitration and distribution law. Rolf has acted as counsel as well as arbitrator in numerous large scale civil disputes before courts as well as arbitral tribunals, in particular post M&A matters and commercial disputes. He has advised industrial clients in several sectors with an emphasis on the automobile industry on the structuring of their distribution networks in Europe. Rolf was born in Frankfurt/Main, Germany, in 1958. He completed his legal education at the University of Frankfurt as well as Berkeley (LLM) and holds the degree of doctor of laws (Dr iur) from the University of Frankfurt/Main. He also was assistant to Prof Fikentscher at the University of Munich. Rolf is the author of a number of articles and publications on litigation, arbitration and distribution law. He is member of the ICC Court for Arbitration representing Germany and heads the advisory board of the German Institution of Arbitration (DIS). He is a frequent speaker at conferences in the fields of arbitration, litigation and distribution law, is co-editor of the German Arbitration Journal (SchiedsVZ) and honorary professor at the University of Frankfurt. Rolf joined Freshfields Bruckhaus Deringer in 1989. He speaks German and English.

Vera Van Houtte holds a Dr. Juris degree from the University of Leuven in Belgium and a LL.M. from Harvard Law School. She is specialised in several areas of law: construction and engineering, industrial projects, public procurement, and energy law as well as arbitration. From 1989 until the end of 2012, she was a Partner at the Brussels office of the Benelux law firm Stibbe. She was involved in major construction and renovation projects in Belgium as well as abroad, acting as counsel and litigator for engineering firms, contractors, developers and their clients, both private enterprises and public authorities. From international construction work, she moved into international arbitration, first as counsel, later as arbitrator. Since retiring from Stibbe, she acts exclusively as an arbitrator (ICC, ICSID, LCIA, DIAC, UNCITRAL, ad hoc). She is a Vice President of the ICC

Court of Arbitration, a Court member of the JAC, a member of the board of the AAA and a member of the board of trustees of the DIAC.

Marco Villiger obtained his legal qualifications in 2000 from the University of LZurich. In 2002, he joined FIFA and acted as Head of Disciplinary until after the 2006 FIFA World Cup GermanyTM. Since 2007, Marco Villiger has been Director of the FIFA Legal Affairs Division. In this capacity, he is currently responsible for the four departments of the Legal Affairs Division: Players' Status (taking care of all international transfer disputes, player's agents), Commercial Legal (Sponsorship agreements, licensing agreements, broadcast agreements, bidding procedures), Disciplinary (doping, suspensions, irregular betting) and Corporate Legal (compliance, litigation, general contracts). Marco Villiger is also a teacher for sports law at the University of Zuric (MASIO), Member of IOC entourage commission and Board member of FIFA Ticketing pty.

Markus Wirth is a Senior Partner in the Litigation and Arbitration practice group of Homburger in Zurich, Switzerland. For many years he has focused on international arbitration. As counsel, he has represented Swiss and foreign companies as well as foreign governments in numerous international arbitration proceedings in Switzerland and elsewhere. Today he acts primarily as an arbitrator. As arbitrator he has served in some 150 international arbitrations with seats in Europe, North America and Asia, in the majority as chairman of the panel or as sole arbitrator, under a variety of institutional rules and in ad hoc proceedings. Chambers Global (editions 2011 | 2012 and 2013) lists Markus Wirth as one of the Most in Demand Arbitrators globally. Mr. Wirth is a former president and honorary president of the Swiss Arbitration Association, a member of the ICC International Court of Arbitration, a fellow of the Chartered Institute of Arbitrators, London, and on the arbitrators' list of several arbitration institutions. He is also a lecturer on arbitration in the University of Zurich's postgraduate programme in international business law and he regularly publishes in the field of international commercial arbitration. Mr. Wirth graduated lic. iur. and Dr. iur. from the University of Zurich and received an LL.M. from the University of Toronto.

ASA CONFERENCE
10 Years of Swiss Rules of International Arbitration
31 January 2014, Basel

Programme

9:00 – 9:15	WELCOME ADDRESS AND INTRODUCTION TO THE CONFERENCE TOPIC	**Elliott Geisinger** Vice President of ASA – Swiss Arbitration Association, Schellenberg Wittmer Ltd, Geneva
9:15 – 9:45	PANEL 1 "PAST AND PRESENT": BACKGROUND AND MAIN CHARACTERISTICS OF THE SWISS RULES	
	Background of the 2004 Rules	**Wolfgang Peter** Python Peter, Geneva
	Background of the 2012 Revision: what were the main objectives?	**Christoph Müller** University of Neuchâtel
	Discussion (Panel and Floor)	
9:45 – 10:45	PANEL 2 KEY FEATURES OF THE SWISS RULES, PART I	Session Chair: **Rolf Trittman** Freshfields Bruckhaus Deringer, Frankfurt
	Consolidation and joinder under the Swiss Rules	**Ruth Stackpool-Moore** HKIAC, Hong Kong
	The arbitral tribunal's jurisdiction for set-off claims and counter-claims	**Vladimir Pavić** University of Belgrade
	Expedited procedure	**Thomas Rohner** Pestalozzi, Zurich
	Discussion (Panel and Floor)	
10:45 – 11:15	COFFEE BREAK	

1:15 – 12:15	**PANEL 3** **KEY FEATURES OF THE SWISS RULES, PART II**	Session Chair: **Vera van Houtte**, Leuven
	Provisional measures and emergency arbitrator	**Christopher Boog,** Schellenberg Wittmer Ltd, Zurich
	Confidentiality	**Pascal Hollander** Hanotiau & van den Berg, Brussels
	Settlement facilitation	**Peter Nobel** Nobel & Hug, Zurich
	Discussion (Panel and Floor)	
12:15 – 12:45	**ASA ADVOCACY PRIZE**	**Michael E. Schneider** President of ASA – Swiss Arbitration Association, LALIVE, Geneva
12.45 – 14:00	**LUNCH**	
14:00 – 15:00	**PANEL 4** **SWISS RULES IN PRACTICE: THE INSIDERS' VIEW**	Session Chair: **Ignacio de Castro,** WIPO Arbitration and Mediation Center, Geneva
	Case handling	**Michael Fischer,** Swiss Chambers' Arbitration Institution, Zurich
	Institutional involvement and costs	**Joya Raha** Swiss Chambers' Arbitration Institution, Geneva
	The workings of the Special Committee and the Arbitration Court	**Philipp Habegger** LALIVE, Zurich[1]
15:00 – 15:30	**COFFEE BREAK**	

[1] As of 1 January 2014.

15:30 – 16:45	**PANEL 5** **PERSPECTIVES FROM USERS, ARBITRATORS AND COUNSEL, AND THE WAY FORWARD**	Session Chair: **Markus Wirth** Homburger, Zurich
	The user's perspective	**François Naef** Merck Serono, Darmstadt **Marco Villiger** FIFA, Zurich
	The counsel's perspective	**Bennar Balkaya** Istanbul **Daniele Favalli** VISCHER, Zurich
	The arbitrator's perspective	**Rudolf Fiebinger** Fiebinger, Polak, Leon & Partner, Vienna **Frank Spoorenberg**, Tavernier Tschanz, Geneva
	Panel discussion: the way forward?	
16:45 – 17:00	**CLOSING ADDRESS**	**Nathalie Voser**, Conference Chair, Schellenberg Wittmer Ltd, Zurich

INTRODUCTION

Launched in 2004, the Swiss Rules of International Arbitration were a major development for arbitration in Switzerland. Instead of a myriad of diverse arbitration rules, the main Swiss chambers of commerce providing arbitration services decided to join forces—and unite their rules into one single Swiss product. Since then, the Swiss Rules have developed into a highly successful venture. To cite just one example: the 2004 Swiss Rules were a modernised version of the 1976 UNCITRAL Arbitration Rules, still in force at the time. When the time came for an update of the UNCITRAL Arbitration Rules, the favour was returned and the Swiss Rules were a major source of inspiration for UNCITRAL's work.

Ten years and one round of revisions later, ASA felt that it was time to take stock, to contemplate what had been accomplished and to look into the future. This made the 10th anniversary of the Swiss Rules an obvious choice for ASA's 2014 winter conference.

The relationship with the Swiss Chambers and the Swiss Rules has always been of major importance for ASA.

ASA is not an arbitration institution having its own arbitration rules. It is independent from all arbitral institutions, including the Swiss Chambers and the Swiss Rules. This characteristic is one of ASA's decisive advantages: its views can never be equated with the interests of a provider of an arbitration product. At the same time, ASA's articles of association state: "The purpose of the Association is to promote the development of arbitration, in Switzerland and abroad". ASA's mission therefore includes taking a strong interest in the Swiss Rules.

It was in this independent capacity as a representative of the Swiss arbitration community that ASA was—with, of course, the Swiss Chambers themselves—one of the driving factors behind the Swiss Rules project from the start. Today, this same independence vis-à-vis the Swiss Chambers enables ASA to retain a critical, if benevolent, spirit when considering the Swiss Rules. The ASA conference of January 2014 was thus the perfect forum to examine the key features of the Swiss Rules, to provide the point of view of users, counsel and arbitrators on the strengths and potential for improvement of the Swiss Rules and to consider the way forward.

Elliott Geisinger
ASA President

Panel 1: "Past and Present": Background and Main Characteristics of the Swiss Rules

The Background of the 2004 Swiss Rules

*Wolfgang Peter**

It is really a great pleasure for me today to speak and be able to look back at ten years of Swiss Rules.[1] My subject is the background of the Swiss Rules 2004 so let me put this in a very concise way because I believe that most of you are quite familiar with what happened ten or 12 years ago.

1. ENVIRONMENT WHEN THE 2004 SWISS RULES WERE DRAFTED

In the 1990s and 2000 a number of European countries already offered institutional arbitration through national arbitration systems; however, Switzerland did not. Switzerland remained fragmented at that time. The Chambers of Commerce and Industry of Zurich, Geneva, Lugano, Basel, Lausanne, Bern had various arbitration rules, but these arbitration rules were quite different from each other and, even worse, did not address modern arbitration development. Therefore, there was not only a lack of unity but also a lack of transparency for observers outside Switzerland. Nobody really understood what was going on. We had not realised the full potential of what Switzerland could have been doing, so in 1997 the idea started to unify these various rules and create one arbitration system.

2. THE PROCESS OF DRAFTING THE 2004 SWISS RULES

My topic is to describe in a few words the process of the drafting of the 2004 Swiss Rules, and I will indeed be short. It is a history of battles and war stories. It was very tough—I can confirm this without hesitation—with three to four years of political lobbying before any breakthrough was achieved. At one stage, one of the Chambers of

---

* Wolfgang Peter is a Founding Partner of Python & Peter in Geneva, Switzerland, where he heads a team specialising in international commercial and investment arbitration. This is a slightly amended version of a presentation given at the conference "10 Years of Swiss Rules of International Arbitration" on 31 January 2014 in Basel and retains the informal speaking style.

1 Swiss Chambers' of International Arbitration, Swiss Rules of International Arbitration (*hereinafter* Swiss Rules).

Commerce threatened us with a court injunction if we continued to run against what it perceived to be its own interests. You can imagine the "good" atmosphere we had in some of these sessions.

We finished by drafting the Swiss Rules, which finally came into force in 2004. One point is important: we could have created an entirely new system but we felt that it was wise to adopt a recognised arbitration system and, therefore, we used the UNCITRAL[2] Arbitration Rules.[3] The UNCITRAL Rules in force in 2004 were those from 1976,[4] already slightly outdated, so there was a need to update them to include modern arbitration practice. They also had to be institutionalised because the UNCITRAL Arbitration Rules are ad hoc rules.

This work was done and we created a case administration system which we called light touch administration. I would simply point out that some of the key features of the Swiss Rules were the creation of an expedited procedure, the addressing of multi-party arbitrations, the inclusion of a most innovative provision on consolidation and joinder as well as on set-off of claims. In 2004, the Swiss Rules were very well accepted and we have the statistics to see how this has evolved over time. They were then slightly amended in 2012 and Christoph Müller is going to speak about that.[5]

3. THE WAY FORWARD: MERGER OF THE ASA AND THE SWISS RULES INTO ONE SINGLE ARBITRATION INSTITUTION

We could say "so far so good", but I did not come here today to speak to you simply about the past. I think we also need to have some serious thoughts about the future because we cannot rest on our laurels.

We are experiencing, and you all know it, economic competition at an unheard of level and the pace of change is very, very fast. We need to anticipate the future; we have to be ready for change. What I am saying here today is my personal opinion. I am not speaking officially or unofficially on behalf of ASA.

It is clear that the Swiss Rules are a good product and we can also say that Switzerland offers an excellent arbitration environment due to its legislation, which is favourable to arbitration, and its arbitration-friendly courts but this does not in itself create a secure future.

---

[2] United Nations Commission on International Trade Law (*hereinafter* UNCITRAL).

[3] UNCITRAL Arbitration Rules as revised in 2010 (*hereinafter* UNCITRAL Arbitration Rules).

[4] UNCITRAL Arbitration Rules 1976.

[5] *See,* Christoph Müller's contribution, *Background of the 2012 Revision: What were the Main Objectives?* in this volume.

Let me make a bit of an extravagant comparison and look at Nokia or Kodak. They had a strong image and leading products in their field and where do they stand now? You all know. We need to secure the future and in doing so we at the same time seek to explore the entire potential that Switzerland as a seat for arbitration has and which is, in my opinion, well beyond what the Swiss Rules are achieving today.

One of the things we can do is continue to improve the Rules as time goes on. This was done in 2012 and may be done in a few years again but, in my opinion, it takes more to shape the future. Therefore, today, I would like to suggest that we take one important step forward: a merger or a joint venture between ASA and the Swiss Chambers' Arbitration Institution in order to form one single arbitration institution.

I know that many of you will say this is radical, but if you think it through, it is the right way to go: for ASA, there is much more strength in the future to be identified with a set of arbitration rules. For the Chambers of Commerce, an enhanced system will provide them with better economic benefits. There is no strength in being separated; strength flows from joining forces.

I could develop a number of arguments but I was reminded to keep to my time so I give you just one hint, one idea. ASA is a unique platform of 1,200 members. If I am not mistaken, we have 400 foreign members, many of them law firms. The awareness of the Swiss Rules among the members of ASA will greatly increase if ASA is the institution which has embodied the Swiss Rules. An ASA member may be aware today that there are Swiss Rules in Switzerland, which is maybe of occasional interest, but after a merger between ASA and the Swiss Rules suddenly the ASA members will see that they are members of an institution which has become an arbitral institution with its own arbitration rules. Quite clearly ASA will become through its arbitration even more international and enter a more international dimension.

I would really want to say that we need the courage to redefine the identity of ASA and seize what I consider to be a great opportunity. There is no reason why we in Switzerland could not do what has been done in England, Germany, Sweden, Austria and other European countries. Take the LCIA,[6] if you want to look at it pragmatically, then you see that it is a national English arbitration institution but they have managed to have a strong international

6 The London Court of International Arbitration (*hereinafter* LCIA).

dimension particularly because they are capitalising on the commonwealth dimension. In addition, the LCIA has all of the arbitration promotion functionalities that ASA has: in other words, the LCIA has incorporated both aspects. This shows that there is no need to separate an arbitration promotion organisation such as ASA and an arbitration administering organisation such as the Swiss Chambers Arbitration Institution. The LCIA successfully comprises both and so do other institutions in Europe and abroad.

Having one institution instead of two would not only strengthen both fields, it would enormously strengthen Switzerland as arbitration hub. It would help us compete in a global market. Therefore, we should not settle for some half-way house of cooperation, some hybrid construction between ASA and the Swiss Rules, but form one national arbitration institution.

ASA, the Swiss Arbitration Association, is ideal for these plans. It has existed for over 40 years and its members form a large pool of competence and experience from which ASA's arbitration activity would enormously benefit.

ASA is an established brand name and we should capitalise on it. In the minds of many people out there in the business community, if you go beyond Switzerland, there is already serious confusion. Most people do not know whether the Swiss Rules are part of ASA or vice versa. People just do not understand the distinction in most places I go, certainly not in Asia and not even in Europe. Instead of trying to explain the difference between two distinct institutions, we should focus on creating one strong institution with enhanced attractiveness. This is my proposal.

Now, what will happen? I know from 1997 when we started the Swiss Rules project, there will immediately be reluctance to such a merger or joint venture. One of the reasons for this will be based on the idea that ASA must be neutral, that it should be open to all arbitration institutions and not favour one. Of course, there appears to be a contrast between this objective of independence and neutrality and ASA itself becoming an arbitration institution, but let us discuss to what extent this should really be seen as a problem.

The credo of ASA has always been that it should be neutral and independent from all other arbitration institutions. But why? What particular purpose do we serve thereby? Moreover, is this a perpetual position that we will have to observe for all times? Why can it not be questioned?

I also ask: what do we fear? What is really the practical downside? Why can we not do what other countries have done successfully? What will we concretely lose? Loss of credibility for ASA in its promotion of arbitration? Why? Do other arbitral institutions lack credibility when they promote arbitration because they also administer arbitrations? ASA could still successfully publish the ASA Bulletin, organize conferences, promote academic thinking, comment on emerging rules and international developments and retain its credibility.

I hear people saying that we will have fewer appointments, that appointments will be impacted, but that has never been justified. People say parties will desert Switzerland. Why would they do this? They have not deserted other countries. I think these fears are irrational. These are the same fears that were expressed back in 1997 when the Swiss Rules project was launched. In hindsight they appear now nonsensical.

In conclusion, I wish to stress that we should again demonstrate three qualities: vision, entrepreneurial courage and energy to take the next step forward: the merger of the ASA and the Swiss Rules into one single arbitration institution.

Background of the 2012 Revision: What Were the Main Objectives?

*Christoph Müller**

1. INTRODUCTION

What were the main objectives of this first revision, only a few years after the entry into force of the Swiss Rules of International Arbitration (*hereinafter* Rules)?

1. Strengthen the supervisory powers conferred upon the arbitral institution;
2. Accelerate the proceedings;
3. Achieve even more flexibility for the arbitral tribunal;
4. Facilitate the consolidation of several proceedings;
5. Improve the control of the costs by the arbitral institution;
6. Grant an emergency relief by emergency arbitrators;
7. Extend the scope of application to domestic arbitration.

Despite these main objectives, the 2012 revision was only a partial and not a general one. The aim was to add improvements based on the several years of experience under the 2004 Rules. The Working Group did not have a more ambitious target simply because the 2004 Rules have by and large worked well. This is also why the starting point of the revision was the former text of the Swiss Rules and not the amended UNCITRAL Arbitration Rules (as revised in 2010).

2. STRENGTHEN THE SUPERVISORY POWERS OF THE ARBITRAL INSTITUTION

The 2004 Rules were based on the 1976 UNCITRAL Arbitration Rules, which were designed for *ad hoc* proceedings. The 2004 version thus already contained several new elements adapting the UNCITRAL ad hoc model to institutional arbitration. This endeavour has been further developed by the following measures in the 2012 revision.

---

* Prof. Dr. Christoph Müller, University of Neuchâtel (Switzerland). This contribution is based on the speech given by the author at the ASA Conference of 31 January 2014. For a more detailed introduction to the 2012 Swiss Rules, see Christoph Brunner, *Part I—Introduction*, in: ARBITRATION IN SWITZERLAND—THE PRACTITIONER'S GUIDE, 327-337 (Manuel Arroyo ed., 2013); Sébastien Besson/Nina Thommesen, *Introduction*, in: SWISS RULES OF INTERNATIONAL ARBITRATION—COMMENTARY, 2nd ed., 1-14 (Tobias Zuberbühler/Christoph Müller/Philipp Habegger eds., Zurich/Basel/Geneva/ Huntington 2013).

First, the Chambers of Commerce founded a new and independent institution, the "Swiss Chambers" Arbitration Institution". This institution then established the Arbitration Court. The Court replaced the former "Arbitration Committee" and the "Special Committee". The new structure is designed to be more centralized. It will insure better coordination of the practice of each Chamber. The Court is assisted by the Secretariat, which continues to work in a decentralized manner and in separate offices.[1]

As a second measure to strengthen the institution, Art. 1(4) extends the supervisory powers of the Arbitration Court. These powers expressly include the competence "to extend the term of office of the arbitral tribunal and to decide on the challenge of an arbitrator on grounds not provided for in the[se] Rules". These are two areas which before potentially fell under the jurisdiction of judicial authorities. They are now clearly within the scope of the Arbitration Court's authority. Art. 1(4) thus gives the broadest possible powers to the arbitral institution. It allows the parties to avoid having to resort to national courts to administer their arbitration.

Under Art. 5(3), the Court now also has "all powers to address" any failure in the constitution of the arbitral tribunal. It can "revoke an appointment made, appoint or reappoint any of the arbitrators". This new provision ensures an appropriate constitution of the arbitral tribunal under all circumstances.

The institutional aspect has been strengthened in yet another way. Art. 3(12) amends the arbitral institution's power to refuse to administer an arbitration when there is "manifestly no agreement to arbitrate referring to these Rules". Under the revised Rules, the Court examines this issue only after—and not before—the notification of the Notice of Arbitration to the Respondent. This allows the Respondent to accept the jurisdiction of the arbitral tribunal or at least the principle of an arbitration under the Swiss Rules.

Finally, the arbitral institution also exercises its expanded supervisory powers through a better control of the costs (see below, section 6).

The organizers of the ASA Conference of January 2014 have conducted a survey among arbitration practitioners regarding their perception of the Swiss Rules. With respect to the degree of involvement of the Swiss Chamber's Arbitration Institution in the arbitration proceedings, 85% of the participants considered that it was "just right".[2]

---

1 Swiss Chambers' Arbitration Institution, Swiss Rules of International Arbitration (June 2012), Appendix A.

2 *See* Annex Swiss Rules Survey.

3. ACCELERATE THE PROCEEDINGS

Art. 41(4) reduces the time limit for the payment of the deposits of costs from 30 to 15 days.

Art. 11(1) introduces a new time limit of 15 days for the challenge of an arbitrator. In comparison: Art. 14(2) ICC Rules provides for a time limit of 30 days. The new Art. 11(2) also provides that if, within another 15 days, the parties do not agree to the challenge or the arbitrator does not withdraw, the Court shall decide on the challenge. These provisions thus bring more clarity and predictability to the challenge proceedings, not only with respect to time.

4. MORE FLEXIBILITY FOR THE ARBITRAL TRIBUNAL

Art. 15(7) introduces a general duty to "act in good faith". This duty applies to "[a]ll participants in the arbitral proceedings". According to this provision it means in particular that the participants are obliged to make "every effort to contribute to the efficient conduct of the proceedings and to avoid unnecessary costs and delays". For arbitrators, this new provision could provide a basis for procedural directions to improve the efficiency of the proceedings. It could also justify decisions on costs adverse to the party causing unnecessary costs and delays.

Art. 15(8) allows the arbitral tribunal to "take steps to facilitate the settlement of the dispute", with the agreement of the parties. This provision clarifies the existing situation with respect to facilitation of amicable settlement by the arbitral tribunal.[3]

According to the new Art. 26(1), the arbitral tribunal may modify, suspend or terminate any interim measures granted. In exceptional circumstances and with prior notice to the parties, it can do so also on its own initiative.

Subsection 3 of Art. 26 expressly allows—as a novelty—for *ex parte* measures by way of a preliminary order.[4]

5. FACILITATE THE CONSOLIDATION OF SEVERAL PROCEEDINGS

Two novelties in the long provision of Art. 4(1) achieve this objective:

---

3 *See,* Markus Wirth's contribution, *Settlement Facilitation,* in this volume.

4 *See,* in this volume Christopher Boog's contribution, *Preliminary Orders and the Emergency Arbitrator: Urgent Interim Relief by an Arbitral Decision Maker in Exception Circumstances,* section 2.

First, in case of consolidation, "the parties to all proceedings shall be deemed to have waived their right to designate an arbitrator". Under the 2004 Rules, only "the parties to the new case" lost this right.

Second, the Court may revoke the appointment and confirmation of arbitrators and confirm (or not) new arbitrators.

The purpose of these two novelties is to guarantee equal rights to the Parties to appoint arbitrators and thus to favour consolidation.[5]

6. IMPROVE THE CONTROL OF THE COSTS BY THE ARBITRAL INSTITUTION

Under Art. 40(4), any determination of the costs, including the determination by the arbitrators of their own fees, is subject to the "approval or adjustment" by the Court. The provision specifies that any such approval or adjustment shall be binding upon the arbitral tribunal. Under the 2004 Rules, the institutional scrutiny was limited to a "consultation". The revision aims at giving the arbitral institution the "last word" on the issue of costs. The arbitrators remain, however, exclusively competent to determine the allocation of costs among the parties.

Under Art. 41(1), the arbitral tribunal will also determine the deposit of costs "after consulting with the Court". Such consultation was not required under the 2004 Rules. In practice, the arbitrators are not required to consult the Court as long as the requested deposits are below the average total costs of the arbitration.

The "Administration of Deposits" is also subject to more detailed rules (see Appendix B Sect. 4.1). The deposits must be held in a separate bank account. This account is to be held by the Secretariat or by the arbitral tribunal, "if so requested by the Secretariat". In practice, the Secretariat systematically requests the arbitrators to establish such a separate bank account. Under the 2004 Rules, the sole arbitrator, or the presiding arbitrator, was exclusively in charge of administering the deposits. The release of part of the deposits to the arbitrators as an advance on costs needs the approval of the Court (see Appendix B Sect. 4.2).

With the entry into force of the 2012 revision, the Court also issued general guidelines for arbitrators on the accounting of expenses (see Appendix B Sect. 3).[6] The Chambers have never used this competence, even though the 2004 Rules had already provided for it.

---

[5] *See*, in this volume Ruth Stackpool-Moore's contribution, *Joinder and Consolidation – Examining Best Practice in the Swiss, HKIAC and ICC Rules*, section 3.2 and 3.3.

[6] These Guidelines are available on https://www.swissarbitration.org/sa/download/guidelines_for_arbitrators_2012.pdf.

The revised Rules also better protect the arbitrators for the time spent on the case before any deposit of costs has been made by the parties. The purpose was to avoid any delay in the conduct of the proceedings due to the arbitrators' legitimate concerns regarding their remuneration.

In order to address this concern, the time limit for the payment of the deposits has been reduced from 30 to 15 days, as mentioned before (see Art. 41(4)). Furthermore, the payment of a provisional deposit has been introduced for expedited procedures (Art. 42(1)(a) and Appendix B Sect. 1.4). Finally, the new Rules provide for a specific deposit in relation to applications for emergency relief by the emergency arbitrator (Art. 43(1)(c) and Appendix B Sect. 1.6).

7. EMERGENCY RELIEF

The 2012 revision also introduced a means for emergency relief by emergency arbitrators in Art. 43. By doing so, the Swiss Chambers' Arbitration Institution followed a general trend of other arbitral institutions.

To this day (24 April 2014), the Secretariat has received only one application for emergency relief proceedings. The President of the Court appointed the emergency arbitrator one day after the Secretariat received the application. One day later, the emergency arbitrator received the case file. 14 days after the transmission of the file, the emergency arbitrator rendered his order of 31 pages. During the emergency proceedings, the parties and the emergency arbitrator held a conference call and a hearing at the place of arbitration. The Parties exchanged two set of written briefs (i.e. the request for emergency relief, the answer to the request for emergency relief, the statement of reply and the statement of rejoinder) and submitted their statements of costs. The case is currently pending before a three-member arbitral tribunal under the Swiss Rules.

Art. 43 applies "unless the parties have agreed otherwise". There is therefore no need for a specific agreement to initiate this new procedure. It is, however, not mandatory and can be "opted out".

The decision of the emergency arbitrator shall have the same effects as a decision of "interim measures of protection" made pursuant to Art. 26 (Art. 43(8)).[7]

---

[7] *See,* in this volume Christopher Boog's contribution, *Preliminary Orders and the Emergency Arbitrator: Urgent Interim Relief by an Arbitral Decision Maker in Exception Circumstances,* section 3.

8. DOMESTIC ARBITRATION

Last but not least, the application of the Swiss Rules to domestic arbitration was a main objective of the 2012 revision Therefore, since 1 June 2012, the Swiss Rules automatically apply not only to international arbitration, but also to domestic arbitration (Introduction Sect. c). They thus replace the former rules of the Chambers governing domestic arbitration. By contrast, the 2004 Rules were not applicable *per se* to domestic arbitration. However, the Chambers decided to administer such arbitrations if the parties so specifically agreed.

Despite this important change in the scope of application, the name "Swiss Rules of *International* Arbitration" was maintained following a heated debate among the members of the Working Group.

9. CONCLUSION

As with every set of arbitration rules, the choices made by the drafters of the 2012 revision are of course open to criticism. According to the survey conducted in the framework of this Conference,[8] further features should be considered for inclusion in a future revision of the Swiss Rules. The survey mentions items such as case management conference, scrutiny process or a more active involvement of the institution in general. Obviously, such features could also have been included in the present revision.

However, from a general standpoint, the 2012 revision has achieved its main objectives. It has improved the Swiss Rules in several respects, in particular by enhancing cost control and by introducing a mechanism for emergency relief.

The new Swiss Rules are a good product meeting the needs of modern institutional arbitration. One can safely advise reference to them in a contract when arbitration as such is appropriate. This is also the result of the survey conducted in the framework of this Conference, as 80% of the participants would recommend the inclusion of the Swiss Rules in an arbitration clause in any situation.[9]

---

8 *See* annex, Swiss Rules Survey.

9 *See* annex, Swiss Rules Survey.

Panel 2: Key Features of the Swiss Rules, Part I

Joinder and Consolidation – Examining Best Practice in the Swiss, HKIAC and ICC Rules

*Ruth Stackpool-Moore**

1. INTRODUCTION

One of the features which currently distinguish leading sets of arbitration rules is the approach they take regarding the handling of "complex disputes." Although most major, as well as emerging, arbitral institutions have revised their rules within the last few years,[1] consensus has yet to emerge on how to best deal with cases involving multiple parties and/or multiple contracts. While provisions on joinder and consolidation can be found in some sets of recently revised rules,[2] they are not present in all,[3] and where they have been included, differences exist between the treatment of the two issues.

---

* Ruth Stackpool-Moore, qualified solicitor of the Supreme Court of New South of Wales and High Court of Australia and England and Wales, is Managing Counsel at the Hong Kong International Arbitration Centre. This contribution is based on a presentation given at the conference "10 Years of Swiss Rules of International Arbitration" on 31 January 2014 in Basel and reflects the views, opinions and positions of the author, and does not necessarily reflect the views, opinions and positions of the Hong Kong International Arbitration Centre.

1 The London Court of International Arbitration (LCIA) is currently in the final stages of introducing new rules, a process already undertaken by the American Arbitration Association (AAA) regarding the rules of its International Centre for Dispute Resolution (ICDR) and the Japan Commercial Arbitration Association (JCCA) in 2014; the Hong Kong International Arbitration Centre (HKIAC), the Kuala Lumpur Regional Centre for Arbitration (KLRCA), the Singapore International Arbitration Centre (SIAC) and the Abu Dhabi Commercial Conciliation & Arbitration Center (ADCCAC) each revised their rules in 2013; as did the International Chamber of Commerce International Court of Arbitration (ICC), the Swiss Chambers" Arbitration Institution and the China International Economic and Trade Arbitration Commission (CIETAC) in 2012 and the Australian Centre for International Commercial Arbitration (ACICA) and the Korean Commercial Arbitration Board (KCAB) in 2011.

2 The provisions in the revised HKIAC, Swiss and ICC Rules are discussed in detail below, but *see also* the LCIA, JCCA and KLRCA Rules.

3 The ICDR and ACICA Rules are silent on the issue of joinder, while other sets of institutional rules require consent in writing of the party to be joined at the time the request for joinder is made (*see*, for example, Art. 24(b) SIAC Rules and Art. 22(1)(viii) LCIA Rules) and in relation to consolidation, many sets of institutional rules, including those of SIAC, ACICA, the KCAB and the AAA's ICDR Rules, contain no provisions to deal with the consolidation of cases.

Before looking at the variations which exist, it is necessary to first consider what practical difference it might make for parties to an arbitration if the rules they select provide the means to handle more complex disputes, and provisions on joinder and consolidation in particular. The second section of this article will therefore touch on the advantages and disadvantages of increased institutional intervention regarding questions of joinder and consolidation from a user's perspective. Having established the advantages of adopting institutional rules which include such provisions, the third section of the article will review a selection of institutional rules which do deal with these issues and examine the various methods adopted to do so.

2. JOINDER AND CONSOLIDATION – MUCH ADO ABOUT NOTHING OR INDISPENSABLE TOOLS IN A PARTY'S ARSENAL?

International commercial relationships, and the disputes which arise from them, increasingly involve a multiplicity of parties and contracts. In 2012, the ICC reported that more than a third of its arbitrations involved more than two parties and that the average number of parties in these cases was four.[4] In general, it has been estimated that about 40% of arbitration cases worldwide involve more than two parties.[5] These figures accord with HKIAC's experience, with over one third of new cases filed under its Administered Rules in 2013 involving multiple parties or multiple contracts.

In all instances some parties will benefit from the ability to include third parties in their arbitration proceedings (otherwise there would be no incentive for a request for their inclusion to be made). In back-to-back sale of goods or construction contacts, for example, the "middle party" will often be interested in having both its upstream and downstream partners involved in proceedings so that all parties will be bound by the determinations of the final award. In this way, the middle party can avoid wasting time and money having to initiate separate proceedings with an uncertain outcome against the downstream partner to recover any damages it would eventually have to pay to its upstream partner for defects or defective work for which it is not ultimately responsible.

---

4 2012 Statistical Report, ICC International Court of Arbitration Bulletin 24 (1), 2013.

5 Nathalie Voser, *Multi-Party Disputes and Joinder of Third Parties, in 50 Years of the New York Convention: ICCA International Arbitration Conference*, 14 ICCA CONGRESS SERIES 343-410, 343 (Albert Jan Van den Berg ed. 2009).

While the presence of a third party is unlikely to serve the interests of all parties equally, it will nevertheless generally serve the interests of international commercial arbitration as a whole, increasing its efficacy in cases where the aggregated case would be more efficiently resolved than several parallel or serial cases.

It is also the case that sometimes one party to an arbitration will have no interest in having a third party join the proceedings or for cases to be consolidated.[6] For example, in pursuing a claim under a construction contract, a party (typically the employer) may consider its interests to be better served if its dispute (usually against the main contractor), is resolved as quickly as possible. In its view, the involvement of a subcontractor in the dispute could complicate the proceedings and increase the time and the cost of arbitration. Further, large parties with abundant funding may also wish to resist consolidation, either because they consider their position to be tenuous in some respect and would like to preserve multiple opportunities to achieve the 'right' outcome in their favour, or because they wish to capitalize on the inequality of resources available to the parties and potentially, by running more than one proceeding, price their opponents out of the game. However, such parties' initial agreement on a set of arbitration rules which promote the quick and efficient resolution of disputes through, amongst others, the inclusion of provisions for consolidation and joinder, should trump this circumstantially strategic behavior, which promotes only one parties' narrow self-interest.

As early as 1987 it was recognised that "consolidation or joinder may be the only adequate means of achieving the ultimate goals of arbitration: fair, efficient, and economical commercial justice."[7] Examining this statement more closely, it is possible to look firstly at the ways in which joinder and consolidation enhance the efficiency and economy of the arbitration process, and as a corollary, how they may also enhance its effectiveness.

Provisions to deal effectively with multi-party or multi-contract situations are likely to enhance the overall efficiency of the arbitration process for one or more of the following reasons:

1) duplicate parallel proceedings necessitated by an inability to join third parties or consolidate related cases require the

---

6 Stavros Brekoulakis, *The Relevance of the Interests of Third Parties in Arbitration: Taking a Closer Look at the Elephant in the Room*, 113(4) PENN STATE LAW REVIEW 1187 (2009).

7 Thomas Stipanowich, *Arbitration and the Multiparty Dispute: The Search for Workable Solutions*, 72 IOWA LAW REVIEW, 500 (1987).

expenditure of additional time and money;

2) the simultaneous resolution of related claims allows arbitrators access to a more complete picture of a transaction and each of the parties' obligations; and

3) the possibility of inconsistent and conflicting decisions on similar or overlapping claims is reduced.[8]

The importance of the third benefit should not be underestimated. Although inconsistent or irreconcilable awards in parallel, overlapping proceedings do not occur often,[9] when they do, they raise serious doubts about arbitration's reliability and the dispositive authority of arbitral awards.[10] Although each of the arbitral awards will have a *res judicata* effect, due to the conflict, one of them must clearly be wrong. As well as undermining confidence in the system of arbitration generally, irreconcilable awards are also likely to frustrate the expectations of the parties to arbitration, who might find that their award is unenforceable if it conflicts with another arbitral award or national judgment.[11] Reducing the risk of multiple and conflicting awards therefore also enhances the effectiveness of the arbitration process as confidence is maintained in the system as a whole and, on an individual level, parties are able to achieve the outcome they bargained for: the certainty and finality of a binding award.

---

[8] Redfern and Hunter, among others, have noted it is generally desirable to deal with all issues in a singular proceeding, rather than in a series of separate proceedings, due to the associated savings of time and money and the avoidance of problems of conflicting decisions on the same issues of law and fact. *See* NIGEL BLACKABY, CONSTANTINE PARTASIDES, ALAN REDFERN, AND MARTIN HUNTER, REDFERN AND HUNTER ON INTERNATIONAL ARBITRATION 149 (2009). Lord Denning also summarised the pitfalls of multiple proceedings in *Abu Dhabi Gas Liquefaction Co v Eastern Bechtel Corp, Bechtel Corp v Ishikawajima Harima Heavy Industries Co Ltd, Eastern Bechtel Corp and Chiyoda Chemical Engineering & Construction Co Ltd v Ishikawajima-harima Heavy Industries Co Ltd*, [1982] 2 Lloyd's Rep 425, where he said "As we have often pointed out, there is a danger in having two separate arbitrations in a case like this. You might get inconsistent findings if there were two separate arbitrators...it is most undesirable that there should be inconsistent findings by two separate arbitrators on virtually the self-same question...It is very desirable that everything should be done to avoid such a circumstance."

[9] *See*, for example, *CME Czech Rep. v Czech Rep.*, 15 World Trade and Arb. Materials 171 (Svea Ct. of Appeals (Sweden) 2003); *R. S. Lauder v Czech Rep.*, 14 World Trade and Arb. Materials 35 (UNCITRAL Arb. Trib. 2002) (Final Award); *CME Czech Rep. v Czech Rep.*, 14 World Trade and Arb. Materials 109 (UNCITRAL Arb. Trib. 2001) (Partial Award).

[10] *Op. cit.* Note 7, Stavros Brekoulakis, p. 1176.

[11] *See*, for example, Stefan Kröll, *§1061—Foreign Awards, in* ARBITRATION IN GERMANY: THE MODEL LAW IN PRACTICE 479-487 (Karl-Heinz Böckstiegel et al. eds., 2007) as referenced in *op. cit.* Note 6, Stavros Brekoulakis, p. 1177.

Arguments made against consolidation and joinder tend to focus on an alleged loss of party autonomy, in respect of the lack of party consent, and the method for appointing the tribunal in the commencement of a multi-party proceeding. However, it is more than arguable that the fundamental principle of party autonomy is not violated by the mechanisms of joinder and consolidation, even when they are implemented on a non-unanimous basis, due to the parties' initial agreement to the chosen institutional rules. The fact that the parties have initially referred to a set of arbitration rules in their arbitration agreement means that they have consented to all the provisions included therein, including those which allow for joinder and consolidation and their consequences. Reference to such rules simply expands the parties' initial consent further than referencing a set of rules which do not.

Detractors often also point to the additional time and cost resulting from an increased number of participants and issues to be resolved in any one dispute. However, this additional burden should not be exaggerated. Under most sets of rules, and indeed under the three sets examined in detail in the third section of this article, consolidation is only considered where there are common issues of law and fact arising from the same or related transactions, where the evidence will often be the same regardless of the number of parties in the proceedings.

A final argument made against multi-party mechanisms relates to a potential loss of confidentiality. Because more parties are involved, more parties will be privy to confidential information shared during the arbitration proceedings. This problem can however easily be resolved through confidentiality agreements or other legal instruments, entered into before or during the proceedings.

Because parties' strategic interests when a dispute has commenced may not necessarily reflect those of a rational economic actor wishing to maximize the economy and efficacy of the arbitration process, their actions at that time are often not beneficial for the arbitration process as a whole. Institutional rules, including provisions implementing the multi-party mechanisms of joinder and consolidation, and parties' agreement to them, prior to this circumstantial strategic influence, provide the means to manage cases to maximize procedural efficiency and fairness. The pressure to adopt such rules has come from the business community, who, as users of arbitration, wish to maximize the cost and time efficiency of their arbitration proceedings. As the increased procedural efficiency and cost effectiveness achieved does not come at the cost of party autonomy or parties' rights of due process, provisions for consolidation and joinder should be welcomed.

3. HOW TO BEST ADDRESS THE ISSUE? EXAMINING THE SWISS, HONG KONG AND PARISIAN APPROACH

3.1 Preliminary Comment

Once it is accepted that provisions on joinder and consolidation enhance the utility of institutional rules by maximizing the procedural efficiency and cost effectiveness of the arbitration process, it is useful to examine and critically analyse the different treatments of the two which currently exist. The three sets of rules selected for review here are the Swiss Rules of International Arbitration 2012 (Swiss Rules), the Hong Kong International Arbitration Centre Administered Arbitration Rules 2013 (HKIAC Rules) and the Rules of Arbitration of the International Chamber of Commerce 2012 (ICC Rules). The basis for the selection lies in all three institutions' comprehensive and detailed provisions dealing with both joinder and consolidation.

In order to usefully compare each set of rules it is necessary for their respective provisions on joinder and consolidation to be familiar. Accordingly, Article 4 of the Swiss Rules, Articles 27 and 28 of the HKIAC Rules and Articles 7 and 10 of the ICC Rules are reproduced in full below.

3.2 The Relevant Rules

3.2.1 Swiss Rules of International Arbitration 2012 (Swiss Rules)

Article 4

1. Where a Notice of Arbitration is submitted between parties already involved in other arbitral proceedings pending under these Rules, the Court may decide, after consulting with the parties and any confirmed arbitrator in all proceedings, that the new case shall be consolidated with the pending arbitral proceedings. The Court may proceed in the same way where a Notice of Arbitration is submitted between parties that are not identical to the parties in the pending arbitral proceedings. When rendering its decision, the Court shall take into account all relevant circumstances, including the links between the cases and the progress already made in the

pending arbitral proceedings. Where the Court decides to consolidate the new case with the pending arbitral proceedings, the parties to all proceedings shall be deemed to have waived their right to designate an arbitrator, and the Court may revoke the appointment and confirmation of arbitrators and apply the provisions of Section II (Composition of the Arbitral Tribunal).

2. Where one or more third persons request to participate in arbitral proceedings already pending under these Rules or where a party to pending arbitral proceedings under these Rules requests that one or more third persons participate in the arbitration, the arbitral tribunal shall decide on such request, after consulting with all of the parties, including the person or persons to be joined, taking into account all relevant circumstances.

3.2.2 HKIAC Administered Arbitration Rules 2013 (HKIAC Rules)

Article 27 – Joinder of Additional Parties

27.1 The arbitral tribunal shall have the power to allow an additional party to be joined to the arbitration provided that, prima facie, the additional party is bound by an arbitration agreement under these Rules giving rise to the arbitration, including any arbitration under Article 28 or 29.

27.2 The arbitral tribunal's decision pursuant to Article 27.1 is without prejudice to its power to subsequently decide any question as to its jurisdiction arising from such decision.

27.3 A party wishing to join an additional party to the arbitration shall submit a Request for Joinder to HKIAC. HKIAC may fix a time limit for the submission of a Request for Joinder.

27.4 The Request for Joinder shall include the following:

(a) the case reference of the existing arbitration;

(b) the names and addresses, telephone numbers, and email addresses of each of the parties, including the additional party;

(c) a request that the additional party be joined to the arbitration;

(d) a reference to the contract(s) or other legal instrument(s) out of or in relation to which the request arises;

(e) a statement of the facts supporting the request;

(f) the points at issue;

(g) the legal arguments supporting the request;

(h) the relief or remedy sought; and

(i) confirmation that copies of the Request for Joinder and any exhibits included therewith have been or are being served simultaneously on all other parties and the arbitral tribunal, where applicable, by one or more means of service to be identified in such confirmation. A copy of the contract(s), and of the arbitration agreement(s) if not contained in the contract(s), shall be annexed to the Request for Joinder.

27.5 Within 15 days of receiving the Request for Joinder, the additional party shall submit to HKIAC an Answer to the Request for Joinder. The Answer to the Request for Joinder shall include the following:

(a) the name, address, telephone and fax numbers, and email address of the additional party and its counsel (if different from the description contained in the Request for Joinder);

(b) any plea that the arbitral tribunal has been improperly constituted and/or lacks jurisdiction over the additional party;

(c) the additional party's comments on the particulars set forth in the Request for Joinder, pursuant to Article 27.4(a) to (g);

(d) the additional party's answer to the relief or remedy sought in the Request for Joinder, pursuant to Article 27.4(h);

(e) details of any claims by the additional party against any other party to the arbitration; and

(f) confirmation that copies of the Answer to the Request for Joinder and any exhibits included therewith have been or are being served simultaneously on all other parties and the arbitral tribunal, where applicable, by one or more means of service to be identified in such confirmation.

27.6 A third party wishing to be joined as an additional party to the arbitration shall submit a Request for Joinder to HKIAC. The provisions of Article 27.4 shall apply to such Request for Joinder.

27.7 Within 15 days of receiving a Request for Joinder pursuant to Article 27.3 or 27.6, the parties shall submit their comments on the Request for Joinder to HKIAC. Such comments may include (without limitation) the following particulars: (a) any plea that the arbitral tribunal lacks jurisdiction over the additional party; (b) comments on the particulars set forth in the Request for Joinder, pursuant to Article 27.4(a) to (g); (c) answer to the relief or remedy sought in the Request for Joinder, pursuant to Article 27.4(h); (d) details of any claims against the additional party; and (e) confirmation that copies of the comments have been or are being served simultaneously on all other parties and the arbitral tribunal, where applicable, by one or more means of service to be identified in such confirmation.

27.8 Where HKIAC receives a Request for Joinder before the date on which the arbitral tribunal is confirmed, HKIAC may decide whether, prima facie, the additional party is bound by an arbitration agreement under these Rules giving rise to the arbitration, including any arbitration under Article 28 or 29. If so, HKIAC may join the additional party to the arbitration. Any question as to the jurisdiction of the arbitral tribunal arising from HKIAC's decision under this Article 27.8 shall be decided by the arbitral tribunal once confirmed, pursuant to Article 19.1.

27.9 HKIAC's decision pursuant to Article 27.8 is without prejudice to the admissibility or merits of any party's pleas.

27.10 Where an additional party is joined to the arbitration, the date on which the Request for Joinder is received by HKIAC shall be deemed to be the date on which the arbitration in respect of the additional party commences.

27.11 Where an additional party is joined to the arbitration before the date on which the arbitral tribunal is confirmed, all parties to the arbitration shall be deemed to have waived their right to designate an arbitrator, and HKIAC may revoke the appointment of any arbitrators already designated or confirmed. In these circumstances, HKIAC shall appoint the arbitral tribunal.

27.12 The revocation of the appointment of an arbitrator under Article 27.11 is without prejudice to:

(a) the validity of any act done or order made by that arbitrator before his or her appointment was revoked; and

(b) his or her entitlement to be paid his or her fees and expenses subject to Schedule 2 or 3 as applicable.

27.13 The parties waive any objection, on the basis of any decision to join an additional party to the arbitration, to the validity and/or enforcement of any award made by the arbitral tribunal in the arbitration, in so far as such waiver can validly be made.

27.14 HKIAC may adjust its Administrative Fees and the arbitral tribunal's fees (where appropriate) after a Request for Joinder has been submitted.

Article 28 – Consolidation of Arbitrations

28.1 HKIAC shall have the power, at the request of a party (the "Request for Consolidation") and after consulting with the parties and any confirmed arbitrators, to consolidate two or more arbitrations pending under these Rules where:

(a) the parties agree to consolidate; or

(b) all of the claims in the arbitrations are made under the same arbitration agreement; or

(c) the claims are made under more than one arbitration agreement, a common question of law or fact arises in both or all of the arbitrations, the rights to relief claimed are in respect of, or arise out of, the same transaction or series of transactions, and HKIAC finds the arbitration agreements to be compatible.

28.2 The party making the request shall provide copies of the Request for Consolidation to all other parties and to any confirmed arbitrators.

28.3 In deciding whether to consolidate, HKIAC shall take into account the circumstances of the case. Relevant factors may include, but are not limited to, whether one or more arbitrators have been designated or confirmed in more than one of the arbitrations, and if so, whether the same or different arbitrators have been confirmed.

28.4 Where HKIAC decides to consolidate two or more arbitrations, the arbitrations shall be consolidated into the arbitration that commenced first, unless all parties agree or HKIAC decides otherwise taking into account the circumstances of the case. HKIAC shall provide copies of such decision to all parties and to any confirmed arbitrators in all arbitrations.

28.5 The consolidation of two or more arbitrations is without prejudice to the validity of any act done or order made by a court in support of the relevant arbitration before it was consolidated.

28.6 Where HKIAC decides to consolidate two or more arbitrations, the parties to all such arbitrations shall be deemed to have waived their right to designate an arbitrator, and HKIAC may revoke the appointment of any arbitrators already designated or confirmed. In these circumstances, HKIAC shall appoint the arbitral tribunal in respect of the consolidated proceedings.

28.7 The revocation of the appointment of an arbitrator under Article 28.6 is without prejudice to:

(a) the validity of any act done or order made by that arbitrator before his or her appointment was revoked;

(b) his or her entitlement to be paid his or her fees and expenses subject to Schedule 2 or 3 as applicable; and

(c) the date when any claim or defence was raised for the purpose of applying any limitation bar or any similar rule or provision.

28.8 The parties waive any objection, on the basis of HKIAC's decision to consolidate, to the validity and/or enforcement of any award made by the arbitral tribunal in the consolidated proceedings, in so far as such waiver can validly be made.

28.9 HKIAC may adjust its Administrative Fees and the arbitral tribunal's fees (where appropriate) after a Request for Consolidation has been submitted.

3.2.3 Rules of Arbitration of the International Chamber of Commerce 2012 (ICC Rules)

Article 7 – Joinder of Additional Parties

1) A party wishing to join an additional party to the arbitration shall submit its request for arbitration against the additional party (the "Request for Joinder") to the Secretariat. The date on which the Request for Joinder is received by the Secretariat shall, for all purposes, be deemed to be the date of the commencement of arbitration against the additional party. Any such joinder shall be subject to the provisions of Articles 6(3)–6(7) and 9. No additional party may be joined after the confirmation or appointment of any arbitrator, unless all parties, including the additional party, otherwise agree. The Secretariat may fix a time limit for the submission of a Request for Joinder.

2) The Request for Joinder shall contain the following information:

   a) the case reference of the existing arbitration;

   b) the name in full, description, address and other contact details of each of the parties, including the additional party; and

   c) the information specified in Article 4(3) subparagraphs c), d), e) and f).

   The party filing the Request for Joinder may submit therewith such other documents or information as it considers appropriate or as may contribute to the efficient resolution of the dispute.

3) The provisions of Articles 4(4) and 4(5) shall apply, mutatis mutandis, to the Request for Joinder.

4) The additional party shall submit an Answer in accordance, mutatis mutandis, with the provisions of Articles 5(1)–5(4). The additional party may make claims against any other party in accordance with the provisions of Article 8.

Article 10 – Consolidation of Arbitrations

The Court may, at the request of a party, consolidate two or more arbitrations pending under the Rules into a single arbitration, where:

a) the parties have agreed to consolidation; or

b) all of the claims in the arbitrations are made under the same arbitration agreement; or

c) where the claims in the arbitrations are made under more than one arbitration agreement, the arbitrations are between the same parties, the disputes in the arbitrations arise in connection with the same legal relationship, and the Court finds the arbitration agreements to be compatible.

In deciding whether to consolidate, the Court may take into account any circumstances it considers to be relevant, including whether one or more arbitrators have been confirmed or appointed in more than one of the arbitrations and, if so, whether the same or different persons have been confirmed or appointed.

When arbitrations are consolidated, they shall be consolidated into the arbitration that commenced first, unless otherwise agreed by all parties.

Having provided the text of the relevant provisions of each set of rules, the remainder of the article will engage in an analysis of the different treatments of consolidation and joinder.

3.3 Analyzing Best Practices for Consolidating Proceedings

While each of the Swiss, HKIAC and ICC Rules provide a mechanism for the consolidation of pending proceedings, the specifics of those mechanisms vary.

Article 4(1) of the Swiss Rules sets forth the basis on which the Swiss Chambers' Arbitration Institution's Arbitration Court (Swiss Chambers' Court) decides whether to consolidate a newly commenced case with other arbitral proceedings already pending under the Swiss Rules. This raises the first points of difference between the provisions of the Swiss Rules and those of the HKIAC and ICC. While the institution, or its court, is the decision maker under each set of rules, unlike the HKIAC or the ICC's International Court of Arbitration (ICC Court), which require an application of one of the parties for the instigation of the consolidation process, on its face the Swiss Chambers' Court has much wider powers, being able to consider consolidation on its own initiative simply on the basis of the submission of a new notice of arbitration.

It has been said that by selecting the Swiss Rules, parties are deemed to have agreed in advance that the Swiss Chambers' Court may decide, in appropriate circumstances, to consolidate future proceedings, so that the Court could—at least theoretically—order consolidation even over the objection of all of the parties.[12] Despite the broad formulation of the text of the provision, it has been suggested in several commentaries that as, prior to the 2012 revisions, the Swiss Chambers' Court had ordered consolidation only in limited and justifiable circumstances, and usually only when it was endorsed by the parties concerned, it is to be expected that the Court, despite enjoying wide powers, will nevertheless continue to adopt a restrictive approach.[13] The secretariat of the *Swiss Chambers' Arbitration Institution* has also reportedly stated in an interview that consolidation should only occur upon the request of one of the parties.[14]

The points raised in the proceeding paragraphs do however also speak to the discretionary nature of the power to consolidate, a feature which is common to each of the sets of rules under discussion. Article 4(1) of the Swiss Rules, Articles 28(1) and 28(4) of the HKIAC Rules and the penultimate paragraph of Article 10 of the ICC Rules require the taking into account of all relevant circumstances when making a decision to consolidate. These relevant circumstances are expressly defined in the Swiss Rules to include "the links between the cases and the progress already made in the pending arbitral proceedings"[15] and, in both the HKIAC and ICC Rules, "whether one or more arbitrators have been designated or confirmed in more than one of the arbitrations, and if so, whether the same or different arbitrators have been confirmed."[16]

One point of difference between the rules is that it is only the Swiss and HKIAC Rules which expressly mandate consultation with

---

[12] Philipp Habegger, *The Revised Swiss Rules of International Arbitration: An Overview of the Major Changes*, 30(2) ASA BULLETIN 276 (2012) referencing BERNARD HANOTIAU, COMPLEX ARBITRATIONS, MULTIPARTY, MULTICONTRACT, MULTI-ISSUE AND CLASS ACTIONS, 166 (The Hague 2005); JULIAN LEW/LOUKAS MISTELIS/STEFAN KRÖLL, COMPARATIVE INTERNATIONAL COMMERCIAL ARBITRATION, N 16.62 (The Hague 2003), and Marc Blessing, *Comparison of the Swiss Rules with the UNCITRAL Rules and others, in The Swiss Rules of International Arbitration"*, ASA SPECIAL SERIES NO 22, 31.

[13] Philipp Habegger, *The Revised Swiss Rules of International Arbitration: An Overview of the Major Changes*, 30(2) ASA BULLETIN 2012, 277.

[14] *See*, LARA PAIR, CONSOLIDATION IN INTERNATIONAL COMMERCIAL ARBITRATION: THE ICC AND SWISS RULES, 46 (2012).

[15] Art. 4(1) Swiss Rules.

[16] Art. 28 HKIAC Rules and Art 10 ICC Rules.

the parties and any confirmed arbitrator in relation to the exercise of this discretion.[17]

Further differences also exist as to how the rules deal with the question of consolidation of cases where different parties are involved and also in respect of cases concerning claims arising out of different arbitration agreements.

Under both the Swiss and HKIAC Rules it is possible for cases to be consolidated where the parties to those proceedings are not the same, regardless of whether or not the claims in the proceedings arise out of the same or different arbitration agreements. The ICC Rules, on the other hand, make a distinction between these two scenarios and, according to Article 10(c), if the claims in the arbitrations are made under more than one arbitration agreement, then for consolidation to be contemplated the arbitrations must be between the same parties, unless all the parties agree otherwise.

The final major difference between the rules relates to the ability of the institution to consolidate cases where arbitrators have already been appointed or confirmed. Both the Swiss and HKIAC Rules provide several consequences for the constitution of the tribunal upon consolidation. First, the parties to the arbitrations are deemed to have waived their right to designate an arbitrator.[18] Second, the institution may revoke the appointment of any arbitrator already designated or confirmed, and third, the institution may appoint the tribunal in respect of the consolidated proceeding.[19] The rationale for these measures is to ensure that all parties to the consolidated proceeding enjoy equal treatment in relation to the appointment of the tribunal.[20]

In contracts, under the ICC Rules, the appointment of arbitrators in more than one of the proceedings is treated as one of the circumstances to be taken in to account in the exercise of the Court's discretion and, if arbitrators have been confirmed in more than one of the proceedings, and those arbitrators are different individuals, then the Secretariat's Guide to the ICC Rules explains that the ICC Court will be unable to consolidate the cases as it does not have the power to constitute a single tribunal absent the voluntary resignation of the

---

17 *See*, Art. 28(1) HKIAC Rules and Art. 4(1) Swiss Rules.

18 *See*, Art. 28(6) HKIAC Rules and Art. 4(1) Swiss Rules.

19 *Ibid.*

20 In relation to the provisions of the Swiss Rules, which are mirrored in Art. 28 HKIAC Rules, Philipp Habegger commented that the provisions "leave more room for, but also allow for better preservation of, equal treatment of the parties in the event of consolidation than any other set of arbitration rules." Philipp Habegger, *The Revised Swiss Rules of International Arbitration*, 5(2) NYSBA NEW YORK DISPUTE RESOLUTION LAWYER 62 (Fall 2012).

arbitrators or their removal by the Court upon the agreement of the parties.[21] This effectively means that consolidation under the ICC Rules is time restricted, becoming unavailable when an arbitrator is confirmed in more than one of the proceedings.

3.4 Analysing Best Practices for Joining Third Parties

3.4.1 Preliminary comment

When the 2012 version of the Swiss Rules was introduced, Article 4(2) on joinder had undergone more limited modification than Article 4(1) dealing with consolidation. According to the Working Group on the revision of the Swiss Rules of International Arbitration there was no intention to change the substance of the provision.[22]

Similarly, in the 2013 revision of the HKIAC rules, while alterations were made to the provisions on joinder, unlike the provisions on consolidation which were completely new, the amended provisions sought to build on and enhance the system which had been in place since 2008.

The most notable features of the provisions on joinder from a comparative perspective relate, first, to the procedural requirements of each set of rules, and second, to their scope of applicability, in terms of who may be joined under each of the provisions.

3.4.2 Procedural requirements

There are three procedural aspects of the joinder provisions which significantly differ between the Swiss, ICC and HKIAC Rules.

The first relates to who is able to make use of the provision.

Under the Swiss and HKIAC Rules it is clear that situations of both joinder and, what is alternately called, intervention, are covered.[23] In other words, it is open to both existing parties to a proceeding to request to join an additional party, as well as for additional parties to submit a request to join—or intervene—in ongoing proceedings. This is not the case under the ICC Rules which explicitly restrict the ability to request joinder to existing parties to the proceedings.[24] As the

---

[21] Jason Fry, Simon Greenberg and Francesca Mazza, *The Secretariat's Guide to ICC Arbitration*, ICC PUBLICATION NO. 729E, para. 3-358 (2012).

[22] *Op. cit.* Note 13, Habegger, p. 278.

[23] *See*, Arts. 27(3) and 27(6) HKIAC Rules and Art. 4(2) Swiss Rules.

[24] *See*, Art. 7(1) ICC Rules which state "[a] ***party*** wishing to join an additional party to the arbitration shall submit its request for arbitration against the additional party (the "Request for Joinder") to the Secretariat..." (emphasis added).

Secretariat's Guide to the ICC Rules provides, the Secretariat "is not even in a position to acknowledge the existence of an arbitration, much less entertain a request for intervention."[25]

The second important procedural difference between the three sets of rules relates to the timing of when a request for joinder, or a request to participate as it should be called under the Swiss Rules, may be made. Each of the three institutions under discussion takes a different approach to this question. Under the Swiss Rules, as it is the arbitral tribunal which is given the power to determine requests to participate, such will only be considered post-constitution.[26] The ICC, on the other hand, specifies in Article 7(1) that "no additional party may be joined after the confirmation or appointment of any arbitrator, unless all parties, including the additional party, agree otherwise," which makes joinder a pre-constitution issue, to be determined by the ICC Court. HKIAC takes a third approach, allowing requests for joinder to be made both pre and post-constitution. If a request for joinder is made prior to the constitution of the tribunal then the issue is one for HKIAC to decide,[27] if made post constitution then it is a matter for the tribunal.[28] According to Article 27(11), if an additional party is joined prior to the confirmation of the tribunal then all parties are deemed to have waived their right to designate an arbitrator and HKIAC, in consultation with the parties, may revoke the appointments of any arbitrators already designated or confirmed. If this occurs then HKIAC will appoint the tribunal. Again, the rationale is to ensure that all parties, including the joined party, enjoy equal treatment in relation to the appointment of the tribunal.

The third significant procedural difference between the rules relates to the form requirements specified. Unlike the ICC and HKIAC Rules, the Swiss Rules do not set out any particular requirements which a request to participate must fulfil. Instead they simply stipulate that if a request is made (in whatever form) the arbitral tribunal will decide on such request "after consulting with all of the parties…taking into account all relevant circumstances."[29] Article 27 of the HKIAC Rues and Article 7 of the ICC Rules, on the other hand, both set out detailed requirements regarding the filing and content of Requests for Joinder and the Answers thereto, including such things as details of the relevant agreements or legal instruments, the facts and legal

---

25 *Op. cit.* Note 22, Jason Fry, Simon Greenberg and Francesca Mazza, para. 3-294.

26 *See,* Art. 4(2) Swiss Rules.

27 Art. 27(8) HKIAC Rules.

28 Art. 27(1) HKIAC Rules.

29 *See,* Art. 4(2) Swiss Rules.

arguments supporting the request as well as any points at issue.[30] The HKIAC Rules go even further, also explicitly providing for all parties to the arbitration to file their comments in relation to the Request for Joinder and specifying what such comments may include.[31] Although more procedurally specific, this reflects the requirement in Article 4(2) of the Swiss Rules that the tribunal consult with all of the parties, a requirement which is absent in the ICC Rules, which provides only for submissions by the requesting party and the party against whom the Request is made.

3.4.3 Who may be joined

When the 2012 revisions to the Swiss Rules were introduced, the change in terminology in the context of who such an application could be made by, or in relation to, from "a third party" to "one or more third persons" in Article 4(2) was important and is the second feature which sets the Swiss, HKIAC and ICC rules apart.

This change had the effect of:

- Making clear that more than one additional third person can be joined in pending proceedings. Something which is possible, although not explicitly stated, under both the ICC and HKIAC Rules.
- Reflecting the idea that the third person to be joined is not, as of the date of the request, a party to the proceedings. A similar idea is conveyed in the HKIAC and ICC Rules by the use of the term "additional party."[32]
- Clarifying that, under the Swiss Rules, it is not necessarily the case that the third person will, upon their joinder, become a "proper party" to the proceeding, that is, it is possible that they may not make any claims or have any claims made against them. If read literally, it may even be the case that some forms of participation may not even require the existence of an arbitration agreement with the person to be joined,[33] meaning that participation by third persons under the Swiss Rules may therefore take other forms, such as "side

---

30 Arts. 27(4) and 27(5) HKIAC Rules and Arts. 7(2) to 7(4) ICC Rules.

31 Art. 27(7) HKIAC Rules.

32 *See*, Arts. 27(1) and 27(6) HKIAC Rules and Art. 7(1) ICC Rules.

33 *Op. cit.* Note 21, Habegger, p. 62.

intervention" or the submission of amicus curiae briefs.[34]

This latter aspect is not possible under the ICC Rules, which specifically requires that the claims being made against the additional party to be set out in the Request for Joinder,[35] and while the HKIAC Rules do not specifically require details of the general nature of any claim be set out in the Request, it must include details of the relief or remedy sought against the additional party, which in practice has the same effect.[36]

The major consequence of the Swiss Rules' allowance of the full spectrum of third person participation is that, if read on the face of its text, it may not be a requirement of the Swiss Rules that the person or persons to be joined be a party to the arbitration agreement. Therefore, under the Swiss Rules, the tribunal may only be required to decide whether the third person to be joined is (or can be regarded as) a party to the arbitration clause(s) forming the basis of the proceedings, in the context of a request for joinder of an additional claimant or respondent. This is a marked contrast to both the HKIAC and ICC Rules. The test under the HKIAC Rules (whether it is HKIAC or the tribunal which is making the decision) is whether, prima facie, the additional party is bound by an arbitration agreement giving rise to the arbitration.[37] Under the ICC Rules, as claims must be made against any additional party to be joined, it is clear that they must necessarily be party to the arbitration agreement giving rise to the dispute and, in fact, if any jurisdictional objection is made the ICC Court will allow the arbitration to proceed only between the parties (including any additional party) with respect to which the Court "is prima facie satisfied that an arbitration agreement under the Rules that binds them all exists."[38]

4. CONCLUSION

Although each of the Swiss, HKIAC and ICC Rules deal with the important issues of joinder and consolidation, and although there are points of similarity between them, overall, the way in which they do so is ultimately very different.

---

34 *Op. cit.* Note 13, Habegger, p. 278.
35 Arts. 7(2)(c) and 4(3)(c) and (e) ICC Rules.
36 Art. 27(4)(h) HKIAC Rules.
37 Arts. 27(1) and 27(8) HKIAC Rules.
38 Art. 6(4)(i) ICC Rules.

Nevertheless, each of the three sets of rules examined provides effective means to manage cases involving multiple parties and/or multiple contracts to maximize procedural efficiency and fairness of the arbitral process, a feature of institutional rules which is particularly important in light of the increasing complexity of international commercial relationships, and the disputes which arise from them.

Jurisdiction of an Arbitral Tribunal over Set-Off under Swiss Rules of International Arbitration

*Vladimir Pavić**

1. INTRODUCTORY COMMENTS

The Swiss Rules of International Arbitration (hereinafter the Swiss Rules) are a decade old (or young, depending on one's perspective). Their content is based upon the UNCITRAL Rules, a tried and tested tool for ad hoc arbitration.[1] Inevitably, initial improvements to the underlying foundation were necessary in order to mold the starting model into a final product more useable in the context of institutional arbitration. Another round of amendments (2012) was introduced to address the ever-changing needs of arbitration users.

The facts presented above resemble to a great extent the stories behind a number of the institutional rules nowadays. Putting aside the peculiar design of the 'institution' (i.e. the supporting institutional structure) administering the Swiss Rules, many of the present institutional rules resemble each other in attempting to provide a flexible and efficient framework and, often, in using the UNCITRAL Rules as the starting point for the solutions they offer. This, in turn, means that the competition between the institutional arbitrations becomes more of a competition between their administrative capacities, reputation and advantages or disadvantages of their geographic locations, rather than a competition between the solutions contained in the respective rules.

The Swiss Rules (both their 2004 and 2012 version), however, do contain a provision which stands out as unique. Art. 21(5) Swiss Rules provides as follows:

> The arbitral tribunal shall have jurisdiction to hear a set-off defence even if the relationship out of which the defence is said to arise is not within the scope of the arbitration clause,

---

* Prof. Dr. Vladimir Pavić, University of Belgrade. This paper is based on a presentation given at the conference "10 Years of Swiss Rules of International Arbitration" on 31 January 2014 in Basel.

[1] Christoph Brunner, *Chapter 3, Part I: Introduction to the Swiss Rules of International Arbitration, in* ARBITRATION IN SWITZERLAND: THE PRACTITIONER'S GUIDE 326 et seq. (Arroyo ed. 2013).

or falls within the scope of another arbitration agreement or forum-selection clause.

This provision has a distinct Swiss flavor. Similar provisions were contained in the arbitration rules of some of the chambers of commerce that now administer the Swiss Rules.[2] Despite the popularity of the Swiss Rules and the high standing of Switzerland as an arbitration venue, the rule contained in Art. 21(5) was, to the best of this author's knowledge, never copied in another set of institutional rules. If anything, the rule has provoked a lively debate on its pros and cons even outside of the commentaries devoted solely to the Swiss Rules.[3] This paper will examine why this might be the case, why there might be some reluctance to follow the Swiss example and whether such reluctance is justified.

In doing so, the paper will first address the notion, legal nature and operation of a set-off (2); its use in the proceedings, distinction from and relation to the counterclaim (3); the (mis)perceived tension between the consent paradigm of arbitration and the set-off (4); the ways in which various arbitration rules address the issue of whether and under which conditions an arbitral tribunal has jurisdiction to decide on a set-off (5); and, finally, the operation and consequences of Art. 21(5) (6) vis-à-vis the solutions which might follow from other institutional rules (7).

2. THE NOTION AND OPERATION OF SET-OFF

Set-off *(lat.: compensatio)* is an operation through which the mutual obligations of a debtor and a creditor are discharged one against the other. The definition offered is a simplification of the myriad of comparative peculiarities and nuances. Different legal systems provide different preconditions, both substantive and procedural, for this to happen.[4] While a set-off is regarded as a substantive defence, subject to

---

[2] *E.g.* International Arbitration Rules of the Zurich Chamber of Commerce, Art. 27.

[3] JEFFREY WAINCYMER, PROCEDURE AND EVIDENCE IN INTERNATIONAL ARBITRATION, 217-254 (2012); Alberto Fortún, *Set-offs Are Not Counterclaims in International Arbitration, in* LIBER AMICORUM BERNARDO CREMADES, 451-469 (Fernández-Ballesteros and Arias eds. 2010); Alexis Mourre, *The Set-off Paradox in International Arbitration,* 24 ARBITRATION INTERNATIONAL 387, 387-404 (2008); Vladimir Pavić, *Counterclaim and Set-Off in International Commercial Arbitration,* 1 BELGRADE LAW REVIEW 101, 101-116 (2006).

[4] If there is a common denominator of such preconditions, it may perhaps be discerned from the Art. 8.1 of the 2010 UNIDROIT Principles, which require that there must be a mutuality of claims between the parties, that the performances owed must be of the same kind, that the party relying on a set-off must be entitled to perform, and the other party's obligation must be ascertained as to its existence and amount, and due. Where the obligations arise out of the same contract, other party's obligation need not be ascertained.

the fulfillment of the substantive rules of the applicable law, it is also the case that in some systems this substantive defence can have effect only thorough a judicial declaration. In such instances, the substantive device is conditional upon its procedural deployment.[5] In the context of adversary proceedings (either before a court or an arbitral tribunal), this might be the result of a situation where the plaintiff or claimant presents its claim (main claim) and the defendant or respondent puts forward the cross-claim it wants to set-off against the main claim. That is why a set-off can seldom be viewed and examined in isolation of the procedural context.

Historically, the operation of the set-off was initially viewed as automatic: the two claims would set off one against the other as soon as the relevant conditions were met, without any need for the parties to be aware of such an automatic operation or rely on it. This extreme and unrealistic position was eventually modified, and the courts settled on a position that the set-off, although automatic in operation, had to be relied upon before the court in order to be taken into account.[6]

Nowadays, the prevalent solution is that the set-off does not operate automatically but requires a positive action, a declaration of one of the parties, which need not be made before the court.[7] However, if the set-off defence is to be considered by the judge, it nevertheless has to be pleaded within the procedural limits and deadlines set by the law, e.g. in the statement of defence or until the main hearing is closed. The effects of the declaration are not uniform. In some systems, the declaration operates so that the mutual obligations are discharged retroactively, at the moment in time when the conditions for their mutual discharge were first met. Other rules provide that the effects of the declaration are only *pro futuro*.[8]

Where the claims may be set-off through a judicial declaration, such a declaration has effect either *ex tunc*, or for the future (*ex nunc*).[9]

---

5 PASCAL PICHONNAZ, LOUISE GULLIFER, SET-OFF IN ARBITRATION AND COMMERCIAL TRANSACTIONS, 17 (2014).

6 PASCAL PICHONNAZ, LOUISE GULLIFER, SET-OFF IN ARBITRATION AND COMMERCIAL TRANSACTIONS, 21 (2014).

7 Among others SWISS CODE OF OBLIGATIONS, Art 124(1); DUTCH CIVIL CODE, Art. 6:127(1); GREEK CIVIL CODE Art. 441; ABGB, Section 1438; SERBIAN LAW ON CONTRACTS AND TORTS, Arts. 336-338; CROATIAN LAW ON CONTRACTS AND TORTS, Arts. 195-197.

8 For an overview of the matter and the legal systems, *see*, PASCAL PICHONNAZ, LOUISE GULLIFER, SET-OFF IN ARBITRATION AND COMMERCIAL TRANSACTIONS, 25 et seq. (2014).

9 PASCAL PICHONNAZ, LOUISE GULLIFER, SET-OFF IN ARBITRATION AND COMMERCIAL TRANSACTIONS, 29 (2014).

English law distinguishes between an "independent" (or "legal") set-off and a "transaction" (or "equitable") set-off. The independent set off can only be used with respect to a court action to offset liquidated and mutual claims and requires a judicial decision. The claims do not need to be connected. A 'transaction' set-off is a substantive defence raised with respect to connected, but not necessarily liquated, claims.[10]

The various ways in which the set-off operates and may be relied upon might be viewed as an indication that there are inherent strengths and weaknesses in the solutions provided. Irrespective of what one views as the ultimately superior concept, this multitude of solutions presents problems even if one takes jurisdiction for granted: the issue of the law applicable to the substantive requirements of set-off (where the claims arise from different transactions, potentially subject to different applicable laws) alone exceeds the scope of this paper.[11]

3. USE OF SET-OFF IN PROCEEDINGS AND DISTINCTION FROM COUNTERCLAIM

Although the set-off is viewed mostly as a substantive defence, it need not be so, as shown above. Where the declaration of a judge is necessary for it to have any effect, procedure cannot be ignored. Even in the systems where a simple out-of-court declaration is sufficient to produce legal effects, those effects might not be observed and

---

[10] The claims have to be "inseparably connected with the transaction giving rise to the claim page so that the title of the plaintiff at law to prosecute his demand is impeached", *The Angelic Grace* [1981] 1 LLOYD'S REP. 288. See, also Peter Aeberli, *Abatements, Setoff and Counterclaims in Arbitration Proceedings*, 3 ARBITRATION AND DISPUTE RESOLUTION LAW JOURNAL 10, 10 (1992); PASCAL PICHONNAZ, LOUISE GULLIFER, SET-OFF IN ARBITRATION AND COMMERCIAL TRANSACTIONS, 108 (2014).

[11] But suffice to say that, where the mechanism is of a procedural nature, the procedural rules of the forum will have the main say on how it is carried out, while the importance of the conflict of law solutions is more prominent where the set-off is of a more substantive nature. Where the main claim and the cross-claim arise out of different relationships, there are several approaches to the matter: application of the *lex causae* of the main claim (this is also the solution of the Art. 17 of the Regulation No. 593/2008 on the Law applicable to Contractual Obligations (Rome I Regulation), OFFICIAL JOURNAL OF THE EUROPEAN UNION L-177, 6-16 (2008) and was a solution earlier advocated by Klaus Peter Berger, *Set-off in International Economic Arbitration*, 15 ARBITRATION INTERNATIONAL 53, 63 (1999) and R.I.V.F. Bertrams, *Set-off in Private International Law, in* COMPARABILITY AND EVALUATION: IN HONOUR OF DIMITRA KOKKINI-IATRIDOU, 153-165 (Boele-Woelki et al. eds., 1994), cumulative application of the laws applicable to the main claim and the cross-claim, application of the lex fori and resort to "general principles of international law" (*see*, FOUCHARD, GAILLARD, GOLDMAN ON INTERNATIONAL COMMERCIAL ARBITRATION, 834 (Gaillard and Savage eds., 1999), invoking, *inter alia*, ICC case no. 3540. *See also*, PASCAL PICHONNAZ, LOUISE GULLIFER, SET-OFF IN ARBITRATION AND COMMERCIAL TRANSACTIONS, 60-74 (2014).

pronounced by the judge unless the reliance on them is admissible in the course of the proceedings (i.e. the defence is raised within the prescribed time limits). This material-procedural dichotomy generates perhaps the most difficulties in dealing with the set-off.

Sometimes the picture is further complicated by the fact that the party resisting the main claim, alongside the possibility to declare a set-off, might also have the possibility to introduce a counterclaim (*Widerklage, demande reconventionelle, domanda riconvenzionale*). While a counterclaim and a set-off might serve a generally similar purpose (defence against the main claim), the role of the set-off defence is to reduce the exposure of the cross-creditor in the ongoing proceedings pursuant to the main claim, but it cannot do more than to reduce it to zero. Thus, there is not a better way to describe it than as a "shield", and the best the shield can do is protect its user. On the other hand, the counterclaim is rather to be viewed as a "sword", a tool that serves not only to defend its bearer but also to go on the attack.[12] Unlike the set-off defence, which will be examined only if the main claim (or at least a portion of it) is found to exist, the counterclaim has a "life" of its own. Thus it can exceed the main claim and will be examined even if the main claim is rejected or found inadmissible and even if the request to compensate it has been withdrawn.

Whether a respondent chooses a set-off defence or a counterclaim will often depend on tactical considerations, taking into account the likelihood of the success of the main claim and its value in relation to the cross-claim. Therefore, while it is true that set-offs can be deployed in the proceedings as "counterclaims in disguise"[13] and that one can resort to counterclaim instead of raising a set-off defence,[14] it is correct to observe: "When claims of money are at stake, which usually is the case in international economic arbitration, set-off and counterclaim are 'only a hair's-breadth away' from each other."[15]

---

[12] The authorship of the popular sword/shield metaphor can be traced to Klaus Peter Berger, *Set-off in International Economic Arbitration*, 15 ARBITRATION INTERNATIONAL 53, 60 (1999).

[13] Klaus Peter Berger, *Set-off in International Economic Arbitration,* 15 ARBITRATION INTERNATIONAL 53, 58 (1999).

[14] Bernard Hanotiau, *Problems Raised by Complex Arbitrations Involving Multiple Contracts—Parties—Issues,* 18 JOURNAL OF INTERNATIONAL ARBITRATION 251, 286 (2001), commenting on ICC case no. 5801.

[15] Klaus Peter Berger, *Set-off in International Economic Arbitration,* 15 ARBITRATION INTERNATIONAL 53, 58 (1999), referencing Philip R. Wood, ENGLISH AND INTERNATIONAL SET-OFF, no. 1-37 *in fine* (1989). European Court of Justice has clearly distinguished between counterclaim and set-off in the case of DANVAERN PRODUCTION A/S V. SCHUHFABRIKEN OTTERBECK GMBH & CO. C-341-93. Perhaps the only country where this distinction has been somewhat blurred are the United States, where a set-off defence has

4. SET-OFF BEFORE AN ARBITRAL TRIBUNAL – CONSENT PARADIGM AND ITS LIMITATIONS

Unlike the state court, which considers the statutory catalogue of jurisdictional grounds in order to determine whether it has competence to adjudicate a particular claim, an arbitration tribunal first considers the consent of the parties. Given that general arbitration agreements, i.e. an arbitration agreement which does not specify the dispute to be submitted to arbitration, are not allowed,[16] a valid arbitration agreement has to circumscribe its scope. While the parties often use inclusive wording to submit to arbitration disputes which both "arise out of" and might be "in connection with" a particular legal relationship, such terms cannot be relied on in order to bring before the tribunal those who are not the parties to the arbitration agreement or disputes which fall outside of its scope. In contrast, the jurisdictional pull of a state court is much stronger and the attraction of jurisdiction may make it competent to accommodate a wider range of parties or claims.

This is not to say that *vis attractiva* of a state court is unlimited: *e.g.* while a party is generally entitled to submit a counterclaim to the court, its right to do so might be conditioned upon the connection of the counterclaim to the main claim.[17] However, by comparison, an arbitral tribunal will administer a much stricter test with respect to the main claim and the counterclaim: both of them can be decided on their merits only if they fall within the ambits of an agreement to arbitrate.

In assessing the scope of their jurisdiction, arbitrators are always weighing two opposing considerations. On the one hand, they consider the importance of arbitration as a flexible and efficient way of dispute resolution (preferably of the entire dispute between the parties). On the other hand, they are aware that, while some of the national legislators are concerned with whether the arbitrators are too

---

been omitted from the federal rules of procedure. However, this does not meant that American courts treat counterclaims and set-off equally, nor that one may put forward claims that have no connection whatsoever with the original cause of action. (Federal Rules of Civil Procedure, 13 (a-b), CHARLES A. WRIGHT, ARTHUR R. MILLER, FEDERAL PRACTICE AND PROCEDURE: FEDERAL RULES OF CIVIL PROCEDURE VOL. 6, 2nd ed. 1426 (1990); INTER-STATE NATIONAL BANK V. LUTHER 221 F.2D 382 (10th Cir. 1955), with certain reservations with regard to subject-matter jurisdiction, *Federman v. Empire Fire & Marine Insurance Co.* 597 F.2d 798 (2nd Cir. 1979).

[16] *See e.g.*, New York Convention, Art. II(1); UNCITRAL Model Law on International Commercial Arbitration (1985) with amendment as adopted in 2006, Art 7.

[17] *See*, Vladimir Pavić, *Counterclaim and Set-Off in International Commercial Arbitration*, 1 BELGRADE LAW REVIEW 101, 102 et seq. (2006); for further references *see*, Christian Koller, *Chapter I: The Arbitration Agreement and Arbitrability - Contemplations on Set-off and Counterclaim in International Commercial Arbitration*, *in* AUSTRIAN ARBITRATION YEARBOOK 59, 63 (Klausegger et al. eds., 2008).

cautious in determining their competence,[18] *all* of them are concerned with arbitrators overstepping their jurisdictional boundaries and have thus put mechanisms to rectify such incursions into the jurisdictional ambit of the state courts.[19]

It is against this background of the consent paradigm that the question arises on how to treat a set-off defence before an arbitral tribunal and whether it raises issues of jurisdiction at all.

A set-off defence might—but need not—arise out of the same legal relationship out of which the main claim arises. If the set-off is seen as a substantive *defence* and its operation automatic, *ex lege* or upon extrajudicial declaration, then it could be argued that whether a tribunal has jurisdiction over the relationship out of which a cross-claim arises is moot. If a tribunal were to ignore a set-off defence for lack of jurisdiction, it would encroach on one party's right of defence and might eventually award the claimant a claim that has already been extinguished.[20] Instead of providing an efficient venue for dispute resolution, arbitration would actually promote the enforcement of claims which have already ceased to exist.[21]

It is even possible to reconcile this position with the consent paradigm. Poudret notes that it is only natural that a claimant who asks the tribunal to rule on its claim has accepted that the tribunal has jurisdiction to rule on any objections against that claim, whatever they may be, including the objection that the claim was affected (diminished or extinguished) through set-off.[22] For Schöll, the consent of the claimant should be examined on a case-by-case basis, paying particular attention to the wording of the arbitration clause and to when it was drafted, prior to or after the dispute arose.[23]

---

[18] *E.g.* while it is possible to revisit a negative jurisdictional decision of a tribunal in Switzerland, it is not possible to under the UNCITRAL Model Law on International Commercial Arbitration.

[19] *See e.g.*, New York Convention, Art. V(1)(c); UNCITRAL Model Law on International Commercial Arbitration (1985) with amendment as adopted in 2006, Art. 34(2)(a)(iii); UNCITRAL Model Law on International Commercial Arbitration Art. 36(1)(a)(iii); English Arbitration Act 1996, Art. 68(2)(b); Serbian Law on Arbitration, Art. 66(1)(3).

[20] Jean-François Poudret, *Compensation et arbitrage, in* LE DROIT EN ACTION 361, 361 (Rapp and Jaccard eds., 1996); Alberto Fortún, *Set-offs Are Not Counterclaims in International Arbitration, in* LIBER AMICORUM BERNARDO CREMADES, 457 (Fernández-Ballesteros and Arias eds. 2010).

[21] Although a debtor might still be entitled to invoke the effect of a set-off declaration at the enforcement stage.

[22] Jean-François Poudret, *Compensation et arbitrage, in* LE DROIT EN ACTION 361, 380 (Rapp and Jaccard eds., 1996). Similarly, Michael Schöll, *Set-Off Defences in International Arbitration*, 26 ASA SPECIAL SERIES 108, 131 (2006).

[23] Michael Schöll, *Set-Off Defences in International Arbitration*, 26 ASA SPECIAL SERIES 108, 132-133 (2006), for a critique of this position *see*, Alexis Mourre, *The Set-off Paradox in*

The opposite argument may be advanced as well: extinguishing, wholly or partially, the main claim pursuant to set-off also effectively recognizes the cross-claim.[24] Coupled with the possibility that, pursuant to the law determined as applicable to the set-off, a cross-claim might not need to be ascertained in order to be set-off against the main claim, this could lead to a situation in which an arbitral tribunal could potentially end up arbitrating *all* disputes between the two parties, and the prohibition of general arbitration clauses would be harder to maintain. Also, where the applicable law only allows a procedural variety of set-off, i.e. set-off which operates only through a judgment of the court, the refusal to hear a set-off defence for lack of jurisdiction does not result in enforcing a main claim which no longer exists.

It is also worth bearing in mind that counterclaims are subject to different admissibility and jurisdictional preconditions. In some jurisdictions, a counterclaim is admissible in litigation only if it is connected to the main claim, can be compensated against the main claim, or is lodged in order to determine the (non)existence of a right or a legal relationship vital for the main claim.[25]

In the context of arbitration, jurisdiction over a counterclaim is entirely subject to the consent paradigm: it has to be within the scope of the arbitration agreement.[26] If the counterclaims and set-offs are indeed a "hair's-breadth away" and if the decision to use one or another can sometimes be purely tactical, rather than inevitable, then having a lower jurisdictional threshold for set-offs than for counterclaims would provide a strong incentive to resort to a set-off as

---

International Arbitration, 24 Arbitration International 387, 395-396 (2008): "Yet, it is hard to understand why the drafting of the arbitral agreement should matter so much. That the arbitration agreement is more or less specific has, for example no bearing on possible counterclaims and set-off defences, which the parties will by definition not have contemplated. The fact page that the arbitration agreement has been concluded before or after the dispute erupted has also little relevance."

[24] Alexis Mourre, *The Set-off Paradox in International Arbitration*, 24 ARBITRATION INTERNATIONAL 387, 394 (2008).

[25] Such is the case in *e.g.* Austria and Serbia. For further references *see*, Christian Koller, *Chapter I: The Arbitration Agreement and Arbitrability - Contemplations on Set-off and Counterclaim in International Commercial Arbitration, in* AUSTRIAN ARBITRATION YEARBOOK 59, 63 (Klausegger et al. eds., 2008) and Vladimir Pavić, *Counterclaim and Set-Off in International Commercial Arbitration*, 1 BELGRADE LAW REVIEW 101, 102 (2006).

[26] GARY BORN, INTERNATIONAL COMMERCIAL ARBITRATION, 3rd ed., 2222 (2014); ALAN REDFERN, MARTIN HUNTER ET AL., REDFERN AND HUNTER ON INTERNATIONAL ARBITRATION, 383 (2009); FOUCHARD, GAILLARD, GOLDMAN ON INTERNATIONAL COMMERCIAL ARBITRATION, 1222 (Gaillard and Savage eds., 1999), and not subject to another dispute resolution clause, *see*, *Société Empresa de Telecomunicaciones de Cuba SA v. Telefonica Antillana SA and SNC Banco Nacional de Comercio Exterior*, COUR D'APPEL DE PARIS IÈRE CHAMBRE, Decision of 16 November 2006.

long as the cross-claim is lower than what the respondent perceives as the likely correct value of the main claim.

5. TREATMENT OF SET-OFF IN ARBITRATION RULES

The problems presented above have no doubt been on the mind of the drafters of many arbitration rules. Today, it is possible to identify at least three ways in which set-offs have been dealt with. Some rules provide restrictions for the introduction of set-off claims and/or set off defences, usually submitting them to the same jurisdictional threshold applicable to counterclaims. Another set of rules does not address the issue explicitly. The third set opens the door wide for the set-off, the most prominent being the Swiss Rules with Art. 21(5) providing for the broad jurisdiction of a tribunal over the set-off claims. Each of these approaches warrants further examination in the following sections.

5.1 Jurisdictional Barriers to the Set-Off

The first option—introducing explicit jurisdictional/admissibility barriers for introduction of set-off defences before the tribunal is present in both the 1976 and the 2010 versions of the UNCITRAL Rules, and a number of institutional rules. The threshold to be cleared varies: *e.g.* 1976 UNCITRAL Rules provide in their Art. 19(3) that

> [...] the respondent may make a counter-claim arising out of the same contract or rely on a claim *arising out of the same contract* for the purpose of a set-off. [Emphasis added]

At the outset, this provision looks very restrictive by requiring that a claim may be advanced as a counterclaim or a set-off only if the cross-claim arises out of the same contract. Thus, it would appear to negate the substantive nature of the set-off defence and greatly restrict the scope of its operation. However, it has been suggested that Art. 19(3) should be interpreted in a more relaxed manner and that it poses no barrier to the use of a cross-claim as a substantive set-off defence whenever the cross-claim is liquid or undisputed (*e.g.* ascertained by a final judgment of a competent tribunal).[27] It might be a stretch to find additional support for this view in the wording used

[27] Alexis Mourre, *The Set-off Paradox in International Arbitration*, 24 ARBITRATION INTERNATIONAL 387, 397 (2008); cf. Alberto Fortún, *Set-offs Are Not Counterclaims in International Arbitration, in* LIBER AMICORUM BERNARDO CREMADES, 461 (Fernández-Ballesteros and Arias eds., 2010).

by the 1976 UNCITRAL Rules, which speaks only about "reliance on a claim for the purpose of a set-off"[28] rather than about a "set-off defence". It is also worth observing that, when agreeing on the text of the arbitration clause, prudent parties will normally broaden the reach of tribunal's jurisdiction over claims not only to those merely "arising out" of the contract but also to those "in relation to" or "in connection with" such contract, thus further broadening the reach of Art. 19(3).

Some institutional rules deal with the jurisdiction over claims for a purpose of a set-off in a manner identical to or reminiscent of the 1976 UNCITRAL Rules, usually subjecting them to the same jurisdictional requirements as those applicable to the counterclaims. If one accepts this interpretation of Art. 19(3) of the 1976 UNCITRAL Rules, however, none of those restrictions would be applicable to liquidated and undisputed claims.

For instance, ACICA Rules allow counterclaims and claims for the purpose of a set-off that are "arising out of, related to, or in connection with" the contract;[29] where the wording of the scope of the arbitration clause is less broad (*e.g.* only "arising out of and in connection with"), it could be construed as a restriction of the jurisdiction the tribunal would otherwise have pursuant to the ACICA Rules.

On the other hand, the Belgrade Rules and the Zagreb Rules provide that counterclaims and set-offs have to stem from the "relationship covered by the arbitration agreement". Thus, they need not arise out of the contract from which the main claim arises but they still have to be covered by the scope of the arbitration agreement.[30]

The ICDR Rules[31] have recently introduced a change. While the 2010 version provided wording[32] similar to the Belgrade and Zagreb Rules, the new 2014 version allows the Respondent to "[...]make any counterclaims covered by the agreement to arbitrate or assert any setoffs[...]"[33] thus keeping the traditional jurisdictional threshold for the counterclaims and lifting it completely for the set-off. It is unclear whether this also means that a set-off of a purely procedural nature is liberated from any jurisdictional constraints as well or whether any set-

---

28 *See*, UNCITRAL Arbitration Rules (1976), Art 19(3) and 19(4).

29 Australian Centre for International Commercial Arbitration (ACICA) Rules Art. 22(3).

30 Rules of the Belgrade Arbitration Center (2014) (*hereinafter* Belgrade Rules), Art. 22(1) ; Rules of Arbitration of the Permanent Arbitration Court at the Croatian Chamber of Commerce (2012) (*hereinafter* Zagreb Rules) Arts. 31 and 32.

31 International Centre for Dispute Resolution.

32 International Dispute Resolution Procedures (Including Mediation and Arbitration Rules) (2010), Art. 3(2): providing that a respondent may make counterclaims or assert set-offs as to any claim *covered by the agreement to arbitrate.*

33 INTERNATIONAL DISPUTE RESOLUTION PROCEDURES (Including Mediation and Arbitration Rules) (2014), Art. 3(2).

off attempt pursuant to the rules is to be viewed as substantive in nature, irrespective of the conflict of law issues.

Since the reference to the "same contract" in the 1976 UNCITRAL Rules was viewed as restrictive, the 2010 version of the UNCITRAL Rules relaxed the jurisdictional threshold, providing a somewhat Pythian wording instead in their Art. 21(3):

> [...] the respondent may make a counterclaim or rely on a claim for the purpose of a set-off *provided that the arbitral tribunal has jurisdiction over it*. [Emphasis added]

Thus, the amended version no longer makes reference to the "same contract" and instead makes a circular definition: a tribunal has jurisdiction over a counterclaim or a claim for the purpose of a set-off provided that it has jurisdiction over it. However, what the conditions are for asserting jurisdiction is not stated, nor is it mentioned whether jurisdictional thresholds are the same for the counterclaims and claims for the purpose of a set-off. So the pendulum has swung the other way, this time in favor of flexibility over certainty.

5.2 Silent or Oblique Treatment

The wording of Art. 21(3) brings 2010 UNCITRAL Rules close to the position of many institutional rules which do not explicitly address the issue of jurisdiction over set-off claims (and sometimes not even the issue of jurisdiction over counterclaims). Some do not mention set-off at all,[34] while the others merely mention the possibility[35] or provide that the value of such claims is relevant for the calculation of the overall value of the dispute and, consequently, for the calculation of the sum to be advanced for costs.[36] Certain rules add that the value of a claim advanced for a purpose of a set-off will not be used for said calculation if it does not create additional workload for the tribunal.[37] This might, at least when it comes to the advance on costs, allow a distinction between claims arising out of a contract other than the one

---

[34] *E.g.* London Court of International Arbitration (LCIA) Rules (1998); Chamber of Arbitration of Milan (cam) Rules (2010); Belgian Centre for Arbitration and Mediation (CEPANI) Rules (2013).

[35] *E.g.* Ljubljana Rules, Art. 7(3).

[36] *E.g.* International Chamber of Commerce (ICC) Rules (2012), Art. 36(7).

[37] *E.g.* Schedule of costs of the Ljubljana Arbitration Center, Art. 2; VIENNA ARBITRATION (VIAC) Rules (2013), Art. 44(6); JAMS International Rules, Art. 33(7); Schedule 1 Registration and Administrative Fees of the Hong Kong International Arbitration Centre (HKIAC), Art. 2(2).

from which the main claim arises and those arising out of the same contract, as well as between liquidated and unliquidated claims.

5.3 Rules Favoring the Set-Off

As noted in literature, the closer one is to the substantive notion of the set-off with regard to its legal nature and its operation, the more it can be seen as essentially an undermining of the main claim and should therefore always be admissible.[38] A number of rules favor such an approach, not providing any jurisdictional test for a claim advanced for the purpose of a set-off and instead providing that its fate will depend purely on the fulfillment of preconditions for the operation of a set-off, whatever those may be. For instance, Art. 25(5) of the SIAC[39] Rules state, "A party may rely on a claim or defence for the purpose of a set-off *to the extent permitted by the applicable law.*" [emphasis added], whereas Art. 33 of the 2007 Rules of the Polish Chamber of Commerce provides that a claim of the respondent may be set-off against that of a claimant if it is "fit for a set-off".[40]

However, the most prominent set of rules in this group are the Swiss Rules, which go a step further, as will be examined below.

6. THE REACH OF ART. 21(5) OF THE SWISS RULES

Just like the SIAC and Polish rules, Art. 21(5) of the Swiss Rules looks at the set-off through "substantive glasses": set-off is primarily a tool of defence against the main claim and should thus be allowed.[41] But then, Art. 21(5) Swiss Rules goes a step further and removes any jurisdictional doubts that the other rules (including those who are essentially silent on the issue of a set-off) might potentially harbor. It provides that a tribunal *shall* have jurisdiction to hear a set-off claim irrespective of the scope of the arbitration clause invoked by the claimant and even where the relationship out of which the set-off defence arises falls within the scope of another arbitration agreement or forum-selection clause. This solution is now mirrored in Art. 377 of

---

38 JEFFREY WAINCYMER, PROCEDURE AND EVIDENCE IN INTERNATIONAL ARBITRATION, 232 (2012). Conversely, at page 233 he states, "The more it is procedural, the more it is seen as an efficiency measure that simply aims to page reduce total transaction costs in resolving multiple claims and thus require independent evidence of consent."

39 Singapore International Arbitration Centre.

40 Art. 26(3) of the previous version of the rules required that a respondent "may raise a plea for setting off where it *relates* to the claim of the claimant." (Emphasis added).

41 Wolfgang Peter, *Some Observations on the New Swiss Rules of International Arbitration*, 22 ASA SPECIAL SERIES 1, 9 (2004).

the Swiss Federal Rules of Civil Procedure[42] and in the somewhat less satisfactory wording in Art. 817bis of the Italian Code of the Civil Procedure.[43]

That the tribunal shall have jurisdiction does not sound like discretion. Rather, it sounds like a command, a command of the sort to which a civil-law ear is attuned: the tribunal's jurisdiction is clear and there is no discretion or a *forum-non-conveniens*-like doctrine to resort to in order to avoid hearing a set-off.[44] Accordingly, the tribunal is competent to hear any and all set-off defences.

What is also clear is that the reach of the Art. 21(5) Swiss Rules is limited to set-offs and is not applicable to counterclaims. Although some propositions and arguments to the contrary were made,[45] the wording[46] and spirit of the Swiss Rules do not provide justification to expand Art. 21(5) Swiss Rules *per analogiam* to counterclaims as well. Art. 21(3) Swiss Rules explicitly reserves the possibility to object to jurisdiction over a counterclaim only—this, coupled with the clear wording of Art. 21(5) Swiss Rules, should be sufficient to differentiate between the two and their treatment.

It follows from the above that the "one step beyond" of Art. 21(5) Swiss Rules, when compared with the other rules, is the removal of any doubts with regard to the tribunal's competence to entertain a set-off defence. Namely, even where the rules are silent on the jurisdiction over a set-off or where they resort to a circular definition (such as in the 2010 UNCITRAL Rules), a lingering question might remain as to whether the scope of the arbitration agreement is still of relevance for accepting jurisdiction over a set-off.

---

42 Previously, Swiss Intercantonal Arbitration Convention (IAC), Art 29 provided: "Where one of the parties pleads a set-off on the basis of a legal relationship in respect of which the arbitral tribunal does not have jurisdiction under the terms of the arbitration agreement, and the parties do not agree to extend the arbitration to cover that legal relationship, the proceedings shall be stayed and a reasonable time shall be allowed to the party making the claim to establish it before the court with jurisdiction."

43 "The arbitrators shall be competent to decide on the objections of set-off, within the limits of the value of the main claim, also if the counterclaimed amount does not fall within the scope of the arbitration agreement."

44 Unless, perhaps, the seat of the tribunal is in a common law jurisdiction allowing to such possibility, *see*, Vladimir Pavić, *Counterclaim and Set-Off in International Commercial Arbitration*, 1 BELGRADE LAW REVIEW 101, 109 (2006).

45 Pierre Karrer leaves open the possibility of applying Art. 21(5) to counterclaims as well (Pierre Karrer, *Arbitration under the Swiss Rules of Arbitration in Switzerland and Elsewhere*, paper presented at 12th Croatian Arbitration Days (December 2004, unpublished, on file with the author p. 6.); *see also*, Franz Kellerhals and Bernhard Berger, *Widerklage und Verrechnung nach den Swiss Rules of International Arbitration*, in MÉLANGES EN L'HONNEUR DE FRANÇOIS KNOEPFLER 207, 223-224 (Bohnet and Wessner eds., 2005).

46 *See e.g.*, the distinction clearly made in Swiss Rules, Arts 3(10), 3(11) and 19(3).

Furthermore, such situations might also raise the issue of whether submitting a relationship from which a possible set-off claim arises to another forum selection or arbitration agreement should be construed as an agreement to exclude such set-off claims and to hear them in separate proceedings. Art. 21(5) Swiss Rules removes all such arguments of potential lack of jurisdiction and thus provides legal certainty, albeit on a pole completely opposite to that provided by Art. 19(3) of the 1976 UNCITRAL Rules.

It should be noted, however, that the parties are free to exclude the operation of Art. 21(5) Swiss Rules and thus again introduce a jurisdictional bar to the admissibility of a claim for a purpose of a set-off. An explicit exclusion will, of course, be sufficient. There are different opinions on whether the submission of a relationship to a specialized arbitration tribunal would be sufficient to exclude any cross-claims arising out of it for the purpose of Art. 21(5) Swiss Rules[47] and whether such explicit exclusion exists where the parties agree on fast-track arbitration for the main claim under the Swiss Rules.[48]

On the other hand, Art. 21(5) Swiss Rules does not state that jurisdiction over a claim advanced for a purpose of a set-off means the substantive preconditions under the law applicable in order to produce the effects sought by the respondent are automatically fulfilled.[49] Thus, the choice of law issues and the differences in substantive laws remain relevant.

7. ART. 21(5) – SOME FURTHER THOUGHTS ON UNDERLYING POLICIES AND CONSIDERATIONS

All is good then with Art. 21(5) Swiss Rules? A survey conducted for the 2014 conference to mark the 10-year anniversary of the Swiss

---

[47] Reto M. Jenny, *Art. 21 [Objections to the jurisdiction of the arbitral tribunal]* in ARBITRATION IN SWITZERLAND: THE PRACTITIONER'S GUIDE, 478, 484 (M. Arroyo et al eds., 2013) opines that such reference would not, in itself, be sufficient to exclude Art. 21(5); but *compare*, W. Wenger, M. Schott, Internationale Schiedsgerichtsbarkeit, Art. 186, BASLER KOMMENTAR INTERNATIONALES PRIVATRECHT, 2ND ED., at para 44. (Honsell et al. eds. 2007).

[48] In favor of treating it as an explicit exclusion, *see*, Michael Schöll, *Set-Off Defences in International Arbitration*, 26 ASA SPECIAL SERIES 108, 133 (2006); P. Habegger, *Das Schiedsverfahren, Art. 377* in BASLER KOMMENTAR, SCHWEIZERISCHE ZIVILPROZESSORDNUNG, at para. 14 (Spühler et al. eds., 2010); for a contrary position, *see*, Reto M. Jenny, *Art. 21 [Objections to the jurisdiction of the arbitral tribunal]* in ARBITRATION IN SWITZERLAND: THE PRACTITIONER'S GUIDE, 478, 484 (M. Arroyo et al eds., 2013).

[49] Reto M. Jenny, *Art. 21 [Objections to the jurisdiction of the arbitral tribunal]* in ARBITRATION IN SWITZERLAND: THE PRACTITIONER'S GUIDE, 478, 487 (M. Arroyo et al eds., 2013).

Rules[50] suggests that it might be: when asked to identify a "special feature" of the Swiss Rules they like the most, over a third of those who participated in the survey (16 out of 44) picked Art. 21(5) Swiss Rules. By comparison, only one participant identified it as the source of major discontent with the Swiss Rules, without stating the reasons.

There is, however, no such thing as a perfect rule. Every rule has to balance opposing policy considerations, most often certainty vs. flexibility. The overview of the arbitral rules dealing with the set-off reveals a gamut, if not of attitudes, then of the ways in which a couple of main ideas are expressed (or implied). Some of those promulgations, on the one hand, although explicit, are flexible at the expense of certainty, avoiding any specific commitment. The 2010 UNCITRAL Rules provide such a rule - one into which the counsel of a party will, no doubt, be able to read many interpretations. On the other hand, a "hard and fast" rule will save parties from needless expense and delay in arguing whether a tribunal does or does not have jurisdiction to hear a particular set-off. Art. 21(5) Swiss Rules is in that respect probably as hard and as fast as it gets, and it is designed to discourage the emergence of a separate jurisdictional or admissibility dispute within the arbitration with regard to the set-off claim.

This clear and firm position has been hailed by some commentators as "fully in line with modern understanding" of set-off and doctrinarily consistent.[51]

However, as with every hard and fast rule, some words of caution are perhaps in order. While the transaction costs are indeed reduced (no protracted arguments about jurisdiction and admissibility of the set-off claim and the possible reduction of the multiplicity of actions), it might be argued that this blanket rule does not distinguish between set-off claims which arise out of related as opposed to wholly different transactions or between those that are ascertained, or easily ascertained, and those that are purely tactical, dilatory or otherwise.[52] All of them have to be equally admitted by the arbitral tribunal.

---

50 Swiss Chambers' Arbitration Institution, Swiss Rules of International Arbitration ("SRIA") - 10 Years of Experience ASA Annual (*hereinafter* Swiss Rules Survey), *see*, Annex Swiss Rules Survey.

51 PASCAL PICHONNAZ, LOUISE GULLIFER, SET-OFF IN ARBITRATION AND COMMERCIAL TRANSACTIONS, 67 et seq. (2014); Alberto Fortún, *Set-offs Are Not Counterclaims in International Arbitration*, in LIBER AMICORUM BERNARDO CREMADES, 451, 463 (Fernández-Ballesteros and Arias eds., 2010) avers "In our experience, the incorporation of Swiss Rules has increased significantly in order to resolve multi-contract situations."

52 *See e.g.*, arguments put forward by JEFFREY WAINCYMER, PROCEDURE AND EVIDENCE IN INTERNATIONAL ARBITRATION, 241 (2012).

Furthermore, the hard and fast nature of the rule could ultimately obfuscate the differences that cannot be simply ignored. Those who stress the substantive nature of the set-off defence argue that it should be differentiated from the counterclaim and thus not subject to the same jurisdictional rules.[53] Art. 21(5) Swiss Rules provides exactly for such differentiation, removing jurisdictional obstacles for set-off. However, given that respondent will always have the option of "dressing up" a counterclaim as a set-off defence and that this will be particularly appealing where its cross-claim appears lower in value than what he perceives as a likely sum to be awarded pursuant the main claim, this might make jurisdictional requirements for the counterclaim largely irrelevant, allowing for a back-door attraction of jurisdiction akin to that before the state court, or even exceeding its effect. This does eventually play into the argument of those who advocate that Art. 21(5) Swiss Rules should be extended to counterclaims as well.[54]

Another good way in which one may attempt to conduct a "stress test" of a particular provision is the juristic equivalent of Kant's first formulation of the categorical imperative: what if everyone adopted the same rule? The question that the tribunal is normally expected to answer is whether it has jurisdiction, and if it does, proceed with the case. In other words, in arbitration there is no equivalent of a *forum non conveniens*—once a tribunal finds that it has jurisdiction, it is on "auto-pilot" of sorts. Whether or not the doctrine of *lis pendens* has any relevance in arbitration is a matter of debate[55] and the principle is not universally accepted in the context of litigation either. This might lead to a situation whereby two tribunals, each considering itself entirely competent as per the applicable rules to decide on the matter, have to deal with the two situations in which the roles of the main claim and

---

53 Alberto Fortún, *Set-offs Are Not Counterclaims in International Arbitration, in* LIBER AMICORUM BERNARDO CREMADES, 459 (Fernández-Ballesteros and Arias eds., 2010).

54 *See*, Pierre Karrer, *Arbitration under the Swiss Rules of Arbitration in Switzerland and Elsewhere*, paper, presented at 12th Croatian Arbitration Days (December 2004, unpublished, on file with the author p. 6.).

55 *See e.g.*, Stavros Brekoulakis, *The Effect of An Arbitral Award and Third Parties in International Arbitration: Res Judicata Revisited*, 16 AMERICAN REVIEW OF INTERNATIONAL ARBITRATION 177, 177 et seq. (2005); Florian Kremslehner, *Chapter III: The Arbitration Procedure - Lis pendens and res judicata in International Commercial Arbitration* in AUSTRIAN ARBITRATION YEARBOOK 127, 127 et seq. (Klausegger et al. eds., 2007) pp. 127 – 162; Bernardo Cremades, Ignacio Madalena, *Parallel Proceedings in International Arbitration*, 24 ARBITRATION INTERNATIONAL 507, 507 et seq. (2008); Anne-Catherine Hahn, *Chapter III: The Award and the Courts, Res Judicata as a Challenge for Arbitral Tribunals*, in AUSTRIAN YEARBOOK ON INTERNATIONAL ARBITRATION 239, 329 et seq. (Klausegger et al. eds., 2014); NADJA ERK, PARALLEL PROCEEDINGS.IN INTERNATIONAL ARBITRATION: A COMPARATIVE EUROPEAN PERSPECTIVE (2014).

the cross-claim are reversed. Whether they could reduce the danger of conflicting decisions by resorting to principles of estoppel, abuse of rights and good faith (to restrict the possibility of raising two claims in different proceedings) remains to be seen.[56] It is also important to note that the emphasis on the substantive nature of the set-off might be used to justify concentration before the state courts of cross-claims which would have otherwise been subject to arbitration agreements. So far, the highest judicial instance of Austria has used precisely such argumentation when it agreed to hear a set-off defence out of the relationship subject to the arbitration agreement,[57] while the courts of Switzerland and Germany refrained from doing so.[58] The Swiss and German courts reasoned that an arbitration agreement effectively introduces a bar to the procedural admissibility of set-off claims; if the legislators were to introduce a provision which would broaden the jurisdiction of the courts alongside the lines of Art. 21(5) Swiss Rules, one would expect that the position of the two courts would be different.

Another possible concern is the situation where a claim exceeding the main claim was tactically "dressed up" as a set-off defence and the cross-claimant now moves to collect the remainder of the debt in another arbitration or a chosen forum or moves to collect it in the entirety (if the set-off defence failed on the merits). Given that the formally binding force of an award will most often be restricted to its operative part, the *res judicata* effects might be viewed differently by the subsequent forum depending on whether the claim for the purpose of a set-off was presented purely as a substantive defence (and thus not addressed and disposed of separately in the holding) or presented as a claim to be ascertained separately and addressed in the operative part of the award.

Finally, the possibility for the respondent to pick and choose which claims to advance for a purpose of a set-off might create a tactical advantage where none was meant to exist in the Swiss Rules. Namely, where a three-member panel is to decide the case, the

---

[56] *See also,* Vladimir Pavić, *Counterclaim and Set-Off in International Commercial Arbitration*, 1 BELGRADE LAW REVIEW 101, 114-115 (2006); JEFFREY WAINCYMER, PROCEDURE AND EVIDENCE IN INTERNATIONAL ARBITRATION, 242 (2012): "Could a tribunal say that the contract later in time is intended to take precedence over the former one as the most recent indication of the intent of the parties? What if instead, an earlier contract referred to arbitration subject to Art. 21 (5) and a later related contract has a choice of forum clause? Would it be held to be a variation of the Art. 21(5) entitlements because it is later in time?"

[57] OGH 14 November 1990 1 Ob 711/89, Sammlung Zivilrecht 63/201.

[58] BGH 22 November 1962 VII ZR 264/61, Neue JuristischeWochenschrift 1963, p. 243; Swiss Federal Tribunal 21 May 1897, ATF 23 I 774 (780 et seq.).

claimant will have to nominate one arbitrator together with its notice of arbitration.[59] It will do so whilst usually having in mind the nature of the claim, the facts surrounding it, legal, linguistic and technical knowledge needed for the resolution of the dispute. The Respondent will do so at a later point in time, together with its answer to the notice of arbitration,[60] which will be expected to contain any counterclaim and/or set-off defence.[61] This will allow him to appoint an arbitrator while taking into account the entirety of the claims submitted. While this misbalance is present to some degree in a number of cases (since the claimant does not know whether and which will be counterclaims submitted by the respondent), the wide open formulation of Art. 21(5) Swiss Rules, including the cross-claims subject to other dispute resolution clauses and the absence of a connexity or relatedness requirement means that the respondent might be in a position to make a much better suited decision when nominating an arbitrator.

8. CONCLUDING REMARKS

Set-off is certainly not easy to grasp. It is a legal institute where substantive and procedural issues intertwine, and where the comparative differences are not merely superficial but often have wide-ranging implications. At the same time, in all of its guises it is a supremely efficient institute, one well-suited to greatly reduce cash-flow issues in business operations. As such, it looks like a perfect fit for arbitration.

Yet, there can hardly be a perfect fit. The issues of applicable law, the type of the set-off resorted to and the paradigm of the consensual nature of arbitration do not help. And, with the counterclaim only a "hair's-breadth away", the plot thickens further.

In absence of a perfect fit, which is the best one? It depends on what one values more—flexibility or certainty. If one strives for certainty, then the institutional rules providing a more straightforward jurisdictional test are to be preferred. This includes Art. 21(5) Swiss Rules, which removes the test completely, making it certain that every set-off defence, irrespective of where it arises, will be admissible. If one favors flexibility, the "silent treatment" of the set-off will provide sufficient latitude for the tribunals to pick and choose along the criteria they deem important: connexity, liquidity of a set-off claim, conflicting dispute resolution clauses and the like. The sheer plethora of possible

---

[59] Swiss Rules, Art. 3(3)(h).
[60] Swiss Rules, Art 3(7)(f).
[61] Swiss Rules, Art 3(10).

considerations, however, might invite the parties to have an "argument within an argument" before the tribunal, and the efficiency goals might be compromised. In light of the fact that such a jurisdictional ruling will potentially be subject to scrutiny of the courts of the *lex loci arbitri*, hard and fast rules (including, but not limited to, Art. 21(5) Swiss Rules) acquire additional appeal.

Expedited Procedure under Art. 42 Swiss Rules

*Thomas Rohner**

1. INTRODUCTION

This publication reflects a presentation given at the ASA Annual Conference 2014. As the time provided for the presentation was limited, this paper will not cover all aspects of this subject but will rather highlight certain important points.

The Expedited Procedure was introduced in the 2004 version of the Swiss Rules. In 2012, 40 percent of all Swiss Chambers' arbitral proceedings were conducted under the Expedited Procedure (Art. 42 Swiss Rules).[1] Due to this positive reaction in the arbitration community,[2] the drafters of the 2012 Swiss Rules have appropriately refrained from significantly modifying Art. 42 Swiss Rules.[3] In light of the popularity of the Expedited Procedure, this article will first deal with the characteristics and the developments that have taken place since the introduction of the Expedited Procedure. Afterwards, an overview of the revised provision will follow. Finally, a selection of particular issues related to the Expedited Procedure will be discussed followed by a short conclusion.

2. CHARACTERISTICS AND DEVELOPMENTS

The Expedited Procedure provides for streamlined arbitral proceedings, as opposed to the ordinary proceedings. Despite the speed of the proceedings, the quality of the arbitrator's work obviously must be maintained. Art. 42 Swiss Rules provides for several features to achieve this.

2.1 Scope of Application

In general, the Expedited Procedure applies to cases where the amount in dispute does not exceed CHF 1,000,000 (Art. 42(2) Swiss

---

* Dr. Thomas Rohner, LL.M., is a Partner with Pestalozzi in Zurich. I would like to thank Lorenz Lauer (MLaw), junior associate with Pestalozzi in Zurich, for his support in preparing this chapter for publication.

1 *Swiss Chambers' Arbitration Institution Newsletter 1/2013*, 1.

2 *Cf. also*, Philipp Habegger, *The Revised Swiss Rules of International Arbitration: An Overview of the Major Changes*, ASA BULLETIN, 269, 293 (2012); Gabrielle Nater-Bass, *How to work with the Swiss Rules: The Counsel's Perspective, in* THE SWISS RULES OF INTERNATIONAL ARBITRATION—FIVE YEARS OF EXPERIENCE, 9 (Rainer Füeg ed., 2009).

3 *Swiss Chambers' Arbitration Institution Newsletter 2/2012*, 2.

Rules). If the amount in dispute exceeds CHF 1,000,000, it is possible for the parties to opt in, i.e. to agree to use the Expedited Procedure. Similarly, the parties can also opt out of the Expedited Procedure even if the amount in dispute is less than CHF 1,000,000.[4] The Court may decide that arbitrating under the Expedited Procedure is not appropriate although the amount in dispute does not exceed CHF 1,000,000. To reach its decision, the Court has to consider all relevant circumstances, such as technical or legal complexity, requests for interim measures or foreseeable difficulties in organizing the hearing.[5]

2.2 Number of Arbitrators

According to Art. 42(2)(b) Swiss Rules, the case will be referred to a sole arbitrator unless the arbitration agreement provides otherwise. As most arbitration agreements provide for an arbitral tribunal of three members, the Court's Secretariat will invite the parties to agree on a sole arbitrator after the dispute has arisen (Art. 42(2)(c) Swiss Rules). The Schedule of Costs provides that, where the parties insist on an arbitral tribunal of more than one arbitrator, the arbitrators' hourly rates will not be less than CHF 350 (Swiss Rules, Appendix B: Schedule of Costs, para. 2.8). This could result in a higher hourly fee for arbitrators of a three-member arbitral tribunal compared to a sole arbitrator, who is confronted with a high workload and a low amount in dispute. The reason for this imbalance is that the sole arbitrator is paid based on a percentage of the amount in dispute.

The aforementioned system of a minimal hourly rate of CHF 350 should encourage the parties to opt for a sole arbitrator and keep the proceedings as streamlined as possible. Although this might work in most cases, it is futile if the respondent refuses to participate in the arbitration at all. Therefore, drafting an arbitration clause providing for one *or* more arbitrators is recommended if the Swiss Rules are chosen to govern the arbitration.[6]

---

[4] Christoph Brunner, *The Swiss Rules of International Arbitration: An Overview for Prospective Users,* GERMAN ARB. J., 233, 248 (2005); *dissenting,* Matthias Scherer, *Acceleration of Arbitration Proceedings—The Swiss Way: The Expedited Procedure under the Swiss Rules of International Arbitration,* GERMAN ARB. J., 229, 230 (2005).

[5] Sandra De Vito Bieri/Raphaëlle Favre Schnyder, *in* SWISS RULES OF INTERNATIONAL ARBITRATION, COMMENTARY, *Art. 42 N. 20* (Tobias Zuberbühler/Christoph Müller/Philipp Habegger eds., 2nd ed. 2013).

[6] Matthias Scherer, *Acceleration of Arbitration Proceedings – The Swiss Way: The Expedited Procedure under the Swiss Rules of International Arbitration,* GERMAN ARB. J., 229, 236 (2005).

2.3 Time Limit of Six Months to Render the Award

An award under the Expedited Procedure will generally be rendered within six months of the transmission of the file to the arbitral tribunal (Art. 42(1)(d) Swiss Rules). The Swiss Rules do not specify whether "six months" means calendar months or consecutive 30-day periods. SCHERER suggests resolving this issue in accordance with Art. 4.2 of the European Convention on the Calculation of Time Limits (SR 0.221.122.3).[7] This provision states that a period is calculated in months end on the day bearing the same number as the *dies a quo*. If the month in which the time limit ends does not have a day with this number, the time limit ends on the last day of this month.

The *dies a quo*, i.e. the beginning of the time limit, is the day after the file was physically received by the arbitral tribunal (Art. 2(2) Swiss Rules).[8]

There is generally no standstill of time limits during court holidays and the like. The end of a time limit is only deferred to the next business day if the expiry day is a public holiday at the place of receipt, not the place of arbitration.[9] If the arbitrators of a three-member arbitral tribunal are based in different jurisdictions, the principle of equality requires that the deadline be equally deferred by the same duration for all arbitrators as this is the case for a deadline common to all parties.[10]

The time limit is observed when the last arbitrator (or the sole arbitrator) signs the award within the time allowed (*cf.* Art. 32(4) Swiss Rules), regardless of when the parties receive it.[11]

2.4 Number of Legal Briefs and Hearing

In addition to the shortening of time limits and the limited number of arbitrators, Art. 42 Swiss Rules provides further means to speed up the arbitration proceedings.

---

7 Matthias Scherer, *Acceleration of Arbitration Proceedings—The Swiss Way: The Expedited Procedure under the Swiss Rules of International Arbitration*, GERMAN ARB. J., 229, 233 (2005).

8 Matthias Scherer, *Acceleration of Arbitration Proceedings—The Swiss Way: The Expedited Procedure under the Swiss Rules of International Arbitration*, GERMAN ARB. J., 229, 233 (2005); Frank Spoorenberg/Isabelle Fellrath, *in* SWISS RULES OF INTERNATIONAL ARBITRATION, COMMENTARY, *Art. 2 N. 22* (Tobias Zuberbühler/Christoph Müller/Philipp Habegger eds., 2nd ed. 2013).

9 Frank Spoorenberg/Isabelle Fellrath, *in* SWISS RULES OF INTERNATIONAL ARBITRATION, COMMENTARY, *Art. 2 N. 22* (Tobias Zuberbühler/Christoph Müller/Philipp Habegger eds., 2nd ed. 2013).

10 *Ibid.*

11 Matthias Scherer, *Acceleration of Arbitration Proceedings – The Swiss Way: The Expedited Procedure under the Swiss Rules of International Arbitration*, GERMAN ARB. J., 229, 233 (2005).

According to Art. 42(1)(b) Swiss Rules, there should be only one exchange of legal briefs and only one evidentiary hearing. The single hearing does not necessarily have to be restricted to one day, but can also take place on several consecutive days. Furthermore, pre-hearing conferences do not count as hearings.[12] Nothing hinders the arbitral tribunal, however, from adjusting the numbers of legal briefs and/or the hearing in light of the specific circumstances of the individual matter. In addition, the same principles of due process and the right to be heard (Art. 190 SPILA)[13] apply under the Expedited Procedure as in the ordinary procedure.[14] Overall, there is no reason to doubt that awards rendered under the framework provided in the Expedited Procedure will meet the necessary quality standards.

2.5 Reasons in the Award

Under the Expedited Procedure, the number of briefs and hearings is generally limited and the reasons in the award need only be in summary form (Art. 42(1)(e) Swiss Rules). The Swiss Rules do not contain more precise guidelines as to how detailed the reasons must be.

2.5.1 Waiver of the reasons

The parties can agree that the arbitral tribunal does not need to give any reasons when rendering their award. Obviously, the arbitral tribunal still needs to have reasons for its award. The waiver of reasoning merely relieves it from its duty of drafting them.[15] Whether such waiver is allowed is not determined by the Swiss Rules but by the applicable *lex arbitri*. In Switzerland, there are several views concerning the validity of such a waiver. According to one scholarly view, the waiver is generally valid but, in the event that the reasons for the award cannot be presented to an appellate instance, it could present practical issues when challenging the award later on.[16] Considering that a waiver of appeals is only valid if neither party is

---

[12] Pierre-Yves Tschanz, *The Chamber of Geneva's Arbitration Rules and their Expedited Procedure*, J'INTL ARB., 51, 52 (1993).

[13] Swiss Private International Law Act, Chapter 12 (1987) (*hereinafter* SPILA).

[14] Matthias Scherer, *Acceleration of Arbitration Proceedings – The Swiss Way: The Expedited Procedure under the Swiss Rules of International Arbitration*, GERMAN ARB. J., 229, 231 (2005).

[15] Sandra De Vito Bieri/Raphaëlle Favre Schnyder, *in* SWISS RULES OF INTERNATIONAL ARBITRATION, COMMENTARY, *Art. 42 N. 18* (Tobias Zuberbühler/Christoph Müller/Philipp Habegger eds., 2nd ed. 2013).

[16] Markus Wirth, *in* BASLER KOMMENTAR INTERNATIONALES PRIVATRECHT, *Art. 189 N. 37* (Heinrich Honsell/Nedim Peter Vogt/Anton K. Schnyder/Stephen V. Berti, eds., 2nd ed. 2007).

domiciled in Switzerland (Art. 192(1) SPILA), another scholarly view holds that the same prerequisite applies should the waiver of reasons result in a waiver of appeals.[17] According to a further opinion, a waiver of reasons is not subject to Art. 192(1) SPILA.[18] Supporting this view is the fact that a waiver of appeals is not allowed in domestic arbitration, but the waiver of reasons is (Art. 384(1)(e) CPC).[19] The Swiss Federal Supreme Court consistently holds that Art. 190(2) SPILA does not include the right to a statement of reasons.[20]

Therefore, a waiver of reasons should be allowed even if one party is domiciled in Switzerland. The party consenting to a waiver needs to consider for itself whether it wants to take the risk of lowering its chances for an appeal. Obviously, an appeal is much more difficult if no written reasons can be presented.

2.5.2 Summary reasons

If the parties do not mutually waive reasons, the arbitral tribunal has to provide them for its decisions. In order to accelerate the time-consuming process of drafting an award, the arbitral tribunal only has to provide reasons for its decision in summary form. As seen above, the lack of reasons does not generally lead to the Swiss Federal Supreme Court to set aside an award. However, the Swiss Federal Supreme Court has held that the arbitral tribunal has a minimal duty to examine and address relevant issues raised by the parties.[21] In addition, the Swiss Rules provide that an award generally has to state its reasons on which it is based, unless the parties have agreed otherwise (Art. 32(3) Swiss Rules).

The question as to how detailed a summary statement of reasons has to be has not been answered yet, not in the Swiss Rules or in the legal literature or in Swiss case law. The summary reasons should contain at least a brief description of the factual circumstances, the parties' main arguments and the arbitral tribunal's decisive considerations. The arbitral tribunal could further limit its references to both evidence and legal sources to a minimum. Having said that, however, it might be in the arbitral tribunal's own interest to provide

---

[17] Anton Heini, *in* ZÜRCHER KOMMENTAR ZUM IPRG, *Art. 189 N. 15* (Girsberger et al. eds., 2nd ed. 2004).

[18] BERNHARD BERGER/FRANZ KELLERHALS, INTERNATIONAL AND DOMESTIC ARBITRATION IN SWITZERLAND, 388-389 (2nd ed. 2010).

[19] Swiss Civil Procedural Code.

[20] DFSC 134 III 186 of 22 January 2008, para. 6.1; DFSC 130 III 125 of 9 December 2003, para. 2.2.

[21] DFSC 133 III 235 of 22 March 2007, para. 5.2.

sufficient reasons as an award which is understood by the losing party is less likely to be challenged.[22]

2.6 More and Faster Proceedings

The past ten years since the Expedited Procedure was introduced in the Swiss Rules have seen two major developments.

First, as mentioned, arbitrating under the Expedited Procedure is popular. In 2012, 40% of the total new cases used the Expedited Procedure. In detail, the statistics are as follows: [23]

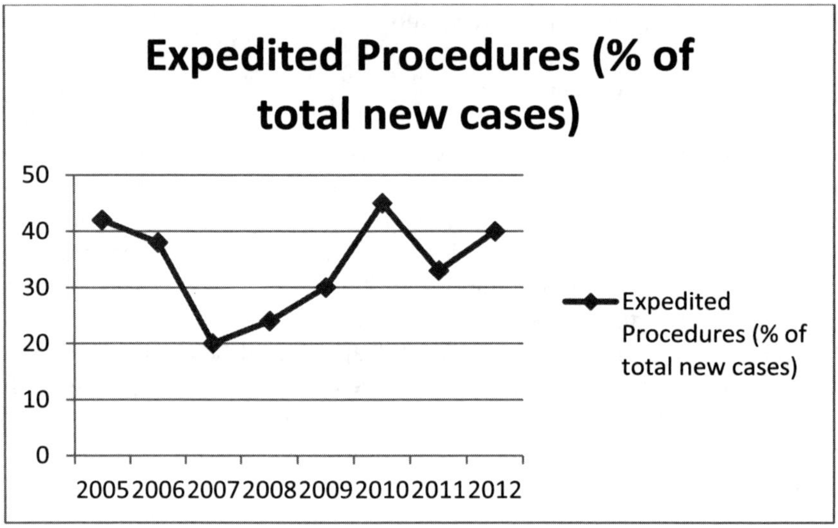

Second, despite a general tendency towards longer arbitration proceedings, the proceedings under the Expedited Procedure under the Swiss Rules show a trend in the opposite direction: While in the period from 2004-2008, the average duration of procedures was 205 days, for the period from 2009 to 2012, this was reduced to approximately 184.5 days.[24]

---

[22] Sébastien Besson/Nina Thommesen, *in* SWISS RULES OF INTERNATIONAL ARBITRATION, COMMENTARY, *Art.* 32 *N.* 22 (Tobias Zuberbühler/Christoph Müller/Philipp Habegger eds., 2nd ed. 2013).

[23] Source: *Swiss Chambers' Arbitration Institution Newsletters*. The statistics are published in the first newsletter of each year.

[24] *Swiss Chambers' Arbitration Institution Newsletter 1/2013, 1.*

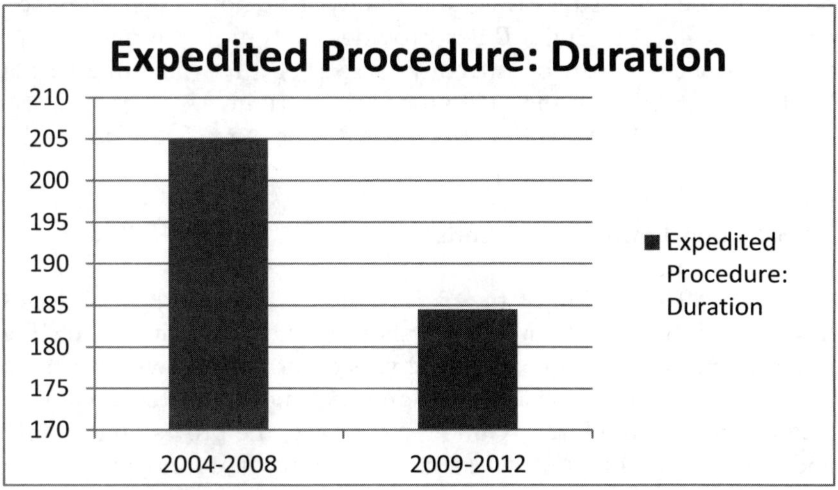

3. THE 2012 REVISION AND ITS CHANGES

The main goal of the 2012 Revision of the Swiss Rules was to make procedures more efficient in terms of both time and cost (and to harmonize the arbitration rules with the CPC[25]).[26] The Expedited Procedure was introduced in 2004 for the same reasons.[27] The past near-decade has shown that the Swiss Rules have been successful in achieving this goal. Consequently, the 2012 Revision contains only minor modifications to the previous set of rules with regard to the Expedited Procedure.

3.1 Provisional Deposit (Art. 42(1)(a) Swiss Rules)

The new Art. 42(1)(a) Swiss Rules requires the claimant to pay a provisional deposit of CHF 5,000. If not paid, the file will not be transmitted to the arbitral tribunal.

Under the 2004 Swiss Rules, the arbitral tribunal had to take the first procedural steps without being certain whether the deposit under Art. 41 Swiss Rules would be transferred or not. To meet the six-month time limit, the arbitral tribunal often could not wait until the parties

---

[25] Philipp Habegger/Anna Masser, *Die revidierte Schweizerische Schiedsordnung (Swiss Rules)*, ANWALTSREVUE, 175, 175 (2012).

[26] Bernd Ehle/Werner Jahnel, *Revision der Swiss Rules – erhöhte Effizienz und Flexibilität*, GERMAN ARB. J., 169, 170, 177 (2012).

[27] Philipp Habegger/Anna Masser, *Die revidierte Schweizerische Schiedsordnung (Swiss Rules)*, ANWALTSREVUE, 175, 177 (2012).

had paid the deposit.[28] This uncertainty has now been removed because Art. 42(1)(a) Swiss Rules provides that, until the payment of the provisional deposit of currently CHF 5,000[29] has been made, the Court will not transmit the file to the arbitral tribunal.[30] Therefore, the six-month period to render the award does not start until the provisional deposit has been paid.[31]

3.2 Shortening Time Limits

In the 2004 version of the Swiss Rules, Art. 42(1)(a) Swiss Rules allowed the Swiss Chambers to shorten the time limits for the appointment of arbitrators. The 2012 version of Art. 42 Swiss Rules no longer contains this provision. This does not mean that the Chambers cannot shorten these limits. Quite the contrary, the provision formerly contained in Art. 42(1)(a) Swiss Rules can now be found in Art. 2(3) Swiss Rules and applies, in principle, to any time limits.[32]

However, whether the six-month time limit set out by Art. 42(1)(d) Swiss Rules can be shortened by the Court is disputed by legal writers.[33] Art. 2(3) Swiss Rules refers to both extending and shortening, but Art. 42(1)(d) Swiss Rules explicitly mentions only the Court's power to extend the deadline. Art. 42 Swiss Rules governs the Expedited Procedure and serves as *lex specialis*. Hence, the Court should not be allowed to shorten the six month deadline. In any event, it is doubtful whether the shortening of the six month deadline is a relevant issue in practice.

---

[28] Bernd Ehle/Werner Jahnel, *Revision der Swiss Rules – erhöhte Effizienz und Flexibilität*, GERMAN ARB. J., 169, 170, 173 (2012).

[29] Swiss Rules, Appendix B: Schedule of Costs, para. 1.4.

[30] *Cf.*, Bernd Ehle/Werner Jahnel, *Revision der Swiss Rules – erhöhte Effizienz und Flexibilität*, GERMAN ARB. J., 169, 170, 179 (2012).

[31] *Cf.*, Art. 42(1)(d) Swiss Rules.

[32] Sandra De Vito Bieri/Raphaëlle Favre Schnyder, *in* SWISS RULES OF INTERNATIONAL ARBITRATION, COMMENTARY, *Art. 42 N. 7a* (Tobias Zuberbühler/Christoph Müller/Philipp Habegger eds., 2nd ed. 2013); Philipp Habegger, *The Revised Swiss Rules of International Arbitration: An Overview of the Major Changes*, ASA BULLETIN, 269, 273 (2012).

[33] *Pro*, Philipp Habegger, *The Revised Swiss Rules of International Arbitration: An Overview of the Major Changes*, ASA BULLETIN, 269, 275 (2012); *contra*, Frank Spoorenberg/Isabelle Fellrath, *in* SWISS RULES OF INTERNATIONAL ARBITRATION, COMMENTARY, *Art. 2 N.* 26 (Tobias Zuberbühler/Christoph Müller/Philipp Habegger eds., 2nd ed. 2013).

4. SOME PRACTICAL ASPECTS FOR AN EFFICIENT PROCEEDING

4.1 The Arbitral Tribunal's Task: Rendering a High Quality Award within the Six-month Time Limit

The six-month time limit means that time is of the essence. Therefore, it is important to initiate the process without delay. The relevant documents, such as the procedural rules and the provisional timetable, should be drafted immediately and a call or meeting with the parties should be set up to discuss the relevant issues. However, not only are the arbitrators required to work quickly, but the cooperation of the parties is needed as well. If the procedural rules and the provisional timetable can be set up within a short time period, valuable time for the rest of the proceedings is gained as the various deadlines are fixed.

4.2 Fixing Time Limits

In fixing the various time limits, it is often helpful to calculate backwards. When is the award due? How much time does the arbitral tribunal need to render the award after the end of the hearings? By calculating backwards the deadlines can be fixed in such a way that they comply with the six-month time restriction.

4.3 Continual Drafting of the Award

It is recommended that the parties' submissions are continually processed upon receipt. This not only ensures that an arbitral tribunal is fully familiar with the file, but even more importantly, it saves valuable time at the end of the proceedings when the award needs to be rendered.

4.4 To Minimize Possible Procedural Surprises

To set a workable timetable, the arbitral tribunal should try to minimize surprises affecting the proceedings. It is, therefore, recommended that the arbitral tribunal try to discover at the beginning of the proceedings whether there are any issues which could possibly have an impact on the proceedings and the timetable. Such issues can include whether, for instance, the parties wish to have settlement talks and, if so, at what stage of the proceedings. In general, the set hearing date should not be affected by possible settlement talks. Often, there is a strong commercial need to settle proceedings under the Expedited Procedure given the lower amounts in dispute as compared with legal fees, costs and management time.

4.5 Number of Legal Briefs

Unsolicited legal briefs should be avoided as they often interfere with the agreed procedural timetable. Although the Swiss Rules generally provide for only one round of legal briefs, under certain circumstances, it can make sense to set a second round at the outset of the proceedings. Again, such planning at the beginning might avoid having to adjust the timetable later.

4.6 Number of Witnesses and Experts

Parties often have at the beginning of the proceedings a good sense of the possible number of witnesses and expert witnesses they intend to call for a hearing. The arbitral tribunal should try to find this out when setting up the provisional timetable. This helps to better plan the proceedings.

4.7 Is a Court Reporter Necessary?

In light of saving time and costs and depending on the circumstances of the individual proceedings, it might be sufficient to simply record the proceedings instead of having a full written transcript. The parties' agreement is needed for such a step.

Finally, the arbitral tribunal should make it clear from the very beginning that extensions of time limits will only be granted under exceptional circumstances.

5. SOME SPECIFIC ISSUES

5.1 The Amount in Dispute as a Determinative Figure

According to Art. 42(2)(a) Swiss Rules, the amount in dispute determines whether the Expedited Procedure is applied. In general, the Expedited Procedure applies if the amount in dispute does not exceed CHF 1,000,000. Specific approval of the parties for the application of the Expedited Procedure is not needed.

5.1.1 The calculation of the amount in dispute

Art. 42(2) Swiss Rules provides that the amount in dispute is "the aggregate of the claim and the counterclaim (or any set-off defense)". The Schedule of Costs provides additional guidance for the determination of the amount in dispute.[34] In general, these provisions also apply to the calculation under Art. 42(2) Swiss Rules.[35] However, contrary to para. 2.4 of the Schedule of Costs, set-off defenses are always included in the calculation, not only if they require significant extra work.[36] In contrast, according to para. 2.5 of the Schedule of Costs, interest claims are not added to the principal claim to calculate the amount in dispute.[37]

5.1.2 Changes of the amount in dispute in the course of the proceedings

The amount in dispute is determined at the beginning of the procedure, i.e. in the Notice of Arbitration, which must contain an indication in this respect (Art. 3(3)(e) *in fine* Swiss Rules). The same requirements apply to the Answer to the Notice of Arbitration (*cf.* Art. 3(7)(c) and 3(10) Swiss Rules).[38] In certain situations, it is possible to submit counterclaims or set-off defenses only in the statement of defense, i.e. after the constitution of the arbitral tribunal (Art. 19(3) Swiss Rules).[39] Art. 3(11) Swiss Rules provides that the Court may rely exclusively on the Notice of Arbitration to determine whether the Expedited Procedure applies in such cases.

The amount in dispute may increase in the course of the proceedings (Art. 20(1) Swiss Rules). If this causes the amount in dispute to exceed CHF 1,000,000 after an Expedited Procedure has been initiated, the question is whether, in such cases, the parties must

---

34 Swiss Rules, Appendix B: Schedule of Costs, paras. 2.4-2.6.

35 Sandra De Vito Bieri/Raphaëlle Favre Schnyder, *in* SWISS RULES OF INTERNATIONAL ARBITRATION, COMMENTARY, *Art. 42 N. 21* (Tobias Zuberbühler/Christoph Müller/Philipp Habegger eds., 2nd ed. 2013).

36 Sandra De Vito Bieri/Raphaëlle Favre Schnyder, *in* SWISS RULES OF INTERNATIONAL ARBITRATION, COMMENTARY, *Art. 42 N. 21* (Tobias Zuberbühler/Christoph Müller/Philipp Habegger eds., 2nd ed. 2013); Matthias Scherer, *Acceleration of Arbitration Proceedings—The Swiss Way: The Expedited Procedure under the Swiss Rules of International Arbitration*, GERMAN ARB. J., 229, 232 (2005).

37 Matthias Scherer, *Acceleration of Arbitration Proceedings—The Swiss Way: The Expedited Procedure under the Swiss Rules of International Arbitration*, GERMAN ARB. J., 229, 232 (2005).

38 Matthias Scherer, *Acceleration of Arbitration Proceedings—The Swiss Way: The Expedited Procedure under the Swiss Rules of International Arbitration*, GERMAN ARB. J., 229, 232 (2005).

39 Bernhard Berger/Stefanie Pfisterer, *in* SWISS RULES OF INTERNATIONAL ARBITRATION, COMMENTARY, *Art. 19 N. 9* (Tobias Zuberbühler/Christoph Müller/Philipp Habegger eds., 2nd ed. 2013).

change to the ordinary procedure. The Expedited Procedure continues if the parties have explicitly agreed to it because they can opt in to the Expedited Procedure regardless of the amount in dispute.[40] Similarly, the Court should grant a modification into an ordinary procedure if requested by both parties.[41] By contrast, the Court has no reason to modify the procedure *ex officio*, i.e. if neither the parties, nor the arbitral tribunal have requested it.[42] The parties will at this stage have agreed to a timetable and presumably want to keep to it. If only one party makes a request to modify the proceedings, scholarly writings on this subject hold that the Court should decide in consideration of all relevant circumstances.[43] This means that new factual and/or legal issues have a different impact on such decisions than the simple increase of the amount in dispute. Due to its general duty to make every effort to ensure efficient conduct of the procedure (Art. 17(7) Swiss Rules) and to treat the parties equally (Art. 15(1) Swiss Rules), the Court should ensure that such a modification is not used as a dilatory tactic by a party.[44]

If the amount claimed or the counterclaim is reduced in the course of the proceedings to an amount below CHF 1,000,000, the question is whether there should be a change from the ordinary proceedings to the Expedited Procedure. The principles as stated above should generally apply. If no party wishes to change the nature of the proceedings, there is no reason to do so. If the Court, however, is asked to decide on such change, the Court will decide in consideration of all relevant circumstances. An important factor should be how much progress has been made in the proceedings. In this sense, a switch to the Expedited Procedure should be granted—if at all—only if the proceedings are at an early stage.[45]

---

[40] Christoph Brunner, *The Swiss Rules of International Arbitration: An Overview for Prospective Users*, GERMAN ARB. J., 233, 248 (2005).

[41] Sandra De Vito Bieri/Raphaëlle Favre Schnyder, *in* SWISS RULES OF INTERNATIONAL ARBITRATION, COMMENTARY, *Art. 42 N. 23* (Tobias Zuberbühler/Christoph Müller/Philipp Habegger eds., 2nd ed. 2013).

[42] Sandra De Vito Bieri/Raphaëlle Favre Schnyder, *in* SWISS RULES OF INTERNATIONAL ARBITRATION, COMMENTARY, *Art. 42 N. 23* (Tobias Zuberbühler/Christoph Müller/Philipp Habegger eds., 2nd ed. 2013).

[43] Sandra De Vito Bieri/Raphaëlle Favre Schnyder, *in* SWISS RULES OF INTERNATIONAL ARBITRATION, COMMENTARY, *Art. 42 N. 24* (Tobias Zuberbühler/Christoph Müller/Philipp Habegger eds., 2nd ed. 2013); Matthias Scherer, *Acceleration of Arbitration Proceedings – The Swiss Way: The Expedited Procedure under the Swiss Rules of International Arbitration*, GERMAN ARB. J., 229, 232 (2005).

[44] Sandra De Vito Bieri/Raphaëlle Favre Schnyder, *in* SWISS RULES OF INTERNATIONAL ARBITRATION, COMMENTARY, *Art. 42 N. 24* (Tobias Zuberbühler/Christoph Müller/Philipp Habegger eds., 2nd ed. 2013).

[45] *Cf.*, Sandra De Vito Bieri/Raphaëlle Favre Schnyder, *in* SWISS RULES OF INTERNATIONAL ARBITRATION, COMMENTARY, *Art. 42 N. 27* (Tobias Zuberbühler/

5.2 The Extension of Time Limits

Art. 42(1)(d) Swiss Rules allows the extension of time limits only in exceptional cases as the speed of the proceeding is of particular importance under the Expedited Procedure.

The Swiss Rules do not specify what is considered to be exceptional circumstances. Scholarly writings refer to situations such as the challenge of an arbitrator, an application of a party to a court, a stay of the proceedings due to pending proceedings abroad, or entirely new and unexpected arguments and/or exhibits of a party.[46] According to the unpublished practice of the Swiss Chambers' Court, the most likely requests to be granted are the ones that the parties and the arbitral tribunal all agreed on and that were filed at an early stage of the proceedings.[47] In one case, an extension was granted because both parties had agreed on the appointment of an expert to prepare a report before the hearing and to be questioned during the hearing.[48]

5.3 Exceeding the Time Limit of Six Months

If an arbitral tribunal takes longer to render its award than the time limit allows, the question arises as to whether such an award can be challenged. In the first instance, the grounds for an appeal largely depend on the applicable *lex arbitri*.

Under Swiss law, the grounds for an appeal to the Swiss Federal Supreme Court are limited.[49] The violation of procedural rules agreed

---

Christoph Müller/Philipp Habegger eds., 2nd ed. 2013); Eliott Geisinger, *The Expedited Procedure under the Swiss Rules of International Arbitration, in* 22 ASA SPECIAL SERIES, 67, 83 (Gabrielle Kaufmann Kohler/Blaise Stucki eds., 2004).

[46] Christoph Brunner, *The Swiss Rules of International Arbitration: An Overview for Prospective Users,* GERMAN ARB. J., 233, 249 (2005); Sandra De Vito Bieri/Raphaëlle Favre Schnyder, *in* SWISS RULES OF INTERNATIONAL ARBITRATION, COMMENTARY, *Art. 42 N. 13* (Tobias Zuberbühler/Christoph Müller/Philipp Habegger eds., 2nd ed. 2013); Matthias Scherer, *Acceleration of Arbitration Proceedings—The Swiss Way: The Expedited Procedure under the Swiss Rules of International Arbitration,* GERMAN ARB. J., 229, 234 (2005).

[47] Sandra De Vito Bieri/Raphaëlle Favre Schnyder, *in* SWISS RULES OF INTERNATIONAL ARBITRATION, COMMENTARY, *Art. 42 N. 14a* (Tobias Zuberbühler/Christoph Müller/Philipp Habegger eds., 2nd ed. 2013), with reference to Zurich Chamber of Commerce case No. 600001-2004.

[48] Sandra De Vito Bieri/Raphaëlle Favre Schnyder, *op. cit.,* with reference to Swiss Chambers' case No. 600251-2011.

[49] *Cf.,* the wording of Art. 190(1) and (2) SPILA and the decision of the Swiss Federal Supreme Court, BGE 130 III 35, cons. 5, ad p. 39 et seq.: *« il s'agit également d'éviter que l'argument tiré de l'imprévisibilité du raisonnement adopté par le tribunal arbitral* ***ne soit détourné pour imposer à l'autorité de recours une révision au fond des sentences arbitrales*** *[…] »*; DFSC 127 III 576 of 10 September 2001, para. 2(b), ASA BULLETIN, 473, 475 (2002).

by the parties, such as the rules of an arbitration institution, is not among them.[50] Similarly, the Swiss Federal Supreme Court has held that the violation of the terms of reference does not justify setting aside an award.[51]

In addition, setting aside an award for violation of the time limit would lead to further delays and thus completely defeat the purpose of the Expedited Procedure as a whole.

Unlike some jurisdictions,[52] Switzerland does not have any statutory provisions limiting the duration of the arbitral tribunal's mandate.[53] Nonetheless, parties can agree to such a limit. In such a case, the arbitral tribunal loses jurisdiction the moment its mandate expires.[54] This was recently confirmed in a decision of the Swiss Federal Supreme Court.[55] As the challenge of an arbitral tribunal's jurisdiction generally constitutes a sufficient reason to set aside an award,[56] the Swiss Federal Supreme Court will interpret the parties' intention in drafting the arbitration agreement. This interpretation is made in accordance with the general rules applicable for the interpretation of private expressions of intent. As a consequence, the Swiss Federal Supreme Court will examine the actual understanding of the parties. If no clear intention can be determined, the declaration is interpreted in an objective way, i.e. in the way the recipient would understand the statement according to the principle of good faith.[57]

With respect to time limitations in arbitration rules, the Appellate Court of Basel has held that exceeding the time limit in Art. 18 ICC Rules 1980 (Art. 30 of the 2012 Rules) was a mere délai d'ordre that did not justify setting aside an award.[58] However, it is possible that the Swiss Federal Supreme Court could decide to set aside an award for exceeding the time limit, if it turned out to be so important to the

---

50 Matthias Scherer, *Acceleration of Arbitration Proceedings – The Swiss Way: The Expedited Procedure under the Swiss Rules of International Arbitration*, GERMAN ARB. J., 229, 235 (2005).

51 DFSC of 24 March 1997, para. 1(a), ASA BULLETIN, 316, 319 (1997).

52 According to JEAN-FRANÇOIS POUDRET/SÉBASTIEN BESSON, COMPARATIVE LAW OF INTERNATIONAL ARBITRATION, 377 (2nd ed. 2007), these are, inter alia, France, Belgium and Italy.

53 Christoph Brunner, *The Swiss Rules of International Arbitration: An Overview for Prospective Users*, GERMAN ARB. J., 233, 249 (2005).

54 BERNHARD BERGER/FRANZ KELLERHALS, INTERNATIONAL AND DOMESTIC ARBITRATION IN SWITZERLAND, 262 (2nd ed. 2010); JEAN-FRANÇOIS POUDRET/SÉBASTIEN BESSON, COMPARATIVE LAW OF INTERNATIONAL ARBITRATION, 382 (2nd ed. 2007).

55 DFSC 4A_490/2013 of 28 January 2014.

56 Art. 190(2)(b) SPILA.

57 DFSC 4P.253/2003 of 25 March 2004 para. 5.3, ASA BULLETIN, 128, 134 (2005).

58 Decision of the Court of Appeals of Basel-City of 2 January 1984, *K.KG v. M.SA and M.G.*, para. 4, ASA BULLETIN, 19, 23 (1985).

parties that they would rather not have arbitrated at all than arbitrated in a procedure that takes longer than six months.[59]

In this sense, the Swiss Federal Supreme Court concluded in the recent decision mentioned that the arbitral tribunal loses jurisdiction the moment its mandate expires.[60] In this case, both the parties and the sole arbitrator agreed on the sole arbitrator's resignation if the award was not rendered by an agreed date. As the sole arbitrator had sent the award only after the agreed date, the Swiss Federal Supreme Court set aside the award.

It remains open whether the Swiss Federal Supreme Court would set aside an award due to a violation of the six-month time limit under Art. 42(1)(d) Swiss Rules, or whether they would decide on a case-by-case basis by applying individual contract interpretation. The question to be asked might be: What were the parties' and arbitrator(s)' intent in concluding their agreement and agreeing on the Swiss Rules? Did such intent also include the application of the time limit of six months under Art. 42(1)(d) Swiss Rules? Were they aware of such time limit?

In any event, it is crucial that the Court carefully monitors the time limit of six months and extends such time limit early enough to avoid a possible lack of jurisdiction and a setting aside request of the losing party. Further, it is the arbitral tribunal's duty to conduct the proceedings in a way that this time limit can be maintained or extended early enough.

6. CONCLUSION

Art. 42 Swiss Rules provides for a successful framework to run proceedings efficiently. Therefore, the drafters of the 2012 Swiss Rules did well by only slightly modifying Art. 42 Swiss Rules. The two minor changes that were made both improved the arbitral tribunal's position and enhanced the flexibility of the proceedings. Overall, Art. 42 Swiss Rules is fit for the future.

---

[59] Sandra De Vito Bieri/Raphaëlle Favre Schnyder, *in* SWISS RULES OF INTERNATIONAL ARBITRATION, COMMENTARY, *Art. 42 N. 17a* (Tobias Zuberbühler/Christoph Müller/Philipp Habegger eds., 2nd ed. 2013).

[60] DFSC 4A_490/2013 of 28 January 2014.

Panel 3: Key Features of the Swiss Rules, Part II

Preliminary Orders and the Emergency Arbitrator: Urgent Interim Relief by an Arbitral Decision Maker in Exceptional Circumstances

*Christopher Boog and Bertrand Stoffel**

1. INTRODUCTION

This paper deals with two selected topics from the broad field of interim relief,[1] governed by Article 26 ("*interim measures of protection*") and Article 43 ("*emergency relief*") of the Swiss Rules of International Arbitration ("Swiss Rules").[2]

The first topic pertains to so-called "preliminary orders" as they are provided for in Article 26(3) of the Swiss Rules. Preliminary orders

---

* Christopher Boog is a Partner in Schellenberg Wittmer's International Arbitration Practice Group. He is based in Singapore and Zurich. Bertrand Stoffel is a Junior Associate of the firm based in Zurich. The views expressed in this paper reflect the views of the authors and not necessarily those of Schellenberg Wittmer Ltd or Schellenberg Wittmer Pte Ltd. This paper is based on a presentation given at the conference "10 Years of Swiss Rules of International Arbitration" on 31 January 2014 in Basel.

[1] The terms "interim relief" and "interim measures" are used here as synonyms. They refer to measures intended to protect a party's rights before and pending the duration of proceedings on the merits, sometimes extending to the time between the decision on the merits and its enforcement. On the definition of interim measures in international arbitration, *see e.g.*, Christopher Boog, *Interim Measures in International Arbitration, in* ARBITRATION IN SWITZERLAND, THE PRACTITIONER'S GUIDE 1355, paras. 1 *et seq.* (Manuel Arroyo ed., 2013).

[2] For a more comprehensive overview of the topic of "interim measures" in international arbitration, *see e.g.*, Christopher Boog, *Interim Measures in International Arbitration, in* ARBITRATION IN SWITZERLAND, THE PRACTITIONER'S GUIDE 1355, paras. 1 *et seq.* (Manuel Arroyo ed., 2013); Georg von Segesser and Christopher Boog, *Interim Measures, in* INTERNATIONAL ARBITRATION IN SWITZERLAND, A HANDBOOK FOR PRACTITIONERS 107, 107 *et seq.* (Elliott Geisinger et al. eds., 2nd edition 2013); for a more comprehensive overview of the topic of the emergency arbitrator, *see*, Baruch Baigel, *The Emergency Arbitrator Procedure under the 2012 ICC Rules: A Juridical Analysis*, 31 JOURNAL OF INTERNATIONAL ARBITRATION 1, 1 *et seq.* (2014); Philipp Habegger, *Article 43 Swiss Rules, in* ARBITRATION IN SWITZERLAND, THE PRACTITIONER'S GUIDE 637, paras. 1 *et seq.* (Manuel Arroyo ed., 2013); Andrea Meier, *Article 43 Swiss Rules, in* SWISS RULES OF INTERNATIONAL ARBITRATION, COMMENTARY 453, paras. 1 *et seq.* (Tobias Zuberbühler et al. eds., 2nd edition 2013); Nathalie Voser and Christopher Boog, *ICC Emergency Arbitrator Proceedings: An Overview*, in 22 ICC BULLETIN SPECIAL SUPPLEMENT 81, 81 *et seq.* (2011).

are orders for interim measures that are rendered by the arbitral tribunal prior to notifying and hearing the party or parties against whom the request for interim relief is directed. In other words, they are *ex parte* orders.

The second topic derives from Article 43(8) of the Swiss Rules and pertains to the legal nature of the emergency arbitrator and the emergency arbitrator's decision, and to what extent such decisions are enforceable in a state court.

These topics are not uncontroversial among international arbitration practitioners and scholars, and opinions differ both with respect to the appropriateness of *ex parte* orders by arbitral tribunals and with respect to the legal nature of the emergency arbitrator as well as his or her decision. The following brief thoughts might add some value to the discussion.

2. PRELIMINARY ORDERS UNDER THE SWISS RULES

2.1 Authority to Issue Preliminary Orders

Article 26(3) of the Swiss Rules provides that, in exceptional circumstances, the arbitral tribunal may grant interim measures by way of a "preliminary order".[3] These interim measures are granted by the arbitral tribunal upon a reasoned request by one party, before such request has been communicated or notified to the party (or parties) against whom the requested measure is directed and—logically—therefore, before the latter has been heard on the request. This mechanism constitutes what is referred to as "*ex parte* interim relief".[4]

Although *ex parte* interim relief is an established feature in court litigation in practically all common and civil law jurisdictions, its admissibility and appropriateness continues to be much disputed in international arbitration. During the discussions leading up to the revisions of both the UNCITRAL Model Law on International Commercial Arbitration as amended in 2006 ("UNCITRAL Model Law") and the UNCITRAL Arbitration Rules (as revised in 2010), for

---

3 Swiss Rules, Article 26(3) provides as follows: "In exceptional circumstances, the arbitral tribunal may rule on a request for interim measures by way of a preliminary order before the request has been communicated to any other party, provided that such communication is made at the latest together with the preliminary order and that the other parties are immediately granted an opportunity to be heard."

4 *See,* Christian Oetiker, *Article 26 Swiss Rules, in* SWISS RULES OF INTERNATIONAL ARBITRATION, COMMENTARY 287, para. 12 (Tobias Zuberbühler et al. eds., 2nd edition 2013); Melissa Magliana, *Article 26 Swiss Rules, in* ARBITRATION IN SWITZERLAND, THE PRACTITIONER'S GUIDE 519, para. 35 (Manuel Arroyo ed., 2013).

example, it became apparent that views differ quite drastically as to whether arbitrators shall have the power to order *ex parte* interim relief.[5] Some of the views advanced against *ex parte* interim relief were that such relief goes against the consensual nature of arbitration, that it violates the principle that the parties to an arbitration be treated equally, or that it is not practical or efficient because the arbitral tribunal lacks the coercive power to enforce *ex parte* measures.[6]

In Switzerland, in turn, it is (and has been for some time) the overwhelmingly predominant view—if not a matter of general consent—that *ex parte* interim measures have their place in arbitration and that arbitral tribunals are vested with the power to grant *ex parte* interim relief.[7] It is accepted that arbitral tribunals shall have the same

---

[5] *See e.g., Report of the Working Group on Arbitration on the work of its thirty-eighth session,* UNICTRAL, Thirty-sixth session, UN Doc. A/CN.9/524 (2003), and *Report of the Working Group on Arbitration and Conciliation on the work of its forty-second session,* UNCITRAL, Thrity-eight session, UN Doc. A/CN.9/573 (2005), available at <http://www.uncitral.org>; *see also,* James E. Castello, *Arbitral Ex Parte Interim Relief, The View in Favor,* 58/3 DISPUTE RESOLUTION JOURNAL 60, 60 and 65 *et seq.* (2003); Yves Derains, *The View Against Arbitral Ex Parte Interim Relief,* 58/3 DISPUTE RESOLUTION JOURNAL 61, 61 *et seq.* (2003).

[6] *See,* Nael Bunni, *Interim Measures in International Commercial Arbitration: A Commentary on the Report by Luis Enrique Graham, in* 50 YEARS OF THE NEW YORK CONVENTION: ICCA INTERNATIONAL ARBITRATION CONFERENCE, 14 ICCA CONGRESS SERIES 583, 602 *et seq.* (Albert Jan van den Berg ed., 2009); Hans van Houtte, *Ten Reasons Against a Proposal for Ex Parte Interim Measures of Protection in Arbitration,* 20 ARBITRATION INTERNATIONAL 85, 85 *et seq.* (2004).

[7] BERNHARD BERGER and FRANZ KELLERHALS, INTERNATIONAL AND DOMESTIC ARBITRATION IN SWITZERLAND para. 1153 (2nd edition 2010); Christopher Boog, *Interim Measures in International Arbitration, in* ARBITRATION IN SWITZERLAND, THE PRACTITIONER'S GUIDE 1355, para. 15 (Manuel Arroyo ed., 2013); Andreas Bucher, *Article 183 PILA, IN* LOI SUR LE DROIT INTERNATIONAL PRIVÉ 1609, para. 8 (Andreas Bucher ed., 2011); DANIEL GIERSBERGER and NATHALIE VOSER, INTERNATIONAL ARBITRATION IN SWITZERLAND para. 859 (2nd edition 2012); Ramon Mabillard, *Article 183 PILA, in* INTERNATIONALES PRIVATRECHT 1861, para. 12 (Heinrich Honsell et al. eds., 3rd edition 2013); Melissa Magliana, *Article 26 Swiss Rules, in* ARBITRATION IN SWITZERLAND, THE PRACTITIONER'S GUIDE 519, para. 36 (Manuel Arroyo ed., 2013); Christian Oetiker, *Article 26 Swiss Rules, in* SWISS RULES OF INTERNATIONAL ARBITRATION, COMMENTARY 287, para. 14 (Tobias Zuberbühler et al. eds., 2nd edition 2013); Frank Vischer, *Article 183 PILA, in* ZÜRCHER KOMMENTAR ZUM IPRG 2015, para. 14 (Daniel Girsberger et al. eds., 2nd edition 2004); Georg von Segesser and Dorothée Schramm, *Swiss Private International Law Act (Chapter 12), art. 183, in* CONCISE INTERNATIONAL ARBITRATION 911, para. 4 (Loukas A. Mistelis ed., 2010); Markus Wirth, *Interim or Preventive Measures in Support of International Arbitration in Switzerland,* 18 ASA BULL. 31, 38 (2000); despite not being specifically mentioned in the Swiss statutes on international and domestic arbitration, the power of arbitral tribunals seated in Switzerland to grant *ex parte* interim measures was explicitly acknowledged by the Expert Commission and the Swiss Federal Council in their preparatory works to the Swiss Code of Civil Procedure of 2008, *see,* Schweizerische Zivilprozessordnung ZPO, Bericht zum Vorentwurf der Expertenkommission (June 2003) 174, and Botschaft zur Schweizerischen Zivilprozessordnung BBl 2006 7399, *see also,* Philipp Habegger, *Article 374 CCP, in* SCHWEIZERISCHE ZIVILPROZESSORDNUNG 2195,

powers as state courts in this respect.[8] The new provision of Article 26(3) of the Swiss Rules thus merely corroborates this general understanding for arbitrations conducted under the Swiss Rules. That being said, it is still commonly stated that *ex parte* measures are rather rare in practice.[9] In our experience, although interim measures are occasionally ordered *ex parte* by arbitral tribunals, this still seems to occur less than in court litigation.

Albeit innovative in containing an express stipulation in favor of *ex parte* interim relief, the Swiss Rules are not the sole institutional arbitration rules providing for such relief today. The Mexico City National Chamber Commerce Arbitration Rules also contain a provision on preliminary orders.[10] Both provisions are inspired by Article 17B and Article 17C of the UNCITRAL Model Law.[11]

By reference in Article 43(1) of the Swiss Rules, Article 26(3) of the Swiss Rules also applies to the emergency arbitrator.[12] In other words, the emergency arbitrator under the Swiss Rules may also grant emergency relief *ex parte*. This may prove particularly helpful to a party in need of urgent interim relief at the very outset of a dispute, before the arbitral tribunal has been constituted. This indeed appears to be a feature unique to the Swiss Rules, whereas the other commonly applied institutional arbitration rules that include an emergency arbitrator only provide for *inter partes*, not however *ex parte* emergency relief.[13]

---

para. 4 (Karl Spühler et al. eds., 2nd edition 2013).

8 *See,* Georg von Segesser and Christopher Boog, *Interim Measures, in* INTERNATIONAL ARBITRATION IN SWITZERLAND, A HANDBOOK FOR PRACTITIONERS 107, 117 (Elliott Geisinger et al. eds., 2nd edition 2013); in an international context, *see also,* ALI YEŞILIRMAK, PROVISIONAL MEASURES IN INTERNATIONAL COMMERCIAL ARBITRATION para. 5-89 (2005).

9 *See e.g.,* Philipp Habegger, *Article 374 CCP, in* SCHWEIZERISCHE ZIVILPROZESSORDNUNG 2195, para. 4 (Karl Spühler et al. eds., 2nd edition 2013); Georg von Segesser and Christopher Boog, *Interim Measures, in* INTERNATIONAL ARBITRATION IN SWITZERLAND, A HANDBOOK FOR PRACTITIONERS 107, 117 (Elliott Geisinger et al. eds., 2nd edition 2013); *see further,* James E. Castello, *Arbitral Ex Parte Interim Relief, The View in Favor,* 58/3 DISPUTE RES. J. 60, 65 (2003).

10 Mexico City National Chamber of Commerce Arbitration Rules, Article 31B and Article 31C.

11 UNCITRAL Model Law, Article 17B(1) provides as follows: "Unless otherwise agreed by the parties, a party may, without notice to any other party, make a request for an interim measure together with an application for a preliminary order directing a party not to frustrate the purpose of the interim measure requested."

12 *See,* Andrea Meier, *Article 43 Swiss Rules, in* SWISS RULES OF INTERNATIONAL ARBITRATION, COMMENTARY 453, para. 13 (Tobias Zuberbühler et al. eds., 2nd edition 2013).

13 *See,* Andrea Meier, *Article 43 Swiss Rules, in* SWISS RULES OF INTERNATIONAL ARBITRATION, COMMENTARY 453, para. 24 (Tobias Zuberbühler et al. eds., 2nd edition 2013); under the ICC Rules of Arbitration, the Secretariat will always notify the

2.2 Prerequisites for Preliminary Orders

Pursuant to Article 26(3) of the Swiss Rules, the arbitral tribunal may grant *ex parte* interim relief "in exceptional circumstances." The Swiss Rules do not itemize the situations in which such relief may be granted, but it is generally understood that "exceptional circumstances" include situations of urgency and situations where notifying the request to the respondent party or parties would risk frustrating the very purpose of the interim measures sought.[14] It is noteworthy, however, that the wording chosen in the Swiss Rules is deliberately broad and may include other (exceptional) circumstances that may not fall strictly within these two categories.[15]

Aside from demonstrating exceptional circumstances, a party seeking *ex parte* interim relief is advised to demonstrate that the "regular" prerequisites for an arbitral tribunal to grant (*inter partes*) interim measures are met, including the existence of a valid arbitration agreement, a valid reason for the granting of such measure (*periculum in mora*) and that it has a reasonable chance of succeeding on the merits of the case (*fumus boni iuris*).[16]

In general terms, it is submitted that the arbitral tribunal should weigh the parties' interests in each individual case in order to establish whether or not *ex parte* relief may be warranted.[17]

---

application for emergency measures to the responding party; however, even if this is not explicitly mentioned in the ICC Rules of Arbitration, it is possible that the emergency arbitrator might issue an initial order after the responding party has been notified of the request, but before the responding party has filed its response, *see*, JASON FRY, SIMON GREENBERG and FRANCESCA MAZZA, THE SECRETARIAT'S GUIDE TO ICC ARBITRATION 298 (2012).

[14] Philipp Habegger, *The Revised Swiss Rules of International Arbitration: An Overview of the Major Changes*, 30 ASA BULL. 269, 287 (2012); Melissa Magliana, *Article 26 Swiss Rules, in* ARBITRATION IN SWITZERLAND, THE PRACTITIONER'S GUIDE 519, para. 36 (Manuel Arroyo ed., 2013); Andrea Meier, *Article 43 Swiss Rules, in* SWISS RULES OF INTERNATIONAL ARBITRATION, COMMENTARY 453, para. 50 (Tobias Zuberbühler et al. eds., 2nd edition 2013).

[15] Philipp Habegger, *The Revised Swiss Rules of International Arbitration: An Overview of the Major Changes*, 30 ASA BULLETIN 269, 287 (2012).

[16] On the requirements for granting interim measures, *see*, e.g., Christopher Boog, *Interim Measures in International Arbitration, in* ARBITRATION IN SWITZERLAND, THE PRACTITIONER'S GUIDE 1355, paras. 28 *et seq.* (Manuel Arroyo ed., 2013).

[17] Nathalie Voser, *Interim Relief in International Arbitration: The Tendency Towards a More Business-Oriented Approach*, 1 DIS. RES. INT'L 171, 177 (2007); *see also*, Christopher Boog, *Interim Measures in International Arbitration, in* ARBITRATION IN SWITZERLAND, THE PRACTITIONER'S GUIDE 1355, para. 32 (Manuel Arroyo ed., 2013); Georg von Segesser and Christopher Boog, *Interim Measures, in* INTERNATIONAL ARBITRATION IN SWITZERLAND, A HANDBOOK FOR PRACTITIONERS 107, 109 *et seq.* (Elliott Geisinger et al. eds., 2nd edition 2013).

Finally, it is worth noting that the arbitral should only grant interim relief on an *ex parte* basis if expressly requested by the party seeking interim relief. *Sua sponta ex parte* orders are impermissible.

2.3 Safeguards in Case of Preliminary Orders

Due to their unilateral nature, *ex parte* interim measures present a certain potential for abuse. It is therefore of primary importance that such measures are not granted without specific safeguards being in place. These specific safeguards must ensure that the procedural rights of the party or parties against whom the preliminary order is directed are respected.

Article 26(3) of the Swiss Rules expressly sets out the most important safeguard by providing that the request must be notified to the respondent party or parties together with any preliminary order and that the respondent party is immediately granted the right to be heard both on the request for interim measures and any measure granted *ex parte*. This obligation includes that the arbitral tribunal or the emergency arbitrator, as the case may be, must reconsider its *ex parte* decision once the respondent has presented its case and then either confirm, modify or lift its decision, as the case may warrant.

Furthermore, the arbitral tribunal may require the requesting party to provide appropriate security pursuant to Article 26(2) of the Swiss Rules. The purpose of such security is to secure potential claims for damages, should the preliminary order later prove to be unjustified. In the case of *ex parte* interim measures where the party against whom the measure is directed has not been granted a possibility to be heard on the request before the measure is ordered, the arbitral tribunal should regularly order the provision of security and should only refrain from doing so as an exception if in exceptional situations it considers it unnecessary or inappropriate, or where the requesting party has provided security on its own motion.[18]

Another safeguard from which arbitral tribunals acting under the Swiss Rules may take inspiration is reflected in Article 17F(1) of the UNCITRAL Model Law, providing that the "arbitral tribunal may require any party promptly to disclose any material change in the circumstances on the basis of which the measure was requested or granted."

---

[18] In this respect, *see*, BERNHARD BERGER and FRANZ KELLERHALS, INTERNATIONAL AND DOMESTIC ARBITRATION IN SWITZERLAND para. 1177 (2nd edition 2010); Christopher Boog, *Article 183 PILS, in* ARBITRATION IN SWITZERLAND, THE PRACTITIONER'S GUIDE 1355, para. 18 (Manuel Arroyo ed., 2013).

2.4 Conclusion

In conclusion, we submit that preliminary orders as provided in Article 26(3) of the Swiss Rules have their legitimate place in international arbitration and are unproblematic insofar as the necessary safeguards are in place. With the express provision in Article 26(3) of the Swiss Rules and the safeguards outlined above at their disposal, arbitral tribunals acting under the Swiss Rules should be more comfortable in the future to order interim relief on an *ex parte* basis in cases that warrant such relief.

That being said, in the course of the ongoing revision of the Swiss law on international arbitration, the Swiss legislator may be well advised to add to Article 183 of the Swiss Private International Law Act ("SPILA") a provision along the lines of Article 26(3) of the Swiss Rules or Article 17B of the UNCITRAL Model Law in order to provide the same level of comfort to arbitral tribunal's seated in Switzerland in *ad hoc* proceedings or arbitral proceedings under other institutional rules that do not contain an express provision allowing for, but also do not forbid *ex parte* relief.

3. THE LEGAL NATURE OF THE EMERGENCY ARBITRATOR AND THE EMERGENCY ARBITRATOR'S DECISION

Article 43(8) of the Swiss Rules stipulates that "[a] decision by the emergency arbitrator shall have the same effects as a decision pursuant to Article 26 [of the Swiss Rules]." This provision is interesting because it touches upon the legal nature or status of an emergency arbitrator's decision, what legal effects such a decision has, and ultimately whether (and how) such a decision may be enforceable in a state court. A closely related, yet distinct and to some extent preliminary, question is what the legal nature of the emergency arbitrator itself is. This question is dealt with first, before turning to the emergency arbitrator's decision.

3.1 An Emergency Arbitrator is an Arbitrator

The legal nature of an emergency arbitrator is still subject to some controversy. Simply put, the question: "What is an emergency arbitrator?", remains debated.

Some argue that an emergency arbitrator cannot qualify as an arbitrator, in particular because the emergency arbitrator lacks the capacity to finally settle a dispute, or because the emergency arbitrator's status will in fact depend on the parties' intention, or because it is not clear whether the emergency arbitration must apply the law in rendering his or her decision.[19]

It is submitted here that an emergency arbitrator is indeed an arbitrator. The emergency arbitrator is not a mediator, adjudicator, conciliator or settlement facilitator. First, there is the name: Why call it an arbitrator if it is not an arbitrator? More importantly, though, the emergency arbitrator has a judicial role.[20] He or she must comply with the minimal procedural guarantees applicable to any arbitral proceedings and must meet the requirements of impartiality and independence, just like any arbitrator.[21] This is expressly stipulated in Article 43(4) and Article 43(6) of the Swiss Rules. The emergency arbitrator's impartiality or independence may be challenged under the same rules and conditions as any other arbitrator, subject only to shortened time-limits pursuant to Article 43(4) of the Swiss Rules, and the Arbitral Tribunal is likely to lift the emergency arbitrator's order in the subsequent arbitration pursuant to Article 43(8) of the Swiss Rules if the emergency arbitrator did not grant the parties an equal and reasonable opportunity to present their case as provided in Article 43(6) of Swiss Rules. And finally, the emergency arbitrator's jurisdiction stems directly from the agreement to arbitrate under the Swiss Rules.[22]

Admittedly, the emergency arbitrator is an arbitrator with a limited mandate, both in terms of time and in terms of subject matter. The emergency arbitrator does not render a final decision over a dispute on the merits. Rather, he or she decides a dispute regarding interim measures that remain in place only for a limited amount of time. This does not, however, change the fact that the emergency arbitrator does so with a judicial function. Nor does anything in the

---

[19] *See e.g.*, Baruch Baigel, *The Emergency Arbitrator Procedure under the 2012 ICC Rules: A Juridical Analysis*, 31 J. INT'L ARB. 1, 6 *et seq. and* 15 *et seq.* (2014); regarding this debate, *see further*, Jason Fry, *The Emergency Arbitrator – Flawed Fashion or Sensible Solution?*, DIS. RES. INT'L 179, 185 *et seq.* (2013).

[20] *See also*, Philipp Habegger, *Article 43 Swiss Rules*, *in* ARBITRATION IN SWITZERLAND, THE PRACTITIONER'S GUIDE 637, para. 41 (Manuel Arroyo ed., 2013); Andrea Meier, *Article 43 Swiss Rules*, *in* SWISS RULES OF INTERNATIONAL ARBITRATION, COMMENTARY 453, paras. 7 and 52 (Tobias Zuberbühler et al. eds., 2nd edition 2013); with regard to the emergency arbitrator under the ICC Rules, *see*, Pierre Mayer and Eduardo Silva Romero, *Le nouveau règlement d'arbitrage de la Chambre de commerce internationale (CCI)*, 2011/4 REVUE ARB. 897, 918-919; Nathalie Voser and Christopher Boog, *ICC Emergency Arbitrator Proceedings: An Overview*, in 22 ICC BULLETIN SPECIAL SUPPLEMENT 81, 86 (2011).

[21] *See*, Andrea Meier, *Article 43 Swiss Rules*, *in* SWISS RULES OF INTERNATIONAL ARBITRATION, COMMENTARY 453, para. 33 (Tobias Zuberbühler et al. eds., 2nd edition 2013).

[22] *See*, Article 43(1) of the Swiss Rules, providing an "opt-out" solution for the emergency arbitrator. In other words, where the parties have agreed to arbitrate their dispute under the Swiss Rules, the emergency relief provisions will apply by default, unless the parties have excluded them.

definition of an "arbitral tribunal" stipulate that a decision maker can only be qualified as an arbitrator if he or she renders a final decision on the merits of a case.[23] This is merely a consequence of the parties' choice to, as a rule, submit a "dispute" to the arbitral tribunal for final settlement. If anything, one might argue that the emergency arbitrator is an arbitrator *sui generis*. What is important is that the emergency arbitrator, as explained above, has a judicial function and renders a decision that is not only contractually binding on the parties, but is binding on the parties as a decision by a judicial authority.

The Swiss Rules do not expressly confirm that an emergency arbitrator under the Swiss Rules is an arbitrator. And rightly so, since—if anything—this is something to be defined by the law at the place where the emergency arbitrator proceedings are seated (*see* Article 43(5) of the Swiss Rules). The Swiss Rules do, however, in our view clearly express the intention of their drafters by providing in Article 43(8) that the emergency arbitrator's decision shall have the same effects as a decision by the arbitral tribunal on interim measures under Article 26 of the Swiss Rules. No one would question that the arbitral tribunal, in rendering a decision under Article 26 of the Swiss Rules, acts as the arbitral tribunal in a judicial role, rendering a judicially binding decision on the parties with regard to the interim relief at issue. Article 43(8) of the Swiss Rules makes plain that the same applies to the emergency arbitrator and his or her decision.

Notably, the Singaporean legislator has recognized the importance of stipulating the legal nature of the emergency arbitrator. For the avoidance of doubt, the most recent revision of the Singapore International Arbitration Act includes in the definition of the "Arbitral Tribunal" in Section 2(1) the emergency arbitrator, providing as follows: "In this Part, unless the context otherwise requires—'arbitral tribunal' means a sole arbitrator or a panel of arbitrators or a permanent arbitral institution, and includes an emergency arbitrator appointed pursuant to the rules of arbitration agreed to or adopted by the parties including the rules of arbitration of an institution or organization." Other jurisdictions are certain to follow the Singaporean lead, and it is submitted that this, too, is an issue which the Swiss legislator may want to consider addressing in the currently ongoing revision of the 12th Chapter of the SPILA.

---

[23] What matters is that the decision maker functions as an arbitral tribunal; regarding the fact that an arbitral tribunal which lacks jurisdiction is an arbitral tribunal nonetheless because of the arbitral nature of its proceedings, *see,* Marco Stacher, *Der unzuständige Schiedsrichter*, 29 SCHWEIZERISCHE ZEITSCHRIFT FÜR ZIVILPROZESS- UND ZWANGSVOLLSTRECKUNGSRECHT 32, 36 *et seq.* (2013).

3.2 The Emergency Arbitrator Renders a Judicially Binding Decision

By reference in Article 43(8) to Article 26 of the Swiss Rules, the emergency arbitrator's decision is binding on the parties under the same principles as a decision by an arbitral tribunal on interim measures pursuant to Article 26 of the Swiss Rules.[24]

The emergency arbitrator's decision is, in other words and as indicated above, not merely contractually binding between the parties, as the case may be for instance regarding the decision by a dispute board or a pre-arbitral referee appointed by separate agreement of the parties and vested with the power to grant interim measures before the initiation of the arbitral proceedings.[25]

Rather, it has the binding force of a judicial decision by an arbitrator, with all its consequences.[26]

3.3 The Emergency Arbitrator's Decision is Enforceable in Court

As a consequence of the above, the emergency arbitrator's decision is, in principle, enforceable in a state court. This does not seem to be disputed.[27] The question is under which provisions.

---

[24] *See also,* Article 43(10) of the Swiss Rules, stipulating situations where the emergency arbitrator's decision "*ceases to be binding on the parties*".

[25] Regarding the decisions by emergency arbitrator under the ICC Rules 2012, *see,* Pierre Mayer and Eduardo Silva Romero, *Le nouveau règlement d'arbitrage de la Chambre de commerce internationale (CCI),* 2011/4 REVUE ARB. 897, 918-919; regarding the decisions by emergency arbitrator under the Stockholm Chamber of Commerce Arbitration Rules, *see,* Patricia Shaughnessy, *Pre-arbitral Urgent Relief: The New SCC Emergency Arbitrator Rules,* 27 JOURNAL OF INTERNATIONAL ARBITRATION 337, 355 *et seq.* (2010); regarding the decisions by a Pre-Arbitral Referee under the ICC Rules for a Pre-arbitral Referee Procedure, *see e.g.,* Klaus Peter Berger, *Die Rechtsstellung des Pre-Arbitral Referees,* 2006 SCHIEDSVZ 176, 176 *et seq.* (2006); Pierre Tercier, *Le référé pré-arbitral,* 22 ASA BULLETIN 464, 474 *et seq.* (2004); *see further,* Cour d'appel de Paris, 29 avril 2003, Société nationale des pétroles du Congo et République du Congo v. Société total Fina Elf E&P Congo, 2003 REVUE DE L'ARBITRAGE 1296, 1296 *et seq.* (2003); Charles Jarrosson, *Note – Cour d'appel de Paris, 29 avril 2003,* 2003 REVUE DE L'ARBITRAGE 1299, 1299 *et seq.* (2003).

[26] Philipp Habegger, *Article 43 Swiss Rules, in* ARBITRATION IN SWITZERLAND, THE PRACTITIONER'S GUIDE 637, para. 41 (Manuel Arroyo ed., 2013); Philipp Habegger, *The Revised Swiss Rules of International Arbitration: An Overview of the Major Changes,* 30 ASA BULL. 269, 303 (2012); Andrea Meier, *Article 43 Swiss Rules, in* SWISS RULES OF INTERNATIONAL ARBITRATION, COMMENTARY 453, para. 52 (Tobias Zuberbühler et al. eds., 2nd edition 2013).

[27] Even by those authors who do not agree that the emergency arbitrator is an arbitrator, *see,* Baruch Baigel, *The Emergency Arbitrator Procedure under the 2012 ICC Rules: A Juridical Analysis,* 31 J. INT'L ARB. 1, 17 (2014).

As with regard to interim measures issued by an arbitral tribunal (under Article 26 of the Swiss Rules or any other, similar provision), in most jurisdictions, including Switzerland, emergency measures granted by an emergency arbitrator will not be enforceable under the Convention on the Recognition and Enforcement of Foreign Arbitral Awards (New York, 1958) ("New York Convention") because these decisions do not qualify as "awards" in terms of Article I of the New York Convention.[28] This is true irrespective of what title the decision is given by the emergency arbitrator ("award", "order" or any other denomination), since most jurisdictions recognize the principle of "substance over form". In other words, the state court faced with a request for recognition and enforcement will look at the content of the emergency arbitrator's decision rather than what it is called in order to decide whether the decision before it falls within the ambit of the New York Convention.[29]

Emergency arbitrator decisions will, however, regularly be enforceable under special enforcement provisions such as, for instance, provisions based on Article 17H and 17I of the UNCITRAL Model Law or, in Switzerland, Article 183(2) SPILA. The most recent revision of the Hong Kong International Arbitration Ordinance even contains an express provision guaranteeing the enforcement of emergency measures just like any tribunal-ordered interim measure, irrespective of whether the measure was granted in Hong Kong or elsewhere. Section 22B(1) of the Hong Kong Arbitration Ordinance of provides that "[a]ny emergency relief granted, whether in or outside Hong Kong, by an emergency arbitrator under the relevant arbitration rules is enforceable in the same manner as an order or direction of the Court that has the same effect, but only with the leave of the Court." In Singapore, the legislator has ensured that enforcement of interim measures granted by an emergency arbitrator is granted by including the emergency arbitrator in the definition of an "arbitral tribunal". Therefore, Section 12(6) of the Singapore International Arbitration Act,

---

[28] For an in-depth analysis of the application of the New York Convention to interim measures, *see*, CHRISTOPHER BOOG, DIE DURCHSETZUNG EINSTWEILIGER MASSNAHMEN IN INTERNATIONALEN SCHIEDSVERFAHREN paras. 294 *et seq*. (2011), with many references to case law and other scholarly writing.

[29] CHRISTOPHER BOOG, DIE DURCHSETZUNG EINSTWEILIGER MASSNAHMEN IN INTERNATIONALEN SCHIEDSVERFAHREN paras. 300 *et seq*. (2011); exceptions may apply in jurisdictions such as the United States of America, usually for lack of special provisions governing the enforcement of tribunal-ordered interim measures; regarding the enforcement of interim measures under the New York Convention in the United States of America, *see*, Restatement of the Law Third, The U.S. Law of International Commercial Arbitration, Tentative Draft No. 2 of 16 April 2012, section 1-1(a) and (q), 28-30, 37-40.

expressly providing for the enforcement of tribunal-ordered interim measures, applies directly also to interim relief granted by an emergency arbitrator.

3.4 Conclusion

In conclusion, we submit that an emergency arbitrator is an arbitrator. He or she has a judicial function and renders a judicially binding decision, which is enforceable in a state court. As mentioned above, interim measures ordered by an emergency arbitrator under the Swiss Rules (or any other rules, for that matter), whilst not being enforceable under the New York Convention, are enforceable under Article 183(2) SPILA already *de lege lata*. Nevertheless, *de lege ferenda*, it might be advisable in light of legal security for the Swiss legislator to follow in the footsteps of the legislators in Singapore and Hong Kong and make express reference to emergency arbitrator decisions and their enforceability in the SPILA.

Confidentiality under Art. 44 Swiss Rules

*Pascal Hollander**

1. INTRODUCTION

For most of the 20th century, arbitration was thought to be confidential. Paradoxically, while many authors (and all arbitration institutions) stressed that confidentiality was one of the most fundamental characteristics of arbitration, very few national laws or arbitration rules had specific provisions thereon.

As arbitration was generally described as being "private justice", this was thought to mean "justice rendered by private judges" but also "justice rendered in private", *i.e.* behind closed doors, not open to the public. It is therefore not surprising that all those who were involved in arbitral proceedings expected commercial arbitration[1] to be confidential by nature.

The legal fragility of this general assumption was highlighted by two famous decisions, the first in 1995 by the High Court of Australia in the "*Esso v. Plowman*" case[2] and the second in 2000 by the Supreme Court of Sweden in the "*Bulbank*" case.[3] In both decisions, the existence of an overarching duty of confidentiality in arbitration was rejected. In the aftermath, many arbitral institutions, and also national lawmakers, realized the need to address the question in one or another way.

The Swiss Chambers did so by introducing Art. 43 in the initial 2004 Swiss Rules, which became Art. 44 of the 2012 Swiss Rules.[4] The text remains, however, almost identical to the 2004 version.[5]

---

* Pascal Hollander is a Founding Partner of Hanotiau & van den Berg in Brussels. This paper is based on a presentation given at the conference "10 Years of Swiss Rules of International Arbitration" on 31 January 2014 in Basel.

1 We will not address in this paper the peculiar situation of investment arbitration, which fundamentally differs from commercial arbitration in that it very frequently implies issues that are of general public interest in the State where the investment was made, therefore justifying that investment arbitral proceedings be given a certain publicity.

2 High Court of Australia, 7 April 1995, Esso Australia Resources Ltd v. Plowman, [1995] HCA 19, XXI Y.B. COMM. ARB., 137 (1996).

3 Supreme Court of Sweden, 27 October 2000, Bulgarian Foreign Trade Bank Ltd v. A.I. Trade Finance Inc., XXVI Y.B. COMM. ARB. 291.

4 Swiss Chambers' Arbitration Institution, The Swiss Chambers of Commerce Association for Arbitration and Mediation 2012 (*hereinafter* Swiss Rules).

5 Minor and purely formal changes were made to the original text by adding newly set-up administrative bodies within the Swiss Chambers, i.e. the members of the board of directors of the Swiss Chambers' Arbitration Institution, the members of the Court and the Secretariat, and the staff of the individual Chambers to the list of persons bound by the confidentiality clause.

Article 44

1. Unless the parties expressly agree in writing to the contrary, the parties undertake to keep confidential all awards and orders as well as all materials submitted by another party in the framework of the arbitral proceedings not already in the public domain, except and to the extent that a disclosure may be required of a party by a legal duty, to protect or pursue a legal right, or to enforce or challenge an award in legal proceedings before a judicial authority. This undertaking also applies to the arbitrators, the tribunal-appointed experts, the secretary of the arbitral tribunal, the members of the board of directors of the Swiss Chambers' Arbitration Institution, the members of the Court and the Secretariat, and the staff of the individual Chambers.

2. The deliberations of the arbitral tribunal are confidential.

3. An award or order may be published, whether in its entirety or in the form of excerpts or a summary, only under the following conditions:

   (a) A request for publication is addressed to the Secretariat;

   (b) All references to the parties' names are deleted; and

   (c) No party objects to such publication within the time-limit fixed for that purpose by the Secretariat.

2. THE LAW APPLICABLE TO THE CONFIDENTIALITY OF ARBITRATION

As we will see, Art. 44 Swiss Rules sets out a very comprehensive regime of confidentiality for proceedings conducted under the Swiss Rules.

Because of the contractual nature of institutional arbitration rules, which parties incorporate by reference to their arbitration agreement, it must first be determined which law(s) govern(s) the confidentiality of arbitration, as it is possible that the rules set forth in Art. 44 could be superseded by public policy or mandatory legal provisions of a law that could potentially be applicable. This situation was explicitly foreseen by Art. 44, since the first exception to the confidentiality regime is the existence of a "legal duty" requiring a party to disclose information pertaining to the arbitration.

It seems therefore important to list all laws that are susceptible of being applied and to check under each of these laws whether they contain public policy or mandatory provisions that could render all or part of Art. 44 Swiss Rules ineffective.

Which potentially applicable laws must be considered?

1) The *lex situs* or law of the place of arbitration: There is no obligation that proceedings conducted under the Swiss Rules be seated in Switzerland. The first law to look at in order to determine if derogations to the regime of Art. 44 are required is therefore the law of the place of arbitration. It seems that, if that law provides for a mandatory confidentiality regime that differs from the one contractually agreed between the parties (by reference to Art. 44) and that must be complied with, any award rendered at the end of a process subject to different confidentiality rules than the ones mandatorily applicable at the place of arbitration would run the risk of being set aside as contrary to public policy. It should be noted, however, that we have no knowledge of an arbitration law that stipulates that arbitration should not be confidential as a matter of public policy. The risk described above appears thus rather limited.

2) The *lex arbitri* or law governing the procedure. This should also be taken into consideration, especially if the parties agreed on a *lex arbitri* that differs from the *lex situs*. One should ensure that such *lex arbitri* will not make the rules set out in Art. 44 ineffective or unenforceable.

3) The *lex partes* or law of the parties. This also plays an important role when it comes to determining possible exceptions to the confidentiality regime of Art. 44 Swiss Rules. As we will see, the parties may be bound by a duty required by the law of the country of which they are a resident or national to disclose information pertaining to arbitral proceedings (e.g. disclosure in a company's financial statements of information capable of affecting the value of publicly traded shares, as required by the law applicable to such company).

4) The *lex loci executionis* or the law of the place where the contract must be performed. This may also play a role. For instance, several countries have laws or regulations requiring a franchisor to disclose to potential franchisees important information about the franchised business before a contract is executed. These laws or regulations generally apply in consideration of the place where the franchise agreement is going to be performed. The required disclosure concerns,

amongst others, the "litigation history" of the franchisor: how many (former) franchisees have sued it in the past three or five years? For which reasons? What was the outcome of such proceedings? These laws or regulations generally do not make a distinction between litigation and arbitration history or even expressly require the disclosure of the franchisor's arbitration history.[6] This comes in direct conflict with the confidentiality of arbitration.

5) Finally, the law of the place of enforcement could also potentially affect the effectiveness of Art. 44 Swiss Rules if it regulated the issue of confidentiality of arbitration as a matter of public policy.[7]

3. THE MATERIAL SCOPE OF CONFIDENTIALITY UNDER ART. 44

Art. 44 Swiss Rules appears to be one of the most comprehensive regimes on confidentiality in any institutional arbitration rules. Yet its wording can give rise to some issues and/or questions.

Subject to exceptions, which we will review under Section 5, Art. 44(1) requires that "the parties undertake to keep confidential all awards and orders as well as all materials submitted by another party in the framework of the arbitral proceedings not already in the public domain."

However, neither the existence of the underlying dispute nor that of the arbitral proceedings as such appears to be included in the subject matter of the confidentiality undertaking. While other institutional rules expressly include the dispute or the arbitration as such as being covered by confidentiality,[8] the absence of such explicit mention in Art. 44(1) Swiss Rules could be interpreted as implying that the dispute itself or the fact that a party initiated arbitral proceedings is not covered by confidentiality. This means that, while the existence of the arbitral proceedings could be disclosed, its outcome may not.

---

6 *See*, C. VON WUNSCHHEIM, *Confidentiality in Arbitration: Help or Hindrance for Franchising Disputes?* Paper presented at the session "Navigating in Calm Seas or Crossing the Roaring Forties: Arbitrating International Distribution and Franchise Disputes", IBA Conference Boston 2013, available at www.ibanet.org.

7 We have not listed above the *lex contractus* as this law seems to be less relevant for assessing the effectiveness of Art. 44 of the Swiss Rules because it does not have, in principle, a bearing on how the arbitral proceedings must be conducted.

8 *See e.g.*, art. 25 of the CEPANI 2013 Rules: "Unless it has been agreed otherwise or there is a legal obligation to disclose, the arbitration proceedings are confidential."

Indeed, Art. 44(1) states that confidentiality extends to awards, which is self-explanatory. It also covers orders, and one should therefore be aware that a procedural timetable or a list of witnesses to be heard may not be disclosed as they are typically recorded in procedural orders. Such is also the case for the name of the court reporter or the interpreter or the venue of the hearing. While these latter elements do not seem very important at first sight, their disclosure could be potentially harmful to the confidentiality of the process.: How would, for instance, a party react if it were faced with journalists waiting in the lobby of the hotel where an arbitral hearing is due to take place because the other party disclosed the venue of the hearing to the press?

Art. 44(1) also states that confidentiality applies to all materials submitted by another party in the framework of the arbitral proceedings not already in the public domain. We must admit that such wording raises some doubt as to the exact meaning of this provision, as it appears to cover only the submissions made by the other party. Does that mean that each party is entitled to disclose its own written submissions and other materials it produces in the arbitration? We do not believe so, as such interpretation would render the whole provision meaningless. Rather, we are of the opinion that this apparent loophole in Art. 44(1) comes from an oversight in the reproduction of the rule that inspired the drafters of Art. 44(1), which is article 30.1 of the LCIA 1998 Rules,[9] and that confidentiality is therefore also meant to cover *all materials in the proceedings created for the purpose of the arbitration*, a mention that appears in that source of inspiration but not in Art. 44(1). By interpreting Art. 44(1) broadly as applying also to 'materials in the proceedings created for the purpose of the arbitration', this would cover not only the parties' own submissions, but also the hearing transcripts, which would otherwise not be covered by the confidentiality undertaking.

Finally, Art. 44(2) Swiss Rules states explicitly that the deliberations of the tribunal are also covered by confidentiality. This does not distinguish arbitration from court litigation, as the "*secret du délibéré*" is a principle that applies to state courts regardless of the publicity of hearings.

---

9 "Unless the parties expressly agree in writing to the contrary, the parties undertake as a general principle to keep confidential all awards in their arbitration, together with all materials in the proceedings created for the purpose of the arbitration and all other documents produced by another party in the proceedings not otherwise in the public domain (...)."

4. THE PERSONAL SCOPE OF THE CONFIDENTIALITY UNDERTAKING

The confidentiality undertaking we just described applies to several players in the arbitral process, not only to the parties. While the first sentence of Art. 44(1) mentions only the parties, the second sentence of Art. 44(1) makes also other participants in the arbitration subject to the confidentiality obligation:

- *The arbitrators*: While it seems quite obvious that arbitrators should refrain from disclosing information about the arbitration, the basis for such duty appears questionable. The obligation to professional secrecy that normally covers the activities of an attorney-at-law (at least for those lawyers subject to such obligation because of their legal or professional rules) may indeed not provide an appropriate basis for the duty of confidentiality of an arbitrator, since acting as an arbitrator substantially differs from acting as counsel. In addition, not all arbitrators are attorneys-at-law and therefore subject to professional secrecy obligations. The explicit mention of the arbitrator as a person bound by the confidentiality undertaking appears thus to serve a meaningful purpose.
- *The tribunal-appointed experts*: One must be careful as the mere fact that tribunal-appointed experts are listed in Art. 44(1) does not seem sufficient to create an obligation which could be enforced against them. Indeed, these experts are not bound by the Swiss Rules as they are not a party to the arbitration agreement designating these Rules. In order for such experts to be bound by confidentiality, it will therefore be necessary that the arbitrators ensure that any expert they appoint agrees to be bound by the confidentiality obligation. This can be achieved either directly, by having the expert signing an express statement of confidentiality reproducing the language of Art. 44(1), or indirectly, by referring to this article (or at least to the Swiss Rules) in the expert's terms of reference, as foreseen by Art. 27(1) of the Rules, on condition that the expert be given an opportunity to read the Rules (for instance, by an indication of the link to the Swiss Chambers' website where the Rules can be accessed), prior to his/her acceptance of these terms of reference.

- *The secretary of the arbitral tribunal*: While it could be reasonably argued that the secretary would be automatically bound by the Swiss Rules by accepting to serve as secretary to an arbitral tribunal acting under said Rules, it is also recommended to have him or her expressly consent to be bound by Art. 44(1) in order to avoid any risk of unenforceability against the secretary, who is neither a party to the arbitration agreement nor a signatory of the terms of reference of the arbitration.

- *The members of the board of directors of the Swiss Chambers' Arbitration Institution, the members of the Court and the Secretariat, and the staff of the individual Chambers*: The issue of whether Art. 44(1) can be enforced against any of these persons does not seem to be problematic as it can be assumed with reasonable certainty that they have consented, upon entering into function (either by signing an employment contract or otherwise) to abide by the Swiss Rules when acting in relation to a Swiss Rules arbitration.

Moreover, it seems that, by analogy with the persons expressly listed in Art. 44(1), other players in the arbitral process should also be bound by a confidentiality undertaking.

- This should be the case for *court reporters* and *interpreters* on condition that, as with tribunal-appointed experts, the arbitral tribunal (or as the case may be the parties) ensures that their attention is drawn to Art. 44(1) of the Rules when retaining their services. The arbitral tribunal should also make its acceptance of their offer for services conditional upon their consent to be bound thereby.

- *Witnesses* (including *expert witnesses*) presented by a party should be deemed as being bound to respect confidentiality even if they have not signed a confidentiality statement due to the duty of confidentiality owed by the party and the position of the witness as "party-dependent" actor in the arbitral process. This means that if a witness (or expert witness) presented by a party makes public disclosures about what happened in the hearing room (or for the expert witness about what he/she wrote in his/her report or saw in the report submitted by the other party's expert witness), the liability of the party who presented that witness could be engaged. It is therefore the responsibility of each party to "educate" the witnesses it presents and draw their attention to the need to respect confidentiality. It should also be noted in this respect that the confidentiality rule of Art. 44(1) cannot be used by someone who testified in arbitral proceedings in order to refuse to testify in other proceedings, before a state court or another arbitral tribunal. The facts on which a witness testifies are indeed not confidential as such (unless this witness had signed a confidentiality agreement before these facts occurred and applying thereto). On the other hand, everything that the witness learned in the framework of arbitral proceedings, either during his or her presence in the hearing room or by his or her preparatory contacts with counsel, is covered by confidentiality.

- With regard to *"independent" witnesses* who may be summoned to appear by an arbitral tribunal, i.e. a witness not put forward by the parties, we do not see how they could be formally bound by Art. 44(1) of the Rules unless they consent to sign a statement of confidentiality before testifying. Indeed, there is no contractual relationship between these independent witnesses and the arbitral tribunal or the parties, which would somehow make Art. 44(1) enforceable against them. It seems therefore wise that an arbitrator should always draw the "independent" witness' attention to the need not to make public statements about what happened during the hearing and ask the witness to promise not to do so, but this will likely remain for that witness a moral commitment rather than a binding legal obligation.
- Finally, *counsels* are of course bound by confidentiality in their capacity as representatives of a party to which Art. 44(1) applies, but also because of their duty to professional secrecy (at least for those lawyers who are subject to such duty because of their legal or professional rules).

5. EXCEPTIONS TO CONFIDENTIALITY

Art. 44(1) provides for several exceptions to the rule of confidentiality.

- The first and most important one is of course the *parties' agreement*. Confidentiality is meant to protect the parties' rights. The parties may thus validly agree that their arbitral proceedings will not be confidential or restrict confidentiality to some of the items foreseen in Art. 44(1). The only requirement is that such an agreement be made in writing.

- The second exception is when disclosure is required by a *legal duty to disclose*. Such a legal duty may affect the parties (*e.g.* duty for a publicly traded company to disclose details of pending disputes in its financial statements or duty for a franchisor to disclose its "litigation and arbitration history" if one of the laws that must be taken into consideration imposes such duties[10]) but also the arbitrators. This is obviously the case for the disclosures that an arbitrator must make when he or she is considered for potential arbitral appointment. In our opinion, the adjective "legal" should be interpreted broadly so that a disclosure obligation on arbitrators foreseen not only by arbitration statutes,[11] but also by rules of arbitral institutions[12] is an exception to confidentiality.
- The *protection or pursuit of a legal right* is also an exception to confidentiality. It seems indeed obvious that a party should be authorized to produce an arbitral award that would constitute the proof of a right challenged by a third party.
- Finally, the *enforcement or challenge of an award* is another obvious exception to confidentiality of arbitration under Art. 44(1) Swiss Rules. One may even ask whether this should have been made a separate exception as it seems that the production of the award before the state court before which an application to set it aside or to enforce it is pending is already comprised within the 'legal duty to disclose' and 'protection or pursuit of a legal right' exceptions.

One should finally stress that Art. 44(2) foresees no exception to the rule of confidentiality of the deliberations of the arbitral tribunal. Yet, it is generally admitted that confidentiality of deliberation does not extend to forbidding noting in the arbitral award that the decision was reached unanimously or only by majority, or to precluding the issuance of a dissenting opinion. The question as to whether such a note or opinion is possible will, however, depend on the *lex arbitri* or *lex situs*.

---

10 *See*, Section 2 above.

11 *See e.g.*, the new Article 1686 of the Belgian Judicial Code (introduced by the Act of 24 June 2013).

12 *See e.g.*, the disclosure obligation provided by Art. 9(2) Swiss Rules.

6. PUBLICATION OF AWARDS

While there seemed to be a consensus that arbitral awards should not be published, the development in recent years of newsletters and magazines publishing information on arbitral proceedings, and sometimes even arbitral awards in a non-redacted format, made it necessary for the drafters of the Swiss Rules to provide for specific rules on the publication of awards. These are set forth by Art. 44(3).

Publication of awards and orders (whether in their entirety or in summary form) or of excerpts thereof is possible if (a) a request for publication is sent to the Chambers' Secretariat, (b) all reference to the parties' names are deleted, and (c) no party objects to the publication within the time limit set by the Secretariat.

These are rather straightforward conditions, which do not raise any issues.

However, one may question whether the mere deletion of the parties' names in the published award is sufficient to preserve confidentiality. Would it not be more appropriate to provide that all elements capable of making the identification of the parties possible should be deleted? This would cover not only names, but also facts that would clearly point to a specific party. However, one should note that if the deletion of the parties' names is not sufficient to guarantee that confidentiality be preserved, any party will most likely object to publication, which means that there is no practical relevance of this issue

Another issue is that the condition that no party should object to publication within the time limit set by the Secretariat seems to make publication of awards a rather theoretical possibility, as one may reasonably assume that the party which lost the arbitration will always object to the publication of the award, even in a sanitized form.

Finally, one should note that no exception is apparently foreseen concerning the prohibition to publish awards or orders (save under the conditions set forth by Art. 44(3). Yet, it seems that, just like in Art. 44(1), the protection or pursuit of a legal right should allow deviating from the strict conditions laid down by Art. 44(3) to publish an award. Consider a dispute concerning a situation where one party disparaged a contractual partner by complaining in the media about its alleged terrible shortcomings in the performance of the contract. If an arbitral tribunal finds that that party did not commit any breach in the performance of the contract, the publication of the award or of an excerpt thereof as ordered by the arbitral tribunal could constitute an appropriate remedy for the disparagement it suffered.

As we do not believe that the drafters of the Swiss Rules intended to restrict the powers of an arbitral tribunal to order the publication of the award if the circumstances of the dispute so justify, it would not be unreasonable to read the exception of protection or pursuit of a legal right as applying not only to the confidentiality rule of Art. 44(1) but also to the publication regime of Art. 44(3).

7. CONCLUSION

Art. 44 Swiss Rules undoubtedly constitutes one of the most comprehensive rules on confidentiality of arbitral proceedings. At the same time, it gives the party the required level of flexibility by allowing them to agree on derogations and provides for a series of logical exceptions. Although some minor improvements in its wording are always possible, Art. 44 nevertheless offers users of the Swiss Rules legal certainty not always available under other rules on the issue of confidentiality of arbitration.

Settlement Facilitation

*Markus Wirth**

Good morning everyone. I am glad to stand in for Peter Nobel. He is an esteemed colleague of mine and I wish him all the best for a quick recovery. He was supposed to speak about settlement facilitation, so that is the topic I will address.

1. THE PROS AND CONS

By settlement facilitation I understand facilitation by the arbitrators. The question is: should it be the rule, should it be an exception or should it be an absolute no go? The approach to that may depend on one's legal background, culture, and social traditions. The same applies to a certain extent to the approach taken by arbitral institutions. Depending on where they are located they may be more open or not towards settlement facilitation.

Let me first briefly address the most repeated reasons for the facilitation of a settlement by the arbitral tribunal and those against it. They are obvious.

First of all, a settlement, if successful, saves time and costs; secondly, a settlement may preserve business relationships; and, third, an often-heard argument is that arbitration is not war but a consensual process so settlement fits the process.

By contrast, there is a widespread approach that says arbitrators, just like judges, should keep to their role: decide the case and not help to reach compromises. A second concern is that if the facilitation fails, the orderly completion of the arbitration may be at risk. I will come back to that.

If we take a step back and look at the arbitral institutions and how they reflect these contrary approaches, we will note that the vast majority of institutional arbitration rules do not even mention settlement facilitation by arbitrators. I refer for instance to the Rules of the London Court of International Arbitration; the United Nations Commission on International Trade Law (UNCITRAL) Rules; the Rules of the International Centre for Dispute Resolution; the Vienna

---

* Markus Wirth is a Senior Partner in the Litigation and Arbitration practice group at Homburger AG in Zurich, Switzerland. This paper slightly amends the presentation given at the conference "10 Years of Swiss Rules of International Arbitration" on 31 January 2014 in Basel and retains the speaking style.

Rules; the Stockholm Rules; and the Rules of the Hong Kong and Singapore Arbitration Centres. Not one word in these rules is lost on the issue of settlement facilitation.

On the other hand we have the Rules of the German Institute of Arbitration (DIS) and the Rules of the Swiss Chambers of Commerce[1] (Swiss Rules). The DIS Rules provide in Section 32.1:

> At every stage of the proceedings, the arbitral tribunal should seek to encourage an amicable settlement of the dispute or of individual issues in dispute.

I read the provision as an invitation to the Arbitral Tribunal not only to encourage the parties to conduct settlement discussions among themselves but, beyond mere encouragement, to also be available to actively facilitate a settlement if so desired by the Parties.

The Swiss Rules explicitly provide for such an active approach. They state in Art. 15(8) as follows:

> With the agreement of each of the parties, the arbitral tribunal may take steps to facilitate the settlement of the dispute before it. Any such agreement by a party shall constitute a waiver of its right to challenge an arbitrator's impartiality based on the arbitrator's participation and knowledge acquired in taking the agreed steps—meaning the agreed facilitation steps.

Along the same lines Appendix IV to the ICC Rules[2] on Case Management Techniques provides in paragraph (h)(ii):

> Where agreed between the parties and the arbitral tribunal, the arbitral tribunal may take steps to facilitate settlement of the dispute, provided that every effort is made to ensure that any subsequent award is enforceable at law.

Even more explicit are the CIETAC Rules which appear to provide for what is sometimes referred to as Med-Arb. Section 45(1)-(3) of the Rules empower the arbitrators as follows:

---

1 Swiss Chambers' Arbitration Institutions, Swiss Rules of International Arbitration 2012 (*hereinafter* Swiss Rules).

2 ICC Rules of Arbitration (as from 1 January 2012).

1. Where both parties wish to conciliate, or where one party wishes to conciliate and the other party's consent has been obtained by the arbitral tribunal, the arbitral tribunal may conciliate the case during the course of the arbitration proceedings ...
2. With the consent of both parties, the arbitral tribunal may conciliate the case in a manner it considers appropriate.

   The arbitral tribunal shall terminate the conciliation proceedings if either party so requests or if the arbitral tribunal believes that further efforts to conciliate will be futile.

How relevant are these facilitation rules in practice? I have looked at the statistics of the Swiss Chambers and can report that of all the cases accepted under the Swiss Rules between 2004 and 2013, 26% were settled. The 26% figure does not differentiate between settlements with the assistance of the arbitral tribunal and those without.[3] However, my experience is that most of the settlements in the arbitrations where I sat were reached during the course of the arbitral process *with* the assistance of the arbitral tribunal and not just by the parties themselves.

This falls in line with the result of the survey that was organized by ASA ahead of this conference. 20% of those who answered the question about the most valued feature of the Swiss Rules referred to settlement facilitation as provided for in Art. 15(8).[4]

2. PRACTICAL ISSUES OF SETTLEMENT FACILITATION

Let me now turn to some practical issues of the settlement facilitation process. What I will mention comes from my personal experiences and preferences. I am perfectly aware that there are different ways to facilitate and often the selection of the successful way to do it will depend on the specific circumstances of the case.

2.1 At What Stage of the Arbitral Proceedings?

The first question that arises when arbitrating under the Swiss Rules and considering applying Art. 15(8) is: at what stage of the arbitral process should facilitation be offered? Usually, as an

---

[3] *See,* Swiss Chambers' Arbitration Institution, Arbitration Statistics 2013, www.swissarbitration.org.

[4] *See,* Annex Swiss Rules Survey, Question 8.

arbitrator, I already refer the parties to Art. 15(8) at the case management conference. I offer to introduce a specific procedural step which I call preliminary views hearing/settlement conference into the procedural timetable. That step identifies how and when settlement facilitation will be conducted unless the parties, before that date, advise the tribunal that they do not want to go through with the exercise.

What is the best time in the provisional timetable to have a preliminary views hearing/settlement conference? It may be immediately after the first exchange of briefs, especially where the case is relatively simple and the parties anticipate submitting comprehensive first briefs. Incidentally, that is the point in time when settlement conferences are regularly scheduled in state court proceedings before the Zurich courts. It goes without saying that settlement at an early stage of the proceedings will provide the best cost savings.

An alternative is to schedule the settlement conference only after the second exchange of briefs. At that time the arbitrators may have a better grasp of the case and of the relevant issues to address in exploring the possibility of a settlement which, as a rule, enhances the chances of reaching a settlement. An additional advantage is that at this point in time the preliminary views hearing/settlement conference may be combined with the pre-hearing conference for the preparation of the evidentiary hearing. The idea is that if the settlement conference bears no results, the conference can be extended to include a discussion of how to structure the forthcoming evidentiary hearing. Such a combination of the settlement conference with a procedural step that is in any event necessary helps to avoid the loss of time resulting from an unsuccessful effort to settle.

An interesting fringe benefit of providing for a settlement conference in the procedural timetable is the mitigating effect this may have on the parties' adversarial rhetoric in their submissions. If they realise that they will meet sometime soon for settlement discussions, they may choose not to use the aggressive language they might otherwise prefer.

There are, of course, also opportunities later on to offer settlement facilitation, e.g. in the course of the evidentiary hearing or at the end of such hearing. Sometimes it is only after one has heard the parties and their witnesses in person that it becomes clear what the parties' real interests are in the dispute. And it may turn out that a form of moral satisfaction is as important as monetary compensation. Even if settlement discussions have not been scheduled to take place at the hearing, it may become clear from the parties' words and acts during the hearing that they are ready to bring the case to an end.

Also, the Arbitral Tribunal may be forced to advise counsel at the end of the evidentiary hearing when wrapping up what it has heard: "Please consider that this is a black and white case: either the claimant wins 100% or the respondent wins 100%. We are not dealing here with a claim that allows us, under the law, to grant more or less damages; either nothing or all. Do you really want to risk ending up 100% on the losing side—and if that happens how will you explain to your board that you missed the chance to get at least a part of what you sought?" I experienced instances where such an analysis had a sobering effect. The parties asked for a break, huddled in their break-out rooms, came back and said they were ready to settle.

The most dramatic settlement I ever experienced at a hearing was some years ago in an arbitration between an Austrian and a German party. The hearing devolved into an extremely aggressive and unpleasant exchange of words between counsel, with the key representatives of the parties eagerly joining in. It got so heated that the court reporter suddenly broke down in tears, and it was not a silent affair, it was heart-breaking crying. It put us all to shame about what had happened. We stopped the hearing and I invited counsel to discuss what had happened between them. After 45 minutes they came back and advised us that they wished to suspend the arbitration and try to find a settlement. Two weeks later we received the written settlement agreement. I would not know what to call this kind of facilitation but surely it was one of the most effective I have ever seen.

2.2 What Safeguards to Provide for?

The second issue I would like to address is safeguards. Before embarking on an attempt to facilitate a settlement, the Arbitral Tribunal should make sure that the parties' agreement to the process is properly recorded. This may be done by obtaining a letter agreement from the parties before the settlement conference or by recording their agreement in the (summary) minutes of the conference. Where the parties' explicit agreement of a settlement conference was provided for in the procedural timetable, that should provide a sufficient record.

As a second safeguard, the arbitral tribunal should obtain the parties' waiver of their right to challenge the arbitrators' impartiality based on their participation in and knowledge acquired during the settlement facilitation. Under Art. 15(8) of the Swiss Rules such a waiver is deemed to be part of the parties' agreement to the process.

Absent such a rule, it is imperative to obtain a specific waiver and have it properly recorded.

Thirdly, it should be made sure that the key representatives of the parties are involved in the process, i.e. that they are present at the settlement conference. After all, it is their case that is sought to be resolved and not the counsels'. Moreover, it cannot be denied that the parties and their counsel may be motivated by different interests when it comes to decide if a case should be settled at an early stage of the proceedings. As arbitrator, you may want to focus on the parties' interests.

2.3 How to Facilitate the Reaching of a Settlement?

There are of course many ways to assist the parties in reaching a settlement—and the best way may be different in each case, depending on the specific circumstances. I personally find it helpful to lay the groundwork for settlement discussions by providing the parties with the arbitral tribunal's preliminary views on the most relevant factual and legal issues of the case. This includes identifying the undisputed issues as well as the disputed ones, and, in respect of the latter, discussing each party's chance to win or to risk losing. The analyses may be provided in hypothetical alternatives depending on the possible outcomes of the further evidentiary procedure: If claimant is able to prove point A, our conclusion will most likely be B. If it turns out that he cannot prove his point, the conclusion will most likely be C, and so on and so forth.

Where the quantum of damages is in dispute, it may be helpful to identify what in the Arbitral Tribunal's view the driving elements or parameters are and how they may be determined or calculated. Such an analysis may then serve as the basis for a joint calculation by the parties or their experts among themselves.

A difficult question is how to deal with the proverbial "elephant in the room" if the arbitrators sense that the dispute is ultimately about something else than what the parties, for jurisdictional reasons, have been able to bring before the arbitral tribunal. What if the tribunal realizes that a settlement may be reachable only if it extends beyond the prayers for relief put forward in the arbitration? Should the tribunal, on its own initiative, address the elephant?

It is important for arbitrators to clarify during the preliminary views process what the basis is on which their views are provided, namely on the basis of the submissions filed so far and of the evidence produced so far. The arbitrators should explicitly and preferably repeatedly make reservations that they may change their minds depending on the further submissions by the parties.

The process of settlement facilitation is of course not without substantial risks. The primary and obvious risk is that the facilitation fails and that, as a result, time is lost and efforts are wasted. In addition, parties that disagree with the preliminary views communicated by the arbitral tribunal may choose to obstruct the further course of the proceedings. Another risk of the process itself is that it requires intensive interaction between the arbitral tribunal and the parties and counsel, and that during such interaction the arbitrators may get entangled in controversial discussions with counsel. Such discussions should be avoided as they may lead arbitrators, in the heat of the moment, to express positions which they have not yet really thought through.

Finally, there is the risk during settlement facilitation to wake up sleeping dogs that is to refer to issues that have not yet been addressed by the parties but which, in the arbitrators' view, are relevant to the case. That can lead to subsequent unsolicited submissions by the parties and a disruption of the procedural timetable. The question then arises as to how to avoid disadvantaging the party that is negatively affected by the coming into play of new issues.

3. CONCLUSION

My personal view is that whether arbitration rules explicitly provide for settlement facilitation or not, and notwithstanding the risks involved with the process, arbitrators should in each case consider offering settlement facilitation to the parties. Thus my recommendation to counsel: Do not hesitate to ask for the arbitral tribunal's assistance but do it only if you are seriously interested in settling the dispute and not merely for tactical reasons. Usually a party's motivation sooner or later becomes clear in the process and neither the counterparty nor the arbitrators appreciate going through a fruitless exercise. And my encouragement to arbitrators: As a part of your service package, offer settlement facilitation. Do it if the parties are willing to try it, protect yourself appropriately, remain flexible in the approach and, if you are successful, party with the parties!

Thank you for your attention.

Panel 4: Swiss Rules in Practice: The Insiders' View

Case Administration

*Michael Fischer**

1. INTRODUCTION

Good afternoon ladies and gentlemen. First of all I would like to express my thanks to the organisers and ASA for this invitation and also to Ignacio de Castro for the kind introduction.

It is truly a great privilege to be invited here to speak before this distinguished audience. In the following presentation I would like to grant you a glimpse behind the institution's and the Secretariat's daily work and responsibilities. The focus of the following presentation lies on the organisational set up of the institution and the interaction between the Secretariat and the Arbitration Court of the institution. I will also provide insight into how cases are administered on a daily basis with a focus on topics of interest to the users. In addition, I would like to take up some questions raised earlier this morning.

2. ORGANISATIONAL STRUCTURE OF SWISS CHAMBERS' ARBITRATION INSTITUTION

The Swiss Chambers' Arbitration Institution has the following organisational structure: the Arbitration Court ("Court") and the Secretariat. The Arbitration Court is comprised of experienced international arbitration practitioners and is assisted in its work by the Secretariat of the Court. It is very important that one distinguishes between the Court, as the body rendering the administrative decisions under the Swiss Rules,[1] and the Secretariat, as the section of the institution in charge of communication with the parties and the arbitral tribunals.

We heard earlier this morning that it might be confusing for foreign users to understand the structure, especially if you have seven

---

* Michael Fischer is Legal Counsel at the Zurich Chamber of Commerce. This is a slightly amended version of a presentation given at the conference "10 Years of Swiss Rules of International Arbitration" on 31 January 2014 in Basel and retains the informal speaking style.

[1] Swiss Chambers' Arbitration Institution, Swiss Rules of International Arbitration 2012 (*hereinafter* Swiss Rules).

addresses where you may file your Notice of Arbitration. Actually, in Art. 3(1) Swiss Rules, it says that the Notice of Arbitration may be filed with any Secretariat, so for the user, and the claimant especially, it does not matter where the Notice of Arbitration is filed. The organisational question of where the case will be administered, i.e. at which office of the Secretariat, is then solely an internal process.

Earlier on the issue was raised as to whether the institution can guarantee a uniform approach with the current organisational structure. As we have learned, it is always the Arbitration Court which renders the administrative decisions and not the offices of the Secretariat. Thus it is always one organisational body, the Arbitration Court, rendering the decisions and you will learn more about it from Philipp Habegger later on.[2]

3. THE FIRST STEPS IN THE CASE ADMINISTRATION

Once a Notice of Arbitration or a Notification for Emergency Relief proceedings are filed with the Secretariat, a Case Administration Committee[3] will be constituted. As a general rule, the Secretariat will designate a Rapporteur and a Vice-Rapporteur among the members of the Court to form the Case Administration Committee and under certain circumstances (i.e. when the 2-member Case Administration Committee would like to obtain further opinions from other Court members regarding a specific issue) two additional members may be included.[4] The employees of the Secretariat do not form part of the Case Administration Committee (i.e. they are not involved in and do not take any administrative decisions).

The Case Administration Committee is empowered to make, within the powers of the Court relating to the case concerned, all decisions which are not expressly delegated to the Court Special Committee or to the Chairperson or Vice-Chairperson.[5]

Once a new case is filed, two Rapporteurs are designated. First, a conflict check amongst the potential Rapporteurs is performed. Members of the Court or their law firms involved in any capacity whatsoever in the proceedings at issue must inform the Secretariat upon becoming aware of such involvement and must refrain from

---

2 For more details, *see*, in this volume Philipp Habegger's contribution, *The Workings of the Special Committee and the Arbitration Court*, section 2.2.

3 Art. 3(1) Swiss Chambers' Arbitration Institution, Internal Rules of the Arbitration Court of the Swiss Chambers' Arbitration Institution 2012 (*hereinafter* Internal Rules 2012).

4 Art. 3(1) Internal Rules 2012.

5 *See*, in this volume Philipp Habegger's contribution, *The Workings of the Special Committee and the Arbitration Court*, section 3.

participating in the discussions or in the decisions of the Court or any of its committees. Such members will not receive any documentation or information pertaining to the proceedings. This is also reflected in Article 9 Internal Rules 2012.

After potential conflicts have been cleared, the Secretariat provides the Case Administration Committee with all relevant information and the draft of the correspondence. Please be aware that all communications from the Court or from any of its committees to the parties or arbitrators concerning the administration of arbitral proceedings will take place exclusively through the Secretariat. All decisions of the Court and any of its committees are communicated by the Secretariat on behalf of the Court so the parties will never directly be in communication with the Court.

Of particular importance and benefit to the users is that the Case Administration Committee consists of the same Rapporteurs from the beginning to the end. There are no ad hoc compositions. Such an approach ensures profound knowledge of the case, which is very beneficial to the decision-making process and the efficiency in administering the proceedings.

4. NOTICE OF ARBITRATION AND ANSWER TO THE NOTICE OF ARBITRATION

Art. 3(3) Swiss Rules states the mandatory requirements of a Notice of Arbitration. I will not go into any of the specific details of what is required but rather give some practical information to you. For the Secretariat, as we have to constitute the Case Administration Committee, it is very useful if we receive the Notice of Arbitration in advance electronically or by fax in order for the internal process to be started.[6] This is in particular very helpful if time is of the essence.

Also it is very important for us that we receive detailed and accurate contact information. This will ensure that the Secretariat can duly and swiftly send the notification letter to the respondent.

How does the institution proceed if there is a request for an extension to file the Answer of Notice of Arbitration? What is the general rule? In line with the current practice of the Court, an extension to file the Answer of Notice of Arbitration beyond an additional 15 days may, as a general rule, be granted up to 30 days without the consent of claimant but only if the respondent, within an additional 15 days, submits the following (if applicable) information:

---

6 *See,* Appendix 1: Sample letter to respondent concerning receipt of Notice of Arbitration and next steps and Appendix 2: Sample letter of receipt of Answer to the Notice of Arbitration.

- respondent's proposal as to the number of arbitrators, if not already agreed upon;
- if the parties' agreement provides for a three-member tribunal, respondent's designation of arbitrators if required by the arbitration clause, the separate arbitration agreement or Art. 8(1) Swiss Rules;
- the proposal as to the seat of arbitration;
- the proposal as to the language of arbitration if not defined in the arbitration clause.

If the parties' agreement provides for a sole arbitrator, in accordance with Art. 7(1) Swiss Rules the parties will be invited to jointly designate a sole arbitrator within 30 days from the date on which the Notice of Arbitration was received by respondent(s), unless the parties' agreement provides otherwise. Should only the respondent(s) request an extension of this time limit, it will only be granted for an additional 15 days, according to the Court's current practice. If, however, both parties jointly request an extension beyond the additional 15 days, the Court will grant such a request.

The purpose of this approach is to provide the Court or the arbitral tribunal at the earliest possible point in time with all the relevant information on procedural issues on which a decision must be rendered rapidly in case of a disagreement between the parties.

5. DECISION AS TO WHETHER OR NOT TO ADMINISTER THE CASE

Professor Müller discussed the strengthening of the institutional supervisory powers concerning the agreement to arbitrate earlier this morning.[7] Here it suffices to say, also from a practical point of view, that the Secretariat will not take any decision with respect to administration and may also not provide any legal advice with respect to the existence, validity or interpretation of an arbitral clause. A claimant must file its Notice of Arbitration, pay the registration fee and then the Court will examine any objection to the arbitration being administered under the Swiss Rules once the time period for the Answer to the Notice of Arbitration has expired.[8]

The standard of review under Art. 3(12) Swiss Rules is that there is manifestly no agreement to arbitrate under the Swiss Rules. The

---

7 *See,* in this volume Christoph Müller's contribution, *Background of the 2012 Revision: What were the Main Objectives?,* section 2.

8 Art. 3(12) Swiss Rules.

refusal to administer an arbitration under the Swiss Rules should, therefore, remain exceptional and is limited to cases where it is clear that no agreement to arbitrate according to the Swiss Rules exists.

As a general rule, the institution will administer a case if an arbitral clause between two parties which may be interpreted as referring to the Swiss Rules exists. The extension of the validity of the clause to third parties or the decision whether several claims between the parties may be administered in the same proceeding will generally be decided by the arbitral tribunal and not by the Court. Ultimately, the main question for the institution with regard to Art. 3(12) Swiss Rules is whether a reference to the Swiss Rules exists, which may give reason to administer the case.

The Court's decision that the arbitration ought to continue will not be definitive. The Court's examination does not limit in any way the arbitral tribunal's power to decide on its own jurisdiction.

6. THE DESIGNATION, APPOINTMENT AND CONFIRMATION OF ARBITRATORS

Other very important issues are the designation, appointment and confirmation of arbitrators.[9] A very practical issue is if a disclosure is made prior to confirmation. If the designation of the arbitrator is made by a party, the parties will generally be invited to comment on the disclosure within a certain time limit. Even if the parties raise no objection, the Court may, under certain circumstances, not confirm the appointee, especially if the disclosed circumstance falls within the scope of the Non-Waivable Red List of the IBA Guidelines on Conflicts of Interest in International Arbitration, which are of course used only as a reference by the Court, as they are not binding.

In the event of a disclosure falling within the ambit of the Non-Waivable Red List, this may also trigger a decision of the Court without inviting the parties to comment. If the appointment is made by the Court, however, the Court will, as a general rule, not confirm an arbitrator if there is any disclosure, unless it is squarely unproblematic.

As you might know, there are no nationality restrictions under the Swiss Rules. Nevertheless, in general, the Court does not appoint arbitrators with the same nationality as the nationality or domicile of the parties. Under certain circumstances, however, the Court may deviate from this rule. This is especially the case if the applicable law and/or language of the arbitration require it. Of course the parties may express their desires regarding the nationality and/or professional

[9] *See*, Appendix 3: Sample form for Consent to Appointment and Statement of Independence.

qualifications of the arbitrators and the Court will take such preference into consideration.

Another important point in practice is Art. 6(1) to (3) Swiss Rules, which deals with the case where the parties have not agreed upon the number of arbitrators. In this situation the Court, taking into account all relevant circumstances, is to decide whether the case should be referred to sole arbitrator or a three-member arbitral tribunal. Art. 6(2) Swiss Rules provides as a rule that the Court will refer the case to a sole arbitrator unless the complexity of the subject matter and/or the amount in dispute justifies that the case be referred to a three-member arbitral tribunal.

There is no amount that would automatically trigger the constitution of an arbitral tribunal consisting of three arbitrators. The Court considers all relevant circumstances on a case by case basis, such as the complexity of the case as well as other considerations such as a party being a State or State-owned corporation. If no specific circumstances exist, the threshold for referring the case to a three-member tribunal in most cases is around CHF 2,000,000.

Art. 6(3) Swiss Rules deals with the situation where the arbitral clause refers to two, three or more arbitrators in an instance in which it appears inappropriate in view of the amount in dispute or other circumstances. The Court shall then invite the parties to agree to refer the case to a sole arbitrator. Again, there is no exact threshold when the Court applies the provision. As a rule of thumb one may say it is below CHF 2,000,000 if there are no other circumstances to be taken into account.

7. FURTHER INFORMATION PROVIDED TO THE INSTITUTION IN THE COURSE OF THE CONDUCT OF THE PROCEEDINGS

Once the arbitral tribunal is constituted, the Secretariat and the Court require certain information during the proceedings: the provisional timetable and any amendments thereof; the request for the deposit on costs; the information on the filing of any counterclaim or set-off defence during the proceedings; the draft award or termination order; the original of any award; and any decisions or procedural orders issued during the proceedings.[10]

---

[10] *See*, Appendix 4: Sample letter concerning constitution of the arbitral tribunal and next steps.

Appendix 1

Sample letter to respondent concerning receipt of notice of arbitration

Courier Service	**Ms Alexandra Smith** Attorney-at-law LAW FIRM & CO 32 Success Street SW1E 6QP London United Kingdom
Courier Service	**Investments International** EXECUTIVE BOARD 12 Rock River Road Cheyenne, WY 82002 United States of America

Zurich, 31 January 2014

Case no 500080-2014

Re: Sparta Co. (Claimant) vs Investments International (Respondent)

Dear Mesdames
Dear Messrs

Confirmation Receipt NoA & Registration Fee

We acknowledge receipt with thanks of the Notice of Arbitration and Exhibits filed in five original copies on 29 January 2014 by Sparta Co., represented by Ms Alexandra Smith, LAW FIRM & CO, against Investments International, as well as the payment of the non-refundable Registration Fee in the amount of CHF 4'500.-, that was received on 28 January 2014.

The Respondent will find herewith the Notice of Arbitration and Exhibits, in original version.

Assigned case number

This matter has been filed under reference **case number 500080-2014** and we would be grateful if the parties could state the complete reference in all future correspondence.

The parties will find enclosed a copy of the Swiss Rules of International Arbitration ("**Swiss Rules**").

Time limit to file Answer to NoA 30 days	The Respondent is hereby invited to file its Answer to Answer to the Notice of Arbitration, **within thirty days from receipt of the Notice of Arbitration**, which has to comply with Article 3(7) to 3(10) of the Swiss Rules.
# arbitrators	The arbitration clause to which reference has been made provides that the case be referred to a three-member arbitral tribunal.
Arbitrator designed	In its Notice of Arbitration, the Claimant designates Ms Samantha Freeman, Attorney-at-law, CONSTRUCTION LAW FIRM, as co-arbitrator.
If Arbitrator no designated	The Claimant is hereby invited to designate a co-arbitrator within **fifteen days from receipt of the present letter**. Pursuant to Article 3(7)(f) of the Swiss Rules, the Respondent is invited to designate a co-arbitrator in its **Answer to the Notice of Arbitration**. We kindly inform the parties that, pursuant to Article 5(1) of the Swiss Rules, the designation of all arbitrators is subject to confirmation by the Court.
If no seat of arbitration	The arbitration clause to which reference has been made does not provide for the seat of the arbitration In its Notice of Arbitration, the Claimant proposes that Zurich be the seat of the arbitration. Pursuant to Article 3(7)(e) of the Swiss Rules, the Respondent is invited to indicate its proposal as to the seat of the arbitration in its **Answer to the Notice of Arbitration**.
Court may decide	Failing an agreement of the parties as to the seat of the arbitration, the Court shall take a decision in this respect, in accordance with Article 16(1) of the Swiss Rules.
If no language of arbitration	The arbitration clause to which reference has been made does not provide for the language of the arbitration. In its Notice of Arbitration, the Claimant proposes that the arbitral proceedings be conducted in English. Pursuant to Article 3(7)(e) of the Swiss Rules, the Respondent is invited to indicate its proposal as to the language of the arbitration in its **Answer to the Notice of Arbitration**.

Court of Arbitral Tribunal may decide

However, and without prejudice to the language of the arbitration, to be agreed upon by the parties or to be decided by the arbitral tribunal pursuant to Article 17 of the Swiss Rules, the Secretariat shall correspond with the parties in English. The parties are also kindly invited to communicate with the Secretariat in English, and to send a copy of all their letters to the other party.

While maintaining strict neutrality between the parties, we are available for any information as may be required regarding the Swiss Rules.

Yours faithfully,

[Name]
Secretariat of the Arbitration Court

Encl.: - Notice of Arbitration and Exhibits, for Respondent
- Swiss Rules of International Arbitration

Swiss Chambers' Arbitration Institution –
Secretariat of the Arbitration Court
– c/o Chamber of Commerce and Industry of Ticino –
Corso Elvezia 16 – P.O. Box 5399 – 6901 Lugano
Tel: +41 (0)91 911 51 11 – Fax: +41 (0)91 911 51 12 –
E-Mail: lugano@swissarbitration.org

Appendix 2

Sample letter of receipt of answer to the notice of arbitration

Courier Service **Ms Alexandra Smith**
Attorney-at-law
LAW FIRM & CO
32 Success Street
SW1E 6QP London
United Kingdom

Courier Service **Mr Steven Miller**
Attorney-at-law
LEGAL CONSULTANTS
Bellestrasse 10
8034 Zurich
Switzerland

Zurich, 3 March 2014

Case no 600080-2014

Re: Sparta Co. (Claimant) vs Investments International (Respondent)

Dear Madam
Dear Sir

Confirmation receipt Answer to NoA

We acknowledge receipt with thanks of the Answer to the Notice of Arbitration and Exhibits filed in five original copies on 3 March 2014 by the Respondent. The Claimant will find enclosed the Answer to the Notice of Arbitration and Exhibits in original version.

Arbitrator designated

In its Answer to the Notice of Arbitration, the Respondent designates Mr John Meyer, Attorney-at-law, LEGAL LAW FIRM, as co-arbitrator.

The Court will invite the two party-nominated arbitrators. After confirmation of the arbitrators by the Court pursuant to Article 5(1) of the Swiss Rules, the Court will set a deadline to the two arbitrators to designate the presiding arbitrator.

We take note that the parties have agreed on Lugano as the seat of arbitration and English as the language or the arbitration.

Yours faithfully,

[Name]
Secretariat of the Arbitration Court

Encl.: - Answer to the Notice of Arbitration and Exhibits, for Claimant

Swiss Chambers' Arbitration Institution –
Secretariat of the Arbitration Court
– c/o Chamber of Commerce and Industry of Ticino –
Corso Elvezia 16 – P.O. Box 5399 – 6901 Lugano
Tel: +41 (0)91 911 51 11 – Fax: +41 (0)91 911 51 12 –
E-Mail: lugano@swissarbitration.org

Appendix 3

Sample Letter of Confirmation of Consent to Appointment, Constitution and Further Steps

Courier Service	**Mrs Andrea Mueller** Attorney-at-law LEVER ATTORNEYS-AT-LAW Rue du Mont-Blanc 48 1201 Geneva Switzerland
Courier Service	**Ms Samantha Freeman** Attorney-at-law CONSTRUCTION LAW FIRM 150 Old Park Lane W1K 1QZ London United Kingdom
Courier Service	**Mr John Meyer** Attorney-at-law LEGAL LAW FIRM 350 Fifth Avenue New York, NY 10118-3299 United States of America

Zurich, 3 April 2014

Case no 500080-2014

Re: Sparta Co. (Claimant) vs Investments International (Respondent)

Dear Mesdames
Dear Sir

We acknowledge receipt with thanks of the Consent to Appointment and Statement of Independence, as well as the curriculum vitae received from Mrs Andrea Mueller, copies of which are enclosed for the co-arbitrators.

We have the pleasure to inform Mrs Andrea Mueller that she has been confirmed by the Court as the presiding arbitrator in the above referred arbitration.

Complete File & Guidelines	The presiding arbitrator will find enclosed the File and Guidelines for Arbitrators.

The arbitral tribunal is henceforth entitled to proceed with the arbitration and invited to communicate directly with the parties.

We would be grateful if, in due course, you could provide us with the following documents:

Provisional Timetable

- **The provisional time-table for the arbitral proceedings** (Article 15(3) of the Swiss Rules), and any further modification thereof. The provisional timetable should contain, if possible, the complete steps of the proceedings, i.e. the time-limits for the filing of the briefs, the date of the hearing(s), as well as an estimate of the date of the interim awards (if any) and of the final award.

Request for deposit on costs

- **The request for the parties' deposit on costs** (Article 41(1), Swiss Rules), as well as a copy of **any request for supplementary deposits** by the parties (Article 41(3), Swiss Rules). **Please be advised that under Article 41 of the Swiss Rules it is the task of the arbitral tribunal to request payment from the parties, after consultation with the Court, of the Advance for Costs. Please also be advised that the request for the Advance on Costs shall include the Administrative Costs as referred to in Article 38(f) and Appendix B of the Swiss Rules.** Based on the information currently available to the Court with respect to the amount in dispute, the Administrative Costs amount to CHF 3'500.- at this stage. For the purpose of requesting deposits from the parties for the Advance on Costs, kindly be advised that in the present case, you are not required to consult the Court for deposits amounting up to a total of CHF *[Admin. Costs + Average Fees [min+max/2] + 10%].*

Counterclaim or set-off defence

- **Any counterclaim or set-off defence** filed during the proceedings without a copy being sent to us. Upon receipt of a counterclaim, you should proceed **only after having received confirmation by us** of the payment of the related Registration Fee by the Respondent (Section 1.5 of Appendix B Swiss Rules). In case of a counterclaim or a set-off defence, please be advised that the Administrative Costs may be reviewed by the Secretariat in accordance with Section 2.4, Appendix B of the Swiss Rules.

Draft award or termination order

- **The draft of the award or termination order**, for approval or adjustment by the Court of the determination on costs which is binding upon the arbitral tribunal in accordance with Article 40(4) of the Swiss Rules.

Original award

- **The original of any award** (Article 32(6) of the Swiss Rules).

Copy decisions & orders

Finally, we would appreciate if you could transmit to us a copy of all your decisions and orders. However, we do not require to be copied on each correspondence between you and the parties throughout the course of the arbitral proceedings. As indicated in our letter sent today to the parties, they have been invited to communicate directly with the arbitral tribunal. A copy of this letter is enclosed for your files.

We thank you in advance for your kind cooperation and remain,

Yours faithfully,

[Name]
Secretariat of the Arbitration Court

Encl.: - Copy of the Consent to Appointment and Statement of Independence and curriculum
- viae received from Mrs Andrea Mueller, for co-arbitrators
- The File and Guidelines for Arbitrators, for presiding arbitrator
- Copy of our letter sent today to the parties, for arbitral tribunal

Cc: - Ms Alexandra Smith, LAW FIRM & CO, London
- Mr Steven Miller, LEGAL CONSULTANTS, Zurich

Swiss Chambers' Arbitration Institution – Secretariat of the Arbitration Court – c/o Chamber of Commerce and Industry of Ticino – Corso Elvezia 16 – P.O. Box 5399 – 6901 Lugano
Tel: +41 (0)91 911 51 11 – Fax: +41 (0)91 911 51 12 – E-Mail:

lugano@swissarbitration.org

Appendix 4
Sample Consent and Statement of Independence Form

Arbitration No: 500080-2014

CONSENT TO APPOINTMENT
and
STATEMENT OF INDEPENDENCE BY THE [SOLE] ARBITRATOR

Surname:... First name: ....

Nationality:..

Address:...

City/Country: ....

(Please fill in the address you wish to be used for correspondence)

Please tick all relevant boxes:

ACCEPTANCE

☐ **I consent** to my appointment as *[Sole]* Arbitrator in this arbitration and I undertake to act in accordance with the Swiss Rules of International Arbitration ("Swiss Rules").

NON-ACCEPTANCE

☐ **I decline** to serve as *[Sole]* Arbitrator.
(If you sign here, simply date and sign the form without completing any other sections.)

AVAILABILITY

☐ **I confirm** to have taken note of Article 15, paragraph 7 Swiss Rules. On the basis of the information presently available to me, I confirm that I will conduct this arbitration diligently, efficiently and in accordance with the Swiss Rules. *[I confirm to comply with the time limits of Article 42, paragraph 1, cipher d) Swiss Rules (Expedited Procedure).]*

PRINCIPAL PROFESSIONAL ACTIVITY

....

INDEPENDENCE

☐ **Nothing to disclose**: I declare that I am, and shall remain, impartial and independent. To the best of my knowledge, and having made due enquiry, there are no facts or circumstances, past or present, likely to give rise to justifiable doubts as to my impartiality or independence. I will declare to the Court and all the parties, for the entire duration of the arbitration, any future fact that could give raise to justifiable doubts as to my impartiality or independence.

☐ **Acceptance with disclosure**: I declare that I am, and shall remain, impartial and independent. However, in accordance with Article 9, paragraph 2 Swiss Rules, I wish to disclose to the Swiss Chambers' Arbitration Institution and to all parties, the matters **on the separate sheet**. To the best of my belief, these circumstances do not impair my impartiality or independence.

FURTHER INFORMATION

Language Skills: List all languages, including your native language, in which you consider yourself able, without the assistance of an interpreter or translator, to:

	conduct a hearing and draft an award	follow and understand oral arguments and testimonies	read and understand documents

COMMENTS

DATE: SIGNATURE:

The information requested in this form will be considered by the Arbitration Court and its Secretariat solely of the purpose of your appointment or confirmation as arbitrator in the Swiss Rules proceedings. The information will remain confidential and will be stored in a case management database system. However, it may be disclosed solely to the parties and their counsel and any confirmed arbitrator in the arbitration proceeding referenced above for the purposes of that proceeding.

Swiss Chambers' Arbitration Institution – Secretariat of the Arbitration Court – c/o Chamber of Commerce and Industry of Ticino – Corso Elvezia 16 – P.O. Box 5399 – 6901 Lugano
Tel: +41 (0)91 911 51 11 – Fax: +41 (0)91 911 51 12 – E-Mail: lugano@swissarbitration.org

Institutional Involvement and Costs

*Joya Raha**

1. INTRODUCTION

Thank you Ignacio de Castro for the introduction and thank you Michael Fischer for this wonderful exposition on how we handle cases in the Secretariat.[1]

Good afternoon ladies and gentlemen. It is a pleasure to be here. I have been asked to address the topic of costs and, specifically, to give a brief overview of the costs of an arbitration in a Swiss Rules[2] proceeding. To do this I will illustrate the Institution's[3] role in three different phases of an arbitration where questions of costs are frequently raised: the advance on costs, the advance payment of arbitrator fees and reimbursement of expenses, and the approval of the costs at the end of the proceedings.

While the question of costs seems to be well documented, I have also read that the subject of costs in an arbitration is not always given the prominence it deserves, especially from a commercial perspective, for clients that have large sums of money on the line. I hope that this brief overview will give you some beneficial insight with respect at least to the Institution's role in arbitration costs. For the practitioners in this room who are very familiar with the nuts and bolts of the Swiss Rules, please excuse some of the basic information that I will present but I believe it is important to review for those who are not as familiar with our little red book.

2. REFRESHER

2.1 Costs (Art. 38 (a) to (g) Swiss Rules)

First, as a refresher, the costs in a Swiss Rules arbitration are comprised of:

---

* Joya Raha is Legal Counsel at the Geneva Chamber of Commerce, Industry and Services. This is a slightly amended version of a presentation given at the conference "10 Years of Swiss Rules of International Arbitration" on 31 January 2014 in Basel, Switzerland.

1 Secretariat of the Arbitration Court, Swiss Chambers' Arbitration Institution (*hereinafter* Secretariat).

2 Swiss Chambers' Arbitration Institution, Swiss Rules of International Arbitration 2012 (*hereinafter* Swiss Rules).

3 Swiss Chambers' Arbitration Institution (*hereinafter* Institution).

- the arbitrator fees and expenses and those of any administrative secretary;
- the cost of expert advice and other assistance that might be required by the arbitral tribunal;
- the travel and other expenses of witnesses;
- reasonable legal representation and assistance, which may include in-house legal counsel costs; and
- the registration fee and administrative costs of the Institution.

2.2 The Institution's Involvement with Regard to Costs (Arts. 38 (a) to (c) and (f) and 40 (4) and Swiss Rules)

The Institution limits its involvement in the costs to those of the arbitral tribunal, meaning:

- the arbitrator fees and expenses, and those of any administrative secretary; and
- the cost of expert advice and other assistance that may be required by the arbitral tribunal.

The Institution also determines its administrative costs, which, as you know, are only charged when the amount in dispute is greater than two million Swiss francs and, as you may know, are usually reduced in cases of settlement.

3. ADVANCE ON COSTS

3.1 Responsibility of Arbitral Tribunal (Art. 41 (1) Swiss Rules and Swiss Rules, Appendix B, Sect. 2)

It is the responsibility of the arbitral tribunal to request the advance on costs from the parties and to be sure that this advance is paid before working on the merits of the case. The philosophy behind the Swiss Rules is to foster collaboration between the Arbitration Court[4] and the arbitral tribunal. The arbitral tribunal is in the best position to assess the amount of work required to render a final award. It is for this reason that the responsibility of determining the advance on costs lies in the

[4] Arbitration Court, Swiss Chambers' Arbitration Institution (*hereinafter* Court).

hands of the arbitral tribunal, with the approval of the Court, as opposed to the Court fixing the advance for the arbitral tribunal.

3.2 Calculation (Swiss Rules, Appendix B, Sect. 2 and 6)

The advance is calculated on the basis of the amount in dispute. The Secretariat calculates a preliminary amount in dispute by taking into account the claim in the Notice of Arbitration and any counterclaim in the Answer to the Notice of Arbitration. When a set-off defence is filed, unlike a counterclaim, no registration fees are due and, in practice, unless it adds to the complexity of the case, the set-off amount is not taken into account when calculating the amount in dispute. On the basis of the preliminary amount in dispute, a range of arbitrator fees—that is, a minimum and maximum—can be calculated by referring to the Schedule of Costs in the Swiss Rules or by using the online cost calculator.

Arbitrators may request from the parties, as was mentioned earlier this morning, without consulting the Court, an amount up to the average fee on the range of arbitrator fees plus 10 percent for their estimated expenses. For those non-math people out there, that is the minimum, plus maximum, divided by two, plus 10 percent for your expenses. The advance must also include the administrative costs, if any, of the Institution.

To address a question that was raised during panel one, the deposit of costs can be held and managed by the Secretariat. This is indeed the practice in the Geneva Secretariat. For each new case that is filed, we open a new and separate account for the deposit of costs and transmit the bank details to the arbitral tribunal.

When the amount in dispute is not quantifiable, the Court will allow the arbitral tribunal to assess the amount of work that would be required to render the final award and propose a figure for the Court's approval. If the amount does not appear to be excessive based on all the elements at hand, the Court will approve the advance. Since this new procedure was instituted under the 2012 Swiss Rules, I have not seen a case where the Court questioned the justification for the first advance on costs that had been requested by the arbitral tribunal.

3.3 Payment (Art. 41 (1), (2) and (4) Swiss Rules)

As a rule, the arbitral tribunal will request the claimant party and the respondent party to pay an equal amount of the advance on costs. In the event that one party defaults on its obligation to pay its share of the advance on costs, the other party will be invited to make the required payment. Although an arbitral tribunal can terminate the proceedings if the advance is not paid in full, in practice, it is extremely rare that this occurs. In our experience, the arbitral tribunal usually suspends the case until the advance is paid in full. In almost all cases, the substitute payment is made.

When a counterclaim is filed and the question of separate deposit of costs is raised, in practice, it is usually only established by the arbitral tribunal upon request of the parties.

In those few cases where a party has requested security of costs, as far as we know, the arbitral tribunals have rejected these requests due to very restrictive conditions that the arbitral tribunals applied in granting these measures. In one case, in fact, the arbitral tribunal not only rejected the respondent party's request for security of costs but rendered an interim award ordering the respondent party to reimburse the claimant for the payment it had made to cover the respondent's share of the advance on costs.

3.4 Additional Advances (Art. 41 (3) Swiss Rules)

During the course of the arbitral proceedings, should an arbitral tribunal require additional advances to cover its estimated work which exceed the amount initially approved by the Court, it is required to submit a request to the Secretariat which will be transmitted to the Court for its approval. The Court will review all the elements of the case to understand the justification of the supplemental advance. A decision is made in just a few days. Under the 2012 Swiss Rules, so far I have only seen a few requests for a supplemental advance on costs, all of which were approved.

Perhaps now is a good time to point out that the fees of the arbitral tribunal fall, on average, around 40 percent below the maximum amount permitted under the Swiss Rules, which is a good thing and appreciated by users.

3.5 Institutional Involvement (Art. 42 (1) (a) Swiss Rules and Swiss Rules, Appendix B, Sect. 1.4)

As far as institutional involvement with the advance on costs, the Institution is responsible to request an advance from the parties in only two situations: under emergency relief proceedings and expedited procedures.

Since we have not had any experience with the relatively new emergency relief proceedings, I will not spend time on it.[5] In the expedited procedures, where a sole arbitrator will render an award within six months from the date that he or she receives the file, a 5,000 Swiss franc provisional deposit is required of the claimant party before the file is communicated to the sole arbitrator. Because six months is a very short amount of time, the 5,000 Swiss franc provisional deposit allows the sole arbitrator to start working immediately on the case after having received the file, with the security of knowing that there are provisions to cover at least the initial steps of the proceedings. This provisional deposit is then considered as partial payment of the claimant's share of the advance on costs to be determined at a later stage by the sole arbitrator, with, of course, the Court's approval.

In nearly all of our expedited cases, the provisional deposit of 5,000 Swiss francs was promptly paid. In the one case where it was not paid, the claimant party withdrew its claim and the case was closed before the official appointment of the sole arbitrator.

A quick side note on the expedited procedure: as you have heard earlier today, it is a cornerstone of the Swiss Rules and well known for its efficiency and reliability. It applies automatically to procedures where the amount in dispute is less than one million Swiss francs and can also be agreed upon by the parties. As a rule, this fast track procedure provides for only one exchange of briefs and can be decided on the basis of documentary evidence only. The arbitrator shall also state the reasons upon which the award is based in summary form, unless the parties agree that no reasons are to be given.

When we compare the average costs of an expedited procedure with the average costs of an ordinary proceeding, we see that expedited cases are 45 percent less expensive overall than ordinary proceedings. We also note that expedited cases that were decided on the basis of documentary evidence only were significantly less expensive, again, around 45 percent less expensive than those cases where a hearing was held.

---

[5] As a post-conference note: On 4 February 2014, the first emergency relief proceeding under the Swiss Rules was filed with the Geneva Secretariat. All required deposits were paid immediately and a Notice of Arbitration was filed simultaneously. The emergency arbitrator rendered a decision within 14 days. Overall, the first emergency relief proceeding was a success. *See*, in this volume Philipp Habegger's paper "*The Swiss Rules in Practice: The Insiders' view: the workings of the Special Committee and the Arbitration Court*", section 5.2.

4. ADVANCE PAYMENT OF ARBITRATOR FEES AND REIMBURSEMENT OF EXPENSES

4.1 Significant Steps (Guidelines for Arbitrators[6] C (b) (5) and (6), Swiss Rules, Appendix B, Sect. 4.2)

My second point is with respect to the arbitral tribunal's request for an advance payment of fees and reimbursement of expenses. According to the guidelines for arbitrators, significant steps in the arbitral proceeding must be completed before advances on fees are made. Significant steps include, but are not limited to, decisions made on requests for document production, hearings held or interim awards rendered—for example, on jurisdiction or time bar.

The Court also looks at the number of hours that have been spent by each member of the arbitral tribunal when the request for an advance on fees is submitted, the duration of the case, the number of documents exchanged between the parties, their length and content, the number of procedural orders rendered by the arbitral tribunal, and, of course, the content of those orders. As you can imagine, decisions are made on a case-by-case basis.

4.2 Expenses (Guidelines for Arbitrators C (b) (4) and Swiss Rules, Appendix B Sect. 3)

Expenses may be reimbursed upon request and only after the accrued unpaid expenses of an arbitrator reach 1,000 Swiss francs. It is advised that expense reports be submitted to the presiding arbitrator or administrative secretary, who will consolidate the reports and submit them to the Secretariat at regular intervals. As a general practice, the presiding arbitrator, or sometimes the administrative secretary, acts as the channel of communication between the Secretariat and arbitral tribunal.

4.3 Disbursement (Guidelines for Arbitrators C (b) (5) and (6) and Swiss Rules, Appendix B Sect. 4.2)

As a rule, no more than 50 percent of the advance can be disbursed to the arbitrators as partial payment of their fees and expenses during the course of the proceedings, bearing in mind, of

---

6 Arbitration Court of the Swiss Chambers' Arbitration Institution, Guidelines for Arbitrators (as effective 1 June 2012), www.swissarbitration.org/sa/download/guidelines_for_arbitrators_2012.pdf.

course, that in all cases the overall costs of the arbitration shall be approved by the Court at the end of the proceedings in accordance with Article 39 Swiss Rules.

Never, in our experience, has an advance payment been made to an arbitrator in an expedited proceeding. For further details on the accounting of expenses, such as *per diem* rates, you can refer to the very short guidelines for arbitrators available online.[7]

4.4 Revocation, Resignation

A delicate question closely linked to advance payment of fees is what happens when an arbitrator ceases to be on the panel for various reasons such as resignation or revocation. In these cases, the arbitral tribunal, once reconstituted, will determine the amount of fees that should be paid to the arbitrator for the work that was completed by the arbitrator during his or her appointment, subject of course to the approval of the Court.

5. APPROVAL OF COSTS

5.1 Court Approval (Arts. 39 (1) and 40 (4) Swiss Rules and Guidelines for Arbitrators C (a))

The third and final phase I wanted to review with you is the determination and approval of costs at the end of the proceedings. As mentioned, arbitrator fees are determined using an *ad valorem* method calculated on the basis of the amount in dispute and taking into account the complexity of the subject matter, the time spent and other relevant circumstances of the case. The arbitral tribunal proposes fees to the Court and the Court reviews the overall costs on a case-by-case basis. It is the Court, and not the Secretariat, that approves the costs. This is important since the members of the Court concentrate their practice on international arbitration and are, therefore, in the best position to make a fair assessment on costs.

5.2 Case Summary

In order to aid the Court in its work, the Secretariat provides the members of the Court with a comprehensive case summary detailing all the elements of the arbitral proceedings. The Court takes into

---

[7] Guidelines for Arbitrators, available at www.swissarbitration.org/sa/download/guidelines_for_arbitrators_2012.pdf, last visited 6 June 2014.

account the complexity of the case and the work completed, the number of hours spent on the case as well as where those hours were spent—for example, dealing with preliminary issues such as jurisdiction or applicable law, rendering an interim award, dealing with copious submissions, rendering decisions on requests for document production, holding hearings and the length of those hearings, the number of procedural orders issued and their content, and the list continues. The efficiency of the arbitral tribunal is also taken into account.

As an aside, while we will ask for the number of hours that each member of the arbitral tribunal spent on the case, this does not need to be indicated in the final award. However, the allocation of the fees amongst the members of the arbitral tribunal must be included in the award. As a rule, the allocation of fees is based on a 40/30/30 or 50/25/25 scheme.

Of all the elements that are reviewed to evaluate the work completed, sometimes it is also relevant to look at the parties' legal representation costs. Other factors, such as the discontinuation of the arbitral proceedings in cases of settlement, are also taken into account.

5.3 In Practice

If there appears to be some concerns after reviewing the detailed case summary, the Court will request further information from the Secretariat, such as certain documents or more precise information on the work that was completed. Over the past few years the Court has, in a few cases, requested that the arbitral tribunal reduce its fees.

It is extremely rare that the fees requested by an arbitrator or an arbitral tribunal exceed the maximum permitted under the schedule of costs. However, this has occurred in expedited procedures where the amount in dispute was very, very small. In a recent case where this occurred, the amount in dispute was 30,000 Swiss francs, allowing for a maximum fee of 3,600 Swiss francs. In the particular circumstances of the case at hand, it was obviously not possible for the sole arbitrator to render a final award for under 4,000 Swiss francs. In this case, the sole arbitrator's fees were fixed at 13,000 Swiss francs.

5.4 Administrative Secretary (Guidelines for Arbitrators A (1-3))

What about administrative secretaries? An administrative secretary is not a fourth arbitrator and his or her assistance to the arbitral tribunal should not increase the overall costs of the arbitration for the parties. The guidelines for arbitrators provide that the fees of an administrative secretary form part of the fees of the arbitral tribunal.

5.5 Tribunal-Appointed Experts (Arts. 27 and 38 (c) Swiss Rules and Guidelines for Arbitrators C (a))

Regarding the costs of tribunal-appointed experts these costs are normally agreed upon by the parties and an advance is made for this purpose. The costs for experts, nonetheless, form part of the costs of the arbitration, subject to approval by the Court. They will, in all cases, be reviewed at some point before the award is rendered, be it when the expert's mandate is completed or at the end of the proceeding.

5.6 Secretariat's Role

The responsibility of the Secretariat is to aid the Court with the review and approval of the costs of the arbitration. The Secretariat will also usually double-check calculations and cross-check figures in the award, despite this not being part of the official services of the Secretariat under the Swiss Rules. We do this as a service to the parties, to be sure that they have an award with no jarring errors that may have to be corrected at a later stage. We feel that it helps to have another pair of eyes on the award.

5.7 Allocation (Art. 40 (1) and (2) Swiss Rules)

The last point I wanted to raise, which is closely linked with the determination of costs, is the question of allocation of costs. It appears that it may be difficult to predict with some certainty whether, and to what extent, a successful party will recover its costs in arbitration. While the Court does not have a role in the allocation of costs between the parties, there are some trends that we can share with you.

The Swiss Rules provide that the costs of the arbitration be borne in principle by the unsuccessful party but that the arbitral tribunal may apportion the costs if it determines that this is reasonable.[8] In practice, the overarching trend is that the costs of the arbitration are apportioned based on the parties' relative degree of success. A pure "costs follow the event" approach, meaning that a successful party, even if only partially successful, would be awarded all of its costs, is not often followed by arbitral tribunals. It is rare to see an arbitral

---

8 Art. 40 (1) Swiss Rules 2012.

tribunal under the Swiss Rules order a losing party to bear 100 percent of the costs unless the successful party won 100 percent of its claim.

With respect to legal representation and assistance, the arbitral tribunal is free to determine which party shall bear the costs or may apportion the costs if it determines that this would be reasonable.[9] In practice, and like the costs of the arbitration, the overarching trend is that legal representation costs are also allocated based on the parties' relative degree of success. This is usually the case even if a party is successful on its claim but not 100 percent successful on the amount of damages. It may be questionable, however, as to whether limiting recoverable party representation costs to the percentage of the damages awarded would be appropriate in some cases, since the time spent by the prevailing party's counsel would have been the same regardless. It is an open question. In any case, when comparing arbitration and litigation, it appears, at least in Switzerland, that the state courts only award a small percentage of the legal representation costs of the prevailing party as compared with arbitration.

Arbitrators are also inclined to apportion costs based on the conduct of the parties and to highlight this in their final awards: both good conduct, such as "the constructive and highly appreciated attitude of both parties" and bad conduct, such as "hardly participated in the proceedings, did not react within the deadlines set, did not participate in the organisation of the arbitration". So conduct counts, too.

6. CONCLUDING COMMENT

On a final note, if you are curious about the overall breakdown of the costs of arbitration, as a whole, the fees and expenses of the arbitral tribunal make up 18 percent of the costs, while the external counsel fees and expenses of the parties make up 80 percent of the arbitration costs. The Institution costs account for 2 percent of the total costs of an arbitration.

Thank you very much for your attention.

---

[9] Art. 40 (2) Swiss Rules 2012.

The Workings of the Special Committee and the Arbitration Court

*Philipp Habegger**

1. INTRODUCTION

1.1 Looking Back: The Arbitration Committee under the Swiss Rules 2004

Five years ago, at a conference in Bern organized by the participating Chambers of Commerce and celebrating five years of the Swiss Rules of International Arbitration,[1] the President of what was then called the Arbitration Committee, which was appointed by the Chambers for the purpose of administering arbitration proceedings under the Swiss Rules 2004,[2] Professor Franz Kellerhals said:[3]

> It came close to a miracle that they [i.e. the authors and the founders of the Swiss Rules] succeeded to overcome the reluctance of board members and directors of the different Chambers of Commerce in Switzerland to give up their beloved local arbitration rules and to vote for a uniform solution, the Swiss Rules.

Professor Kellerhals also emphasized that the authors and promoters of the Swiss Rules in "their wisdom did not push the idea of uniformity too far" in that they provided for uniform rules for international arbitration in Switzerland, but not for a centralized administration of the proceedings.[4]

---

* Dr. Philipp Habegger, LL.M., is a Partner in the Arbitration Practice Group of LALIVE in Zurich and he has served as Chairman of the Arbitration Court of the Swiss Chambers' Arbitration Institution since 2013. From 2010 to 2013, he served as a member of the Arbitration Court and its predecessor, the Arbitration Committee. This paper is based on a presentation given at the conference "10 Years of Swiss Rules of International Arbitration" on 31 January 2014 in Basel.

[1] Swiss Chambers' Arbitration Institution, Swiss Rules of International Arbitration (*hereinafter* Swiss Rules). Terms in capital letters which are not defined in this contribution are those from the Swiss Rules (2004) and the Swiss Rules (2012) respectively.

[2] Swiss Rules (2004), Introduction (d) and (e).

[3] *See*, Franz Kellerhals, *Highlights from the Arbitration Committee*, in: The Swiss Rules of International Arbitration—Five Years of Experience, 25 (Rainer Füeg ed. 2009).

[4] Kellerhals, *above* n 3, p. 25.

There was, of course, a danger of a decentralized administration: the risk that each Chamber would administer the Swiss Rules *"à sa propre façon"*. The authors of the Swiss Rules addressed that risk by setting up the "National Arbitration Committee" and the "Special Committee" with a view to ensuring a uniform and consistent application of the Swiss Rules by the local administrators.

The Special Committee would not only be responsible for administrative decisions of a particularly critical and sensitive nature (such as the challenge of arbitrators) but would also provide advice on issues of the interpretation and uniform application of the Swiss Rules upon enquiry of a local committee. It would then report to the National Arbitration Committee, where these open issues concerning the interpretation and application of the Swiss Rules were discussed in plenum.

However, this organization had its drawbacks and led to a rather confusing structure[5] which many—in particular foreign—users failed to understand. In order for the structure to be reflected in the Rules, the Swiss Rules 2004 provided:[6]

> In order to ensure the administration of arbitrations under these Rules, the Chambers have appointed an Arbitration Committee (hereinafter the "Arbitration Committee"), which shall exercise the powers vested in the Chambers under these Rules, so that **any reference to the Chambers in these Rules shall be deemed to refer to the Arbitration Committee**. [Emphasis added]

1.2 Did the National and Special Committees Meet the Expectations?

Without doubt, the Special Committee substantially contributed to clarify many open issues in connection with the Swiss Rules. It also made its decisions and advice public through different channels, such as the Newsletter, special publications and at conferences and seminars in Switzerland and abroad.

Indeed, despite an increase in new cases brought before the Swiss Chambers, the number of consultations brought before the Special Committee by the local committees decreased between 2004 and 2009,[7] showing that a certain harmonization in practice had been achieved

5 *See*, Kellerhals, *above* n 3, 26.

6 Introduction (d) Swiss Rules 2004(emphasis added).

7 Kellerhals, *above*, n 3, 28.

and the number of unresolved issues regarding the uniform application of the Swiss Rules could be reduced over time.

However, practitioners regularly involved in Swiss Rules proceedings still perceived that there were differences in the way matters were handled depending on which Chamber administered a case. Moreover, the "federalist" approach in the organisation of the Swiss Chambers led to the rather confusing structure, which reflected the attempt to reach a balance between local autonomy and centralized supervision as well as the interdependence of local and national bodies. Again, especially foreign users—but not only—were frequently confused by this structure.

2. THE NEW ORGANISATION

2.1 Organisational Independence of the Arbitration Court from the Chambers (Introduction (b) Swiss Rules)

With the entry into force of the Swiss Rules 2012, a separate legal entity from the Chambers, the "Swiss Chambers' Arbitration Institution", a Swiss "Verein",[8] has begun providing the arbitration services offered by the Chambers.[9] This entity is organized as an association in order to increase its organizational independence from the Chambers.[10]

With the revised Rules, the former Arbitration Committee has become the Arbitration Court ("Court"), established by the Swiss Chambers' Arbitration Institution for the same purpose, i.e. the administration of arbitration proceedings under the Swiss Rules.[11]

No member of the board of the Swiss Chambers' Arbitration Institution and no member of management of any participating Chamber of Commerce act as a member of the Court under the Swiss Rules.[12]

As with the Arbitration Committee under the Swiss Rules 2004, the Court may delegate the power to take certain decisions under the

---

8 Art. 60 et seq. Swiss Civil Code of 10 December 1907 (Status as of 1 July 2013) [*hereinafter* Swiss Civil Code].

9 Introduction (b) Swiss Rules 2012.

10 Habegger, *The Revised Swiss Rules of International Arbitration – an Overview of the Major Changes*, 2 ASA BULL. 2012, 273. As to the principle of institutional independence see Urs Weber-Stecher, *Principles of Good Governance and Organization of Arbitral Institutions, in* ARBITRAL INSTITUTIONS UNDER SCRUTINY, ASA SPECIAL SERIES NO. 40, 37-53, 40 et seq. (Habegger et al. eds. 2013).

11 Introduction (b) Swiss Rules 2012.

12 A list of the members of the Court and of the Secretariat is available on the website www.swissarbitration.org, last visited 27 May 2014.

Swiss Rules 2012 to one or more members or committees.[13] However, the Swiss Rules 2012 themselves no longer distinguish between the administering body as a whole and its committees. The detailed internal organization of the Court is now governed exclusively by the Internal Rules,[14] which are easier to amend should changes to the organization become necessary.

The Swiss Rules 2012, for the first time, make express reference to the Secretariat of the Court ("Secretariat"), which assists the Court in its work.[15] The provisions in the Swiss Rules 2012 attempt to distinguish precisely and consistently between the Court, as the body rendering administrative decisions under the Rules, and the Secretariat, as the unit of the institution in charge of communications with parties and arbitral tribunals.

While the Secretariat continues to work in a decentralized manner,[16] the distinction between "local" and "national" Secretariats and Arbitration Committees[17] has been formally abandoned in the Internal Rules. The Swiss Chambers' Arbitration Institution functions as one organization with several offices (*Geschäftsstellen, bureaux*).[18]

2.2 Internal Organisation of the Arbitration Court

2.2.1 Bodies involved in the case administration

2.2.1.1 The bodies involved in case administration include:

- the Case Administration Committees
- the Special Committee
- the Chairperson/Vice-Chairpersons of the Court

A Case Administration Committee is formed for each new case[19] and will follow the case from beginning to end.[20] It is "empowered [...]

[13] *See e.g.,* Introduction (e), Arts.11, 12 and 16 Swiss Rules 2004 and Introduction (b) Swiss Rules 2012.

[14] *See,* Arts. 1 and 5 Swiss Chambers' Arbitration Institution, Internal Rules of the Arbitration Court of the Swiss Chambers' Arbitration Institution 2012 (*hereinafter* Internal Rules 2012).

[15] Introduction (b) Swiss Rules 2012.

[16] *See,* Appendix A Swiss Rules 2012.

[17] Arts. 3, 4 and 5 Swiss Chambers' Court of Arbitration and Mediation, Internal Rules 2010, (*hereinafter* Internal Rules 2010), *available at* www.swissarbitration.org/sa/download/internal_rules_2010.pdf.

[18] Art. 3(1) and Appendix A Swiss Rules 2012.

[19] Art. 3(1) Internal Rules. Other authors address the work of the Case Administration Committees in their contributions to this publication; *See e.g.,* Michael Fischer's contribution, *Case Administration,* in this volume.

to make all decisions within the powers of the Court relating to the case concerned, which are not expressly delegated to the Court Special Committee [...] or the Chairperson or any Vice-Chairperson [...]."[21] The work of the Special Committee and the Chairperson is discussed in sections 3 and 5 below.

2.2.1.2 Bodies not involved in the case administration

Other bodies of the Court not directly involved in case administration include

- the plenary session of the Court
- the Know-How Working Group
- the Rules Revision Working Group

The plenary session of the Court (the "Plenary Session") is not directly involved in case administration. It plays, however, an important role in shaping and defining the Court's practice as will be discussed in section 4 below.

The **Know-How Working Group** is not involved in case administration either. A team of Court members in cooperation with the Secretariat collects and reviews all administrative decisions rendered since 2004 with a view to publish and make transparent the Court's practice in administering proceedings under the Swiss Rules. The goal is to increase the transparency of the Court's work, to increase predictability for the users and to further enhance their confidence in the process. It is a standing working group and it is expected to keep publishing certain relevant administrative decisions on a rolling basis.

To ensure that administrative decisions, rendered by any of these bodies, are made known to the Know-How Working Group, Art. 5(2) Internal Rules provides that the Chairperson, the Vice-Chairperson, or any committee must report to the Court "if they have encountered any issue of interpretation of any provision of the Swiss Rules or have rendered a decision inducing a change of practice in the administration of arbitration proceedings". It will then be for the plenary session of the Court to discuss how to define or amend any practice and for the

---

[20] This is in contrast to other institutional rules, such as the ICC Rules, where committees dealing with administrative decisions are not formed as a standing body for each case but on an ad-hoc basis for each session. At these sessions, decisions relating to a number of different cases are taken.

[21] Art. 3(2) Internal Rules.

Court's Know-How Working Group to make the practice available to Court members and transparent to users.[22]

While there are no immediate plans to revise the Swiss Rules again, the Court considered it appropriate to set up a standing **Rules Revision Working Group** to monitor and record current developments in order to propose amendments to the Swiss Rules to the Swiss Chambers' Arbitration Institution and provide a first point of assistance to any future body charged with a revision of the Swiss Rules.

3. THE COURT SPECIAL COMMITTEE (ART. 4 INTERNAL RULES)

3.1 Jurisdiction of the Court Special Committee

Pursuant to Art. 4(4) Internal Rules, the Special Committee has the power to render administrative decisions considered of particular importance or concerning particularly critical issues. The list in Art. 4(4) Internal Rules is exhaustive. It includes the following items:

- Direct appointment of an arbitrator (i.e. instances when a party/the parties or the co-arbitrators are being deprived of their entitlement to designate an arbitrator);[23]
- Challenge of an arbitrator;[24]
- Removal of an arbitrator;[25]
- Revocation of arbitrator appointment(s) with a view to ensure the proper constitution of the arbitral tribunal;[26]
- Non-replacement of an arbitrator (i.e. continuation of the proceedings with a truncated tribunal after the closure of the proceedings);[27]
- Determination of the seat of arbitration;[28]
- Decisions relating to consolidation.[29]

---

22 For further information on the Plenary Session *see*, below section 4.

23 Arts. 5(2)(b) and 13(2)(a) Swiss Rules.

24 Art. 11 Swiss Rules.

25 Art. 13 Swiss Rules.

26 Art. 5(3) Swiss Rules.

27 Art. 13(2) in conjunction with Art. 29 Swiss Rules.

28 Art. 16(1) Swiss Rules.

29 Art. 4(1) Swiss Rules.

While this contribution will not address how these issues are dealt with on the merits by the Special Committee, two changes compared to the Swiss Rules 2004 are notable.

First, the Special Committee is no longer consulted by a local Committee to decide whether or not a case is to be administered by the Swiss Chambers' Arbitration Institution under the Swiss Rules. Now the Case Administration Committee decides without further ado whether "there is manifestly no agreement to arbitrate referring to these Rules".[30]

Second, the Special Committee now has the power to make any decision in relation to consolidation, whereas under the Swiss Rules 2004 it was only consulted by a local Committee.[31] The transfer of the decision making power from the Case Administration Committee to the Special Committee in the context of consolidation became necessary due to the additional powers granted to the Court under the Swiss Rules 2012, i.e. the power to revoke arbitrator appointments in order to preserve the equal treatment of the parties in the constitution of the arbitral tribunal when consolidating proceedings.[32]

3.2 The Work of the Special Committee in 2012-2014

In 2012 the Special Committee made six determinations of the seat of arbitration,[33] handled six requests for advice by local committees on issues of consolidation of proceedings[34] and one inquiry whether the proceedings should be administered under the Swiss Rules.[35] The amount of time the Special Committee needed to render its decisions or to provide advice varied between 3 and 28 calendar days. In the instance where it took the Special Committee 28 calendar days, an additional round of submissions was filed by the parties on a challenge of an arbitrator after the Special Committee had already begun deliberating.

In 2013 the Special Committee made seven decisions, of which three concerned the seat of the arbitration,[36] one dealt with a request by a party for consolidation of cases (which was rejected)[37] and three dealt with challenges to arbitrators.[38] Two challenges were rejected and one

---

30 *Compare*, Art. 3(6) Swiss Rules 2004 to Art. 3(12) Swiss Rules 2012.

31 Art. 4(1) Swiss Rules 2004; Kellerhals, *above* n 2, 24.

32 Art. 4(1) Swiss Rules 2012. *See* Habegger, *above* n 10, 277 et seq.

33 Art. 16(1) Swiss Rules.

34 Art. 4(1) Swiss Rules 2004.

35 Art. 3(6) Swiss Rules 2004.

36 Art. 16(1) Swiss Rules.

37 Art. 4(1) Swiss Rules 2012.

38 Art. 11 Swiss Rules.

was accepted. There was also one application to remove an arbitrator but no decision[39] was ultimately needed, as the parties finally agreed to replace an arbitrator whose health did not permit him to continue to act. Finally, the Special Committee provided advice to the Case Administration Committee in one case where it was doubtful whether the case should be administered under the Swiss Rules.[40] The respective decisions or advice in 2013 were made within 1 to 12 calendar days.

In 2014, as of 31 May 2014, the Special Committee handled one challenge of an arbitrator,[41] which was rejected within two working days, and it determined the seat of arbitration[42] in two cases within two working days each. Moreover, it granted within three working days one request to consolidate two cases at the request of the identical 42 parties in the two proceedings.[43]

3.3 How Does the Special Committee Operate in Practice?

The Special Committee is comprised of seven members plus the Chairperson and the two Vice-chairpersons of the Court, i.e. a total of ten members.[44] In addition, there are five substitute members. For a decision to be valid, at least five members of the Special Committee have to participate in the decision making process.[45]

If the Secretariat receives a request or the Case Administration Committee initiates an action which requires a decision of the Special Committee pursuant to Art. 4 Internal Rules:

- the Secretariat in cooperation with the Case Administration Committee gathers the comments from the parties and/or the arbitrators (depending on the decision to be taken);
- the Secretariat in cooperation with the Case Administration Committee determines the documents and, if deemed necessary, prepares a summary of facts to be submitted to the Special Committee;
- the Secretariat checks whether any law firm of a member of the Special Committee has a conflict of interest (i.e. is involved

39 Art. 12 Swiss Rules.
40 Art. 3(12) Swiss Rules 2012.
41 Art. 11 Swiss Rules.
42 Art. 16(1) Swiss Rules.
43 Art. 4(1) Swiss Rules.
44 Art. 4(1+2) Internal Rules.
45 Art. 4(4) Internal Rules.

as arbitrator or counsel of record in the matter concerned) and informs the Chairperson/Vice-Chairperson when transferring the file to him/her.

- the Chairperson (or a Vice-Chairperson if the Chairperson is conflicted or otherwise unavailable) conducts a conflict of interest and availability check by e-mail/Doodle inquiry with all non-conflicted members of the Special Committee and ensures that the required quorum for a decision[46] can be reached, either by electronic communication (e-mail) or, if need be, by telephone conference and preferably within 3 business days.
- the Chairperson checks whether the file is complete or otherwise requests additional information from the Secretariat/Case Administration Committee.
- the Chairperson submits the file to the participating members of the Special Committee. A proposal of the Chairperson on how to decide will only be included in instances where the decision to be taken squarely falls within an established practice of the Court.[47] In all other instances the Chairperson will express his/her opinion last.
- the Chairperson collects the opinions expressed by the members of the Special Committee (by e-mail or in a telephone conference) and communicates the decision of the Special Committee to the Secretariat.
- the Secretariat communicates the decision of the Special Committee as the decision of the Court[48] to the parties and the arbitrators.

---

[46] Art. 4(4) Internal Rules.

[47] *E.g.*, with regard to the determination of the seat of arbitration, it is the established practice of the Court to name Geneva or Zurich as the seat in instances where the arbitration clause refers to the former arbitration rules of the Geneva Chamber of Commerce and Industry (CCIG Rules) or the International Arbitration Rules of the Zurich Chamber of Commerce (ZCC Rules), because Art. 3 CCIG and Art. 4 ZCC Rules, respectively, provided for Geneva or Zurich as the seat of arbitration absent any agreement by the parties on the seat.

[48] The Rules themselves do not distinguish which body of the Court renders which administrative decision (*see* above section 2.1). As a consequence of the Court's power to delegate the power to make decisions pursuant to the Court's Internal Rules (Introduction (b) Swiss Rules), all administrative decisions are rendered in the name of and by the Court.

The above process has shown to work very smoothly and since its implementation has considerably reduced the average time needed for the decisions by the Special Committee.

While no reasons for a decision are usually provided,[49] the Case Administration Committee is charged with preparing a summary of the facts and the decision, both of which are to be submitted to the Know-How Working Group for inclusion into the database and for possible publication in a Newsletter or on the website of the Swiss Chambers' Arbitration Institution.

4. PLENARY SESSION (ARTICLE 5 INTERNAL RULES)

Art. 5(2) Internal Rules provides that the Plenary Session is "to define a common practice so as to ensure consistent and efficient administration of arbitration proceedings" under the Swiss Rules.

For this purpose the frequency of Plenary Sessions has been increased from one to two per year since the Swiss Rules 2012 came into force.

By way of illustration one may mention the issues and practices which were discussed and/or decided at some of the more recent Plenary Sessions of the Court:

- **Art. 3(5):** Defining in general terms which information missing in the Notice of Arbitration is in any event to be requested from Claimant within an additional non-extendable time limit not exceeding 15 days.[50]
- **Art. 3(7):** With a view to accelerate the constitution of the arbitral tribunal in the event the Respondent requests an extension of time to file the Answer to the Notice of Arbitration beyond an additional 15 days, such extension may be granted up to 30 days without the consent of the Claimant, but only if the Respondent submits certain information within an additional period of time of 15 days.[51]
- Drafting a standard response to address informal inquiries by a prospective Claimant before the filing of the Notice of

[49] Arts. 5(1), 11(3), 12(2) Swiss Rules.

[50] Note that pursuant to the wording of Art. 3(5) (and Art. 3(9)) Swiss Rules, the Secretariat is not required to request a party to provide missing information if a Notice of Arbitration or an Answer to the Notice of Arbitration is incomplete and may therefore continue with the administration of the proceedings and in particular with the process of constituting the arbitral tribunal.

[51] *See*, Michael Fischer's contribution, *Case Administration*, in this volume.

Arbitration as to whether a case will be administered based on a specific wording of an arbitration clause.[52]

- **Art. 5(1):** Definition of the practice as to whether an arbitrator is to be confirmed if the language of the arbitration is in dispute and the Statement of Acceptance completed by that arbitrator indicates that he/she is not in a position to follow and understand oral arguments and testimony and/or to read and understand documents in one or more of the languages under discussion. Similarly, whether to confirm a sole/ presiding arbitrator if he/she is not in a position to conduct a hearing and draft an award in any of the languages under discussion.
- **Arts. 5(3), 7(3), 8(2), 8(5):** Discussion as to whether and, if so, under which circumstances, the Court when making appointments may appoint a presiding or sole arbitrator of the nationality of one of the parties.[53]
- **Art. 13 (or prior to the application of art. 13):** Defining steps for escalating communications between the Court/Secretariat and an arbitrator who does not comply with his/her duties (such as not providing the Secretariat with copies of procedural decisions, the provisional timetable, requests for deposits from the parties, or information on developments as to the amount in dispute [e.g. because of an introduction of a counter-claim or a set-off defence] etc.) before the Court sends, on its own motion, a written warning pursuant to Art. 13(1) Swiss Rules.
- **Art. 34; Appendix B Section 2 footnote 2:** Defining the method to determine Administrative Costs if proceedings are terminated prior to a final award.

---

[52] *I.e.*, how to address inquiries by potential parties who wish to know whether the case will be administered pursuant to Art. 3(12) without first filing a Notice of Arbitration.

[53] The requirement that the sole or presiding arbitrator be of national neutrality is the practice under many sets of international arbitration rules (*see* e.g. Art. 13(5) ICC Rules, Art. 6(1) London Court of International Arbitration (LCIA) Rules 1998). The Swiss Rules, in contrast, do not contain a specific requirement of national neutrality (*see* Bühler/Feit, in: Zuberbühler/Müller/Habegger (Eds.), Swiss Rules of International Arbitration–Commentary, 2nd Ed., 2013, Art. 7 N 17-21, Art. 8 N 13; Dickenmann, in: Arroyo (Ed.), Arbitration in Switzerland - The Practitioner's Guide, 2013, Art. 7 Swiss Rules N 25, Art. 8 Swiss Rules N 36). The question is whether the Court, when making appointments, should take into account "the advisability of appointing an arbitrator of a nationality other than the nationalities of the parties" (*see* Art. 6(7) UNCITRAL Rules) and how this is to be balanced against other factors.

- **Art. 38(a):** Defining the process to determine the fees and expenses for an arbitrator who has ceased to be in office (as a consequence of a successful challenge,[54] successful request for removal,[55] agreement by the parties on the replacement of an arbitrator,[56] resignation or death of an arbitrator[57]) by the newly constituted arbitral tribunal and drafting of the related amendment to the Guidelines for Arbitrators.[58]
- **Art. 41(1):** Defining the method of calculation and notification together with the transmission of the file[59] of the range of an advance on costs and Administrative Costs which may be fixed by the arbitral tribunal without the need to further consult with the Court.[60]
- **Art. 42(2):** Defining the instances in which the Court should decide that the Expedited Procedure is not to apply despite the amount in dispute not exceeding CHF 1,000,000.

5. CHAIRPERSON AND VICE-CHAIRPERSONS OF THE COURT (ARTICLE 6 INTERNAL RULES)

5.1 Jurisdiction of the Chairperson

The competences of the Chairperson, or of one of his/her Vice-Chairpersons in case of the Chairperson's unavailability, are confined to issues relating to emergency relief proceedings:[61]

---

54 Art. 11 Swiss Rules.

55 Art. 12 Swiss Rules.

56 *See*, Frey/Aebi, *Art. 13, in*: SWISS RULES OF INTERNATIONAL ARBITRATION – COMMENTARY, 2ND ED., Art. 13 N 10, (Zuberbühler/Müller/Habegger eds., 2013); Gordon-Vrba/Vock, *Art. 11 and Art. 13, in*: ARBITRATION IN SWITZERLAND – THE PRACTITIONER'S GUIDE, Art. 11 N 20-21 and Art. 13 N 4 (Arroyo ed., 2013); Marguerat, *Art. 11, in*: SWISS RULES OF INTERNATIONAL ARBITRATION – COMMENTARY, 2ND ED., Art. 11 N 26, (Zuberbühler/Müller/Habegger eds. 2013).

57 *See*, Frey/Aebi, *above* n *56*, Art. 13 N 11-18; Gordon-Vrba/Vock, *above n 56*, Art. 13 Swiss Rules N 7-8.

58 The Guidelines for Arbitrators are available on the website www.swissarbitration.org/sa/download/guidelines_for_ arbitrators_2012.pdf, last visited 27 May 2014.

59 Art. 5(5) Swiss Rules.

60 Art. 41(1) Swiss Rules 2012 (in contrast to Art. 41(1) Swiss Rules 2004) requires the arbitral tribunal to consult with the Court prior to requesting a deposit from the parties. The aim of this practice is to provide the arbitral tribunal upon transmitting the file to it with a cap up to which it may request deposits from the parties without the need to consult and to thus reduce the number of necessary consultations.

61 Emergency Relief is a new feature of the Swiss Rules 2012 and is governed by Art. 43 Swiss Rules.

- Appointment, challenge and removal of an emergency arbitrator;[62]
- Determination of the seat of the emergency relief proceedings.[63]

Due to the (purported) urgency in emergency relief proceedings, these decisions are taken by only one member of the Court, i.e. the Chairperson or one Vice-Chairperson.

With regard to the appointment of an emergency arbitrator, the Chairperson has a non-exhaustive list of potential emergency arbitrators. The individuals on this list have already declared in writing their interest in principle to sit as emergency arbitrator under the applicable terms and conditions,[64] subject, of course, to availability and complete independence and impartiality when approached on a specific matter.

Other administrative decisions in connection with emergency relief proceedings, such as extensions of time,[65] are made by the Case Administration Committee. It is also in charge of monitoring the arbitration proceedings on the merits, which are supposed to be initiated at the latest within ten days after the filing of the application for emergency relief.[66]

5.2 The First Emergency Relief Proceedings in February 2014

At the time of the ASA Conference of 31 January 2014, no application for emergency relief proceedings had yet been filed and thus no experiences could be reported. However, the Secretariat had been approached with an informal inquiry by a potential respondent in emergency relief proceedings as to whether the Court would accept the filing of a *"Schutzschrift"* / *"mémoire préventif"*[67] and, if so, under what terms. Upon consultation with some Court members, the Secretariat advised the inquiring party of the requirement to pay a registration fee and of the period of time during which the *Schutzschrift* would be kept

---

62 Art. 43(2+4) Swiss Rules.

63 Art. 43(5) Swiss Rules.

64 *I.e.*, duty to render a decision on the emergency application within 15 days after receipt of the file (Art. 43(7) Swiss Rules), fees of the emergency arbitrator being in principle capped at CHF 20'000 (Section 2.9 Appendix B Swiss Rules), no possibility to serve as arbitrator in any subsequent arbitration on the merits unless parties agree (Art. 43(11) Swiss Rules).

65 Art. 43(7) Swiss Rules.

66 Art. 43(3) Swiss Rules.

67 *See*, for state court proceedings in Switzerland, Art. 270 Swiss Civil Procedure Code (Civil Procedure Code, CPC) of 19 December 2008 (Status as of 1 May 2013).

on file by the Secretariat. Ultimately, no *Schutzschrift* was filed. Whether the payment of a registration fee and, if so, in what amount, and whether the period of keeping the *Schutzschrift* on file will become standard practice may be a matter to be defined by a future Plenary Session.[68]

The first application for emergency relief was filed with the Geneva office of the Secretariat on 4 February 2014 by a Swiss company requesting injunctions against a Canadian company under a dispute arising out of a cooperation agreement between the parties dated 24 August 2006 and governed by Swiss law and submitted to the Swiss Rules.[69] The Secretariat informed the Chairman of the Court about the application on the same day by telephone and by email of 17:49 CET.

By 18:42 CET the Chairman had approached five candidates from the non-exhaustive list of potential emergency arbitrators by e-mail as follows:

> Dear Mr/Mrs X.
>
> I am approaching you for a potential appointment as emergency arbitrator under the Swiss Rules of International Arbitration. If you are interested and available (i.e. both free of conflict of interest and in a position to render a decision on the application within 15 days from the transfer of the file to you pursuant to Article 43(7) Swiss Rules), I would appreciate your indication by returning the attached Statement of Independence duly completed by email both to me and Ms Joya Raha of the Geneva Secretariat of the Arbitration Court at the latest by tomorrow 5 February 2014, 2 pm CET. As you will be aware, the fees of an emergency arbitrator may exceed CHF 20'000 in exceptional circumstances and with the approval of the Court only.

---

68 *See*, above section 4.

69 Note in this context that parties that have entered into a Swiss Rules arbitration agreement prior to 1 June 2012, i.e. prior to the entry into force of the emergency relief provisions (Art. 43 Swiss Rules), without having expressly excluded the application of the revised Swiss Rules, are, in principle, deemed to have impliedly consented to the emergency relief provisions (*see*, Habegger, *above* n 10, 273; Habegger, *Art. 43, in* ARBITRATION IN SWITZERLAND – THE PRACTITIONER'S GUIDE, Art. 43 n 69 (Arroyo ed., 2013); Meier, *Art. 43, in* SWISS RULES OF INTERNATIONAL ARBITRATION – COMMENTARY, 2ND ED., Art. 43 n 4 (Zuberbühler/Müller/Habegger eds., 2013).

> You will find the identity of the parties and some further information below. Kindly note that, according to our reading of the application for emergency relief, no ex parte relief is requested.
>
> Finally, in light of the time pressure inherent in emergency relief proceedings, please be advised that this inquiry is made to several potential emergency arbitrators simultaneously and that any appointment will only form the subject of a further decision by myself in accordance with Art. 6 of the Internal Rules of the Arbitration Court of the Swiss Chambers' Arbitration Institution.

Having received, by 5 February 2014, 09:55 CET, three replies of candidates unavailable to act (for reasons of conflict of interest or due to other pressing commitments), the Chairman sent the e-mail invitation to three additional candidates before 10:30 CET.

By 5 February 2014, 14:00 CET, the Chairman had received two positive responses. He appointed a Belgian national who was notified of the appointment by the Secretariat via e-mail the same afternoon and who received the file on 6 February 2014.

The emergency arbitrator issued draft procedural rules and a draft provisional timetable on 6 February 2014 and held a conference call with the parties on 7 February 2014. The answer to the request for emergency relief was filed on 11 February 2014, the reply on 13 February 2014, and the rejoinder on 15 February 2014. A hearing took place in Geneva on 18 February 2014 and the parties filed their statement of costs on 19 February 2014.

The emergency arbitrator issued his order ruling on the application for emergency relief on 20 February 2014. He partially granted the applicant's request that the respondent be enjoined from disclosing the contents of the cooperation agreement and from using documents, tools, research and analytical techniques, structure information and explanations said to be in the possession of the applicant. He rejected the applicant's requests that the respondent be enjoined from making further contact with the applicant's suppliers and contacts and that the respondent be enjoined from taking further actions that might reduce the value of the goodwill commonly created by the parties as well as the applicant's request that he be permitted to withhold payments received. As to the request for a penalty, the emergency arbitrator found that he did not have the authority to impose a penalty for noncompliance with the non-disclosure order.

This first experience proved that emergency relief proceedings under the Swiss Rules work well and that no adjustments will need to be made as to the manner in which they are administered.

6. A PERSONAL VISION OF THE CHAIRMAN OF THE COURT FOR THE FUTURE

The future development of the Swiss Chambers' Arbitration Institution is, of course, a matter for its members at the level of the general assembly and the board of the Swiss Chambers' Arbitration Institution. The Swiss Rules are a product of the seven participating Chambers of Commerce and it is their prerogative how to develop the Swiss Rules further. If I may nevertheless convey a personal wish list in my capacity as Chairman of the Court,[70] I would consider the following:

- the addition of foreign members to the Court to promote diversity, to build up know-how and expertise and to further the international acceptance of the Swiss Rules;[71]
- the improvement of the cohesion amongst members of the Secretariat and the increase in their independence from the Chambers by, e.g., having them formally employed by the Swiss Chambers' Arbitration Institution instead of an individual Chamber;[72]
- the development of the technical facilities available to the Secretariat and the Court members, e.g. an improved intranet;
- the facilitating of financial matters for parties and arbitral tribunals by running only one bank account for payment of Registration Fees[73] and deposits;[74]

---

[70] The following reflects entirely the author's personal opinion and does not represent the views of the Court.

[71] *See*, Weber-Stecher, *above* n *10*, 44 footnote 30, referring to Section A Clause 1 of the Constitution of the LCIA Arbitration Court ("The Arbitration Court shall [...] consist of up to thirty-five members appointed by the Board of Directors of the LCIA on the recommendation of the Court, of whom up to six shall be from the United Kingdom and the remainder from other countries".); Stockholm Chamber of Commerce (SCC) Rules Art. 3 Appendix I ("*[...] The Board shall include both Swedish and non-Swedish nationals*").

[72] As to the independence of bodies involved in case administration from other bodies of the institution (such as, e.g., the board of directors), *see*, Weber-Stecher, *above* n 10, 38 ss.

[73] Arts. 3(3)(i), 5(5), Appendix A and Section 1 Appendix B Swiss Rules.

[74] Art. 41, Appendix A and Sections 1.4 and 1.6 Appendix B Swiss Rules.

- the increased marketing and the related availability of additional financial means for the marketing of the Swiss Rules;[75]
- the further increase in the transparency of the work of the Secretariat and the Court,[76] such as by making publicly available the outcome of administrative decisions of interest or administrative practices (e.g. by way of a FAQ section on the Swiss Chambers' Arbitration Institution's website);[77]
- the opening of offices of the Secretariat abroad in the mid and long term.[78]

While the above may be overreaching at least for the immediate future and will inevitably need time for discussion and implementation, I would not like to end without thanking my colleagues in the Arbitration Court and the members of the Secretariat for the time, effort and diligence they put in securing the efficient, diligent and pragmatic administration of Swiss Rules proceedings and making the Swiss Rules a successful and reliable product deserving the trust of parties, counsel and arbitrators.

---

[75] One should be mindful of the financial limitations in this context, however. The seven Chambers of Commerce being the members of the Swiss Chambers' Arbitration Institution do not have the benefit of mandatory membership of companies and the related income by way of mandatory membership fees as, e.g., the Austrian Federal Economic Chamber which "runs" the Vienna International Arbitration Centre (VIAC).

[76] As to the request for transparency *see*, Weber-Stecher, *above* n 8, p. 51 ss.

[77] *See e.g.*, www.lcia.org/Frequently_Asked_Questions.aspx for the LCIA.

[78] An international presence would certainly assist in having the Swiss Rules perceived as a truly international product. Consider in this context the opening of offices by the ICC in Hong Kong and New York or by the LCIA in Dubai, New Delhi and Mauritius.

Panel 5: Perspectives from Users, Arbitrators and Counsel, and the Way Forward

The Swiss Rules from the Users' Perspective: A Pharmaceutical Company

*François Naef**

1. SUITABILITY OF ARBITRATION FOR A GLOBAL COMPANY

Merck Serono, a division of Merck, is a global pharmaceutical and chemical company that generates around EUR 5.9 billion turnover per year, has 15,000 employees around the world and operates in more than 70 countries. Until 2012, it had significant operations in Switzerland since the pharmaceutical operations of Serono and then Merck Serono were until that time headquartered in Geneva. It still has approximately 800 people working in Switzerland.

As a global company it is regularly involved in a variety of legal disputes around the world, mainly concerning contract issues but, being an innovative research and development company, also many patent disputes arise. Merck Serono typically subjects commercial transactions to ordinary court proceedings and would submit to arbitration in two main instances: (i) commercial transactions in emerging markets where there is uncertainty about the quality of justice in the ordinary courts, and (ii) patent disputes, where arbitration is a convenient way to avoid or limit the potential impact on discussions on the validity of patents.

1.1 In Case of Arbitration the Relevant Criteria are the Choice of the Applicable Law and of the Arbitration Rules

Merck Serono has in the past used many types of arbitration rules including those of the International Chamber of Commerce (ICC), World Intellectual Property Organization (WIPO), the American

* François Naef joined Merck Serono in the year 2007, acted first as General Counsel and later as Group General Counsel and Chairman of the Board. He was also the former chairman of the Geneva Chamber of Commerce. This is an amended version of a presentation given at the conference "10 Years of Swiss Rules of International Arbitration" on 31 January 2014 in Basel and retains the informal speaking style.

Arbitration Association (AAA) and the Swiss Rules of International Arbitration of Swiss Chambers' Arbitration Institutions (Swiss Rules). As a result, Merck Serono has a relatively broad experience in using different rules.

1.2 The Applicable Law

When Merck Serono selects arbitration, it typically takes the following approach.

First, although it may not always receive everything it wants in a negotiation, it will typically first try to look for what it believes will be the best law applicable to the transaction. This is a key element because selecting a particular law will provide better predictability or even answers on what Merck Serono perceives as potential risks or other legal issues affecting the transaction. For example, Merck Serono would not typically choose Belgian law for a distribution contract. American laws on contract issues are also generally avoided because the rules of contract interpretation under American law are not desirable. Swiss law is one of the preferred laws, particularly for international commercial transactions (excluding the area of intellectual property), as it is relatively well accepted on a worldwide basis and generally not too difficult to negotiate.

In fact, the applicable law is generally something which Merck Serono will fight harder for than the arbitration rules themselves. This is because experience has shown that all arbitration rules have their pros and cons and it is difficult to predict at the time of contract negotiation which procedural rules may, at the end of the day, offer the best leverage or the best support for a future dispute. As previously stated, the most important factor is the substantive laws to be applied to the dispute and the location where the dispute might take place. This will then lead to a conclusion about the arbitration rules to be selected.

1.3 The Choice of Swiss Rules

In my experience and taking into account what has been said above, it would be atypical to conduct the arbitration under the Swiss Rules in Switzerland and at the same time apply foreign law. It is the law and the seat chosen which then lead to the choice of the applicable arbitration rules.

On the issue of efficiency, experience has shown that the time, cost and complexity of the arbitration are much more dependent on the arbitrators than on the rules. The fact that Merck Serono has traditionally subject arbitration in Switzerland to the Swiss Rules is probably more due to the fact that these rules are generally well accepted and they also reflect the cultural approach to dispute resolution that is known and favored in Switzerland.

2. THE FUTURE OF THE SWISS RULES

From the perspective and experience of an in-house lawyer working in a large international company not based in Switzerland, the future success of Swiss Rules depends on three factors.

First, the continuing attractiveness of Swiss law as a body of law that offers appropriate solutions in a world moving quickly with new technical solutions. Given that the choice of law is the primary focus before the procedural set-up, it is the quality of Swiss laws and their ability to cope with new technologies that will be an important factor for the success of arbitration in Switzerland, and therefore the Swiss Rules.

Second, the continuing attractiveness of Switzerland as a place of choice for arbitration will be important. This can take the form of the general attributes of the country as well as its neutrality, political stability, predictability of the legal system, quality of legal services, expertise in arbitration as well as access to facilities. The promotion of the Swiss Rules should not be underestimated. At the end of the day, the Swiss Rules are a product and like every product they need to be marketed if they are to be used. Of course the general condition of the country is important for the success of the rules but also the way they are internationally promoted as a product.

Finally, an issue which sometimes raises difficult discussions within the arbitration world is a "split award". In other words, an arbitral award that does not necessarily addresses the legal point in question but where it instead appears that the arbitrators had an end result in their minds and worked backwards in the reasoning process to arrive at the result. This sometimes results in arbitrators giving a little bit to each party but not necessarily addressing the legal point that the parties were looking for confirmation of. The consequence is that it makes it more difficult for future disputes to be settled because the legal point has not been answered. This is one of the main risks and frustrations that in-house counsels face from time to time in arbitration. In most cases, where a multinational company decides to pursue arbitration rather than settle, it is because there are fundamental principles at stake to which an affirmative decision is sought. When the result of the arbitration is that there is no decision (positive or negative) on these principles, it does not reflect well on the arbitration rules although it may have nothing to do directly with the rules but rather with the arbitrators.

The Swiss Rules from the Users' Perspective: A Sports Organization

*Marco Villiger**

1. INTRODUCTION

As the international governing body of football, FIFA is involved in three distinct kinds of disputes within the area of sport. To address these matters, FIFA relies on three different dispute resolution systems.

2. NON-COMMERCIAL DISPUTES: DISPUTES RESULTING FROM THE FIELD OF PLAY

The first category of disputes concerns those that take place on the field of play, where the referee acts as policeman, prosecutor and judge. Prior to the introduction of referees in 1882, it was the role of the two team captains to decide whether there was a foul play or any other violations of the Laws of the Game. Considering the amount of discussions captains have with referees in today's matches, it is obvious how important the role of the referee is during the game.

3. NON-COMMERCIAL DISPUTES: DISPUTES BETWEEN MEMBERS OF THE FIFA

The second area where disputes can arise in football is between the (direct or indirect) members of FIFA, i.e. the confederations, member associations, leagues, clubs, players and player's agents.

As stakeholders in the game, they are directly or indirectly affiliated to FIFA and fall under its statutes. The FIFA Statutes contain an arbitration clause which requires that all disputes be finally decided by the Court of Arbitration for Sport (CAS).[1]

---

* Marco Villiger joined Fédération Internationale de Football Association (FIFA) in the year 2002, acted first as Head of Disciplinary until the 2006 FIFA World Cup™ in Germany and since 2007 has been Director of the FIFA Legal Affairs Division. This is an amended version of a presentation given at the conference "10 Years of Swiss Rules of International Arbitration" on 31 January 2014 in Basel.

1 *See*, Arts. 66-68 FIFA Statutes 2013, which require disputes between FIFA, members, confederations, leagues, clubs, players, officials and licensed match agents and players' agents to be conducted according the CAS Code without recourse to the ordinary courts of law, unless specifically provided for in the FIFA regulations. Associations are also mandated to require their leagues, clubs, players and officials to submit to the jurisdiction of the CAS.

The CAS is an institutionalized arbitration court with a centralized administration. It has the advantage of being able to provide fast decisions and is available 24-hours a day. This is necessary, for example, when there are issues concerning whether a player has been cleared to play or has been suspended due to a possible doping case.

4. COMMERCIAL DISPUTES FACED BY FIFA

The third, and the most relevant kind of disputes for international commercial arbitration, are those disputes that FIFA encounters with its co-contractors. In this area, FIFA relies fully on the Swiss Rules of International Arbitration of Swiss Chambers' Arbitration Institutions.[2] FIFA has a strong practice of incorporating arbitration clauses referring to the Swiss Rules in all of its commercial agreements, including its sponsorship, broadcasting, licensing, bidding and hosting agreements.

With respect to hosting, such an arbitration clause will be relevant to the future FIFA World Cups™ to be held in Brazil, Russia and Qatar. In the unlikely event that such countries breach their hosting agreements, the disputes would be a prominent case of a FIFA dispute being arbitrated under the Swiss Rules.

5. ADVANTAGES OF THE SWISS RULES

In handling disputes, FIFA uses arbitration rather than the ordinary courts because it is confidential, quick[3] and cost efficient.[4] These virtues are reflected in the Swiss Rules as well as in Swiss law. In particular, with regard to the confidentiality, Article 44 of the Swiss Rules is one of the few arbitration rules that provide that, subject to certain exceptions, the parties, arbitrators, experts, secretary, Swiss Chambers' Arbitral Institution, members of the Court and Secretariat and the staff of the individual Chambers have a comprehensive duty of confidentiality.

---

[2] Swiss Chambers' of International Arbitration, Swiss Rules of International Arbitration (*hereinafter* Swiss Rules).

[3] Expedited proceedings are available under Article 42 of the Swiss Rules. Unless there are exceptional circumstances, the award shall be made within six months from the date on which the Secretariat transmitted the file to the arbitral tribunal.

[4] The rules relating to costs can be found at Articles 30-41 of the Swiss Rules. The administrative costs under the Swiss Rules are modest in comparison to other institutions as a result of the light touch of the Swiss Rules Court during the proceedings. Further, the parties can foresee the costs using the costs calculator on the website of the Swiss Chambers' Arbitral Institution and the Swiss Rules Court monitors all decisions relating to costs.

Confidentiality is important to FIFA. The amount of media attention each case involving FIFA attracts makes it undesirable to use the ordinary courts. In addition, when lodging a complaint against a commercial party, it is not just important to win, but also to receive a rapid decision. Mediation procedures are not attractive because of the cost and time involved. However, if FIFA does decide to pursue mediation, then it must be both cost and time efficient.

The introduction of a provision for an emergency arbitrator into the Swiss Rules is definitely useful.[5] As an organization with a global mandate and international co-contractors, the fact that enforcement of awards issued under the Swiss Rules is well-established worldwide is an important consideration, as is the level of autonomy accorded to the parties and the legal framework under which the Swiss Rules operate.

6. CONCLUSION

Whilst arbitration under the CAS is more appropriate for sports related disputes amongst direct and indirect members of FIFA, FIFA favors the Swiss Rules for all commercial matters because of their cost efficiency, quick procedures and confidentiality. Insisting on other arbitration rules for these matters by the counter-party is somewhat of a deal breaker for FIFA.

Generally speaking, our agreements will also be subject to Swiss substantive law. Although a discussion is sometimes required with some of our counterparties, we find that, overall, Swiss law and the Swiss Rules are widely accepted internationally.

---

5 *See*, Art. 43 Swiss Rules.

Counsel's Perspective on the Swiss Rules

*Bennar Balkaya**

As a panel member, I was asked the following question: "When selecting arbitration rules, as a party counsel, what speaks for and what against choosing the Swiss Rules?" This article provides my response, based on my own personal experience.

1. WHAT SPEAKS FOR THE SWISS RULES?

As a party counsel dealing mainly with commodity disputes in the iron and steel market and as a frequent user of the Swiss Rules, I opt for the Swiss Rules mainly due to the efficiency and the flexibility of the proceedings.

1.1 Time Efficiency

Time, cost and efficiency might not always be sought by the business users. However, given the current economic situation in the world, such considerations do become more of an issue as business users look for ways in tough times to cut down on costs but without endangering efficiency and quality.

Time may be quite significant for parties in tight markets. Especially in commodity trading, disputing parties cannot afford a long-lasting dispute resolution process and need a speedy resolution. These are my clients' priority needs, which I have in mind when, as a counsel, I advise my clients about the best possible arbitration rules. In that respect Swiss Rules meet the needs of my clients.

The Swiss Rules stipulate that all participants in the arbitral proceedings shall act in good faith, make every effort to contribute to the efficient conduct of the proceedings and avoid unnecessary costs and delays.[1] In order to achieve that, the Swiss Rules were amended so that the process for initiating arbitration and confirming arbitrators was made more efficient and the time limits for paying deposits at the

---

* Bennar Balkaya, LL.M., MCIArb., is a Lawyer in Turkey and a member of the CIArb Board of Management. This is an amended version of a presentation given at the conference "10 Years of Swiss Rules of International Arbitration" on 31 January 2014 in Basel and retains the informal speaking style.

1 Art. 15(7) Swiss Chambers' Arbitration Institution, Swiss Rules of International Arbitration (June 2012) (*hereinafter* Swiss Rules).

beginning of the procedure were shortened.[2] In addition, the submission of all documents and other evidence on which the parties rely is required together with the Statement of Claim and Defence respectively.[3] All these features of the Swiss Rules contribute to the efficiency.

Moreover, the availability of an expedited procedure has a lot of advantages. The Swiss Rules provide that the award shall be made within six months from the date on which the Secretariat transmitted the file to the arbitral tribunal.[4] The efficiency of arbitration proceedings under the Swiss Rules could be attributed to the availability of the expedited procedures.

In today's world, time and cost efficiency are the main priorities for most users. People want value for their money and in that regard when the claim is not so high or the dispute is not so complex or, as it is the case in commodity trading, when the disputes are frequent, expedited proceedings appeal to the parties, especially in tight markets, which are usually active markets where every day counts. In practice, when the client is negotiating a contract and the counsel is drafting an arbitration clause, it is not always easy to predict what the nature of the dispute will be, but at that point Swiss Rules also allow for voluntary expedited proceedings,[5] which can help the parties in dispute.[6]

The statistics of the Swiss Chambers show that 42% of the cases in 2013 were conducted in an expedited way.[7] This is the highest figure since the launching of the Swiss Rules in 2004.[8]

According to the results of a survey about the Swiss Rules, 60.47% of the survey participants responded that the expedited proceedings for small amounts in dispute are an advantage that distinguishes the

---

2 Art. 41(4) Swiss Rules.

3 Arts. 18(3) and 19(2) Swiss Rules.

4 Art. 42(1)(d) Swiss Rules.

5 Art. 42(1) Swiss Rules.

6 It should also be noted that the arbitral proceedings are automatically conducted in accordance with an expedited procedure where the amount in dispute, representing the aggregate of the claim and the counterclaim (or any set-off defence), does not exceed CHF 1,000,000, unless the Court decides otherwise, having taken into account all relevant circumstances, Art. 42(2) Swiss Rules.

7 Swiss Chambers' Arbitration Institution, Arbitration Statistics 2013 (*hereinafter* Arbitration Statistics 2013), *available at* www.swissarbitration.org/sa/download/statistics_2013.pdf.

8 Swiss Chambers' Arbitration Institution, Newsletter—1/2014, *available at* www.swissarbitration.org/sa/download/newsletter_2014_1.pdf.

Swiss Rules from other institutional rules[9] and 70.45% found the expedited procedures to be one of the most valued special features.[10]

In my experience with the expedited procedures under the Swiss Rules, there were usually no surprises in terms of achieving the time limit and the procedure worked quite well. The transmission of the file to the arbitrators upon payment of a provisional advance makes this procedure efficient right from the beginning.[11] Besides, knowing more or less when you should expect an award is another attractive feature of the Swiss Rules in order to enable the counsel to respond to the client as to when the arbitration is likely to be over.

Looking at various cases, excluding certain complex ones, where I acted as a counsel under the Swiss Rules, the length of the proceedings was six to eleven months in normal proceedings and approximately five months for documents-only cases. In addition, where the proceedings were conducted in an expedited way, the arbitrators were mostly strict with the time limit of six months to render the award, even when a witness hearing was conducted.

1.2 Cost Efficiency

As to the costs of the proceedings in terms of efficiency, the payment mechanism under the Swiss Rules is quite straightforward.

As per the Swiss Rules, parties are required to deposit the advance for costs directly to the arbitrator's account based on the schedule of costs[12] and, under the expedited procedure upon payment of the provisional advance, the file is transmitted to the arbitrators without any delays.[13] Given that cost efficiency is usually connected to speed or time efficiency, minimum intervention of the Institution and more direct contact between the parties and the arbitrators makes this mechanism quite efficient and saves time.

Moreover, the availability of expedited procedures under the Swiss Rules has a positive effect on costs. The transmission of the file to the arbitral tribunal upon payment of the provisional deposit allows the tribunal to start working on the file as soon as they receive it, without waiting for the payment of the deposits on advance for the

---

9 Annex Swiss Rules Survey, Question No.6 "Which advantages distinguishes the Swiss Rules from other institutional rules?"

10 Annex Swiss Rules Survey, Question No.8 "Which of the following 'special features' of the Swiss Rules do you value most?"

11 Art. 5(5) Swiss Rules.

12 Under the revised Swiss Rules, the arbitral tribunal has to consult with the Court about the deposit to be requested from the parties, Art. 41(1) and Art. 41(3) Swiss Rules.

13 Art. 42(1)(a) Swiss Rules and Section 1.4 of Appendix B Swiss Rules.

costs. This immediate start also contributes to ensure compliance with the six-month time limit to render the award.

Other than that, generally the costs under the Swiss Rules do not dramatically differ as compared with other major institutions' cost schedules. This seems to correspond to the perception of the users: according to the results of the survey about the Swiss Rules, 85.71% responded that the fee structure is competitive compared to other rules.[14]

Consequently, my personal experience with the Swiss Rules shows that in terms of costs and speed the advantage of using Swiss Rules mainly lies in the simplicity of the payment mechanism, the minimum intervention by the Institution to this mechanism, the transmission of the file to the arbitral tribunal without delay allowing the tribunal to start working on the file as soon as possible and the availability of the expedited procedure, all of which function properly.

1.3 Flexibility of the Proceedings

As is the case with efficiency, the flexibility of the proceedings is equally significant for a counsel when selecting arbitration rules.

Like many other arbitration rules, the Swiss Rules gives flexibility to the parties for the choice of arbitrators subject to confirmation by the court,[15] for the choice of law[16] and the language.[17] The Swiss Rules further allow the parties to conduct their arbitration outside Switzerland.[18]

1.4 Availability of the Swiss Rules in Various Languages

In addition to English, French, German and Italian, the Swiss Rules are available in nine more languages including Turkish, Arabic, Chinese, Czech, Greek, Polish, Portuguese, Russian and Spanish.[19]

Although this alone is not amongst the main reasons why as a counsel I opt for the Swiss Rules, the availability of the rules in one's native language is helpful, in particular when clients or the in-house counsels of the clients who are not fluent in a foreign language would

---

14 Annex Swiss Rules Survey, Question No.9 "Is the fee structure of the SRIA competitive compared to other arbitration rules?"

15 Art. 5(1) Swiss Rules.

16 Art. 33(1) Swiss Rules.

17 Art. 17(1) Swiss Rules.

18 Art. 1(2) Swiss Rules.

19 The Swiss Rules can be accessed at www.swissarbitration.org/sa/en/rules.php, last visited 14.05.2014.

like to have information on or review the relevant rules applying to the arbitration proceeding concerned.

Moreover, this has a positive effect during the enforcement stage in terms of both cost and time. It is often the case that the local counsel in the enforcing country are required to provide information to the relevant state court on the rules applicable to the arbitration award subject to the enforcement. In that respect the availability of the Swiss Rules in various languages turns into an advantage, allowing the counsels to save time and costs on the translation of the rules to the local language of the enforcing country.

1.5 Ease of Enforcement

I have already pointed out that one of the advantages of the Swiss Rules in the recognition phase is the availability of the Swiss Rules in many different languages. There are other factors which account for the fact that Swiss Rules awards do not pose any hurdles in the enforcement phase: the Swiss Rules provide that the arbitrators shall be and remain at all times impartial and independent of the parties[20] and ensure equal treatment of the parties and their right to be heard.[21] The well-respected Swiss Rules and the reliability of the Swiss Chambers' Arbitration Institution make it easy to enforce an award in another country, which is a relief for counsel.

This also applies to the arbitration awards rendered under other major arbitration institutions' rules and is not specifically a distinctive advantage of arbitrations conducted under the Swiss Rules; however, this is one of the numerous advantages of opting for Swiss Rules. A process under another institution's rules could be more cost and time efficient, but this alone will not mean much to ensure ease of enforcement unless the institution is well-respected and reliable.

1.6 Role of the Swiss Chambers' Arbitration Institution

The role of the Swiss Chambers' Arbitration Institution through the seven Swiss Chambers has significant importance particularly in terms of efficiency. The Chambers are highly responsive when their assistance is required, not only at the initial stage but also after the end of the arbitration proceeding.

---

[20] Art. 9(1) Swiss Rules.

[21] Art. 15(1) Swiss Rules; *see also,* Art. 182(3) Swiss Private International Law Act, Chapter 12 (1987) (*hereinafter* SPILA).

In my experience, at the initial stage of the proceedings it takes approximately two weeks for the Chambers to appoint an arbitrator where the parties could not agree on a certain arbitrator. Moreover, it is a relief for a party counsel to know that an appropriate person will be appointed by the Chambers, thanks to the quality and pool of the arbitrators available to the Chambers.

Besides, as mentioned above, the files are transmitted by the Chambers to the arbitral tribunals as soon as possible without undue delays, which is one of the Institution's contributions to efficiency.

Moreover, the requirements of the state courts where enforcement of the arbitration award is sought may vary from country to country. In particular, when an enforcing court requires validation of the arbitration awards rendered in Switzerland or asks for information on the Swiss Rules, the assistance of the Institution plays an important role, especially if you are a counsel practicing outside Switzerland. Accordingly, with regards to the Institution's role after the end of the proceedings, the Swiss Chambers assist counsels in terms of obtaining validation from the competent authorities in Switzerland and giving information on the Swiss Rules where necessary. As is known, post purchase customer satisfaction is ensured by providing extra effort, not promised before purchase, to serve customers who have purchased. Therefore, I consider this a post 'purchase service' of the Institution to ensure customer satisfaction.

My experience shows that the Chambers have always been quite responsive and efficient in handling these requests and quality of the services offered is undoubtedly praiseworthy.

1.7 Role of the Swiss Federal Supreme Court

Selecting Switzerland as the seat of arbitration has significant advantages in terms of possible applications for the challenge of the arbitration award rendered in this country.

In my personal experience with arbitrations conducted under the Swiss Rules in Switzerland, only a few times were the relevant arbitration awards challenged by the non-prevailing parties, which is why I was involved in the proceedings at the Swiss Federal Supreme Court.

My experience as a foreign counsel shows that the Supreme Court and the Secretary General's Office of the Court are easily accessible and responsive to the questions of the foreign counsels on certain procedural issues at the initial stage and during the course of the proceedings.

Moreover, I find that the Supreme Court is very efficient when an attestation as to the finality of the relevant arbitration award subject to the challenge is required by the relevant enforcing country courts following the dismissal of a challenge.

As a result, the Supreme Court can be reached easily and is efficient and responsive, which is a serious advantage for foreign counsel.

2. WHAT SPEAKS AGAINST THE SWISS RULES?

It is surely beyond doubt that the various advantages of selecting the Swiss Rules greatly override any possible disadvantages. The only downside could be the perception of foreigners as to the seat of the Swiss Chambers' Arbitration Institution, in particular when the counterparty is a Swiss company.

In fact even if the offices of the Secretariat of Institution are based in Switzerland, the Swiss Chambers administers cases with parties from Western Europe, Eastern Europe and former USSR, Northern America, Asia, Middle East and others[22] and that such a perception of one of the parties when the other party is from a country where the relevant arbitration institution is located about whether or not the other party will have the home advantage could also apply to the other regional arbitration institutions and is not specifically the case for the Swiss Chambers' Arbitration Institution.

The various road shows held in the last couple of years by the Swiss Arbitration Association were in my view very useful not only for the promotion of arbitration in Switzerland, but also for the promotion of the Swiss Rules. I believe that by promoting the Swiss Rules more and raising the awareness of the practitioners and users abroad, the perception of "made in Switzerland" could be enhanced to show the international character of the Swiss Chambers' Arbitration Institution in terms of administering cases. Moreover, as seen in the survey results, 79.55% responded that they would welcome more promotion and marketing efforts of the Institution.[23]

3. CONCLUSION

My experience with the Swiss Rules has only been related to the proceedings with the seat of arbitration in Switzerland and mainly

---

22 Arbitration Statistics 2013.

23 Annex Swiss Rules Survey, Question No.13 "Would you welcome more promotion and marketing efforts by the Swiss Chambers' Arbitration Institution?"

with Swiss law being applied. This is also what I advise my clients about the advantages when arbitrating under the Swiss Rules: neutrality, cultural diversity in Switzerland, arbitration friendliness with minimal interference by the state courts and extensive experience of the Swiss Federal Supreme Court concerning challenges to arbitral awards.

Among other things, efficiency and flexibility of the process are the main reasons why, as a counsel, I opt for the Swiss Rules. This has been, in my view, successfully achieved with the Rules, most importantly, without hindering the flexibility of the process and party autonomy.

Finally, I believe that the Swiss Rules should be made known more widely to be more competitive in the market and to raise the awareness of its international character.

Counsel's Perspective on the Model of Decentralized Administration

*Daniele Favalli**

1. INTRODUCTION

Thank you for being here at this late hour. We were asked by Markus Wirth to do our presentation in an "Article 42 Swiss Rules-style", in other words, quickly and I will try to do my best.

When I was presented with these questions, I thought about what my friends say about lawyers giving presentations and answering questions. Usually, they tell me that only lawyers can talk a lot without answering a question or turn things upside down. I will try to do the opposite and answer the questions specifically. The answers should serve as food for thought for the panel discussion. Hopefully, I will answer some questions myself, but some may have to be answered by the audience.

The following question was posed by this panel's moderator: "Is the model of an 'institution light' with a decentralized administration of arbitral proceedings a suitable one, *e.g.*, as regards accessibility, securing procedural efficiency, and cost control?" In essence, the question is to be divided into three parts: one is accessibility of the institution from a counsel's perspective; the second one should address securing procedural efficiency and cost control; and, this is to be balanced against the term of the 'institution light', a decentralized institution and what can be said about it.

2. ACCESSIBILITY

If we look at whether a light and decentralised institution has a positive impact on accessibility, *i.e.*, whether it is relatively easy for parties to approach the institution, perhaps the first thought that comes to mind is: yes, it does. The various administrative offices are local and therefore speak the local language (French, German or Italian) in addition to English, and are in proximity to counsel, which may be a psychological effect only. However, do proceedings perhaps depend as well on where they take place? Is there a risk or perhaps a

* Daniele Favalli is a Partner in the Dispute Resolution Team of VISCHER in Zurich, Switzerland. This is a slightly amended version of a presentation given at the conference "10 Years of Swiss Rules of International Arbitration" on 31 January 2014 in Basel and retains the informal speaking style.

lack of predictability because Switzerland has several administrative bodies, *i.e.*, one in Zurich, one in Geneva, one in Basel, etc.? Does it matter whether you are in Zurich or Geneva or elsewhere? Obviously, counsel and advocates, where predictability is of key importance, will assess this question and decide whether the answer has an impact on the issue of where to file for arbitration in Switzerland.

From my personal experience the answer to this question is "no", the differences are minimal and, thus far, I have not filed for arbitration in one place because I did not want to file for arbitration in another specific venue in Switzerland.

Perhaps the more important issue here is how the competition between various centralized administrations, *e.g.*, the International Chamber of Commerce (ICC) Secretariat, and the Swiss Rules administration is to be considered. We should be aware that we benefit from federalism, but it brings the downside of having more than one administration under Swiss Rules. If administration in Switzerland was in one place only and the Swiss Rules were to speak with one voice, it is likely that the Swiss Rules could attract more arbitration proceedings. In other words, we pay a price for local accessibility and one could imagine that, in the future and with the increased importance of other arbitration hubs, arbitration in Switzerland should, if compared on an international level, increase its efforts to compete with institutions abroad.

Finally, despite the above mentioned risk of the lack of a unified Swiss arbitration voice, there is the benefit of having more than one personalized and approachable administration. It is helpful to know what and who you get regardless of where you are. In other words, the rather small and personalized administrative teams are a specific feature of Swiss Rules arbitration and do guarantee utmost accessibility.

3. PROCEDURAL EFFICIENCY

If we look at the issue of procedural efficiency, there are, at least, three issues to be considered from a counsel's perspective.

The first issue may be summarized as follows: Are combined forces (*i.e.*, a centralized administration) more efficient and perhaps more receptive to counsel issues because they have greater experience regarding procedural issues as they simply handle more cases? This may perhaps be the case. The issue at stake, however, is how much the increase in procedural efficiency is going to be. Overall, the benefit with respect to efficiency may be rather minimal. Just because there is only one centralized administration, the increase in procedural efficiency will not necessarily be significant.

The next point which perhaps you would want to reflect on is whether the scrutiny of awards lowers procedural efficiency or whether it just lengthens the process (*i.e.*, the duration of the proceedings) up to the award. From a counsel perspective—and this is perhaps a bit provocative—the question is whether arbitrators need to be supervised by the institution when rendering the award? The trust in the arbitrators, often nominated by the parties upon recommendation of their counsel, is of great importance and, therefore, the scrutiny of the award is not most important, at least, from a counsel perspective. In other words, the scrutiny of awards does in fact increase the duration of the proceedings. It does, however, not significantly increase, at least with respect to Switzerland, the quality and/or the efficiency of the arbitration. In turn, not having the award scrutinized by the institution does not increase procedural efficiency either, but will shorten the proceedings accordingly.

The last and likely most important point with respect to procedural efficiency is the assumption that procedural efficiency does not depend on the administration, but, more importantly, on how swift the arbitration proceedings themselves are. Specifically, procedural efficiency does depend on the arbitration rules and the process embedded therein. Under the Swiss Rules, many of you have experienced that awards under expedited procedure are indeed issued within six months after the transmission of the file to the arbitrator. This is a Swiss Rules reality, which I think is impressive to a lot of practitioners and, most importantly, to the parties who are the users of the rules after all. Swift proceedings which lead to a decision within a reasonable amount of time are procedurally efficient and are what the users of arbitration will, among other things, be looking for. From a counsel's perspective, procedural efficiency means, therefore, predictable mechanisms to resolve disputes and a short time-frame within which the businesses know about their legal positions and claims. In turn, uncertainty for a long period of time is what businesses do not appreciate and we, the lawyers, need to be aware of.

4. COST CONTROL

The last issue to be addressed relates to the issue of cost control. If we look at the Swiss system of decentralized institutions (or arbitration administrations in general), cost control of the administrative costs is a negligible element in the big scheme of things.

We know that the bulk part of the costs are those of the arbitrators and, in particular, attorneys' fees, not administrative fees. Of course every dollar and every Swiss franc counts but administrative costs are not going to make a big impact on the question of cost control. In my limited experience, the cost of administration has never been the decisive element to agree to one set of rules or another.

One may think that a light administration is less costly than a large administration. One may, however, also think that several light administrations are more costly than one (perhaps larger/heavier) administration. Again, the issue of cost control with respect to administrative fees does not appear to be a relevant issue, at least in disputes involving significant amounts of money.

A much more effective method of cost control would be for the administration to review attorneys' fees since the scrutiny of attorneys' fees is, to my knowledge, not addressed in any arbitration rules. Although the users may welcome a scrutiny of arbitration fees by arbitral institutions, the cost control of attorneys' fees should and has to remain under the control of the parties who, after all, retained their counsel.

Finally, one can conclude that costs may be controlled by the type of arbitrator that the parties choose. If the arbitrator is cost aware and procedurally efficient, this will have a positive effect on costs. Accordingly, the extent of time granted by the arbitrator to file written submissions, the willingness to allow for discovery, the length of witness hearings, the number of rounds of written submissions, the number of witnesses and experts to be heard, etc. have a direct impact on the attorneys' fees. Again, the selection of the arbitrator is, perhaps, the most significant element of this equation.

Thank you for your attention.

An Arbitrator's View: Can Party Autonomy Hinder Procedural Efficiency?

Rudolf Fiebinger and Christoph Hauser***

1. INTRODUCTION

International commercial arbitration offers parties a number of advantages over litigation before national courts. In choosing arbitration, parties to a contract are to a large extent free to decide numerous aspects of the resolution of possible disputes arising out of their business relationship, such as the arbitrators, the language and the seat.[1] These can be very important issues to parties to international contracts and, in practice, they are, especially considering that the use of arbitration clauses is today more popular than ever.[2] From the point of view of an arbitrator, the procedural rules according to which a dispute is resolved can mean a number of constraints. In particular, various sets of rules give arbitrators different scopes of discretion in deciding the conduct of the proceedings. While most arbitration rules stipulate the primacy of any agreements between the parties on particular issues, some omit such wording. While this does not constitute a wanton license for arbitrators to disrespect the parties' will, it does play a psychological role in that it strengthens an arbitrator's position in discussing procedural points with the parties. In any case, overriding an agreement of the parties would not withstand a later challenge of the award: national procedural laws and the New York Convention allow for the setting aside or refusal of enforcement of arbitral awards which are the result of arbitrators not respecting the procedural agreement of the parties to the proceedings.[3]

---

* Rudolf Fiebinger is Co-Founding Partner of Fiebinger Polak Leon Attorneys-At-Law and head of the firm's litigation and international arbitration group. This contribution is based on a presentation given at the conference "10 Years of Swiss Rules of International Arbitration" on 31 January 2014 in Basel.

** Christoph Hauser is an Associate with Fiebinger Polak Leon Attorneys-at-Law.

1 *See e.g.*, Art. 18, 22 of the 2012 Rules of Arbitration of the International Chamber of Commerce (*hereinafter* ICC Rules"), Art. 16, 25, 26 Rules of Arbitration of the International Arbitral Centre of the Austrian Federal Economic Chamber in Vienna, and Art. 7, 8, 16, 17 Swiss Rules of International Arbitration of the Swiss Chambers of Commerce Association for Arbitration and Mediation (*hereinafter* Swiss Rules).

2 GARY B. BORN, INTERNATIONAL COMMERCIAL ARBITRATION 92 *ff* (2nd ed., 2014).

3 Article V(1)(d) New York Convention on the Recognition and Enforcement of Foreign Arbitral Awards (*hereinafter* New York Convention).

It is important to bear in mind that certain aspects of international arbitration, although often perceived by parties as advantageous, can also have disadvantages. This can, for example, be the case in expedited proceedings. Where the length of an arbitration is limited beforehand, a final award is generally arrived at more quickly than in an ordinary arbitration, which usually takes several years. However, under expedited proceedings, parties will not have any realistic possibility of presenting their arguments to the same extent as in a "standard" arbitration, *i.e.* one without pre-set time constraints. When using such procedural tools that can bring both advantages and disadvantages to the parties, it is important for arbitral tribunals to carefully balance the interests of all participants to the arbitration and to involve them in the preparation and execution of procedural decisions. Institutional arbitration rules can aid arbitrators in achieving this.

2. STARTING POINT

2.1 Party Autonomy

Party autonomy is a basic tenet of international commercial arbitration. It is the parties' agreement (usually contained in an arbitration clause of a contract) which allows a dispute to be referred to arbitration.[4] Accordingly, parties have great liberty in deciding various aspects of the arbitral process. This liberty can roughly be divided into two parts: the autonomy enjoyed by the parties before proceedings are commenced and the autonomy during the proceedings themselves.[5] The first part concerns choices such as the law applicable to the case, the place and language of arbitration and any particular prerequisites that might be required of an arbitrator or chairperson.[6] These choices are mostly reflected in the arbitration clause.

Party autonomy plays a second, very important role in arbitration. Once an arbitral tribunal has been constituted or a sole arbitrator appointed, it is largely up to the parties to decide on how to proceed, *i.e.* how many rounds of and which time frames for written submissions, etc.[7] In other words, the conduct of the proceedings

---

4 *See e.g.*, Elektrim SA v. Vivendi Universal SA (No 2) [2007] 2 Lloyd's L.R. 8, 19; NIGEL BLACKABY/MARTIN HUNTER/CONSTANTINE PARTASIDES/ALAN REDFERN, REDFERN AND HUNTER ON INTERNATIONAL ARBITRATION para 6.08 (2009).

5 Michael Pryles, *Limits to Party Autonomy in Arbitral Procedure*, 24 J. INT'L. ARB. 327, 328-336 (2007).

6 Charles Chatterjee, *The Reality of the Party Autonomy Rule in International Arbitration*, 20 J. INT'L. ARB. 539, 540 (2003).

7 *E.g.* Art. 14(1)(ii) 1998 Arbitration Rules of the London Court of International Arbitration (*hereinafter* LCIA Rules).

(which themselves exist only by virtue of the parties' agreement) is again the result of an agreement by the parties. The freedom that party autonomy grants is one of the main reasons why parties to international contracts choose arbitration over the jurisdiction of state courts. The possibility of selecting a decision maker with certain expertise as well as the flexibility and the possibility of influencing the arbitral procedure itself are features unique to arbitration and are largely perceived as benefits of this form of dispute resolution.[8] After all, they stand in stark contrast to national judicial systems, in which the parties are not afforded any great share of autonomy in the organization of the proceedings but must accept the rules as they are.[9] The principle of party autonomy is enshrined in virtually every legal order dealing with arbitration. In particular, the UNCITRAL Model Law and the New York Convention recognize the primacy of party autonomy over the arbitral process. These two legal orders strongly influence most national arbitration laws, which in turn influence arbitrations seated in their respective countries.[10] In other words, the legal framework which parties cannot opt out of, *i.e.* the *lex arbitri* and the New York Convention, contains rules in which party autonomy is established and cannot be limited.

2.1.1 Party autonomy in the UNCITRAL Model Law

The UNCITRAL Model Law on International Commercial Arbitration[11] was adopted in 1985 and amended in 2006. It serves as a basis for the harmonization and improvement of national procedural laws and covers all stages of the arbitral process.[12] States are encouraged to make as few modifications as possible when incorporating the UNCITRAL Model Law into their national legal systems.[13] As of May 2, 2014, 66 countries have adopted legislation

---

8 See, Queen Mary University of London, *2013 International Arbitration Survey: Corporate Choices, in* 8 INTERNATIONAL ARBITRATION: INDUSTRY PERSPECTIVES (2013).

9 GARY B. BORN, INTERNATIONAL COMMERCIAL ARBITRATION 85 (2nd ed., 2014).

10 *See, e.g.* Art. 1506 of the French Code of Civil Procedure (Code de procédure civile, *hereinafter* CCP); section 2 of the 1996 English Arbitration Act (*hereinafter* EAA); Art. 176(1) and (2) of the Swiss Private International Law Act (Bundesgesetz über das Internationale Privatrecht, *hereinafter* SPILA); section 577(1) and (2) of the Austrian Code of Civil Procedure (Zivilprozessordnung, *hereinafter* ZPO).

11 UNCITRAL Model Law on International Commercial Arbitration, (1985) with amendments as adopted 2006 (*hereinafter* UNCITRAL Model Law).

12 UNCITRAL Model Law on International Commercial Arbitration, United Nations Publication Sales No. E.08.V.4, Part Two: Explanatory Note by the UNCITRAL secretariat on the 1985 Model Law on International Commercial Arbitration as amended in 2006, para 2.

13 *Ibid*, para 3.

based on the UNCITRAL Model Law as their procedural law dealing with arbitration.[14] Chapter V of the UNCITRAL Model Law sets out the framework for the conduct of arbitral proceedings.

First, Art 18 UNCITRAL Model Law stipulates that the parties are to be treated equally; each party must be given a full opportunity to present its case.[15] These are fundamental rights of due process laid down in a number of other legal instruments, most notably in Art 6 of the European Convention on Human Rights and a number of national constitutional laws.[16] A violation of these fundamental guarantees of due process would almost always amount to a violation of public policy, leading to the possibilities of challenge or non-enforcement of the award in question.[17] Second, Art 19(1) UNCITRAL Model Law grants the parties to the arbitration the freedom to agree on the procedure to be followed by the arbitral tribunal, subject to the mandatory provisions of the UNCITRAL Model Law.[18] Failing an agreement by the parties, the tribunal is granted discretion to conduct the arbitration in such a manner as it considers appropriate.[19] This system can be understood as a three-step hierarchy: mandatory provisions—party agreement—tribunal discretion.

The procedural guarantees granted by Arts. 18 and 19 of the UNCITRAL Model Law have found their way into a number of important *leges arbitri*.[20] By virtue of these arbitration laws, arbitral tribunals—whether acting under institutional rules or not—would, therefore, also be under the obligation to respect party autonomy and to grant a fair trial in arbitrations seated in these jurisdictions.

2.1.2 Party autonomy in the New York Convention

The New York Convention regulates the recognition and enforcement of foreign arbitral awards in signatory states. This international treaty has been extremely successful: it has been ratified by 149 countries, creating a uniform framework for the recognition and

---

[14] Status of conventions and model laws, United Nations 47th General Assembly (2014) Document A/CN.9/806 19.

[15] Art. 18 UNCITRAL Model Law.

[16] *See e.g.*, Art. 6 European Convention on Human Rights; Art. 24 Costituzione della Repubblica Italiana (Constitution of the Italian Republic); Art. 45(1) Konstytucja Rzeczpospolitej Polskiej (Constitution of the Republic of Poland).

[17] *See*, Art. 36(1)(b)(ii) UNCITRAL Model Law; Art. 5(2)(b) New York Convention.

[18] UNCITRAL Model Law on International Commercial Arbitration, United Nations Publication XXX, Part Two, para 34.

[19] *See*, Art. 19(2) UNCITRAL Model Law.

[20] *See e.g.*, Arts. 1464, 1510, and 1511 CCP; sections 33 and 34 EAA; Art. 182 SPILA; section 594(1) and (2) ZPO.

enforcement of awards worldwide.[21] This wide acceptance is generally viewed as one of the main benefits of international commercial arbitration.[22] As does the UNCITRAL Model Law, the New York Convention recognizes the paramount role of party autonomy among the grounds for which the recognition and enforcement of a foreign arbitral award can be refused. According to Art. V(1)(d) New York Convention, parties have the right to agree on the composition of the arbitral tribunal and arbitral procedure. To determine the composition of the tribunal and the arbitral procedure, parties may select any rules they wish—national, institutional, or even rules they have drafted themselves.[23] If an arbitral tribunal does not respect the agreement of the parties on composition or procedure, an award can be refused recognition and enforcement.[24] Party autonomy has limits under the New York Convention, as it does under the UNCITRAL Model Law. Art. V (2)(a) and (b) New York Convention allow for the refusal of recognition and enforcement if the subject matter of the dispute is not arbitrable or if the recognition and enforcement were contrary to public policy. The threshold for both tests is not the substantive law chosen by the parties but the law of the country where enforcement is being sought. These two grounds for the refusal of enforcement are to be taken into consideration directly by the court or authority which the party seeking enforcement has applied to.[25] Apart from the *ex officio* grounds for refusal, a party against whom enforcement is being sought can *inter alia* object to the application for recognition and enforcement and demonstrate that it was not given proper notice of the appointment of the arbitrator or of the arbitration proceedings or that it was otherwise unable to present its case.[26] An award rendered on this basis would be contrary to the fair trial guarantees in place in many countries.[27]

---

[21] Status of conventions and model laws, United Nations General Assembly Document A/CN.9/806 14 *ff*.

[22] GARY B. BORN, INTERNATIONAL COMMERCIAL ARBITRATION 77 (2nd ed., 2014).

[23] Patricia Nacimiento, *Article V(1)(d), in* RECOGNITION AND ENFORCEMENT OF FOREIGN ARBITRAL AWARDS: A GLOBAL COMMENTARY ON THE NEW YORK CONVENTION 281, 283 (Herbert Kronke et al. eds., 2010); Stefan Michael Kröll/Peter Kraft, *Part II - Commentary on the German Arbitration Law (10th Book of the German Code of Civil Procedure), Chapter VII—Recourse Against the Award, § 1059 – Application for Setting Aside , in* ARBITRATION IN GERMANY: THE MODEL LAW IN PRACTICE para 67 (Karl-Heinz Böckstiegel et al., eds., 2007).

[24] Art. V(1)(d) New York Convention.

[25] Art. V(2) New York Convention.

[26] Art. V(1)(b) New York Convention.

[27] *Supra*, footnote 16.

2.2 Procedural Efficiency

The possibility of highly efficient dispute resolution is widely seen as one of the most positive features of international commercial arbitration.[28] This is, in part, due to the fact that arbitral proceedings result in a decision that is not subject to general appeal, but to judicial scrutiny in only a limited number of cases of gross violation of parties' rights and public policy. Thus, an arbitral award's finality shortens the time for the resolution of disputes in that, even if an arbitration should be lengthy and very complex, it will only be decided by one instance. To decide the same case before state courts would, in the usual case of a three-tier court system in civil matters, almost certainly take longer.

Arbitration also offers parties the possibility to craft tailor-made procedural rules and timetables with the arbitral tribunal or sole arbitrator.[29] This can allow the tribunal to take the specific needs of the case or of the parties into account, *e.g.* the need for hearings on jurisdiction, the need or desire for expert reports and the possibility to comment on such reports. Whether the procedure is efficient and how this efficiency will be implemented in practice greatly depends on the personality of the arbitrator(s) who are to decide the dispute. While it is generally a delicate psychological exercise to head an arbitral tribunal or serve as sole arbitrator, it is all the more so to discipline unruly parties or to convince parties that it might be best to take certain measures which might restrict party autonomy, albeit in favor of quicker proceedings. Procedural efficiency in arbitration can be a particularly decisive factor for parties domiciled in countries with overburdened judicial systems. Delays in justice can occur both in states with reasonably well-funded courts but also in countries with budgetary or other endemic organizational deficiencies.[30] Parties enter into arbitration agreements with the best intentions in mind. However, it can then happen that things do not develop as planned and that the arbitral proceedings end up not being very different from proceedings before ordinary state courts. This issue, and in particular the reasons, for such situations as well as possible solutions will be explored in the following sections.

---

28 GARY B. BORN, INTERNATIONAL COMMERCIAL ARBITRATION 85 (2nd ed., 2014).

29 *See e.g.*, Philipp A. Habegger, *Chapter 12, Part V: Saving Time and Costs in Arbitration, in* ARBITRATION IN Switzerland: THE PRACTITIONER'S GUIDE 1393 (Manuel Arroyo, ed., 2013).

30 GARY B. BORN, INTERNATIONAL COMMERCIAL ARBITRATION 87 (2nd ed., 2014), referring to Indian courts which can take up to three decades to finally decide an issue.

2.3 Too Much Party Autonomy Can Lead to Less Procedural Efficiency

Although the arbitral procedures offer every possibility for procedural efficiency, for making the arbitration "lean", it is often surprising to hear "high costs" and "long duration" cited as criticisms to international commercial arbitration.[31] However, the practice underlying this criticism is, at least in part, due to the parties themselves. With only one instance in which to plead, parties often overstate their case. This can lead to submissions of extraordinary length and/or the agreement of the parties to a large number of exchanges of submissions on the merits of the case. Parties may also agree on particularly long deadlines to file submissions, which might not always be absolutely necessary.[32] Different remuneration schemes can lead to different points of view: On the one hand, while arbitrators are usually, particularly under institutional arbitration rules, paid a lump-sum fee, albeit dependent on the amount in dispute, party representatives commonly apply hourly rates to their services.[33] On the other hand, counsel will go out of their way to help clients win their cases; this can generate more costs.[34]

The ones to suffer are, in such cases, the arbitrators and the parties themselves. The arbitrators must potentially deal with a much larger caseload than expected when accepting the mandate to arbitrate. The parties are the ones who must pay for the possibilities granted to them by the flexibility of arbitration.

This flexibility, if used very broadly by the parties, can therefore result in extremely high costs and long duration of arbitral proceedings. While it is true that parties can utilize every opportunity to state every possible aspect of their case, this comes at a cost—and parties are usually all but pleased by high costs, having chosen arbitration *inter alia* in order to avoid such costs.

---

31 GARY B. BORN, INTERNATIONAL COMMERCIAL ARBITRATION 85 *f* (2nd ed., 2014).

32 Michael Pryles, *Limits to Party Autonomy in Arbitral Procedure,* 24 J. INT'L. ARB. 3, 327 (2007).

33 Christian Wolf/Sven Hasenstab, Hybride Verfahrensgestaltung internationaler Schiedsverfahren, 9 RIW 612, 615 f. (2011).

34 ICC Publication 843, *Techniques for Controlling Time and Costs in Arbitration, Report from the ICC Commission on Arbitration*, Introduction [unnumbered page] (2007), citing statistics provided by the ICC International Court of Arbitration based on ICC cases that went to a final award in 2003 and 2004 which showed that, of the total costs incurred by the parties in presenting their cases, 82% were incurred for lawyers' fees and expenses, expenses related to witness and expert evidence, and other costs excluding arbitrators' fees and expenses and the administrative expenses of the ICC.

2.4 How to Deal with This Issue

Various sets of institutional arbitration rules deal with the conflict between party autonomy and procedural efficiency in order to respond to potential users' needs. In general, the result is similar from institution to institution. However, there are fine nuances which might make one set of rules more favorable than another.

It is important to note that the possible solutions to any issues in arbitral proceedings—and in particular to the issue highlighted above—will vary depending on the point of view from which one considers them. An arbitrator might favor arbitration rules limiting party autonomy in certain instances or giving the arbitrator the possibility to, at times, override the parties' wishes in favor of more efficiency. On the other hand, parties will probably be more in favor of rules containing mandatory instruments aimed at increasing procedural efficiency, *e.g.* procedural timetables, case management conferences, etc., without at the same time limiting party autonomy.

The following section highlights two possible solutions to the conflict between party autonomy and procedural efficiency.

3. POSSIBLE SOLUTIONS

3.1 Party Autonomy and Procedural Efficiency under the ICC Rules

The ICC Rules deal with the interplay of party autonomy and procedural efficiency in Arts. 19 and 22. Art. 19 ICC Rules establishes a hierarchy of the different sources of authority:

> Rules Governing the Proceedings
> The proceedings before the arbitral tribunal shall be governed by the Rules and, where the Rules are silent, by any rules which the parties or, failing them, the arbitral tribunal may settle on, whether or not reference is thereby made to the rules of procedure of a national law to be applied to the arbitration.

This three-tier hierarchy determines the rules applicable to the proceedings. First, the ICC Rules themselves are applicable. If they are silent, the proceedings should be governed by any agreements between the parties; if these are lacking, the arbitral tribunal can decide which rules to apply.[35] Although the ICC Rules are placed one step above the parties' agreement in the hierarchy of Art. 19, this does not narrow the scope of party autonomy and the importance it is afforded. After all, the ICC Rules also apply by virtue of an agreement between the parties.

This three-tier system is, of course, in reality a four-tier hierarchy: arbitral tribunals must first take the *lex arbitri* into consideration, before the ICC Rules. And in addition to the *lex arbitri*, arbitrators will usually also bear in mind the provisions of Art. V New York Convention, since these could limit the enforceability of their awards. The four-tier hierarchy is thus supplemented by the New York Convention.

Art. 19 ICC Rules makes a global reference to the "Rules". This reference is substantiated, among others, in Art. 22 ICC Rules, of which paragraphs 1, 2, and 4 are particularly noteworthy:

> 1. The arbitral tribunal and the parties shall make every effort to conduct the arbitration in an expeditious and cost-effective manner, having regard to the complexity and value of the dispute.
> 2. In order to ensure effective case management, the arbitral tribunal, after consulting the parties, may adopt such procedural measures as it considers appropriate, provided that they are not contrary to any agreement of the parties.
>
> (...)
>
> 4. In all cases, the arbitral tribunal shall act fairly and impartially and ensure that each party has a reasonable opportunity to present its case.

Art. 22 ICC Rules gives guidelines on how to conduct proceedings efficiently. According to Art. 22(1), the two main guidelines of ICC proceedings should be cost-effectiveness and speed – these two principles limit the tribunal's discretion granted by Art. 19 ICC Rules.[36] Cost-effectiveness and speed can be achieved through effective case management by arbitral tribunal. Art. 22(2) ICC Rules gives the tribunal the competence to adopt the procedural measures it considers appropriate. However, the arbitral tribunal must first consult with the parties and may only adopt such measures which are not

---

[35] *Cf.*, JASON FRY/SIMON GREENBERG/FRANCESCA MAZZA, THE SECRETARIAT'S GUIDE TO ICC ARBITRATION para 3-709 (2012).

[36] Art. 22(1) ICC Rules.

contrary to the parties' agreement.[37] This limitation on the arbitral tribunal's discretion is in line with the position party autonomy is given in Art. 19 ICC Rules.[38]

Art. 22(4) of the ICC Rules introduces a further limitation on the discretion granted to a tribunal in Art. 19 ICC Rules. Arbitrators must—according to the explicit requirement of Art. 22(4)—act fairly and impartially and afford each party a reasonable opportunity to present its case.[39] This limitation is in line with the New York Convention and the UNCITRAL Model Law and a large number of *leges arbitri*.

In practice, an arbitral tribunal will confer with the parties in order to find solutions to procedural issues. Only when the parties are both—and this is rarely the case—unwilling to cooperate, it might happen that a tribunal must make important procedural decisions without seeking a prior agreement.

3.2 Party Autonomy and Procedural Efficiency under the Swiss Rules

The Swiss Rules govern the relationship between party autonomy and procedural efficiency in their Art. 15:

> GENERAL PROVISIONS
> Article 15
>
> 1. Subject to these Rules, the arbitral tribunal may conduct the arbitration in such manner as it considers appropriate, provided that it ensures equal treatment of the parties and their right to be heard.
>
> (...)
>
> 7. All participants in the arbitral proceedings shall act in good faith, and make every effort to contribute to the efficient conduct of the proceedings and to avoid unnecessary costs and delays. The parties undertake to comply with any award or order made by the arbitral tribunal or emergency arbitrator without delay.

On its face, Art. 15(1) Swiss Rules gives an arbitral tribunal a wide margin of discretion within which to operate. This can be very

---

[37] Art. 22(2) ICC Rules.

[38] *Cf.*, JASON FRY/SIMON GREENBERG/FRANCESCA MAZZA, THE SECRETARIAT'S GUIDE TO ICC ARBITRATION para 3-804 (2012).

[39] Art. 22(4) ICC Rules.

positive, contributing to the possibility of more procedural efficiency. However, party autonomy is such an important principle in international commercial arbitration that it cannot realistically have been the intention of the drafters of the Swiss Rules to override party autonomy by a decision of the tribunal. In practice, the discretion that Art. 15(1) Swiss Rules affords to arbitral tribunals is subject to a number of constraints. First, and most importantly, arbitral tribunals are not, as just mentioned, in a realistic position to disregard party autonomy. This is primarily because, while it is not explicitly mentioned in Art. 15 Swiss Rules, party autonomy is almost omnipresent in the most important *leges arbitri* and it occupies an important position in the New York Convention.[40] It is further widely accepted that it is one of an arbitrator's most significant obligations to render an award that is enforceable.[41] Such enforceability includes—particularly where the assets of the losing party are located abroad—an award's conformity to the New York Convention, meaning that Art. V(1)(d) New York Convention cannot be disregarded by an arbitral tribunal. On the other hand and while it has been argued that, even though the Swiss Rules do not contain any express provision in this regard, it is primarily for the parties to agree on detailed provisions governing the arbitral procedure as a consequence of party autonomy,[42] Art. 15(1) Swiss Rules on its face does not fully support this view, since party autonomy could also be understood to grant parties the possibility of adopting a set of rules which (fully) confers the discretion of procedural decisions on the decision maker. This would mean that parties could opt out of their autonomy by virtue of their very autonomy. This appears to be the case of the Swiss Rules: apart from the constraints placed on the arbitral tribunal by the Swiss Rules themselves,[43] the *leges arbitri* and the New York Convention, the wording of Art. 15(1) Swiss Rules does not support a primary competence of the parties to decide on the manner in which to conduct the proceedings.

For the reasons explained, the hierarchy of rules applicable to the proceedings must contain party agreements, even if not explicitly referenced in Art. 15(1) Swiss Rules. The hierarchy is, therefore, similarly to the ICC Rules, four-fold. First, mandatory provisions of the applicable *lex arbitri* must be taken into account—here it is advisable

---

40 *See infra*, 2.1.1 and 2.1.2.

41 GARY B. BORN, INTERNATIONAL COMMERCIAL ARBITRATION 1993 (2nd ed., 2014); *cf.* Art. 41 ICC Rules.

42 Michael Lazopoulos, *Chapter 3, Part II: Commentary on the Swiss Rules, Article 15 [General provisions], in* ARBITRATION IN SWITZERLAND: THE PRACTITIONER'S GUIDE 446 (Manuel Arroyo, ed., 2013).

43 *Cf.*, Art. 15(7) Swiss Rules.

for arbitrators to also bear in mind the provisions of the New York Convention. Next are the mandatory provisions of the Swiss Rules, followed by agreements between the parties and then the rules established by the arbitral tribunals.

Apart from the hierarchy of applicable rules in the *leges arbitri*, the Swiss Rules themselves place further constraints on an arbitral tribunal's discretion. Art. 15(1) Swiss Rules stipulates that the parties must be treated equally and guaranteed the right to be heard; this is in line with widespread constitutional guarantees, the New York Convention, and many *leges arbitri*. Art. 15(7) Swiss Rules *inter alia* requires all participants in the arbitration to act in good faith and make every effort to contribute to the efficient conduct of the proceedings and to avoid unnecessary costs and delays. This provision obligates both the arbitral tribunal and the parties. The wording of the provision ("*shall*") implies that this obligation cannot be freely disposed of by the parties. By choosing the Swiss Rules, the parties, thus, renounce a part of their party autonomy in favor of a higher degree of procedural efficiency. While the validity of such a provision could be debated if one takes the position that party autonomy cannot be renounced, Art. 15(7) Swiss Rules at least gives the participants in the arbitration, *i.e.* the tribunal and the parties, a valid basis for discussion to optimize the proceedings' effectiveness.

Although it can be argued that Art(15) Swiss Rules gives arbitral tribunals the possibility of disregarding agreements between the parties, the Swiss *lex arbitri*, which is the most significant *lex arbitri* for arbitration under the Swiss Rules,[44] gives party autonomy an important position. Art. 182(1) and (2) SPILA give the parties the primacy over the conduct of the arbitration, followed by a subsidiary competence of the arbitral tribunal:

> 1 The parties may, directly or by reference to rules of arbitration, determine the arbitral procedure; they may also submit the arbitral procedure to a procedural law of their choice.
>
> 2 If the parties have not determined the procedure, the Arbitral Tribunal shall determine it to the extent necessary, either directly or by reference to a statute or to rules of arbitration.[45]

---

[44] At least 97 percent of arbitrations under the Swiss Rules between 2004 and 2013 were seated in Switzerland, *cf.* Swiss Chambers' Arbitration Institution – Arbitration Statistics 2013 2, available at https://www.swissarbitration.org/sa/download/statistics_2013.pdf.

[45] Translation from *Elliott Geisinger/Pierre Ducret, Chapter 5: The Arbitral Procedure, in* INTERNATIONAL ARBITRATION IN SWITZERLAND: A HANDBOOK FOR PRACTITIONERS 74

While parties choosing the Swiss Rules make use of the second alternative in Art. 182(1) and (2) SPILA (*"by reference to rules of arbitration"*), the right of parties to determine the arbitral procedure "directly" is almost certainly not excluded by such reference. This would not be in line with the guiding principle of party autonomy and is not necessarily supported by the wording of Art. 182(1) SPILA. If these alternatives were mutually exclusive, it would most probably contain wording along the lines of "or, in the alternative", instead of a simple *"or"*. Moreover, Swiss *lex arbitri* does not contain any provision whereby a procedural agreement of the parties—in this case an agreement to choose to arbitrate disputes under the Swiss Rules—is irrevocable, contrary to other *leges arbitri*.[46] One might therefore argue that the Swiss Rules are a *lex specialis* to the *lex arbitri* and could therefore be on a higher hierarchic level than the (non-mandatory) provision of the Art 182(2) SPILA.

The Swiss Rules, in many provisions, do in fact repeatedly make reference to the principle of party autonomy (*e.g.* by including wording such as "unless the parties have agreed otherwise").[47] It is also the general understanding that an arbitral tribunal operating under the Swiss Rules and seated in Switzerland is bound by the parties' procedural agreements.[48] An arbitral tribunal can therefore not simply derogate any agreements made by the parties.

This is particularly true in light of the possible consequences of such behavior by an arbitral tribunal. On the one hand, as mentioned, an award that has been made in proceedings in which a tribunal has derogated agreements made by the parties could risk not being enforceable under the New York Convention. On the other hand, parties would have the possibility to challenge an arbitrator by agreement under Art. 11(1) and (2) Swiss Rules—this decision would override any decision taken by the Arbitration Court of the Swiss Chambers' Arbitration Institution.[49]

In any case, Art. 15(1) Swiss Rules, when taken together with Art. 15(7), gives arbitrators a valuable tool to promote more procedural efficiency, with wording that is more precise, and thus clearer, than

---

(Elliot Geisinger, Nathalie Voser, eds., 2nd ed., 2013).

46 GABRIELLE KAUFMANN-KOHLER/ANTONIO RIGOZZI, ARBITRAGE INTERNATIONAL 346 *f* (2nd ed., 2010).

47 *See e.g.*, Arts. 6(1), 8(1), and 16(1) Swiss Rules.

48 GABRIELLE KAUFMANN-KOHLER / ANTONIO RIGOZZI, ARBITRAGE INTERNATIONAL 346 (2nd ed., 2010).

49 Lucy Gordon-Vrba/Dominik Vock, *Chapter 3, Part II: Commentary on the Swiss Rules, Article 11 [Independence and challenge of arbitrators, III]*, *in* ARBITRATION IN Switzerland: THE PRACTITIONER'S GUIDE 429 (Manuel Arroyo, ed., 2013).

Art. 19 ICC Rules. Even though it does not necessarily exclude an agreement of the parties to the contrary, it can help a tribunal to convince parties to take steps that, while limiting the parties' freedom at first, will ultimately benefit the parties.

4. CONCLUDING REMARKS

Putting aside the nuances contained in institutional rules and *leges arbitri* which might allow arbitral tribunals to override the wishes of parties, it is important to note that, in reality, arbitral tribunals will seldom want to "trample" on the wishes of the parties who have, at least indirectly, nominated them.[50] Arbitrators are, nowadays, very concerned with their reputation, as it is often, if not most commonly, their personal standing which led to their nomination by a party or its counsel.[51]

Also, arbitral tribunals and sole arbitrators are well advised not to disregard any agreements of the parties because such disregard could lead to the setting aside of an arbitral award and, in any case, could lead to the refusal of recognition and enforcement of a foreign arbitral award.[52] While not all countries which have adopted the UNCITRAL Model Law have implemented the inconsistency of an arbitral procedure with the agreement of the parties as grounds to set aside arbitral awards, others have.[53] Art. 34(2)(iv) UNCITRAL Model Law can be understood widely, to include even terms of reference and procedural orders which have been agreed on by and with the parties.[54] In situations in which parties jeopardize the efficiency of their arbitration by asserting "too much" party autonomy, it is therefore important for arbitrators to exhibit prudent behavior and delicately inquire as to other possibilities of proceeding. For parties, the choice of the right arbitrator is more important today than ever. For arbitrators, this is an opportunity to display resoluteness and guide the parties to a result which they will not regret.

---

[50] Even where an arbitrator is appointed by an arbitral institution, the institution's right of appointment arises from the parties' prior agreement to arbitrate under that institution's rules.

[51] GARY B. BORN, INTERNATIONAL COMMERCIAL ARBITRATION 2013 (2nd ed., 2014); *cf.* Queen Mary University of London, *2013 International Arbitration Survey: Corporate Choices in International Arbitration: Industry Perspectives* 22 (2013).

[52] *Cf.* Art. V(1)(d) New York Convention.

[53] Art. 34(2) (iv) Model Law; *cf.* Art. 190 SPILA, section 611 ZPO. For an example of a country that has implemented this option, *see* section 1059 para 2 item 1 (d) of the German Code of Civil Procedure (*Zivilprozessordnung*)

[54] *See,* Oberlandesgericht Frankfurt am Main 26 Sch 13/10, judgment of February 17, 2011, available at http://www.lareda.hessenrecht.hessen.de/jportal/portal/t/124j/page/bslaredaprod.psml/.

An Arbitrator's Perspective: A Few Reflections about the Case Administration under the Swiss Rules

*Frank Spoorenberg**

This paper stems from a panel discussion during the ASA Conference of 31 January 2014. The panel was asked the following question: "Is the model of an 'institution light' with a decentralized administration of arbitral proceedings a suitable one, for instance as regards accessibility, securing procedural efficiency and cost control?" The panel was further asked to give some thoughts as to the way forward for the Swiss Chambers' Arbitration Institution (also the "Institution").

This paper intends to reflect the author's contribution during the conference and to continue the discussion. It first examines whether the Swiss Rules arbitrations are correctly labeled as a "light touch" approach to administered arbitrations and, if so, what the consequences are in terms of efficiency and accessibility (1). Then, it analyzes whether the decentralization is indeed an issue (2) and discusses four possible improvements (3).

1. NATURE OF THE CASE ADMINISTRATION UNDER THE SWISS RULES

1.1. The Swiss Rules Represent a "Light Touch" Approach to Administered Arbitrations

Swiss Rules[1] arbitrations can be categorized as "light touch" administration, whether with respect to the organization in place or to the Institution's interference with the arbitration process.

The Institution is composed of the Court of Arbitration (the "Court") and the Secretariat of the Court (the "Secretariat"). The character of the Swiss Chambers' Arbitration Institution, in particular the absence of any scrutiny of the award apart from the decision on

* Frank Spoorenberg is a Partner with Tavernier Tschanz, Geneva. In this paper, the author expresses his own opinion. He does not –and does not intend to– express any opinion on behalf of the Arbitration Court of the Swiss Chambers' Arbitration Institution, of which he is currently one of the two vice-chairpersons.

1 Swiss Chambers' Arbitration Institution, Swiss Rules of International Arbitration (June 2012) (*hereinafter* Swiss Rules).

costs, results in very reasonable needs in terms of staff.[2] In effect, although the Secretariat is composed of staff of the seven chambers of commerce which enacted the Swiss Rules, the overall number of these members is very limited.

1.2. Consequences of "Light Touch" Administration in Terms of Efficiency

In theory, a "light touch" administration could entail the risk of an underequipped institution not able to cope with the requirements of an efficient arbitration process. The efficiency of an arbitration institution is often measured by the reasonableness of its costs and its responsiveness. The question is how well the Swiss Chambers' Arbitration Institution performs in terms other those measurements.

1.2.1. Efficiency: cost-wise

One requirement of accessibility is that the administrative fees do not exceed what is reasonable. An arbitral institution cannot seriously pretend that the arbitration services offered are accessible if the range of its fees actually limits such services to a minority of powerful groups of companies or well-off individuals.

Statistics show, however, that the costs of the Swiss Rules arbitrations are reasonable. The administrative costs are reported to represent two percent of the total arbitration costs and, for disputes under two million Swiss francs, there are no costs. As to the arbitrators' fees, the same statistics report that they represent eighteen percent of the total arbitration costs.[3]

1.2.2. Efficiency: response-wise

As a premise, one should admit that no arbitral institution holds the key to efficiency in arbitral proceedings in any specific case. The key lies much more in the hands of the arbitrators and, even more so, in those of the parties' counsel. However, it is true that an institution cannot pretend to contribute to this efficiency if each of its interventions results in the derailment of the procedural timetable.

---

2 Art. 40 (4) Swiss Rules. The absence of a requirement of terms of reference which would have to be scrutinized by the Institution is another factor reducing the staffing needs.

3 *See*, Joya Raha's contribution, *Institutional Involvement and Costs*, section 6, in this volume.

This is certainly not an issue with the Swiss Chambers' Arbitration Institution, which is reported to be very responsive. In the author's experience, the Swiss Chambers' Arbitration Institution responds in a matter of days. For instance, the Court's determination on the arbitral tribunal's draft decision on costs is issued within two to four working days from the communication of the draft award to the Secretariat. The same applies to the arbitrator's appointment, be it further to, or in the absence of, a nomination by the parties. Equally rapid are the decisions within the purview of the Court's Special Committee.[4] For instance, in 2013, it only took two working days for the Special Committee to deal with and decide on a challenge of an arbitrator.[5] The Special Committee's decisions on the seat of the arbitration are equally or even more rapid.

The responsiveness of the Institution can be attributed to two main factors. First, the Secretariat is very quick to respond. In this respect, the staff members of the Chambers of Commerce who compose the Secretariat must be praised for their eagerness to assist. Secondly, the Court members always make sure to react promptly to the Secretariat's queries.

Of course, one could argue that this effectiveness would probably be affected if the Court had to scrutinize draft awards in their entirety and not only the costs section. Such scrutiny would require a substantial preparatory work of the Secretariat in order to enable the Court to decide within an acceptable time frame. As a consequence, not only would the response time of the Institution be longer but the staffing needs would also increase. It is enough to consider, *mutatis mutandis*, the resources that the ICC needs in order to ensure a comprehensive and high quality scrutiny.

Whether the Swiss Rules should be amended so as to provide for a full scrutiny of awards is an issue which exceeds the scope of this paper. We will thus restrict ourselves to one comment. On the one hand, the ICC Rules provide for such scrutiny,[6] and it is commonly accepted that this scrutiny and its quality are one of—if not, the—landmark(s) of ICC arbitration. On the other hand, the Swiss Rules arbitrations are among the arbitrations administered with a light touch. Statistics show that they are also fast.[7] However, the speed of Swiss

---

4 For a list of the areas reserved to the Special Committee; see, Art. 4 Internal Rules of the Arbitration Court of the Swiss Arbitration Institution.

5 Art. 11 (2) Swiss Rules.

6 Art. 33 International Chamber of Commerce, International Court of Arbitration, Arbitration Rules (2012), [*hereinafter* ICC Rules].

7 Statistics report that in 2013 the average duration of an arbitration proceeding under the ordinary procedure was eleven months and seven months for those under the

Rules arbitrations is not the result of the absence of scrutiny. Practitioners know that the length of proceedings depends almost entirely on the arbitral tribunal, the parties and their counsel, and only marginally on the institutional arbitration rules, at least with respect to the rules of reputable arbitration institutions. Nevertheless, it is not disputable that the scrutiny of draft awards by the Institution would have repercussions on the Institution in terms of its staffing and on the length of the proceedings. Therefore, our preliminary conclusion would be not to duplicate an essential feature of another arbitration institution, all the more so if that feature might in turn change the nature of the Swiss Rules arbitrations in terms of its light touch administration.

2. DECENTRALIZATION V. CENTRALIZATION IS NOT AN ISSUE

The Secretariat takes care of the day-to-day administrative management of the cases. Since the Secretariat is composed of staff members of the Chambers of Commerce of the seven cantons which adopted the Swiss Rules,[8] the Swiss Rules arbitrations may appear decentralized in this respect. The risk of such an organization is that, in theory, the respective practice of the chambers may differ. However, this is of no practical concern.

This organization could be an issue if there were room for materially differing local practices, but this is not the case. The practice can only differ where interpretation of the rules is required. All of the issues where interpretation could be of concern are handled by the Court: e.g. confirmation of arbitrators or, if required, determination of the place of arbitration.[9] It follows that the Secretariat exclusively deals with administrative issues.

The (unique) Court guarantees the unity of practice. It is composed of twenty-seven practitioners, who meet regularly *in persona*, as with the court of other institutions such as the International Chamber of Commerce (ICC) or London Court of International Arbitration (LCIA). The purpose of the plenary sessions is to ensure "consistent and efficient administration of arbitration proceedings."[10]

---

expedited procedure.

8 Swiss Chambers of Commerce in Basel, Bern, Geneva, Neuchâtel, Ticino, Vaud and Zurich.

9 Arts. 5 and 16(1) Swiss Rules.

10 Art. 5 of the Internal Rules of the arbitration court of the Swiss Chambers' Arbitration Institution (*hereinafter* Internal Rules). According to this same provision: "The Chairperson, the Vice-Chairpersons and the committees must report to the Court if they

Moreover, decisions which are subject to some discretion are entrusted to the Court's Special Committee of seven members, which further guarantees a uniform practice. These decisions relate to the correction of a failure in the constitution of the arbitral tribunal,[11] the appointment of a replacement arbitrator,[12] the challenge of an arbitrator,[13] the removal of an arbitrator,[14] the revocation of an arbitrator,[15] the non-replacement of an arbitrator after the closure of the proceeding,[16] the determination of the seat of the arbitration and the consolidation of proceedings.[17]

The decisions that do not fall within the ambit of the Court's Special Committee are taken by the administration committee in charge of the case (the "Case Administration Committee").[18] Each proceeding is assigned to a specific Case Administration Committee, which remains the same throughout the arbitration. Therefore, the same Court members will follow the case from start to finish. Such permanence is certainly a source of comfort for the parties and arbitrators, especially in relation to the Court's power to review the arbitral tribunal's decision on costs.

Therefore, while it is a fact that the Secretariat has staff in multiple locations, i.e. different cantons, delocalization is not an issue since it does not affect the coherence of the practice. This coherence is ensured by the Court's plenary sessions with respect to the overall proceedings under the Swiss Rules and, for each particular proceeding, by the permanent composition of the Special Administration Committee in charge.

---

have encountered an issue of interpretation of any provision of the Swiss Rules or have rendered a decision inducing a change of practice in the administration of arbitration proceedings pending under the Swiss Rules. The Court may at such time define a common practice in order to ensure consistent and efficient administration of arbitration proceedings."

[11] *See*, Art. 5(3) Swiss Rules.

[12] *See*, Art. 13(2)(a) Swiss Rules.

[13] *See*, Art. 11 Swiss Rules.

[14] *See*, Art. 12 Swiss Rules.

[15] *See*, Art. 5(3) Swiss Rules.

[16] *See*, Art. 13(2)(b) Swiss Rules.

[17] Art. 4 Internal Rules and *see also*, Art. 4(1) Swiss Rules.

[18] A reservation should be made for the decisions which, in the context of the emergency proceedings, are entrusted to the Chairperson of the Court or one of the Vice-Chairpersons, i.e. the appointment of the emergency arbitrator (Swiss Rules, Art. 43[2]), the challenge of an emergency arbitrator (Swiss Rules, Art. 43[4]), the removal of an emergency arbitrator (Swiss Rules, Art. 43[4]) and determination of the seat of the emergency relief proceedings (Swiss Rules, Art. 43[5]).

3. IS THERE ROOM FOR IMPROVEMENT?

Whether as counsel for a party, arbitrator or Court member, the author of the present paper has never been frustrated by an event which could be attributed to a malfunctioning of the Institution or an outdated practice. A different assessment would be alarming for a ten-year-old arbitration institution when its rules have just been reviewed and revised. Although it may seem premature to devote time and energy to trying to improve something that is working well, the author would like to suggest four points for reflection.

3.1. One Focused Entity with a Fulltime Staff

The present paper has endeavored to report the author's experience that the administration by the Institution, be it the Secretariat or the Court, is responsive and quick. There was no different experience expressed by the other panelists of the ASA conference of 31 January 2014. Thus, there seems to be consensus in this respect.

Would the assessment remain the same if the number of proceedings were to increase dramatically and to reach, for instance, the numbers of proceedings which are administered by the ICC? There is no need for detailed projections to anticipate that the Institution, in its current structure and organization, would be overwhelmed by such an increase.

The question is whether the Swiss Chambers' Arbitration Institution should anticipate such an increase. In particular, should the staff of the Secretariat be increased?

Launching a program now to increase the number of employees with an eye to a possible increase in cases in the future sounds rather premature. However, after ten years of existence, it may be a good time for the Institution to reflect on whether it has the most rationalized organization. To outline what such an organization should be obviously exceeds the scope of the present paper. However, a few submissions might be put forward here.

There is no reason why the Swiss Chambers' Arbitration Institution would contradict the quite natural principle according to which synergies are generated by gathering in one location people who simultaneously do the same work in different places. Suffice it to say how much easier it would be to coordinate work, exchange information or collect statistics. Moreover, gathering the Secretariat staff members in one location would generate additional working capacity, which would then give the Institution the flexibility to cope with an increase in the number of cases, at least up to a certain level.

This additional working capacity would also allow staff members to dedicate more time to tasks that they may find difficult to include in their current workload. Areas where efforts would be welcome are numerous. For instance, as with any product, the Swiss Rules need more promotion and marketing. There is no need for in-depth studies to conclude that promotion and marketing would be much more powerful if they were carried out by a professional or even a team of professionals, working full time for the Swiss Chambers' Arbitration Institution. No need for in-depth studies either, to acknowledge that the visibility of the Swiss Rules, and thus their market share, would be greater if this team of professionals were under the leadership of one person, who could be a full-time executive director or secretary.

Gathering the staff in one location under one leader in order to act in a coordinated manner seems to depict the mission of a centralized entity. Why not? This entity would have under its one roof a team of professionals who would be fully dedicated to one goal from sunrise to sunset: the Swiss Rules, only the Swiss Rules and their market share. Is it a mere dream? First, what is wrong with dreaming? Dreams are often our best counselor. Secondly and more importantly, it is not quite a dream but, in the author's understanding, the subject-matter of a motion that is currently being considered by the Chambers of Commerce and that should be fully supported.

3.2. Option for the Arbitral Tribunal's Fees Computed on a Time-Spent Basis

The present paper reflects the consensus that arbitration fees and administrative costs represent the smallest part of arbitration costs. The Swiss Rules system based on an *ad valorem* schedule is no exception.[19] Yet, these costs, more particularly the arbitrators' fees, may generate some frustration on the parties' part when these costs are perceived as too high or, on the arbitrators' part, when they are perceived as too low. An example of a rather high risk for such frustrations is when the parties reach a settlement. On the one hand, the parties have dedicated a lot of time, effort and financial resources to the settlement. A kind of exhaustion may then add to their feeling of release and achievement which a settlement normally generates. Such exhaustion might sometimes turn into incomprehension, not to say exasperation, when the arbitration costs, especially the arbitrators'

---

19 Swiss Rules, Appendix B.

fees, are disclosed and it is discovered that they are almost the same as they would have been had the proceedings not been settled. Conversely, arbitrators might feel the same way when the settlement arises quite late in the process, for instance shortly before the hearing or when the drafting of the award is well advanced, and the fees as confirmed by the arbitral institution, in their opinion, do not appropriately reflect the work done. Whether justified or not, these possible frustrations should be anticipated to the extent possible.

Certain parties and arbitrators may feel more comfortable if the arbitrators' fees are computed on an hourly basis.[20] Without seeking to be exhaustive, the pros and cons of such computations are worth discussing briefly.

Once the hourly rate is established, there should be little room for objection or frustration, but would this really be the case? Parties may not be convinced by the necessity or efficiency of all the hours that the arbitrators have dedicated to the case and the questioning of those hours would also generate frustration. One could think of two remedies. First, preemptively, such issues may be avoided, or at least the risk of such doubts arising may be considerably reduced, by a careful screening of the candidate arbitrators. Secondly, a posteriori, an overcharging arbitrator would not go unnoticed for long and is likely to be sanctioned by the market.

Now the question would be whether fees calculated on an hourly rate basis would remunerate more adequately the work accomplished than an *ad valorem* computation. Legitimate doubts remain. In particular, would such computation not be a premium to inefficiency? Why should the time spent prevail over other circumstances which may be even more relevant? These circumstances should also include the efficiency of the arbitrators, as some may be more efficient in a specific industry or type of dispute than others.[21]

These legitimate doubts as to the adequacy of a fee computed on an hourly rate basis confirm that such system should not be imposed upon the parties but they should be given this option if they so wish.

---

20 As for instance the arbitrations under the LCIA Arbitration Rules, effective 1 January 2014, (*hereinafter* LCIA Rules), Appendix Schedule of costs.

21 In this respect, Art. 39 Swiss Rules provides that the arbitral tribunal's fees must be "reasonable in amount, taking into account the amount in dispute, the complexity of the subject-matter of the arbitration, the time spent and any other relevant circumstances of the case, including the discontinuation of the arbitration proceedings in case of settlement."; *see also,* Marco Stacher, *Art. 39,* in SWISS RULES OF INTERNATIONAL ARBITRATION, COMMENTARY, Art. 39 N. 3 (Zuberbühler, Müller, Habegger eds, 2nd ed, 2013).

The Swiss Rules could be amended and refer expressly to this option.[22] In order to avoid the discomfort that could arise should a party want to decline a time-spent-basis fee, which presumably would come from an arbitral tribunal, the Swiss Rules could provide that an agreement on such an option must be made before the constitution of the arbitral tribunal.

3.3. An Internationally Composed Arbitration Court for International Arbitrations?

This paper has emphasized that the Court is a single instance and thus a centralized body. Looking at its current composition, one should also say that the Court's members are almost all Swiss and all Swiss-based.

Should this composition not be reviewed, first for the benefit of practitioners and users and, second, for the benefit of the Court itself?

From the practitioners' perspective, there is little doubt that the Swiss-based counsel and arbitrators have no real concern about the Court's "Swiss-based" composition. It may actually be quite a comfort for these practitioners to know that any Court's interference in their arbitrations will be led by colleagues who have the same legal and cultural background. Admittedly, however, practitioners from other parts of the world may feel more comfortable if there were some compatriots on the panel.

From the Court's perspective, it is quite obvious that the Court would gain in wisdom if all the topics that the Court has to deal with were discussed with a multinational and multicultural input. To put it simply, since the vast majority of the proceedings conducted under the Swiss Rules are international arbitrations, it would not be incongruous that this international nature be reflected in the Court's composition. Of course, one could argue that part of the efficiency and responsiveness of the Court might be explained by the simple fact that all its members live close-by and it is true that proximity helps (suffice it to mention the absence of a time difference). Although proximity may contribute to efficiency, it is certainly not a necessary pre-requisite. Besides, other reputable arbitration institutions have shown the way.[23]

---

22 *See e.g.,* Hong Kong International Arbitration Centre, HKIAC Administered Arbitration Rules (2013 Edition) (*hereinafter* HKIAC Rules), Art. 10 provide for such an option.

23 For instance, the LCIA went as far as to provide for a cap for the UK-based practitioners in the composition of the LCIA Court (up to six UK-based members Constitution of the LCIA Arbitration Court, adopted 1990, amended 1998, 2002, 2008,

Reversing the Rule of Art. 42(e) Swiss Rules?

Statistics show that the expedited procedure as in Art. 42 Swiss Rules has been very popular among users.[24] Those who have experienced those procedures, especially as arbitrators, may have had the feeling that the concept actually results in maintaining almost all the steps of standard arbitration proceedings but cuts short the time periods between each step, thus putting pressure on parties and arbitrators.

A significant part of this pressure may arise out of the time that is required for the drafting of the award and that reduces accordingly the time available for the parties' pleadings. The expedited procedure thus expressly authorizes the arbitrators to state the reasons on which the award is based in a summary form.[25] However, it is difficult to assess how much this latitude actually eases the burden on arbitrators. More often than not, in practice, the awards issued in expedited procedure are so complete and detailed that it is actually hard to tell how they could have been different if the case had been conducted under the ordinary procedure.

A possible way to ease the arbitrators' burden and thereby to release time for the parties' pleadings may be to reverse the rules of Art. 42(e) Swiss Rules so as to provide that the award will not set out the reasons for the decision unless the parties have agreed otherwise. This may, however, open the way to frustration for the parties and raise concern at the enforcement stage, depending on where enforcement is sought.

4. CONCLUSION

A few remarks by way of conclusion: The assessment that the Swiss Rules arbitrations fall under the category of "light touch" administered arbitrations is certainly true. Considering the achievements in terms of responsiveness, noting for instance how fast the tribunals are constituted or, more generally, how fast the Court reaches its decisions, one could reasonably and rightly believe that the Swiss Rules should stay that way.

2009, 2010 and 2011, Art. A.1). Similarly, the Board of the Arbitration Institute of the Stockholm Chamber of Commerce (the "SCC") must include both Swedish and non-Swedish nationals; however, there is no cap for Swedish nationals (Art. 3 of Appendix I to the Arbitration Rules of the SCC).

24 *See,* annex Swiss Rules Survey, Cases under the expedited procedure represented 38% of the cases since 2004 throughout 2013.

25 Art. 42(e) Swiss Rules.

However, this *satisfecit* should not mean that there is no room for improvement. On the contrary, intense competition and the globalization will very soon—if they have not done so already—make the current organization outdated. It may have been sufficient when it was about picking up some cases in our neighboring countries. Now the whole world is the hunting ground for arbitration institutions. The structure must be adapted accordingly, which in the author's view means a centralized entity run by one leader whose only focus would be the development of Swiss Rules arbitration.

Closing Address

*Nathalie Voser**

Dear Conference Participants,

Dear Session Chairs and Panelists,

It has been a long and intensive day and I will be very brief in my closing address.

First of all, I would like to thank whole-heartedly all the speakers of today. I know they have been preparing this conference very diligently and with a lot of effort. The same thank you goes to all the Session Chairs. Without their guidance and coordination, we would not have had the quality of the presentations and discussions we had today.

Moreover, I would like to thank the participants for their active contribution to the floor discussions.

Today, we first looked into the past and heard where the Swiss Rules came from, when they were drafted in 2004 and where we stand after the revision of 2012.

With panels two and three, we turned to the key features of the Swiss Rules which distinguish these rules from other institutional rules.

Some of them are more particular than others. In my view, this is the case for the expedited procedure, the consolidation and joinder as well as the jurisdiction of an arbitral tribunal over set-off claims. Others can also be found in other institutional rules in the same or a similar way. This is the case for provisional measures and emergency arbitrator, confidentiality and settlement facilitation.

The results of the survey showed that the expedited procedure for small amounts in dispute is one of the features that the users of the Swiss Rules value most. In fact, over 75% mentioned this as a positive aspect. But also the confidentiality, the consolidation and joinder and finally the settlement facilitation provisions ranked quite high on the list of positive aspects of the Swiss Rules.

The presentations of the special features and the following discussion hopefully showed you where the Swiss Rules distinguish

---

* Nathalie Voser is a dispute resolution Partner of Schellenberg Wittmer Ltd in Zurich, Switzerland where she co-heads the arbitration team. She was the Conference Chair of the conference "10 Years of Swiss Rules of International Arbitration" on 31 January 2014 in Basel.

themselves from other arbitration rules and will help you when advising clients in which situations the Swiss Rules are a better option than other institutional rules.

The fourth panel explored how Swiss Rules arbitration is administered. I hope that this insight will help you to better understand the mechanism of decisions taken by the Swiss Rules bodies such as the Special Committee and the Arbitration Court.

Last but not least, in the fifth panel we gave the word to the users, arbitrators and counsel. They focused on why they prefer or would choose the Swiss Rules from their respective points of view and also on the "institutional light" aspect of the Swiss Rules, which is probably the main distinguishing feature of the Swiss Rules as compared to other institutional rules with regard to the administration. While, according to the survey, 85% thought that the administration was just right, some people think that the administration is too light and, in particular, there should be more scrutiny. This will have to be carefully considered by the administrative and governing bodies of the Swiss Rules.

What is the way forward? Based on the survey, an overwhelming majority wanted to have more promotion and marketing efforts by the Swiss Chambers' Arbitration Institution as well as more seminars, workshops and conferences on the Swiss Rules.

With regard to the content of the Swiss Rules, I was surprised to see that a large majority of 76% would welcome the introduction of a management conference. And a quarter of the respondents would value a scrutiny process of the content of the award. In my view these are probably the two main issues that the governing body of the Swiss Rules will have to seriously consider in a future revision of the Swiss Rules.

As most of you will know, today, the 31 January 2014, is the Chinese Lunar New Year's Day and we are entering the year of the horse. The horse is said to be spirited and energetic; it is born to race and thrives in competition. It is a good year to start a new business and generally for "taking off".

Let us hope that this conference was the start for the Swiss Rules, not only into 2014 but into the next decade and that the people responsible for the promotion of the Swiss Rules will use the good fortune and positive energy of the year of the horse to launch not only a successful 2014 but also a successful new decade for the Swiss Rules.

Appendix A:

Swiss Rules of International Arbitration (Swiss Rules)

MODEL ARBITRATION CLAUSE

Any dispute, controversy, or claim arising out of, or in relation to, this contract, including the validity, invalidity, breach, or termination thereof, shall be resolved by arbitration in accordance with the Swiss Rules of International Arbitration of the Swiss Chambers' Arbitration Institution in force on the date on which the Notice of Arbitration is submitted in accordance with these Rules.

The number of arbitrators shall be ... ("one", "three", "one or three");

The seat of the arbitration shall be ... (name of city in Switzerland, unless the parties agree on a city in another country);

The arbitral proceedings shall be conducted in ... (insert desired language).

INTRODUCTION

(a) In order to harmonise their rules of arbitration the Chambers of Commerce and Industry of Basel, Bern, Geneva, Neuchâtel, Ticino, Vaud and Zurich in 2004 replaced their former rules by the Swiss Rules of International Arbitration (hereinafter the "Swiss Rules" or the "Rules").

(b) For the purpose of providing arbitration services, the Chambers founded the Swiss Chambers' Arbitration Institution. In order to administer arbitrations under the Swiss Rules, the Swiss Chambers' Arbitration Institution has established the Arbitration Court (hereinafter the "Court"), which is comprised of experienced international arbitration practitioners. The Court shall render decisions as provided for under these Rules. It may delegate to one or more members or committees the power to take certain decisions pursuant to its Internal Rules.[1] The Court is assisted in its work by the Secretariat of the Court (hereinafter the "Secretariat").

---

[1] The Internal Rules are available on the website www.swissarbitration.org.

(c) The Swiss Chambers' Arbitration Institution provides domestic and international arbitration services, as well as other dispute resolution services, under any applicable law, in Switzer- land or in any other country.

SECTION I. INTRODUCTORY RULES

SCOPE OF APPLICATION

Article 1

1. These Rules shall govern arbitrations where an agreement to arbitrate refers to these Rules or to the arbitration rules of the Chambers of Commerce and Industry of Basel, Bern, Geneva, Neuchâtel, Ticino, Vaud, Zurich, or any further Chamber of Commerce and Industry that may adhere to these Rules.
2. The seat of arbitration designated by the parties may be in Switzerland or in any other country.
3. This version of the Rules shall come into force on 1 June 2012 and, unless the parties have agreed otherwise, shall apply to all arbitral proceedings in which the Notice of Arbitration is submitted on or after that date.
4. By submitting their dispute to arbitration under these Rules, the parties confer on the Court, to the fullest extent permitted under the law applicable to the arbitration, all of the powers required for the purpose of supervising the arbitral proceedings otherwise vested in the competent judicial authority, including the power to extend the term of office of the arbitral tribunal and to decide on the challenge of an arbitrator on grounds not provided for in these Rules.
5. These Rules shall govern the arbitration, except if one of them is in conflict with a provision of the law applicable to the arbitration from which the parties cannot derogate, in which case that provision shall prevail.

NOTICE, CALCULATION OF PERIODS OF TIME

Article 2

1. For the purposes of these Rules, any notice, including a notification, communication, or proposal, is deemed to have been received if it is delivered to the addressee, or to its habitual residence, place of business, postal or electronic

address, or, if none of these can be identified after making a reasonable inquiry, to the addressee's last-known residence or place of business. A notice shall be deemed to have been received on the day it is delivered.

2. A period of time under these Rules shall begin to run on the day following the day when a notice, notification, communication, or proposal is received. If the last day of such a period is an official holiday or a non-business day at the residence or place of business of the addressee, the period is extended until the first business day which follows. Official holidays or non-business days are included in the calculation of a period of time.
3. If the circumstances so justify, the Court may extend or shorten any time-limit it has fixed or has the authority to fix or amend.

NOTICE OF ARBITRATION AND ANSWER TO THE NOTICE OF ARBITRATION

Article 3

1. The party initiating arbitration (hereinafter called the "Claimant" or, where applicable, the "Claimants") shall submit a Notice of Arbitration to the Secretariat at any of the addresses listed in Appendix A.
2. Arbitral proceedings shall be deemed to commence on the date on which the Notice of Arbitration is received by the Secretariat.
3. The Notice of Arbitration shall be submitted in as many copies as there are other parties (hereinafter called the "Respondent" or, where applicable, the "Respondents"), together with an additional copy for each arbitrator and one copy for the Secretariat, and shall include the following:
   (a) A demand that the dispute be referred to arbitration;
   (b) The names, addresses, telephone and fax numbers, and e-mail addresses (if any) of the parties and of their representative(s);
   (c) A copy of the arbitration clause or the separate arbitration agreement that is invoked;
   (d) A reference to the contract or other legal instrument(s) out of, or in relation to, which the dispute arises;

(e) The general nature of the claim and an indication of the amount involved, if any;

(f) The relief or remedy sought;

(g) A proposal as to the number of arbitrators (i.e. one or three), the language, and the seat of the arbitration, if the parties have not previously agreed thereon;

(h) The Claimant's designation of one or more arbitrators, if the parties' agreement so requires;

(i) Confirmation of payment by check or transfer to the relevant account listed in Appendix A of the Registration Fee as required by Appendix B (Schedule of Costs) in force on the date the Notice of Arbitration is submitted.

4. The Notice of Arbitration may also include:

(a) The Claimant's proposal for the appointment of a sole arbitrator referred to in Article 7;

(b) The Statement of Claim referred to in Article 18.

5. If the Notice of Arbitration is incomplete, if the required number of copies or attachments are not submitted, or if the Registration Fee is not paid, the Secretariat may request the Claimant to remedy the defect within an appropriate period of time. The Secretariat may also request the Claimant to submit a translation of the Notice of Arbitration within the same period of time if it is not submitted in English, German, French, or Italian. If the Claimant complies with such directions within the applicable time-limit, the Notice of Arbitration shall be deemed to have been validly filed on the date on which the initial version was received by the Secretariat.

6. The Secretariat shall provide, without delay, a copy of the Notice of Arbitration together with any exhibits to the Respondent.

7. Within thirty days from the date of receipt of the Notice of Arbitration, the Respondent shall submit to the Secretariat an Answer to the Notice of Arbitration. The Answer to the Notice of Arbitration shall be submitted in as many copies as there are other parties, together with an additional copy for each arbitrator and one copy for the Secretariat, and shall, to the extent possible, include the following:

(a) The name, address, telephone and fax numbers, and e-mail address of the Respondent and of its representative(s);

(b) Any plea that an arbitral tribunal constituted under these Rules lacks jurisdiction;

(c) The Respondent's comments on the particulars set forth in the Notice of Arbitration referred to in Article 3(3)(e);

(d) The Respondent's answer to the relief or remedy sought in the Notice of Arbitration referred to in Article 3(3)(f);

(e) The Respondent's proposal as to the number of arbitrators (i.e. one or three), the language, and the seat of the arbitration referred to in Article 3(3)(g);

(f) The Respondent's designation of one or more arbitrators if the parties' agreement so requires.

8. The Answer to the Notice of Arbitration may also include:

   (a) The Respondent's proposal for the appointment of a sole arbitrator referred to in Article 7;

   (b) The Statement of Defence referred to in Article 19.

9. Articles 3(5) and (6) are applicable to the Answer to the Notice of Arbitration.

10. Any counterclaim or set-off defence shall in principle be raised with the Answer to the Notice of Arbitration. Article 3(3) is applicable to the counterclaim or set-off defence.

11. If no counterclaim or set-off defence is raised with the Answer to the Notice of Arbitration, or if there is no indication of the amount of the counterclaim or set-off defence, the Court may rely exclusively on the Notice of Arbitration in order to determine the possible application of Article 42(2) (Expedited Procedure).

12. If the Respondent does not submit an Answer to the Notice of Arbitration, or if the Respondent raises an objection to the arbitration being administered under these Rules, the Court shall administer the case, unless there is manifestly no agreement to arbitrate referring to these Rules.

CONSOLIDATION AND JOINDER

Article 4

1. Where a Notice of Arbitration is submitted between parties already involved in other arbitral proceedings pending under these Rules, the Court may decide, after consulting with the parties and any confirmed arbitrator in all proceedings, that

the new case shall be consolidated with the pending arbitral proceedings. The Court may proceed in the same way where a Notice of Arbitration is submitted between parties that are not identical to the parties in the pending arbitral proceedings. When rendering its decision, the Court shall take into account all relevant circumstances, including the links between the cases and the progress already made in the pending arbitral proceedings. Where the Court decides to consolidate the new case with the pending arbitral proceedings, the parties to all proceedings shall be deemed to have waived their right to designate an arbitrator, and the Court may revoke the appointment and confirmation of arbitrators and apply the provisions of Section II (Composition of the Arbitral Tribunal).

2. Where one or more third persons request to participate in arbitral proceedings already pending under these Rules or where a party to pending arbitral proceedings under these Rules requests that one or more third persons participate in the arbitration, the arbitral tribunal shall decide on such request, after consulting with all of the parties, including the person or persons to be joined, taking into account all relevant circum- stances.

SECTION II. COMPOSITION OF THE ARBITRAL TRIBUNAL

CONFIRMATION OF ARBITRATORS

Article 5

1. All designations of an arbitrator made by the parties or the arbitrators are subject to confirmation by the Court, upon which the appointments shall become effective. The Court has no obligation to give reasons when it does not confirm an arbitrator.
2. Where a designation is not confirmed, the Court may either:
   (a) invite the party or parties concerned, or, as the case may be, the arbitrators, to make a new designation within a reasonable time-limit; or
   (b) in exceptional circumstances, proceed directly with the appointment.

3. In the event of any failure in the constitution of the arbitral tribunal under these Rules, the Court shall have all powers to address such failure and may, in particular, revoke any appointment made, appoint or reappoint any of the arbitrators and designate one of them as the presiding arbitrator.
4. If, before the arbitral tribunal is constituted, the parties agree on a settlement of the dispute, or the continuation of the arbitral proceedings becomes unnecessary or impossible for other reasons, the Secretariat shall give advance notice to the parties that the Court may terminate the proceedings. Any party may request that the Court proceed with the constitution of the arbitral tribunal in accordance with these Rules in order that the arbitral tribunal determine and apportion the costs not agreed upon by the parties.
5. Once the Registration Fee and any Provisional Deposit have been paid in accordance with Appendix B (Schedule of Costs) and all arbitrators have been confirmed, the Secretariat shall transmit the file to the arbitral tribunal without delay.

NUMBER OF ARBITRATORS

Article 6

1. If the parties have not agreed upon the number of arbitrators, the Court shall decide whether the case shall be referred to a sole arbitrator or to a three-member arbitral tribunal, taking into account all relevant circumstances.
2. As a rule, the Court shall refer the case to a sole arbitrator, unless the complexity of the subject matter and/or the amount in dispute justify that the case be referred to a three-member arbitral tribunal.
3. If the arbitration agreement provides for an arbitral tribunal composed of more than one arbitrator, and this appears inappropriate in view of the amount in dispute or of other circumstances, the Court shall invite the parties to agree to refer the case to a sole arbitrator.
4. Where the amount in dispute does not exceed CHF 1,000,000 (one million Swiss francs), Article 42(2) (Expedited Procedure) shall apply.

APPOINTMENT OF A SOLE ARBITRATOR

Article 7

1. Where the parties have agreed that the dispute shall be referred to a sole arbitrator, they shall jointly designate the sole arbitrator within thirty days from the date on which the Notice of Arbitration was received by the Respondent(s), unless the par- ties' agreement provides otherwise.
2. Where the parties have not agreed upon the number of arbitrators, they shall jointly designate the sole arbitrator within thirty days from the date of receipt of the Court's decision that the dispute shall be referred to a sole arbitrator.
3. If the parties fail to designate the sole arbitrator within the applicable time-limit, the Court shall proceed with the appointment.

APPOINTMENT OF ARBITRATORS IN BI-PARTY OR MULTI-PARTY PROCEEDINGS

Article 8

1. Where a dispute between two parties is referred to a three-member arbitral tribunal, each party shall designate one arbitrator, unless the parties have agreed otherwise.
2. If a party fails to designate an arbitrator within the time-limit set by the Court or resulting from the arbitration agreement, the Court shall appoint the arbitrator. Unless the parties' agreement provides otherwise, the two arbitrators so appointed shall designate, within thirty days from the confirmation of the second arbitrator, a third arbitrator who shall act as the pre- siding arbitrator of the arbitral tribunal. Failing such designation, the Court shall appoint the presiding arbitrator.
3. In multi-party proceedings, the arbitral tribunal shall be constituted in accordance with the parties' agreement.
4. If the parties have not agreed upon a procedure for the constitution of the arbitral tribunal in multi-party proceedings, the Court shall set an initial thirty-day time-limit for the Claimant or group of Claimants to designate an arbitrator, and set a sub- sequent thirty-day time-limit for the

Respondent or group of Respondents to designate an arbitrator. If the party or group(s) of parties have each designated an arbitrator, Article 8(2) shall apply to the designation of the presiding arbitrator.

5. Where a party or group of parties fails to designate an arbitrator in multi-party proceedings, the Court may appoint all of the arbitrators, and shall specify the presiding arbitrator.

INDEPENDENCE AND CHALLENGE OF ARBITRATORS

Article 9

1. Any arbitrator conducting an arbitration under these Rules shall be and shall remain at all times impartial and independent of the parties.
2. Prospective arbitrators shall disclose to those who approach them in connection with a possible appointment any circumstances likely to give rise to justifiable doubts as to their impartiality or independence. An arbitrator, once designated or appointed, shall disclose such circumstances to the parties, unless they have already been so informed.

Article 10

1. Any arbitrator may be challenged if circumstances exist that give rise to justifiable doubts as to the arbitrator's impartiality or independence.
2. A party may challenge the arbitrator designated by it only for reasons of which it becomes aware after the appointment has been made.

Article 11

1. A party intending to challenge an arbitrator shall send a notice of challenge to the Secretariat within 15 days after the circumstances giving rise to the challenge became known to that party.
2. If, within 15 days from the date of the notice of challenge, all of the parties do not agree to the challenge, or the challenged arbitrator does not withdraw, the Court shall decide on the challenge.

3. The decision of the Court is final and the Court has no obligation to give reasons.

REMOVAL OF AN ARBITRATOR

Article 12

1. If an arbitrator fails to perform his or her functions despite a written warning from the other arbitrators or from the Court, the Court may revoke the appointment of that arbitrator.
2. The arbitrator shall first have an opportunity to present his or her position to the Court. The decision of the Court is final and the Court has no obligation to give reasons.

REPLACEMENT OF AN ARBITRATOR

Article 13

1. Subject to Article 13(2), in all instances in which an arbitrator has to be replaced, a replacement arbitrator shall be designated or appointed pursuant to the procedure provided for in Articles 7 and 8 within the time-limit set by the Court. Such procedure shall apply even if a party or the arbitrators had failed to make the required designation during the initial appointment process.
2. In exceptional circumstances, the Court may, after consulting with the parties and any remaining arbitrators:
   (a) directly appoint the replacement arbitrator; or
   (b) after the closure of the proceedings, authorise the remaining arbitrator(s) to proceed with the arbitration and make any decision or award.

Article 14

If an arbitrator is replaced, the proceedings shall, as a rule, resume at the stage reached when the arbitrator who was replaced ceased to perform his or her functions, unless the arbitral tribunal decides otherwise.

SECTION III. ARBITRAL PROCEEDINGS

GENERAL PROVISIONS

Article 15

1. Subject to these Rules, the arbitral tribunal may conduct the arbitration in such manner as it considers appropriate, provided that it ensures equal treatment of the parties and their right to be heard.
2. At any stage of the proceedings, the arbitral tribunal may hold hearings for the presentation of evidence by witnesses, including expert witnesses, or for oral argument. After consulting with the parties, the arbitral tribunal may also decide to conduct the proceedings on the basis of documents and other materials.
3. At an early stage of the arbitral proceedings, and in consultation with the parties, the arbitral tribunal shall prepare a provisional timetable for the arbitral proceedings, which shall be provided to the parties and, for information, to the Secretariat.
4. All documents or information provided to the arbitral tribunal by one party shall at the same time be communicated by that party to the other parties.
5. The arbitral tribunal may, after consulting with the parties, appoint a secretary. Articles 9 to 11 shall apply to the secretary.
6. The parties may be represented or assisted by persons of their choice.
7. All participants in the arbitral proceedings shall act in good faith, and make every effort to contribute to the efficient conduct of the proceedings and to avoid unnecessary costs and delays. The parties undertake to comply with any award or order made by the arbitral tribunal or emergency arbitrator without delay.
8. With the agreement of each of the parties, the arbitral tribunal may take steps to facilitate the settlement of the dispute before it. Any such agreement by a party shall constitute a waiver of its right to challenge an arbitrator's impartiality based on the arbitrator's participation and knowledge acquired in taking the agreed steps.

SEAT OF THE ARBITRATION

Article 16

1. If the parties have not determined the seat of the arbitration, or if the designation of the seat is unclear or incomplete, the Court shall determine the seat of the arbitration, taking into account all relevant circumstances, or shall request the arbitral tribunal to determine it.
2. Without prejudice to the determination of the seat of the arbitration, the arbitral tribunal may decide where the proceedings shall be conducted. In particular, it may hear witnesses and hold meetings for consultation among its members at any place it deems appropriate, having regard to the circumstances of the arbitration.
3. The arbitral tribunal may meet at any place it deems appropriate for the inspection of goods, other property, or documents. The parties shall be given sufficient notice to enable them to be present at such an inspection.
4. The award shall be deemed to be made at the seat of the arbitration.

LANGUAGE

Article 17

1. Subject to an agreement of the parties, the arbitral tribunal shall, promptly after its appointment, determine the language or languages to be used in the proceedings. This determination shall apply to the Statement of Claim, the Statement of Defence, any further written statements, and to any oral hearings.
2. The arbitral tribunal may order that any documents annexed to the Statement of Claim or Statement of Defence, and any supplementary documents or exhibits submitted in the course of the proceedings in a language other than the language or languages agreed upon by the parties or determined by the arbitral tribunal shall be accompanied by a translation into such language or languages.

STATEMENT OF CLAIM

Article 18

1. Within a period of time to be determined by the arbitral tribunal, and unless the Statement of Claim was contained in the Notice of Arbitration, the Claimant shall communicate its Statement of Claim in writing to the Respondent and to each of the arbitrators. A copy of the contract, and, if it is not contained in the contract, of the arbitration agreement, shall be annexed to the Statement of Claim.
2. The Statement of Claim shall include the following particulars:
   (a) The names and addresses of the parties;
   (b) A statement of the facts supporting the claim;
   (c) The points at issue;
   (d) The relief or remedy sought.
3. As a rule, the Claimant shall annex to its Statement of Claim all documents and other evidence on which it relies.

STATEMENT OF DEFENCE

Article 19

1. Within a period of time to be determined by the arbitral tribunal, and unless the Statement of Defence was contained in the Answer to the Notice of Arbitration, the Respondent shall communicate its Statement of Defence in writing to the Claimant and to each of the arbitrators.
2. The Statement of Defence shall reply to the particulars of the Statement of Claim set out in Articles 18(2)(b) to (d). If the Respondent raises an objection to the jurisdiction or to the proper constitution of the arbitral tribunal, the Statement of Defence shall contain the factual and legal basis of such objection. As a rule, the Respondent shall annex to its Statement of Defence all documents and other evidence on which it relies.
3. Articles 18(2)(b) to (d) shall apply to a counterclaim and a claim relied on for the purpose of a set-off.

AMENDMENTS TO THE CLAIM OR DEFENCE

Article 20

1. During the course of the arbitral proceedings, a party may amend or supplement its claim or defence, unless the arbitral tribunal considers it inappropriate to allow such amendment having regard to the delay in making it, the prejudice to the other parties, or any other circumstances. However, a claim may not be amended in such a manner that the amended claim falls outside the scope of the arbitration clause or separate arbitration agreement.
2. The arbitral tribunal may adjust the costs of the arbitration if a party amends or supplements its claims, counterclaims, or defences.

OBJECTIONS TO THE JURISDICTION OF THE ARBITRAL TRIBUNAL

Article 21

1. The arbitral tribunal shall have the power to rule on any objections to its jurisdiction, including any objection with respect to the existence or validity of the arbitration clause or of the separate arbitration agreement.
2. The arbitral tribunal shall have the power to determine the existence or the validity of the contract of which an arbitration clause forms part. For the purposes of Article 21, an arbitration clause which forms part of a contract and which provides for arbitration under these Rules shall be treated as an agreement independent of the other terms of the contract. A decision by the arbitral tribunal that the contract is null and void shall not entail *ipso jure* the invalidity of the arbitration clause.
3. As a rule, any objection to the jurisdiction of the arbitral tribunal shall be raised in the Answer to the Notice of Arbitration, and in no event later than in the Statement of Defence referred to in Article 19, or, with respect to a counterclaim, in the reply to the counterclaim.
4. In general, the arbitral tribunal should rule on any objection to its jurisdiction as a preliminary question. However, the

arbitral tribunal may proceed with the arbitration and rule on such an objection in an award on the merits.

5. The arbitral tribunal shall have jurisdiction to hear a set-off defence even if the relationship out of which the defence is said to arise is not within the scope of the arbitration clause, or falls within the scope of another arbitration agreement or forum-selection clause.

FURTHER WRITTEN STATEMENTS

Article 22

The arbitral tribunal shall decide which further written statements, in addition to the Statement of Claim and the Statement of Defence, shall be required from the parties or may be presented by them and shall set the periods of time for communicating such statements.

PERIODS OF TIME

Article 23

The periods of time set by the arbitral tribunal for the communication of written statements (including the Statement of Claim and Statement of Defence) should not exceed forty-five days. However, the arbitral tribunal may extend the time-limits if it considers that an extension is justified.

EVIDENCE AND HEARINGS

Article 24

1. Each party shall have the burden of proving the facts relied on to support its claim or defence.
2. The arbitral tribunal shall determine the admissibility, relevance, materiality, and weight of the evidence.
3. At any time during the arbitral proceedings, the arbitral tribunal may require the parties to produce documents, exhibits, or other evidence within a period of time determined by the arbitral tribunal.

Article 25

1. The arbitral tribunal shall give the parties adequate advance notice of the date, time, and place of any oral hearing.
2. Any person may be a witness or an expert witness in the arbitration. It is not improper for a party, its officers, employees, legal advisors, or counsel to interview witnesses, potential witnesses, or expert witnesses.
3. Prior to a hearing and within a period of time determined by the arbitral tribunal, the evidence of witnesses and expert witnesses may be presented in the form of written statements or reports signed by them.
4. At the hearing, witnesses and expert witnesses may be heard and examined in the manner set by the arbitral tribunal. The arbitral tribunal may direct that witnesses or expert witnesses be examined through means that do not require their physical presence at the hearing (including by videoconference).
5. Arrangements shall be made for the translation of oral statements made at a hearing and for a record of the hearing to be provided if this is deemed necessary by the arbitral tribunal having regard to the circumstances of the case, or if the parties so agree.
6. Hearings shall be held *in camera* unless the parties agree otherwise. The arbitral tribunal may order witnesses or expert witnesses to retire during the testimony of other witnesses or expert witnesses.

INTERIM MEASURES OF PROTECTION

Article 26

1. At the request of a party, the arbitral tribunal may grant any interim measures it deems necessary or appropriate. Upon the application of any party or, in exceptional circumstances and with prior notice to the parties, on its own initiative, the arbitral tribunal may also modify, suspend or terminate any interim measures granted.
2. Interim measures may be granted in the form of an interim award. The arbitral tribunal shall be entitled to order the provision of appropriate security.

3. In exceptional circumstances, the arbitral tribunal may rule on a request for interim measures by way of a preliminary order before the request has been communicated to any other party, provided that such communication is made at the latest together with the preliminary order and that the other parties are immediately granted an opportunity to be heard.
4. The arbitral tribunal may rule on claims for compensation for any damage caused by an unjustified interim measure or preliminary order.
5. By submitting their dispute to arbitration under these Rules, the parties do not waive any right that they may have under the applicable laws to submit a request for interim measures to a judicial authority. A request for interim measures addressed by any party to a judicial authority shall not be deemed to be incompatible with the agreement to arbitrate, or to constitute a waiver of that agreement.
6. The arbitral tribunal shall have discretion to apportion the costs relating to a request for interim measures in an interim award or in the final award.

TRIBUNAL-APPOINTED EXPERTS

Article 27

1. The arbitral tribunal, after consulting with the parties, may appoint one or more experts to report to it, in writing, on specific issues to be determined by the arbitral tribunal. A copy of the expert's terms of reference, established by the arbitral tribunal, shall be communicated to the parties.
2. The parties shall give the expert any relevant information or produce for the expert's inspection any relevant documents or goods that the expert may require of them. Any dispute between a party and the expert as to the relevance of the required information, documents or goods shall be referred to the arbitral tribunal.
3. Upon receipt of the expert's report, the arbitral tribunal shall communicate a copy of the report to the parties, which shall be given the opportunity to express, in writing, their opinion on the report. A party shall be entitled to examine any document on which the expert has relied in the report.

4. At the request of any party, the expert, after delivery of the report, may be heard at a hearing during which the parties shall have the opportunity to be present and to examine the expert. At this hearing, any party may present expert witnesses in order to testify on the points at issue. Article 25 shall be applicable to such proceedings.
5. Articles 9 to 11 shall apply to any expert appointed by the arbitral tribunal.

DEFAULT

Article 28

1. If, within the period of time set by the arbitral tribunal, the Claimant has failed to communicate its claim without showing sufficient cause for such failure, the arbitral tribunal shall issue an order for the termination of the arbitral proceedings. If, within the period of time set by the arbitral tribunal, the Respondent has failed to communicate its Statement of Defence without showing sufficient cause for such failure, the arbitral tribunal shall order that the proceedings continue.
2. If one of the parties, duly notified under these Rules, fails to appear at a hearing, without showing sufficient cause for such failure, the arbitral tribunal may proceed with the arbitration.
3. If one of the parties, duly invited to produce documentary or other evidence, fails to do so within the period of time determined by the arbitral tribunal, without showing sufficient cause for such failure, the arbitral tribunal may make the award on the evidence before it.

CLOSURE OF PROCEEDINGS

Article 29

1. When it is satisfied that the parties have had a reasonable opportunity to present their respective cases on matters to be decided in an award, the arbitral tribunal may declare the proceedings closed with regard to such matters.
2. The arbitral tribunal may, if it considers it necessary owing to exceptional circumstances, decide, on its own initiative or upon the application of a party, to reopen the proceedings on

the matters with regard to which the proceedings were closed pursuant to Article 29(1) at any time before the award on such matters is made.

WAIVER OF RULES

Article 30

If a party knows that any provision of, or requirement under, these Rules or any other applicable procedural rule has not been complied with and yet proceeds with the arbitration without promptly stating its objection to such non-compliance, it shall be deemed to have waived its right to raise an objection.

SECTION IV. THE AWARD

DECISIONS

Article 31

1. If the arbitral tribunal is composed of more than one arbitrator, any award or other decision of the arbitral tribunal shall be made by a majority of the arbitrators. If there is no majority, the award shall be made by the presiding arbitrator alone.
2. If authorized by the arbitral tribunal, the presiding arbitrator may decide on questions of procedure, subject to revision by the arbitral tribunal.

FORM AND EFFECT OF THE AWARD

Article 32

1. In addition to making a final award, the arbitral tribunal may make interim, interlocutory, or partial awards. If appropriate, the arbitral tribunal may also award costs in awards that are not final.
2. The award shall be made in writing and shall be final and binding on the parties.
3. The arbitral tribunal shall state the reasons upon which the award is based, unless the parties have agreed that no reasons are to be given.

4. An award shall be signed by the arbitrators and it shall specify the seat of the arbitration and the date on which the award was made. Where the arbitral tribunal is composed of more than one arbitrator and any of them fails to sign, the award shall state the reason for the absence of the signature.
5. The publication of the award is governed by Article 44.
6. Originals of the award signed by the arbitrators shall be communicated by the arbitral tribunal to the parties and to the Secretariat. The Secretariat shall retain a copy of the award.

APPLICABLE LAW, AMIABLE COMPOSITEUR

Article 33

1. The arbitral tribunal shall decide the case in accordance with the rules of law agreed upon by the parties or, in the absence of a choice of law, by applying the rules of law with which the dispute has the closest connection.
2. The arbitral tribunal shall decide as *amiable compositeur* or *ex aequo et bono* only if the parties have expressly authorised the arbitral tribunal to do so.
3. In all cases, the arbitral tribunal shall decide in accordance with the terms of the contract and shall take into account the trade usages applicable to the transaction.

SETTLEMENT OR OTHER GROUNDS FOR TERMINATION

Article 34

1. If, before the award is made, the parties agree on a settlement of the dispute, the arbitral tribunal shall either issue an order for the termination of the arbitral proceedings or, if requested by the parties and accepted by the arbitral tribunal, record the settlement in the form of an arbitral award on agreed terms. The arbitral tribunal is not obliged to give reasons for such an award.
2. If, before the award is made, the continuation of the arbitral proceedings becomes unnecessary or impossible for any reason not mentioned in Article 34(1), the arbitral tribunal shall give advance notice to the parties that it may issue an

order for the termination of the proceedings. The arbitral tribunal shall have the power to issue such an order, unless a party raises justifiable grounds for objection.

3. Copies of the order for termination of the arbitral proceedings or of the arbitral award on agreed terms, signed by the arbitrators, shall be communicated by the arbitral tribunal to the par- ties and to the Secretariat. Where an arbitral award on agreed terms is made, Articles 32(2) and (4) to (6) shall apply.

INTERPRETATION OF THE AWARD

Article 35

1. Within thirty days after the receipt of the award, a party, with notice to the Secretariat and to the other parties, may request that the arbitral tribunal give an interpretation of the award. The arbitral tribunal may set a time-limit, as a rule not exceeding thirty days, for the other parties to comment on the request.
2. The interpretation shall be given in writing within forty-five days after the receipt of the request. The Court may extend this time limit. The interpretation shall form part of the award and Articles 32(2) to (6) shall apply.

CORRECTION OF THE AWARD

Article 36

1. Within thirty days after the receipt of the award, a party, with notice to the Secretariat and to the other parties, may request the arbitral tribunal to correct in the award any errors in computation, any clerical or typographical errors, or any errors of similar nature. The arbitral tribunal may set a time-limit, as a rule not exceeding thirty days, for the other parties to comment on the request.
2. The arbitral tribunal may within thirty days after the communication of the award make such corrections on its own initiative.
3. Such corrections shall be in writing, and Articles 32(2) to (6) shall apply.

ADDITIONAL AWARD

Article 37

1. Within thirty days after the receipt of the award, a party, with notice to the Secretariat and the other parties, may request the arbitral tribunal to make an additional award as to claims presented in the arbitral proceedings but omitted from the award. The arbitral tribunal may set a time-limit, as a rule not exceeding thirty days, for the other parties to comment on the request.
2. If the arbitral tribunal considers the request for an additional award to be justified and considers that the omission can be rectified without any further hearings or evidence, it shall complete its award within sixty days after the receipt of the request. The Court may extend this time-limit.
3. Articles 32(2) to (6) shall apply to any additional award.

COSTS

Article 38

The award shall contain a determination of the costs of the arbitration. The term "costs" includes only:

(a) The fees of the arbitral tribunal, to be stated separately as to each arbitrator and any secretary, and to be determined by the arbitral tribunal itself in accordance with Articles 39 and 40(3) to (5);

(b) The travel and other expenses incurred by the arbitral tribunal and any secretary;

(c) The costs of expert advice and of other assistance required by the arbitral tribunal;

(d) The travel and other expenses of witnesses, to the extent such expenses are approved by the arbitral tribunal;

(e) The costs for legal representation and assistance, if such costs were claimed during the arbitral proceedings, and only to the extent that the arbitral tribunal determines that the amount of such costs is reasonable;

(f) The Registration Fee and the Administrative Costs in accordance with Appendix B (Schedule of Costs);

(g) The Registration Fee, the fees and expenses of any emergency arbitrator, and the costs of expert advice and of other assistance required by such emergency arbitrator, determined in accordance with Article 43(9).

Article 39

1. The fees and expenses of the arbitral tribunal shall be reasonable in amount, taking into account the amount in dispute, the complexity of the subject-matter of the arbitration, the time spent and any other relevant circumstances of the case, including the discontinuation of the arbitral proceedings in case of settlement. In the event of a discontinuation of the arbitral proceedings, the fees of the arbitral tribunal may be less than the minimum amount resulting from Appendix B (Schedule of Costs).
2. The fees and expenses of the arbitral tribunal shall be determined in accordance with Appendix B (Schedule of Costs).
3. The arbitral tribunal shall decide on the allocation of its fees among its members. As a rule, the presiding arbitrator shall receive between 40% and 50% and each co-arbitrator between 25% and 30% of the total fees, in view of the time and efforts spent by each arbitrator.

Article 40

1. Except as provided in Article 40(2), the costs of the arbitration shall in principle be borne by the unsuccessful party. However, the arbitral tribunal may apportion any of the costs of the arbitration among the parties if it determines that such apportionment is reasonable, taking into account the circumstances of the case.
2. With respect to the costs of legal representation and assistance referred to in Article 38(e), the arbitral tribunal, taking into account the circumstances of the case, shall be free to deter mine which party shall bear such costs or may apportion such costs among the parties if it determines that an apportionment is reasonable.
3. If the arbitral tribunal issues an order for the termination of the arbitral proceedings or makes an award on agreed terms,

it shall determine the costs of the arbitration referred to in Articles 38 and 39 in the order or award.

4. Before rendering an award, termination order, or decision on a request under Articles 35 to 37, the arbitral tribunal shall submit to the Secretariat a draft thereof for approval or adjustment by the Court of the determination on costs made pursuant to Articles 38(a) to (c) and (f) and Article 39. Any such approval or adjustment shall be binding upon the arbitral tribunal.

5. No additional costs may be charged by an arbitral tribunal for interpretation, correction, or completion of its award under Articles 35 to 37, unless they are justified by the circumstances.

DEPOSIT OF COSTS

Article 41

1. The arbitral tribunal, once constituted, and after consulting with the Court, shall request each party to deposit an equal amount as an advance for the costs referred to in Articles 38(a) to (c) and the Administrative Costs referred to in Article 38(f). Any Provisional Deposit paid by a party in accordance with Appendix B (Schedule of Costs) shall be considered as a partial payment of its deposit. The arbitral tribunal shall provide a copy of such request to the Secretariat.

2. Where a Respondent submits a counterclaim, or it otherwise appears appropriate in the circumstances, the arbitral tribunal may in its discretion establish separate deposits.

3. During the course of the arbitral proceedings, the arbitral tribunal may, after consulting with the Court, request supplementary deposits from the parties. The arbitral tribunal shall provide a copy of any such request to the Secretariat.

4. If the required deposits are not paid in full within fifteen days after the receipt of the request, the arbitral tribunal shall notify the parties in order that one or more of them may make the required payment. If such payment is not made, the arbitral tribunal may order the suspension or termination of the arbitral proceedings.

5. In its final award, the arbitral tribunal shall issue to the parties a statement of account of the deposits received. Any unused amount shall be returned to the parties.

SECTION V. OTHER PROVISIONS

EXPEDITED PROCEDURE

Article 42

1. If the parties so agree, or if Article 42(2) is applicable, the arbitral proceedings shall be conducted in accordance with an Expedited Procedure based upon the foregoing provisions of these Rules, subject to the following changes:

   (a) The file shall be transmitted to the arbitral tribunal only upon payment of the Provisional Deposit as required by Section 1.4 of Appendix B (Schedule of Costs);

   (b) After the submission of the Answer to the Notice of Arbitration, the parties shall, as a rule, be entitled to submit only a Statement of Claim, a Statement of Defence (and counterclaim) and, where applicable, a Statement of Defence in reply to the counterclaim;

   (c) Unless the parties agree that the dispute shall be decided on the basis of documentary evidence only, the arbitral tribunal shall hold a single hearing for the examination of the witnesses and expert witnesses, as well as for oral argument;

   (d) The award shall be made within six months from the date on which the Secretariat transmitted the file to the arbitral tribunal. In exceptional circumstances, the Court may extend this time-limit;

   (e) The arbitral tribunal shall state the reasons upon which the award is based in summary form, unless the parties have agreed that no reasons are to be given.

2. The following provisions shall apply to all cases in which the amount in dispute, representing the aggregate of the claim and the counterclaim (or any set-off defence), does not exceed CHF 1,000,000 (one million Swiss francs), unless the Court decides otherwise, taking into account all relevant circum- stances:

   (a) The arbitral proceedings shall be conducted in accordance with the Expedited Procedure set forth in Article 42(1);

   (b) The case shall be referred to a sole arbitrator, unless the arbitration agreement provides for more than one arbitrator;

(c) If the arbitration agreement provides for an arbitral tribunal composed of more than one arbitrator, the Secretariat shall invite the parties to agree to refer the case to a sole arbitrator. If the parties do not agree to refer the case to a sole arbitrator, the fees of the arbitrators shall be determined in accordance with Appendix B (Schedule of Costs), but shall in no event be less than the fees resulting from the hourly rate set out in Section 2.8 of Appendix B.

EMERGENCY RELIEF

Article 43

1. Unless the parties have agreed otherwise, a party requiring urgent interim measures pursuant to Article 26 before the arbitral tribunal is constituted may submit to the Secretariat an application for emergency relief proceedings (hereinafter the "Application"). In addition to the particulars set out in Articles 3(3)(b) to (e), the Application shall include:

   (a) A statement of the interim measure(s) sought and the reasons therefore, in particular the reason for the purported urgency;

   (b) Comments on the language, the seat of arbitration, and the applicable law;

   (c) Confirmation of payment by check or transfer to the relevant account listed in Appendix A of the Registration Fee and of the deposit for emergency relief proceedings as required by Section 1.6 of Appendix B (Schedule of Costs).

2. As soon as possible after receipt of the Application, the Registration Fee, and the deposit for emergency relief proceedings, the Court shall appoint and transmit the file to a sole emergency arbitrator, unless

   (a) there is manifestly no agreement to arbitrate referring to these Rules, or

   (b) it appears more appropriate to proceed with the constitution of the arbitral tribunal and refer the Application to it.

3. If the Application is submitted before the Notice of Arbitration, the Court shall terminate the emergency relief

proceedings if the Notice of Arbitration is not submitted within ten days from the receipt of the Application. In exceptional circumstances, the Court may extend this time-limit.

4. Articles 9 to 12 shall apply to the emergency arbitrator, except that the time-limits set out in Articles 11(1) and (2) are shortened to three days.
5. If the parties have not determined the seat of the arbitration, or if the designation of the seat is unclear or incomplete, the seat of the arbitration for the emergency relief proceedings shall be determined by the Court without prejudice to the determination of the seat of the arbitration pursuant to Article 16(1).
6. The emergency arbitrator may conduct the emergency relief proceedings in such a manner as the emergency arbitrator considers appropriate, taking into account the urgency inherent in such proceedings and ensuring that each party has a reasonable opportunity to be heard on the Application.
7. The decision on the Application shall be made within fifteen days from the date on which the Secretariat transmitted the file to the emergency arbitrator. This period of time may be extended by agreement of the parties or, in appropriate circumstances, by the Court. The decision on the Application may be made even if in the meantime the file has been transmitted to the arbitral tribunal.
8. A decision of the emergency arbitrator shall have the same effects as a decision pursuant to Article 26. Any interim measure granted by the emergency arbitrator may be modified, suspended or terminated by the emergency arbitrator or, after transmission of the file to it, by the arbitral tribunal.
9. The decision on the Application shall include a determination of costs as referred to in Article 38(g). Before rendering the decision on the Application, the emergency arbitrator shall submit to the Secretariat a draft thereof for approval or adjustment by the Court of the determination of costs. The costs shall be payable out of the deposit for emergency relief proceedings. The determination of costs pursuant to Articles 38(d) and (e) and the apportionment of all costs among the parties shall be decided by the arbitral tribunal. If no arbitral tribunal is constituted, the determination of costs pursuant to

Articles 38(d) and (e) and the apportionment of all costs shall be decided by the emergency arbitrator in a separate award.

10. Any measure granted by the emergency arbitrator ceases to be binding on the parties either upon the termination of the emergency relief proceedings pursuant to Article 43(3), upon the termination of the arbitral proceedings, or upon the rendering of a final award, unless the arbitral tribunal expressly decides otherwise in the final award.

11. The emergency arbitrator may not serve as arbitrator in any arbitration relating to the dispute in respect of which the emergency arbitrator has acted, unless otherwise agreed by the parties.

CONFIDENTIALITY

Article 44

1. Unless the parties expressly agree in writing to the contrary, the parties undertake to keep confidential all awards and orders as well as all materials submitted by another party in the framework of the arbitral proceedings not already in the public domain, except and to the extent that a disclosure may be required of a party by a legal duty, to protect or pursue a legal right, or to enforce or challenge an award in legal proceedings before a judicial authority. This undertaking also applies to the arbitrators, the tribunal-appointed experts, the secretary of the arbitral tribunal, the members of the board of directors of the Swiss Chambers' Arbitration Institution, the members of the Court and the Secretariat, and the staff of the individual Chambers.

2. The deliberations of the arbitral tribunal are confidential.

3. An award or order may be published, whether in its entirety or in the form of excerpts or a summary, only under the following conditions:

   (a) A request for publication is addressed to the Secretariat;

   (b) All references to the parties' names are deleted; and

   (c) No party objects to such publication within the time-limit fixed for that purpose by the Secretariat.

EXCLUSION OF LIABILITY

Article 45

1. Neither the members of the board of directors of the Swiss Chambers' Arbitration Institution, the members of the Court and the Secretariat, the individual Chambers or their staff, the arbitrators, the tribunal-appointed experts, nor the secretary of the arbitral tribunal shall be liable for any act or omission in connection with an arbitration conducted under these Rules, except if the act or omission is shown to constitute intentional wrongdoing or gross negligence.
2. After the award or termination order has been made and the possibilities of correction, interpretation and additional awards referred to in Articles 35 to 37 have lapsed or have been exhausted, neither the members of the board of the Swiss Chambers' Arbitration Institution, the members of the Court and the Secretariat, the individual Chambers or their staff, the arbitrators, the tribunal-appointed experts, nor the secretary of the arbitral tribunal shall be under an obligation to make statements to any person about any matter concerning the arbitration. No party shall seek to make any of these persons a witness in any legal or other proceedings arising out of the arbitration.

Offices of the Secretariat of the Arbitration Court

Swiss Chambers' Arbitration Institution
Arbitration Court Secretariat
c/o Basel Chamber of Commerce
Aeschenvorstadt 67
P.O. Box
CH-4010 Basel
Telephone: +41 61 270 60 50
Fax: +41 61 270 60 05
E-mail: basel@swissarbitration.org Bank details: UBS AG, CH-4002 Basel Account No: 292-10157720.0
Clearing No: 292
Swift Code: UBSWCHZH80A Iban: CH98 0029 2292 10157720 0

c/o Chamber of Commerce and Industry of Bern
Kramgasse 2
P.O. Box 5464
CH-3001 Bern
Telephone: +41 31 388 87 87
Fax: +41 31 388 87 88
E-mail: bern@swissarbitration.org Bank details: BEKB
Account No: KK 16 166.151.0.44 HIV Kanton Bern Clearing No: 790
Swift Code: KBBECH22
Iban: CH35 0079 0016 1661 5104 4

c/o Geneva Chamber of Commerce, Industry and Services
4, Boulevard du Théâtre
P.O. Box 5039
CH-1211 Geneva 11
Telephone: +41 22 819 91 11
Fax: +41 22 819 91 36
E-mail: geneva@swissarbitration.org
Bank details: UBS SA, Rue du Rhône 8, 1204 Genève Account No: 279-HU108533.1
Clearing No: 279
Swift Code: UBSWCHZH80A Iban: CH13 0027 9279 HU1085331

c/o Neuchâtel Chamber of Commerce and Industry
4, rue de la Serre
P.O. Box 2012
CH-2001 Neuchâtel Telephone: +41 32 727 24 27

Fax: +41 32 727 24 28
E-mail: neuchatel@swissarbitration.org Bank details: BCN, Neuchâtel
Account No: C0029.20.09
Clearing No: 766
Swift Code: BCNNCH22
Iban: CH69 0076 6000 C002 9200 9

c/o Chamber of Commerce and Industry of Ticino
Corso Elvezia 16
P.O. Box 5399
CH-6901 Lugano
Telephone: +41 91 911 51 11
Fax: +41 91 911 51 12
E-mail: lugano@swissarbitration.org
Bank details: Banca della Svizzera Italiana (BSI), Via Magatti 2, CH-6901 Lugano
Account No: A201021A Clearing No: 8465 Swift Code: BSILCH22
Iban: CH64 0846 5000 0A20 1021 A

c/o Chamber of Commerce and Industry of Vaud
Avenue d'Ouchy 47
P.O. Box 315
CH-1001 Lausanne Telephone: +41 21 613 35 31
Fax: +41 21 613 35 05
E-mail: lausanne@swissarbitration.org
Bank details: Banque Cantonale Vaudoise, 1001 Lausanne Account No: CO 5284.78.17
Clearing No: 767
Swift Code: BCVLCH2LXX
Iban: CH44 0076 7000 U528 4781 7

c/o Zurich Chamber of Commerce
Selnaustrasse 32
P.O. Box 3058 CH-8022 Zurich
Telephone: +41 44 217 40 50
Fax: +41 44 217 40 51
E-mail: zurich@swissarbitration.org
Bank details: Credit Suisse, CH-8070 Zurich Account No: 497380-01
Clearing No: 4835
Swift Code: CRESCHZZ80A
Iban: CH62 0483 5049 7380 0100 0

Schedule of Costs
(effective as of 1 June 2012)

(All amounts in this Appendix B are in Swiss francs, hereinafter "CHF")

1. REGISTRATION FEE AND DEPOSITS

1.1 When submitting a Notice of Arbitration, the Claimant shall pay a non-refundable Registration Fee of

- CHF 4,500 for arbitrations where the amount in dispute does not exceed CHF 2,000,000;
- CHF 6,000 for arbitrations where the amount in dispute is between CHF 2,000,001 and CHF 10,000,000;
- CHF 8,000 for arbitrations where the amount in dispute exceeds CHF 10,000,000.

1.2 If the amount in dispute is not quantified, the Claimant shall pay a non-refundable Registration Fee of CHF 6,000.

1.3 The above provisions shall apply to any counterclaim.

1.4 Under the Expedited Procedure, upon receipt of the Notice of Arbitration, the Court shall request the Claimant to pay a Provisional Deposit of CHF 5,000.

1.5 If the Registration Fee or any Provisional Deposit is not paid, the arbitration shall not proceed with respect to the related claim(s) or counterclaim(s).

1.6 A party applying for Emergency Relief shall pay a non-refundable Registration Fee of CHF 4,500 and a deposit as an advance for the costs of the emergency relief proceedings of CHF 20,000 together with the Application. If the Registration Fee and the deposit are not paid, the Court shall not proceed with the emergency relief proceedings.

1.7 In case of a request for the correction or interpretation of the award or for an additional award made pursuant to Articles 35, 36 or 37, or where a judicial authority remits an award to the arbitral tribunal, the arbitral tribunal may request a supplementary deposit with prior approval of the Court.

2. FEES AND ADMINISTRATIVE COSTS

2.1 The fees referred to in Articles 38(a) and (g) shall cover the activities of the arbitral tribunal and the emergency arbitrator, respectively, from the moment the file is transmitted until the final award, termination order, or decision in emergency relief proceedings.

2.2 Where the amount in dispute exceeds the threshold specified in Section 6 of this Appendix B, Administrative Costs[2] shall be payable to the Swiss Chambers' Arbitration Institution, in addition to the Registration Fee.

2.3 As a rule, and except for emergency relief proceedings, the fees of the arbitral tribunal and the Administrative Costs shall be computed on the basis of the scale in Section 6 of this Appendix B, taking into account the criteria of Article 39(1). The fees of the arbitral tribunal, the deposits requested pursuant to Article 41, as well as the Administrative Costs may exceed the amounts set out in the scale only in exceptional circumstances and with prior approval of the Court.

2.4 Claims and counterclaims are added for the determination of the amount in dispute. The same rule applies to set-off defences, unless the arbitral tribunal, after consulting with the parties, concludes that such set-off defences will not require significant additional work.

2.5 Interest claims shall not be taken into account for the calculation of the amount in dispute. However, when the interest claims exceed the amount claimed as principal, the interest claims alone shall be taken into account for the calculation of the amount in dispute.

2.6 Amounts in currencies other than the Swiss franc shall be converted into Swiss francs at the rate of exchange applicable at the time the Notice of Arbitration is received by the Secretariat or at the time any new claim, counterclaim, set-off defence or amendment to a claim or defence is filed.

---

2 Chambers' Arbitration Institution, in addition to the Registration Fee. In the event of a discontinuation of the arbitral proceedings (Article 39(1)), the Swiss Chambers' Arbitration Institution may, in its discretion, decide not to charge all or part of the Administrative Costs.

2.7 If the amount in dispute is not quantified, the fees of the arbitral tribunal and the Administrative Costs shall be determined by the arbitral tribunal, taking into account all relevant circumstances.

2.8 Where the parties do not agree to refer the case to a sole arbitrator as provided for by Article 42(2) (Expedited Procedure), the fees of the arbitrators shall be determined in accordance with the scale in Section 6 of this Appendix B, but shall not be less than the fees resulting from the application of an hourly rate of CHF 350 (three hundred fifty Swiss francs) for the arbitrators.

2.9 The fees of the emergency arbitrator shall range from CHF 2,000 to CHF 20,000. They may exceed CHF 20,000 only in exceptional circumstances and with the approval of the Court.

3. EXPENSES

The expenses of the arbitral tribunal and the emergency arbitrator shall cover their reasonable disbursements for the arbitration, such as expenses for travel, accommodation, meals, and any other costs related to the conduct of the proceedings. The Court shall issue general guidelines for the accounting of such expenses.[3]

4. ADMINISTRATION OF DEPOSITS

4.1 The Secretariat or, if so requested by the Secretariat, the arbitral tribunal, is to hold the deposits to be paid by the parties in a separate bank account which is solely used for, and clearly identified as relating to, the arbitral proceedings in question.

4.2 With the approval of the Court, part of the deposits may from time to time be released to each member of the arbitral tribunal as an advance on costs, as the arbitration progresses.

5. TAXES AND CHARGES APPLICABLE TO FEES

Amounts payable to the arbitral tribunal or emergency arbitrator do not include any possible value added taxes (VAT) or other taxes or

3 The guidelines are available at www.swissarbitration.org

charges that may be applicable to the fees of a member of the arbitral tribunal or emergency arbitrator. Parties have a duty to pay any such taxes or charges. The recovery of any such taxes or charges is a matter solely between each member of the arbitral tribunal, or the emergency arbitrator, on the one hand, and the parties, on the other.

6. SCALE OF ARBITRATOR'S FEE AND ADMINISTRATIVE COSTS

6.1 Sole Arbitrator

Amount in Dispute (in Swiss francs)		**Administrative Costs**	**Sole Arbitrator**	
			Minimum	Maximum
0 –	300,000	–	4% of amount	12% of amount
300,001 –	600,000	–	12,000 + 2% of amount over 300,000	36,000 + 8% of amount over 300,000
600,001 –	1,000,000	–	18,000 + 1.5% of amount over 600,000	60,000 + 6% of amount over 600,000
1,000,001 –	2,000,000	–	24,000 + 0.6% of amount over 1,000,000	84,000 + 3.6% of amount over 1,000,000
2,000,001 –	10,000,000	4,000 + 0.2% of amount over 2,000,000	30,000 + 0.38% of amount over 2,000,000	120,000 + 1.5% of amount over 2,000,000
10,000,001 –	20,000,000	20,000 + 0.1% of amount over 10,000,000	60,400 + 0.3% of amount over 10,000,000	240,000 + 0.6% of amount over 10,000,000
20,000,001 –	50,000,000	30,000 + 0.05% of amount over 20,000,000	90,400 + 0.1% of amount over 20,000,000	300,000 + 0.2% of amount over 20,000,000
50,000,001 –	100,000,000	45,000 + 0.01% of amount over 50,000,000	120,400 + 0.06% of amount over 50,000,000	360,000 + 0.18% of amount over 50,000,000
100,000,001 –	250,000,000	50,000	150,400 + 0.02% of amount over 100,000,000	450,000 + 0.1% of amount over 100,000,000
> 250,000,000		50,000	180,400 + 0.01% of amount over 250,000,000	600,000 + 0.06% of amount over 250,000,000

6.2 Three Arbitrators[4]

Amount in dispute (in Swiss francs)		Administrative costs	Three-member arbitral tribunal	
			Minimum	Maximum
0 –	300,000	–	10% of amount	30% of amount
300,001 –	600,000	–	30,000 + 5% of amount over 300,000	90,000 + 20% of amount over 300,000
600,001 –	1,000,000	–	45,000 + 3.75% of amount over 600,000	150,000 + 15% of amount over 600,000
1,000,001 –	2,000,000	–	60,000 + 1.5% of amount over 1,000,000	210,000 + 9% of amount over 1,000,000
2,000,001 –	10,000,000	4,000 + 0.2% of amount over 2,000,000	75,000 + 0.95% of amount over 2,000,000	300,000 + 3.75% of amount over 2,000,000
10,000,001 –	20,000,000	20,000 + 0.1% of amount over 10,000,000	151,000 + 0.75% of amount over 10,000,000	600,000 + 1.5% of amount over 10,000,000
20,000,001 –	50,000,000	30,000 + 0.05% of amount over 20,000,000	226,000 + 0.25% of amount over 20,000,000	750,000 + 0.5% of amount over 20,000,000
50,000,001 –	100,000,000	45,000 + 0.01% of amount over 50,000,000	301,000 + 0.15% of amount over 50,000,000	900,000 + 0.45% of amount over 50,000,000
100,000,001 –	250,000,000	50,000	376,000 + 0.05% of amount over 100,000,000	1,125,000 + 0.25% of amount over 100,000,000
> 250,000,000		50,000	451,000 + 0.025% of amount over 250,000,000	1,500,000 + 0.15% of amount over 250,000,000

4 The fees of an arbitral tribunal consisting of more than one arbitrator represent those of a sole arbitrator plus 75 % for each additional arbitrator, i.e. 250% of the fees of a sole arbitrator for a three-member tribunal.

Appendix B:

Comparison of the 2004 and 2012 Swiss Rules of International Arbitration

Swiss Rules of International Arbitration Version 2004	**Swiss Rules of International Arbitration Revision 2012**
Swiss Rules of International Arbitration (Swiss Rules)	**Swiss Rules of International Arbitration (Swiss Rules)**
MODEL ARBITRATION CLAUSE	*MODEL ARBITRATION CLAUSE*
Any dispute, controversy or claim arising out of or in relation to this contract, including the validity, invalidity, breach or termination thereof, shall be resolved by arbitration in accordance with the Swiss Rules of International Arbitration of the Swiss Chambers of Commerce in force on the date when the Notice of Arbitration is submitted in accordance with these Rules.	Any dispute, controversy, or claim arising out of, or in relation to, this contract, including the validity, invalidity, breach, or termination thereof, shall be resolved by arbitration in accordance with the Swiss Rules of International Arbitration of the Swiss Chambers' Arbitration Institution in force on the date on which the Notice of Arbitration is submitted in accordance with these Rules.
The number of arbitrators [1]shall be ... (one or three);	The number of arbitrators[1] shall be ... ("one", "three", "one or three");
The seat of the arbitration shall be ... (name of city in Switzerland, unless the parties agree on a city abroad);	The seat of the arbitration shall be ... (name of city in Switzerland, unless the parties agree on a city in another country);
The arbitral proceedings shall be conducted in ..... (insert desired language).	The arbitral proceedings shall be conducted in ..... (insert desired language).

[1] For the sake of convenience only the masculine form is used within these Rules.

Swiss Rules of International Arbitration Version 2004	**Swiss Rules of International Arbitration Revision 2012**
INTRODUCTION	*INTRODUCTION*
*(a)*In the past, six Chambers of Commerce and Industry in Switzerland had their own different rules of arbitration for the resolution of international commercial disputes. *(b)* In order to promote institutional arbitration in Switzerland and to harmonise the existing rules of arbitration, the Chambers of Commerce and Industry of Basel, Bern, Geneva, Ticino, Vaud and Zurich, joined by Neuchâtel in 2008, (hereinafter collectively "the Chambers") have adopted the present uniform rules, the Swiss Rules of International Arbitration (hereinafter the "Rules"), which replace the Chambers' former rules of international arbitration. These Rules are based on the UNCITRAL Arbitration Rules, to which two types of changes and additions have been made: i. Changes and additions required to adapt the UNCITRAL Arbitration Rules to institutional arbitration; ii. Changes and additions reflecting modern practice and comparative law in the field of international arbitration. These changes and additions have been deliberately kept to a minimum. A comparative version of these Rules, in which the modifications to the UNCITRAL Arbitration Rules are	a) In order to harmonise their rules of arbitration the Chambers of Commerce and Industry of Basel, Bern, Geneva, Neuchâtel, Ticino, Vaud and Zurich in 2004 replaced their former rules by the Swiss Rules of International Arbitration (hereinafter the "Swiss Rules" or the "Rules"). ~~(b) The Swiss Rules are based on the UNCITRAL Arbitration Rules (Version 1976), to which two three types of changes and additions have been made[2]:~~ ~~i. Changes and additions required to adapt the UNCITRAL Arbitration Rules to institutional arbitration while keeping the special features of the Swiss Rules recognized by modern arbitration practice;~~ ~~ii. Changes and additions increasing the efficient and cost-effective resolution of the dispute;~~ ~~iii. Changes and additions in order to use these Rules for domestic arbitration in Switzerland as well.~~ b) For the purpose of providing arbitration services, the Chambers founded the Swiss Chambers' Arbitration Institution ~~as an arbitral institution~~. In order to administer arbitrations under the Swiss Rules, the Swiss Chambers' Arbitration Institution has established the Arbitration Court (hereinafter the "Court"), which is comprised of experienced international arbitration practitioners. The Court shall render decisions as provided for under these Rules. It

[2] ~~A comparative version of these Rules, in which the modifications to the UNCITRAL Arbitration Rules are italicised, is available on the website www.swissarbitration.org~~.

Swiss Rules of International Arbitration Version 2004	**Swiss Rules of International Arbitration Revision 2012**
italicised, is available on the website of the Chambers: www.sccam.org. *(c)* When a Notice of Arbitration is submitted to one of the Chambers listed in Appendix A, an arbitral tribunal shall be constituted in accordance with these Rules. *(d)* In order to ensure the administration of arbitrations under these Rules, the Chambers have appointed an Arbitration Committee (hereinafter the "Arbitration Committee"), which shall exercise the powers vested in the Chambers under these Rules, so that any reference to the Chambers in these Rules shall be deemed to refer to the Arbitration Committee. *(e)* The Arbitration Committee is comprised of experienced practitioners of international arbitration. The Arbitration Committee shall designate from among its members the person or persons who will assist the Chambers in the administration and monitoring of the arbitral proceedings. In addition, the Arbitration Committee has designated from among its members a Special Committee (hereinafter the "Special Committee"), which shall render decisions under Articles 11 and 12 on the challenge and revocation of arbitrators and under Article 16 on the seat of arbitration, and advise the Chambers on other procedural matters that may arise in relation to the application of these Rules.	may delegate to one or more members or committees the power to take certain decisions pursuant to its Internal Rules[3]. The Court is assisted in its work by the Secretariat of the Court (hereinafter the "Secretariat"). c) The Swiss Chambers' Arbitration Institution provides domestic and international arbitration services, as well as other dispute resolution services, under any applicable law, in Switzerland or in any other country.

[3] The Internal Rules are available on the website www.swissarbitration.org.

Swiss Rules of International Arbitration Version 2004	**Swiss Rules of International Arbitration Revision 2012**
Section I. Introductory rules	**Section I. Introductory Rules**
SCOPE OF APPLICATION **Article 1**	*SCOPE OF APPLICATION* **Article 1**
1. These Rules shall govern international arbitrations, where an agreement to arbitrate refers to these Rules, or to the arbitration rules of the Chambers of Commerce and Industry of Basel, Bern, Geneva, Ticino, Vaud, Zurich and any further Chamber of Commerce and Industry that may adhere to these Rules.	1. These Rules shall govern ~~international~~ arbitrations where an agreement to arbitrate refers to these Rules or to the arbitration rules of the Chambers of Commerce and Industry of Basel, Bern, Geneva, Neuchâtel, Ticino, Vaud, Zurich, or any further Chamber of Commerce and Industry that may adhere to these Rules.
2. The parties are free to designate the seat of the arbitration in Switzerland or elsewhere.	2. The seat of arbitration designated by the parties may be in Switzerland or in any other country.
3. These Rules shall come into force on January 1st, 2004 and, unless the parties have agreed otherwise, shall apply to all arbitral proceedings in which the Notice of Arbitration is submitted on or after that date.	3. This version of the Rules shall come into force on ,1 June 2012 and, unless the parties have agreed otherwise, shall apply to all arbitral proceedings in which the Notice of Arbitration is submitted on or after that date.
	4. By submitting their dispute to arbitration under these Rules, the parties confer on the Court, to the fullest extent permitted under the law applicable to the arbitration, all of the powers required for the purpose of supervising the arbitral proceedings otherwise vested in the competent judicial authority, including the power to extend the term of office of the arbitral tribunal and to decide on the challenge of an arbitrator on grounds not provided for in these Rules.
	5. These Rules shall govern the

Swiss Rules of International Arbitration Version 2004	**Swiss Rules of International Arbitration Revision 2012**
	arbitration, except if one of them is in conflict with a provision of the law applicable to the arbitration from which the parties cannot derogate, in which case that provision shall prevail.
NOTICE, CALCULATION OF PERIODS OF TIME **Article 2** 1. For the purposes of these Rules, any notice, including a notification, communication or proposal, is deemed to have been received if it is physically delivered to the addressee or if it is delivered to its habitual residence, place of business or mailing address, or, if none of these can be found after making reasonable inquiry, then at the addressee's last-known residence or place of business. Notice shall be deemed to have been received on the day it is so delivered.	*NOTICE, CALCULATION OF PERIODS OF TIME* **Article 2** 1. For the purposes of these Rules, any notice, including a notification, communication, or proposal, is deemed to have been received if it is ~~physically~~ delivered to the addressee, or ~~if it is delivered~~ to its habitual residence, place of business, postal or electronic address, or, if none of these can be identified after making a reasonable inquiry, ~~then at~~ to the addressee's last-known residence or place of business. A notice shall be deemed to have been received on the day it is delivered.
2. For the purposes of calculating a period of time under these Rules, such period shall begin to run on the day following the day when a notice, notification, communication or proposal is received. If the last day of such period is an official holiday or a non-business day at the residence or place of business of the addressee, the period is extended until the first business day which follows. Official holidays or non-business days occurring during the running of the period of time are included in calculating the period.	2. ~~For the purpose of calculating~~ A period of time under these Rules~~,~~ ~~such period~~ shall begin to run on the day following the day when a notice, notification, communication, or proposal is received. If the last day of such a period is an official holiday or a non-business day at the residence or place of business of the addressee, the period is extended until the first business day which follows. Official holidays or non-business days are included in the calculation of a period of time.
3. If the circumstances so justify, the Chambers may extend the time-limits provided in Section I (Introductory	3. If the circumstances so justify, the Court may extend or shorten any ~~the~~ time-limit~~s~~ it has fixed or has the

Swiss Rules of International Arbitration Version 2004	Swiss Rules of International Arbitration Revision 2012
Rules) and Section II (Composition of the arbitral tribunal), as well as any time-limits that they have set.	authority to fix or amend. ~~provided in Section I (Introductory Rules), Section II (Composition of the arbitral tribunal) and Section V (Expedited Procedures), the term of office of the arbitral tribunal and any time-limits it has fixed or has the authority to amend. extend in lieu of a court or judicial authority to the extent the law applicable to the arbitration allows.~~
NOTICE OF ARBITRATION AND ANSWER TO THE NOTICE OF ARBITRATION **Article 3** 1. The party initiating recourse to arbitration (hereinafter called the "Claimant" or, where applicable, "Claimants") shall submit a Notice of Arbitration to the Chambers at any of the addresses listed in Appendix A.	*NOTICE OF ARBITRATION AND ANSWER TO THE NOTICE OF ARBITRATION* **Article 3** 1. The party initiating arbitration (hereinafter called the "Claimant" or, where applicable, the "Claimants") shall submit a Notice of Arbitration to the Secretariat at any of the addresses listed in Appendix A.
2. Arbitral proceedings shall be deemed to commence on the date on which the Notice of Arbitration is received by the Chambers.	2. Arbitral proceedings shall be deemed to commence on the date on which the Notice of Arbitration is received by the Secretariat.
3. The Notice of Arbitration shall be submitted in as many copies as there are other parties (hereinafter called the "Respondent" or, where applicable, "Respondents"), together with an additional copy for each arbitrator and one copy for the Chambers, and shall include the following:	3. The Notice of Arbitration shall be submitted in as many copies as there are other parties (hereinafter called the "Respondent" or, where applicable, the "Respondents"), together with an additional copy for each arbitrator and one copy for the Secretariat, and shall include the following:
(a) A demand that the dispute be referred to arbitration;	*(a)* A demand that the dispute be referred to arbitration;
(b) The names, addresses, telephone and fax numbers and e-mail addresses (if any) of the parties and of their counsel;	*(b)* The names, addresses, telephone and fax numbers, and e-mail addresses (if any) of the parties and of their representative(s) ~~counsel~~;
(c) A copy of the arbitration clause or the separate arbitration	*(c)* A copy of the arbitration clause or the separate arbitration

Swiss Rules of International Arbitration Version 2004	**Swiss Rules of International Arbitration Revision 2012**
agreement that is invoked;	agreement that is invoked;
(d) A reference to the contract or other legal instrument(s) out of or in relation to which the dispute arises;	*(d)* A reference to the contract or other legal instrument(s) out of, or in relation to, which the dispute arises;
(e) The general nature of the claim and an indication of the amount involved, if any;	*(e)* The general nature of the claim and an indication of the amount involved, if any;
(f) The relief or remedy sought;	*(f)* The relief or remedy sought;
(g) A proposal as to the number of arbitrators (i.e. one or three), if the parties have not previously agreed thereon;	*(g)* A proposal as to the number of arbitrators (i.e. one or three), the language, and the seat of the arbitration, if the parties have not previously agreed thereon;
	(h) The Claimant's designation of ~~an~~ one or more arbitrators, ~~for the purpose of constituting a three-member arbitral tribunal referred to in Article 8~~, if the parties' agreement so requires;
(h) The payment, by check or transfer to the account of the Chamber to which the Notice of Arbitration is submitted as listed in Appendix A, of the Registration Fee as required by Appendix B (Schedule of the Costs of Arbitration) in force on the date when the Notice of Arbitration is submitted.	*(i)* Confirmation of payment by check or transfer to the relevant account listed in Appendix A of the Registration Fee as required by Appendix B (Schedule of ~~the~~ Costs ~~of Arbitration~~) in force on the date the Notice of Arbitration is submitted.
4. The Notice of Arbitration may also include:	4. The Notice of Arbitration may also include:
(a) The Claimant's proposals for the appointment of a sole arbitrator referred to in Article 7;	*(a)* The Claimant's proposal for the appointment of a sole arbitrator referred to in Article 7;
(b) The Claimant's designation of	~~(b) The Claimant's designation of~~

Swiss Rules of International Arbitration Version 2004	**Swiss Rules of International Arbitration Revision 2012**
an arbitrator, for the purpose of constituting a three-member arbitral tribunal referred to in Article 8;	an arbitrator, for the purpose of constituting a three-member arbitral tribunal referred to in Article 8;
(c) The Statement of Claim referred to in Article 18.	*(b)* The Statement of Claim referred to in Article 18.
5. If the Notice of Arbitration is incomplete or if the copies or attachments are not submitted in the required number, or if the Registration Fee is not paid, the Chambers may request the Claimant to remedy the defect within an appropriate period of time. The Chambers may also request within such time-limit a translation of the Notice of Arbitration if it is not submitted in English, German, French or Italian. If the Claimant complies with such directions within the applicable time-limit, the Notice of Arbitration shall be deemed to have been validly filed on the date when the initial version was received by the Chambers.	5. If the Notice of Arbitration is incomplete, or if the required number of copies or attachments are not submitted in the required number, or if the Registration Fee is not paid, the Secretariat may request the Claimant to remedy the defect within an appropriate period of time. The Secretariat may also request within such time-limit the Claimant to submit a translation of the Notice of Arbitration within the same period of time if it is not submitted in English, German, French, or Italian. If the Claimant complies with such directions within the applicable time-limit, the Notice of Arbitration shall be deemed to have been validly filed on the date on which the initial version was received by the Secretariat.
6. The Chambers shall provide without delay a copy of the Notice of Arbitration and of any exhibits included therewith to the Respondent, unless the Chambers decide, after consultation with the Special Committee, that there is manifestly no agreement to arbitrate referring to these Rules.	6. The Secretariat shall provide, without delay, a copy of the Notice of Arbitration together with any exhibits included therewith to the Respondent. unless the Chambers decide, after consultation with the Special Committee, that there is manifestly no agreement to arbitrate referring to these Rules.
7. Within thirty days from receipt of the Notice of Arbitration, the Respondent shall submit to the Chambers an Answer to the Notice of Arbitration. This Answer to the Notice of Arbitration shall be submitted in as many copies as there are other parties, together with an additional	7. Within thirty days from the date of receipt of the Notice of Arbitration, the Respondent shall submit to the Secretariat an Answer to the Notice of Arbitration. The Answer to the Notice of Arbitration shall be submitted in as many copies as there are other parties, together with

Swiss Rules of International Arbitration Version 2004	**Swiss Rules of International Arbitration Revision 2012**
copy for each arbitrator and one copy for the Chambers, and shall, to the extent possible, include the following:	an additional copy for each arbitrator and one copy for the Secretariat, and shall, to the extent possible, include the following:
(a) The name, address, telephone and fax numbers and e-mail address (if any) of the Respondent and of its counsel (if different from the description contained in the Notice of Arbitration);	*(a)* The name, address, telephone and fax numbers, and e-mail address ~~(if any)~~ of the Respondent and of its representative(s);
(b) Any plea that an arbitral tribunal constituted under these Rules lacks jurisdiction;	*(b)* Any plea that an arbitral tribunal constituted under these Rules lacks jurisdiction;
(c) The Respondent's comments on the particulars set forth in the Notice of Arbitration, pursuant to Article 3, paragraph 3(e);	*(c)* The Respondent's comments on the particulars set forth in the Notice of Arbitration, referred to in Article 3(3)(e);
(d) The Respondent's answer to the relief or remedy sought in the Notice of Arbitration, pursuant to Article 3, paragraph 3(f);	*(d)* The Respondent's answer to the relief or remedy sought in the Notice of Arbitration, referred to in Article 3(3)(f);
(e) The Respondent's proposal as to the number of arbitrators (i.e. one or three), if the parties have not previously agreed thereon, pursuant to Article 3, paragraph 3(g).	*(e)* The Respondent's proposal as to the number of arbitrators (i.e. one or three), the language, and the seat of the arbitration, ~~if the parties have not previously agreed thereon~~, referred to in Article 3(3)(g);
	(f) The Respondent's designation of one or more arbitrators if the parties' agreement so requires.
8. The Answer to the Notice of Arbitration may also include:	8. The Answer to the Notice of Arbitration may also include:
(a) The Respondent's proposals for the appointment of a sole arbitrator referred to in Article 7;	*(a)* The Respondent's proposal for the appointment of a sole arbitrator referred to in Article

Swiss Rules of International Arbitration Version 2004	Swiss Rules of International Arbitration Revision 2012
	7;
(b) The Respondent's designation of an arbitrator for the purpose of constituting a three-member arbitral tribunal referred to in Article 8;	~~*(b)* The Respondent's designation of an arbitrator for the purpose of constituting a three-member arbitral tribunal referred to in Article 8;~~
(c) The Statement of Defence referred to in Article 19.	*(c)* The Statement of Defence referred to in Article 19.
	9. ~~The Swiss Chambers' Court shall provide without delay a copy of provisions of~~ Articles 3(5) and (6) are applicable to the Answer to the Notice of Arbitration ~~and of any exhibits included therewith to the Claimant~~.
9. Any counterclaim or set-off defence shall in principle be raised with the Respondent's Answer to the Notice of Arbitration. The provisions of Article 3, paragraph 3 are applicable to the counterclaim or set-off defence.	10. Any counterclaim or set-off defence shall in principle be raised with the Answer to the Notice of Arbitration. ~~The provisions of~~ Article 3(3) is ~~are~~ applicable to the counterclaim or set-off defence.
10. If no counterclaim or set-off defence is raised with the Respondent's Answer to the Notice of Arbitration, or if there is no indication of the amount of the counterclaim or set-off defence, the Chambers may rely exclusively on paragraph 3 (e) of the present Article 3 in order to determine the possible application of Article 42, paragraph 2 (Expedited Procedure).	11. If no counterclaim or set-off defence is raised with the Answer to the Notice of Arbitration, or if there is no indication of the amount of the counterclaim or set-off defence, the Court may rely exclusively on the Notice of Arbitration ~~of this Article 3~~ in order to determine the possible application of Article 42(2) (Expedited Procedure).
11. The Chambers shall provide without delay a copy of the Answer to the Notice of Arbitration and of any exhibits included therewith to the Claimant.	12. If the Respondent does not submit an Answer to the Notice of Arbitration, or if the Respondent raises an objection to the arbitration being administered under these Rules, the Court shall administer the case, unless there is manifestly no agreement to arbitrate referring to these Rules.
12. Once the Registration Fee has been paid and all arbitrators have been confirmed, the Chambers shall	

Swiss Rules of International Arbitration Version 2004	**Swiss Rules of International Arbitration Revision 2012**
transmit without delay the file to the sole arbitrator or to the arbitral tribunal. 13. The parties may be represented or assisted by persons of their choice. The names and addresses of such persons must be communicated in writing to the other party and the Chambers; such communication must specify whether the appointment is being made for purposes of representation or assistance.	
CONSOLIDATION OF ARBITRAL PROCEEDINGS (JOINDER), PARTICIPATION OF THIRD PARTIES **Article 4** 1. Where a Notice of Arbitration is submitted between parties already involved in other arbitral proceedings pending under these Rules, the Chambers may decide, after consulting with the parties to all proceedings and the Special Committee, that the new case shall be referred to the arbitral tribunal already constituted for the existing proceedings. The Chambers may proceed likewise where a Notice of Arbitration is submitted between parties that are not identical to the parties in the existing arbitral proceedings. When rendering their decision, the Chambers shall take into account all circumstances, including the links between the two cases and the progress already made in the existing proceedings. Where the Chambers decide to refer the new case to the existing arbitral tribunal, the parties to the new case shall be deemed to have waived their right to designate an arbitrator.	*CONSOLIDATION ~~OF ARBITRAL PROCEEDINGS, PARTICIPATION OF THIRD PARTIES~~ AND JOINDER* **Article 4** 1. Where a Notice of Arbitration is submitted between parties already involved in other arbitral proceedings pending under these Rules, the Court may decide, after consulting with the parties and any confirmed arbitrator in all proceedings, that the new case shall be consolidated with the pending arbitral proceedings. The Court may proceed in the same way where a Notice of Arbitration is submitted between parties that are not identical to the parties in the pending arbitral proceedings. When rendering its decision, the Court shall take into account all relevant circumstances, including the links between the ~~two~~ cases and the progress already made in the pending arbitral proceedings. Where the Court decides to consolidate the new case with the pending arbitral proceedings, the parties to all proceedings shall be deemed to have waived their right to designate an arbitrator, and the Court may

Swiss Rules of International Arbitration Version 2004	**Swiss Rules of International Arbitration Revision 2012**
2. Where a third party requests to participate in arbitral proceedings already pending under these Rules or where a party to arbitral proceedings under these Rules intends to cause a third party to participate in the arbitration, the arbitral tribunal shall decide on such request, after consulting with all parties, taking into account all circumstances it deems relevant and applicable.	revoke the appointment and confirmation of arbitrators and apply the provisions of Section II (Composition of the Arbitral Tribunal). 2. Where one or more third persons request to participate in arbitral proceedings already pending under these Rules or where a party to pending arbitral proceedings under these Rules requests that one or more third persons participate in the arbitration, the arbitral tribunal shall decide on such request, after consulting with all of the parties, including the person or persons to be joined, taking into account all relevant circumstances.
Section II. Composition of the arbitral tribunal *CONFIRMATION OF ARBITRATORS* **Article 5** 1. All designations of a sole arbitrator or of the arbitrators composing a three-member arbitral tribunal, made by the parties or the arbitrators, are subject to confirmation by the Chambers, upon which the appointments shall become effective. The Chambers have no obligation to give reasons when they do not confirm an arbitrator.	**Section II. Composition of the Arbitral Tribunal** *CONFIRMATION OF ARBITRATORS* **Article 5** 1. All designations of an ~~sole~~ arbitrator ~~or of the arbitrators composing a three-member arbitral tribunal~~ made by the parties or the arbitrators are subject to confirmation by the Court, upon which the appointments shall become effective. The Court has no obligation to give reasons when it does not confirm an arbitrator.
2. Where a designation is not confirmed, the Chambers may	2. Where a designation is not confirmed, the Court may either
(a) either invite the party or parties concerned, or the arbitrators, as the case may be, to make a new designation within a reasonable time-limit; or	*(a)* invite the party or parties concerned, or, as the case may be, the arbitrators, to make a new designation within a reasonable time-limit; or
(b) proceed directly with the appointment.	*(b)* in exceptional circumstances, proceed directly with the

Swiss Rules of International Arbitration Version 2004	Swiss Rules of International Arbitration Revision 2012
	appointment. 3. In the event of any failure in the constitution of the arbitral tribunal under these Rules, the Court shall have all powers to address such failure and may, in particular, revoke any appointment made, appoint or reappoint any of the arbitrators and designate one of them as the presiding arbitrator. 4. If, before the arbitral tribunal is constituted, the parties agree on a settlement of the dispute, or the continuation of the arbitral proceedings becomes unnecessary or impossible for other reasons, the Secretariat shall give advance notice to the parties that the Court may terminate the proceedings. Any party may request that the Court proceed with the constitution of the arbitral tribunal in accordance with these Rules in order that the arbitral tribunal determine and apportion the costs not agreed upon by the parties. 5. Once the Registration Fee and any Provisional Deposit have been paid in accordance with Appendix B (Schedule of Costs) and all arbitrators have been confirmed, the Secretariat shall transmit the file to the arbitral tribunal without delay.
NUMBER OF ARBITRATORS **Article 6** 1. If the parties have not agreed upon the number of arbitrators, the Chambers shall decide whether the case shall be referred to a sole arbitrator or to a three-member arbitral tribunal, taking into account all relevant circumstances.	*NUMBER OF ARBITRATORS* **Article 6** 1. If the parties have not agreed upon the number of arbitrators, the Court shall decide whether the case shall be referred to a sole arbitrator or to a three-member arbitral tribunal, taking into account all relevant circumstances.

Swiss Rules of International Arbitration Version 2004	**Swiss Rules of International Arbitration Revision 2012**
2. As a rule, the Chambers shall refer the case to a sole arbitrator, unless the complexity of the subject matter and/or the amount in dispute justify that the case be referred to a three-member arbitral tribunal.	2. As a rule, the Court shall refer the case to a sole arbitrator, unless the complexity of the subject matter and/or the amount in dispute justify that the case be referred to a three-member arbitral tribunal.
3. If the arbitration agreement provides for a three-member arbitral tribunal and if this appears inappropriate in view of the amount in dispute or of other circumstances, the Chambers shall advise the parties that they may wish to agree to refer the dispute to a sole arbitrator.	3. If the arbitration agreement provides for an arbitral tribunal composed of ~~a three-member arbitral tribunal~~ more than one arbitrator, and this appears inappropriate in view of the amount in dispute or of other circumstances, the Court shall invite the parties ~~that they may wish~~ to agree to refer the case to a sole arbitrator.
4. Where the amount in dispute does not exceed CHF 1'000'000 (one million Swiss francs), the provisions of Article 42, paragraph 2 (Expedited Procedure), shall apply.	4. Where the amount in dispute does not exceed CHF 1'000'000 (one million Swiss francs), ~~the provisions of~~ Article 42(2) (Expedited Procedure) shall apply.
APPOINTMENT OF A SOLE ARBITRATOR **Article 7** 1. Where two or more parties have agreed that the dispute shall be referred to a sole arbitrator, they shall jointly designate the sole arbitrator within thirty days from the date when the Notice of Arbitration was received by the Respondent(s) unless the parties' agreement provides otherwise.	*APPOINTMENT OF A SOLE ARBITRATOR* **Article 7** 1. Where the parties have agreed that the dispute shall be referred to a sole arbitrator, they shall jointly designate the sole arbitrator within thirty days from the date on which the Notice of Arbitration was received by the Respondent(s), unless the parties' agreement provides otherwise.
2. Where the parties have not agreed upon the number of arbitrators, they shall jointly designate the sole arbitrator within thirty days from the date when the Chambers' decision that the dispute shall be referred to a sole arbitrator was received by them.	2. Where the parties have not agreed upon the number of arbitrators, they shall jointly designate the sole arbitrator within thirty days from the date of receipt of the Court's decision that the dispute shall be referred to a sole arbitrator.

Swiss Rules of International Arbitration Version 2004	**Swiss Rules of International Arbitration Revision 2012**
3. If the parties fail to designate the sole arbitrator within the applicable time-limit, the Chambers shall proceed with the appointment.	3. If the parties fail to designate the sole arbitrator within the applicable time-limit, the Court shall proceed with the appointment.
APPOINTMENT OF ARBITRATORS IN BI-PARTY OR MULTI-PARTY PROCEEDINGS **Article 8** 1. Where a dispute between two adverse parties is referred to a three-member arbitral tribunal, each party shall designate one arbitrator, unless the parties have agreed otherwise.	*APPOINTMENT OF ARBITRATORS IN BI-PARTY OR MULTI-PARTY PROCEEDINGS* **Article 8** 1. Where a dispute between two parties is referred to a three-member arbitral tribunal, each party shall designate one arbitrator, unless the parties have agreed otherwise.
2. If a party fails to designate an arbitrator within the time-limit set by the Chambers or resulting from the arbitration agreement, the Chambers shall appoint the arbitrator. Unless the parties' agreement provides otherwise, the two arbitrators so appointed shall designate, within thirty days from the confirmation of the second arbitrator, a third arbitrator who shall act as the presiding arbitrator of the arbitral tribunal. Failing such designation, the Chambers shall appoint the presiding arbitrator.	2. If a party fails to designate an arbitrator within the time-limit set by the Court or resulting from the arbitration agreement, the Court shall appoint the arbitrator. Unless the parties' agreement provides otherwise, the two arbitrators so appointed shall designate, within thirty days from the confirmation of the second arbitrator, a third arbitrator who shall act as the presiding arbitrator of the arbitral tribunal. Failing such designation, the Court shall appoint the presiding arbitrator.
3. In multi-party proceedings, the arbitral tribunal shall be constituted in accordance with the parties' agreement.	3. In multi-party proceedings, the arbitral tribunal shall be constituted in accordance with the parties' agreement.
4. If the parties have not agreed upon a procedure for the constitution of the arbitral tribunal in multi-party proceedings, the Chambers shall set an initial thirty-day time-limit for the Claimant or group of Claimants to designate an arbitrator and set a subsequent thirty-day time-limit for the Respondent or group of Respondents to designate an	4. If the parties have not agreed upon a procedure for the constitution of the arbitral tribunal in multi-party proceedings, the Court shall set an initial thirty-day time-limit for the Claimant or group of Claimants to designate an arbitrator, and set a subsequent thirty-day time-limit for the Respondent or group of Respondents to designate an

Swiss Rules of International Arbitration Version 2004	**Swiss Rules of International Arbitration Revision 2012**
arbitrator. If the group or groups of parties have each designated an arbitrator, Article 8, paragraph 2 shall apply by analogy to the designation of the presiding arbitrator.	arbitrator. If the party or group(s) of parties have each designated an arbitrator, Article 8(2) shall apply to the designation of the presiding arbitrator.
5. Where a party or group of parties fail(s) to designate an arbitrator in multiparty proceedings, the Chambers may appoint all three arbitrators and shall specify the presiding arbitrator.	5. Where a party or group of parties fails to designate an arbitrator in multi-party proceedings, the Court may appoint all of the ~~three~~ arbitrators, and shall specify the presiding arbitrator.
INDEPENDENCE AND CHALLENGE OF ARBITRATORS (Articles 9 to 12)	*INDEPENDENCE AND CHALLENGE OF ARBITRATORS* ~~*(Articles 9 to 12)*~~
Article 9 1. All arbitrators conducting an arbitration under these Rules shall be and remain at all times impartial and independent of the parties.	**Article 9** 1. Any arbitrator conducting an arbitration under these Rules shall be and shall remain at all times impartial and independent of the parties.
2. A prospective arbitrator shall disclose to those who approach him in connection with his possible appointment any circumstances likely to give rise to justifiable doubts as to his impartiality or independence. An arbitrator, once appointed or chosen, shall disclose such circumstances to the parties unless they have already been informed by him of these circumstances.	2. Prospective arbitrators shall disclose to those who approach them in connection with a possible appointment any circumstances likely to give rise to justifiable doubts as to their impartiality or independence. An arbitrator, once designated or appointed, shall disclose such circumstances to the parties, unless they have already been so informed.
Article 10 1. Any arbitrator may be challenged if circumstances exist that give rise to justifiable doubts as to the arbitrator's impartiality or independence.	**Article 10** 1. Any arbitrator may be challenged if circumstances exist that give rise to justifiable doubts as to the arbitrator's impartiality or independence.
2. A party may challenge the arbitrator appointed by it only for reasons of which it becomes aware	2. A party may challenge the arbitrator designated by it only for reasons of which it becomes aware

Swiss Rules of International Arbitration Version 2004	Swiss Rules of International Arbitration Revision 2012
after the appointment has been made.	after the appointment has been made.
Article 11 1. If the arbitrator being challenged does not withdraw, the Special Committee shall decide on the challenge. 2. The decision of the Special Committee is final. The Special Committee has no obligation to give reasons.	**Article 11** 1. A party intending to challenge an arbitrator shall send a notice of challenge to the Secretariat within 15 days after the circumstances giving rise to the challenge became known to that party. 2. If, within 15 days from the date of the notice of challenge, all of the parties do not agree to the challenge, or the challenged arbitrator does not withdraw, the Court shall decide on the challenge. 3. The decision of the Court is final and the Court has no obligation to give reasons.
Article 12 1. If an arbitrator fails to perform his functions despite a written warning from the other arbitrators or from the Chambers, the Special Committee may revoke the appointment of that arbitrator. 2. The arbitrator shall have an opportunity to present his position to the Special Committee. The decision of the Special Committee is final. The Special Committee has no obligation to give reasons.	*REMOVAL OF AN ARBITRATOR* **Article 12** 1. If an arbitrator fails to perform his or her functions despite a written warning from the other arbitrators or from the Court, the Court may revoke the appointment of that arbitrator. 2. The arbitrator shall first have an opportunity to present his or her position to the Court. The decision of the Court is final and the Court has no obligation to give reasons.
REPLACEMENT OF AN ARBITRATOR **Article 13** 1. If an arbitrator designated by a party deceases or becomes unable to perform his functions due to any reasons beyond his control, the Chambers shall set a time-limit for the	*REPLACEMENT OF AN ARBITRATOR* **Article 13** ~~1. If an arbitrator designated by a party deceases or becomes unable to perform his functions due to any reasons beyond his control, the Swiss Chambers' Court shall set a~~

Swiss Rules of International Arbitration Version 2004	**Swiss Rules of International Arbitration Revision 2012**
party having designated that arbitrator to designate a replacement arbitrator. This rule also applies if an arbitrator has been successfully challenged, has been otherwise removed or has resigned.	~~time-limit for the party having designated that arbitrator to designate a replacement arbitrator. This rule also applies if an arbitrator has been successfully challenged, has been otherwise removed or has resigned.~~
2. If the party concerned fails to designate a replacement arbitrator within the applicable time-limit, the Chambers shall appoint a replacement arbitrator.	~~2. If the party concerned fails to designate a replacement arbitrator within the applicable time-limit, the Swiss Chambers' Court shall appoint a replacement arbitrator.~~ 1. Subject to Article 13(2), in all instances in which an arbitrator has to be replaced, a replacement arbitrator shall be designated or appointed pursuant to the procedure provided for in Articles 7 and 8 within the time-limit set by the Court. Such procedure shall apply even if a party or the arbitrators had failed to make the required designation during the initial appointment process. 2. In exceptional circumstances, the Court may, after consulting with the parties and any remaining arbitrators: (a) directly appoint the replacement arbitrator; or (b) after the closure of the proceedings, authorise the remaining arbitrator(s) to proceed with the arbitration and make any decision or award.
CONSEQUENCES OF THE REPLACEMENT OF AN ARBITRATOR	~~*CONSEQUENCES OF THE REPLACEMENT OF AN ARBITRATOR*~~
Article 14 If an arbitrator is replaced, the proceedings shall as a rule resume at	**Article 14** If an arbitrator is replaced, the proceedings shall, as a rule, resume

Swiss Rules of International Arbitration Version 2004	**Swiss Rules of International Arbitration Revision 2012**
the stage where the arbitrator who was replaced ceased to perform his functions, unless the arbitral tribunal decides otherwise.	at the stage reached when the arbitrator who was replaced ceased to perform his or her functions, unless the arbitral tribunal decides otherwise.
Section III. Arbitral proceedings	**Section III. Arbitral Proceedings**
GENERAL PROVISIONS **Article 15** 1. Subject to these Rules, the arbitral tribunal may conduct the arbitration in such manner as it considers appropriate, provided that it ensures equal treatment of the parties and their right to be heard.	*GENERAL PROVISIONS* **Article 15** 1. Subject to these Rules, the arbitral tribunal may conduct the arbitration in such manner as it considers appropriate, provided that it ensures equal treatment of the parties and their right to be heard.
2. At any stage of the proceedings, the arbitral tribunal may hold hearings for the presentation of evidence by witnesses, including expert witnesses, or for oral argument. After consulting with the parties, the arbitral tribunal may also decide to conduct the proceedings on the basis of documents and other materials.	2. At any stage of the proceedings, the arbitral tribunal may hold hearings for the presentation of evidence by witnesses, including expert witnesses, or for oral argument. After consulting with the parties, the arbitral tribunal may also decide to conduct the proceedings on the basis of documents and other materials.
3. At an early stage of the arbitral proceedings and in consultation with the parties, the arbitral tribunal shall prepare a provisional time-table for the arbitral proceedings, which shall be provided to the parties and, for information, to the Chambers.	3. At an early stage of the arbitral proceedings, and in consultation with the parties, the arbitral tribunal shall prepare a provisional timetable for the arbitral proceedings, which shall be provided to the parties and, for information, to the Secretariat.
4. All documents or information supplied to the arbitral tribunal by one party shall at the same time be communicated by that party to the other party.	4. All documents or information provided to the arbitral tribunal by one party shall at the same time be communicated by that party to the other parties.
5. The arbitral tribunal may, after consulting with the parties, appoint a secretary. Article 9 of these Rules shall apply by analogy to the	5. The arbitral tribunal may, after consulting with the parties, appoint a secretary. Articles 9 to 11 ~~of these Rules~~ shall apply to the secretary.

Swiss Rules of International Arbitration Version 2004	Swiss Rules of International Arbitration Revision 2012
secretary.	
6. All participants in the arbitral proceedings shall act in accordance with the requirements of good faith.	6. The parties may be represented or assisted by persons of their choice. ~~The names, addresses, telephone and fax numbers and e-mail addresses of such persons must be communicated in writing to all parties and to the Swiss Chambers' Court. Such communication must specify whether the appointment is being made for purposes of representation or assistance.~~
	7. All participants in the arbitral proceedings shall act in good faith, and make every effort to contribute to the efficient conduct of the proceedings and to avoid unnecessary costs and delays. The parties undertake to comply with any award or order made by the arbitral tribunal or emergency arbitrator without delay.
	8. With the agreement of each of the parties, the arbitral tribunal may take steps to facilitate the settlement of the dispute before it. Any such agreement by a party shall constitute a waiver of its right to challenge an arbitrator's impartiality based on the arbitrator's participation and knowledge acquired in taking the agreed steps.
SEAT OF THE ARBITRATION **Article 16** 1. If the parties have not determined the seat of the arbitration, or if such designation is unclear or incomplete, the Special Committee shall determine the seat of the arbitration taking into account all relevant circumstances, or shall request the arbitral tribunal to determine the seat.	*SEAT OF THE ARBITRATION* **Article 16** 1. If the parties have not determined the seat of the arbitration, or if the designation of the seat is unclear or incomplete, the Court shall determine the seat of the arbitration, taking into account all relevant circumstances, or shall request the arbitral tribunal to determine it.

Swiss Rules of International Arbitration Version 2004	**Swiss Rules of International Arbitration Revision 2012**
2. Without prejudice to the determination of the seat of the arbitration, the arbitral tribunal may decide where the proceedings shall be conducted. In particular, it may hear witnesses and hold meetings for consultation among its members at any place it deems appropriate, having regard to the circumstances of the arbitration.	2. Without prejudice to the determination of the seat of the arbitration, the arbitral tribunal may decide where the proceedings shall be conducted. In particular, it may hear witnesses and hold meetings for consultation among its members at any place it deems appropriate, having regard to the circumstances of the arbitration.
3. The arbitral tribunal may meet at any place it deems appropriate for the inspection of goods, other property or documents. The parties shall be given sufficient notice to enable them to be present at such inspection.	3. The arbitral tribunal may meet at any place it deems appropriate for the inspection of goods, other property, or documents. The parties shall be given sufficient notice to enable them to be present at such an inspection.
4. The award shall be deemed to be made at the seat of the arbitration.	4. The award shall be deemed to be made at the seat of the arbitration.
LANGUAGE **Article 17** 1. Subject to an agreement by the parties, the arbitral tribunal shall, promptly after its appointment, determine the language or languages to be used in the proceedings. This determination shall apply to the Statement of Claim, the Statement of Defence, and any further written statements and, if oral hearings take place, to the language or languages to be used in such hearings.	*LANGUAGE* **Article 17** 1. Subject to an agreement of the parties, the arbitral tribunal shall, promptly after its appointment, determine the language or languages to be used in the proceedings. This determination shall apply to the Statement of Claim, the Statement of Defence, any further written statements, and to any oral hearings.
2. The arbitral tribunal may order that any documents annexed to the Statement of Claim or Statement of Defence, and any supplementary documents or exhibits submitted in the course of the proceedings, delivered in their original language, shall be accompanied by a translation into the language or languages agreed upon by the parties or determined by the arbitral tribunal.	2. The arbitral tribunal may order that any documents annexed to the Statement of Claim or Statement of Defence, and any supplementary documents or exhibits submitted in the course of the proceedings in a language other than the language or languages agreed upon by the parties or determined by the arbitral tribunal shall be accompanied by a translation into such language or

Swiss Rules of International Arbitration Version 2004	**Swiss Rules of International Arbitration Revision 2012**
	languages.
STATEMENT OF CLAIM **Article 18** 1. Unless the Statement of Claim was contained in the Notice of Arbitration, within a period of time to be determined by the arbitral tribunal, the Claimant shall communicate its Statement of Claim in writing to the Respondent and to each of the arbitrators. A copy of the contract, and of the arbitration agreement if not contained in the contract, shall be annexed thereto.	*STATEMENT OF CLAIM* **Article 18** 1. Within a period of time to be determined by the arbitral tribunal, and unless the Statement of Claim was contained in the Notice of Arbitration, the Claimant shall communicate its Statement of Claim in writing to the Respondent and to each of the arbitrators. A copy of the contract, and, ~~of the arbitration agreement~~ if it is not contained in the contract, of the arbitration agreement, shall be annexed to the Statement of Claim.
2. The Statement of Claim shall include the following particulars:	2. The Statement of Claim shall include the following particulars:
(a) The names and addresses of the parties;	*(a)* The names and addresses of the parties;
(b) A statement of the facts supporting the claim;	*(b)* A statement of the facts supporting the claim;
(c) The points at issue;	*(c)* The points at issue;
(d) The relief or remedy sought.	*(d)* The relief or remedy sought.
3. As a rule, the Claimant shall annex to its Statement of Claim all documents it deems relevant.	3. As a rule, the Claimant shall annex to its Statement of Claim all documents and other evidence on which it relies~~it deems relevant~~.
STATEMENT OF DEFENCE **Article 19** 1. Within a period of time to be determined by the arbitral tribunal and unless the Statement of Defence was contained in the Answer to the Notice of Arbitration, the Respondent shall communicate its Statement of Defence in writing to the Claimant and	*STATEMENT OF DEFENCE* **Article 19** 1. Within a period of time to be determined by the arbitral tribunal, and unless the Statement of Defence was contained in the Answer to the Notice of Arbitration, the Respondent shall communicate its Statement of Defence in writing to

Swiss Rules of International Arbitration Version 2004	**Swiss Rules of International Arbitration Revision 2012**
to each of the arbitrators.	the Claimant and to each of the arbitrators.
2. The Statement of Defence shall reply to the particulars (b), (c) and (d) of the Statement of Claim (Article 18, paragraph 2). If the Respondent has raised an objection to the jurisdiction or to the proper constitution of the arbitral tribunal, the Statement of Defence shall contain the factual and legal basis of such objection. As a rule, the Respondent shall annex to its Statement of Defence all documents on which it relies for its defence.	2. The Statement of Defence shall reply to the particulars of the Statement of Claim set out in Articles 18(2)(b) to (d). If the Respondent raises an objection to the jurisdiction or to the proper constitution of the arbitral tribunal, the Statement of Defence shall contain the factual and legal basis of such objection. As a rule, the Respondent shall annex to its Statement of Defence all documents and other evidence on which it relies.~~on which it relies for its defence.~~
3. The provisions of Article 18, paragraphs 2 (b) – (d), shall apply to a counterclaim and a claim relied on for the purpose of a set-off.	3. ~~The provisions of~~ Articles 18(2)(b) to (d) shall apply to a counterclaim and a claim relied on for the purpose of a set-off.
AMENDMENTS TO THE CLAIM OR DEFENCE **Article 20** 1. During the course of the arbitral proceedings either party may amend or supplement its claim or defence unless the arbitral tribunal considers it inappropriate to allow such amendment having regard to the delay in making it or prejudice to the other party or any other circumstances. However, a claim may not be amended in such a manner that the amended claim falls outside the scope of the arbitration clause or separate arbitration agreement.	*AMENDMENTS TO THE CLAIM OR DEFENCE* **Article 20** 1. During the course of the arbitral proceedings, a ~~either~~ party may amend or supplement its claim or defence, unless the arbitral tribunal considers it inappropriate to allow such amendment having regard to the delay in making it, the prejudice to the other parties, or any other circumstances. However, a claim may not be amended in such a manner that the amended claim falls outside the scope of the arbitration clause or separate arbitration agreement.

Swiss Rules of International Arbitration Version 2004	**Swiss Rules of International Arbitration Revision 2012**
2. The arbitral tribunal may adjust the costs of the arbitration if a party amends or supplements its claims, counterclaims or defences.	2. The arbitral tribunal may adjust the costs of the arbitration if a party amends or supplements its claims, counterclaims, or defences.
PLEAS AS TO THE JURISDICTION OF THE ARBITRAL TRIBUNAL **Article 21** 1. The arbitral tribunal shall have the power to rule on objections that it has no jurisdiction, including any objections with respect to the existence or validity of the arbitration clause or of the separate arbitration agreement.	*OBJECTIONS TO THE JURISDICTION OF THE ARBITRAL TRIBUNAL* **Article 21** 1. The arbitral tribunal shall have the power to rule on any objections to its jurisdiction, including any objection with respect to the existence or validity of the arbitration clause or of the separate arbitration agreement.
2. The arbitral tribunal shall have the power to determine the existence or the validity of the contract of which an arbitration clause forms a part. For the purposes of Article 21, an arbitration clause which forms part of a contract and which provides for arbitration under these Rules shall be treated as an agreement independent of the other terms of the contract. A decision by the arbitral tribunal that the contract is null and void shall not entail *ipso jure* the invalidity of the arbitration clause.	2. The arbitral tribunal shall have the power to determine the existence or the validity of the contract of which an arbitration clause forms a part. For the purposes of Article 21, an arbitration clause which forms part of a contract and which provides for arbitration under these Rules shall be treated as an agreement independent of the other terms of the contract. A decision by the arbitral tribunal that the contract is null and void shall not entail *ipso jure* the invalidity of the arbitration clause.
3. As a rule, a plea that the arbitral tribunal does not have jurisdiction shall be raised in the Answer to the Notice of Arbitration, but in no event later than in the Statement of Defence referred to in Article 19, or, with respect to a counterclaim, in the reply to the counterclaim.	3. As a rule, any objection to the jurisdiction of the arbitral tribunal shall be raised in the Answer to the Notice of Arbitration, and in no event later than in the Statement of Defence referred to in Article 19, or, with respect to a counterclaim, in the reply to the counterclaim.
4. In general, the arbitral tribunal should rule on a plea concerning its jurisdiction as a preliminary question. However, the arbitral tribunal may proceed with the arbitration and rule	4. In general, the arbitral tribunal should rule on any objection to its jurisdiction as a preliminary question. However, the arbitral tribunal may proceed with the

Swiss Rules of International Arbitration Version 2004	**Swiss Rules of International Arbitration Revision 2012**
on such a plea in its final award.	arbitration and rule on such an objection in an award on the merits. ~~its final award.~~
5. The arbitral tribunal shall have jurisdiction to hear a set-off defence even when the relationship out of which this defence is said to arise is not within the scope of the arbitration clause or is the object of another arbitration agreement or forum-selection clause.	5. The arbitral tribunal shall have jurisdiction to hear a set-off defence even if the relationship out of which the defence is said to arise is not within the scope of the arbitration clause, or falls within the scope of another arbitration agreement or forum-selection clause.
FURTHER WRITTEN STATEMENTS **Article 22** The arbitral tribunal shall decide which further written statements, in addition to the Statement of Claim and the Statement of Defence, shall be required from the parties or may be presented by them and shall set the periods of time for communicating such statements.	*FURTHER WRITTEN STATEMENTS* **Article 22** The arbitral tribunal shall decide which further written statements, in addition to the Statement of Claim and the Statement of Defence, shall be required from the parties or may be presented by them and shall set the periods of time for communicating such statements.
PERIODS OF TIME **Article 23** The periods of time set by the arbitral tribunal for the communication of written statements (including the Statement of Claim and Statement of Defence) should not exceed forty-five days. However, the arbitral tribunal may extend the time-limits if it concludes that an extension is justified.	*PERIODS OF TIME* **Article 23** The periods of time set by the arbitral tribunal for the communication of written statements (including the Statement of Claim and Statement of Defence) should not exceed forty-five days. However, the arbitral tribunal may extend the time-limits if it ~~concludes~~ considers that an extension is justified.
EVIDENCE AND HEARINGS (Articles 24 and 25) **Article 24** 1. Each party shall have the burden of proving the facts relied on to support	*EVIDENCE AND HEARINGS* ~~*(Articles 24 and 25)*~~ **Article 24** 1. Each party shall have the burden of proving the facts relied on to

Swiss Rules of International Arbitration Version 2004	**Swiss Rules of International Arbitration Revision 2012**
its claim or defence.	support its claim or defence.
2. The arbitral tribunal may, if it considers it appropriate, require a party to deliver to the tribunal and to the other party, within such a period of time as the arbitral tribunal shall decide, a summary of the documents and other evidence which that party intends to present in support of the facts in issue set out in its Statement of Claim or Statement of Defence.	2. The arbitral tribunal shall determine the admissibility, relevance, materiality, and weight of the evidence. tribunal may, if it considers it appropriate, require a party to deliver to the tribunal and to the other party, within such a period of time as the arbitral tribunal shall decide, a summary of the documents and other evidence which that party intends to present in support of the facts in issue set out in its Statement of Claim or Statement of Defence.
3. At any time during the arbitral proceedings the arbitral tribunal may require the parties to produce documents, exhibits or other evidence within such a period of time as the tribunal shall determine.	3. At any time during the arbitral proceedings, the arbitral tribunal may require the parties to produce documents, exhibits, or other evidence within a period of time determined by the arbitral tribunal.
Article 25 1. In the event of an oral hearing, the arbitral tribunal shall give the parties adequate advance notice of the date, time and place thereof.	**Article 25** 1. The arbitral tribunal shall give the parties adequate advance notice of the date, time, and place of any oral hearing.
2. Any person may be a witness or an expert witness. If witnesses or expert witnesses are to be heard, at least fifteen days before the hearing each party shall communicate to the arbitral tribunal and to the other party the names and addresses of the witnesses or expert witnesses it intends to present, the subject upon and the languages in which such witnesses or expert witnesses will give their testimony. 3. The arbitral tribunal shall make arrangements for the translation of oral statements made at a hearing and for a record of the hearing if	2. Any person may be a witness or an expert witness in the arbitration. If witnesses or expert witnesses are to be heard, at least fifteen days before the hearing each party shall communicate to the arbitral tribunal and to the other party the names and addresses of the witnesses or expert witnesses it intends to present, the subject upon and the languages in which such witnesses or expert witnesses will give their testimony. It is not improper for a party, its officers, employees, legal advisors, or counsel to interview witnesses, potential witnesses, or expert witnesses.

Swiss Rules of International Arbitration Version 2004	**Swiss Rules of International Arbitration Revision 2012**
either is deemed necessary by the tribunal under the circumstances of the case, or if the parties have agreed thereto and have communicated such agreement to the tribunal at least fifteen days before the hearing.	3. Prior to a hearing and within a period of time determined by the arbitral tribunal, the evidence of witnesses and expert witnesses may be presented in the form of written statements or reports signed by them. 4. At the hearing, witnesses and expert witnesses may be heard and examined in the manner set by the arbitral tribunal. The arbitral tribunal may direct that witnesses or expert witnesses be examined through means that do not require their physical presence at the hearing (including by videoconference). 5. Arrangements shall be made for the translation of oral statements made at a hearing and for a record of the hearing to be provided if this is deemed necessary by the arbitral tribunal having regard to the circumstances of the case, or if the parties so agree.
4. Hearings shall be held *in camera* unless the parties agree otherwise. The arbitral tribunal may require the retirement of any witness or witnesses or expert witnesses during the testimony of other witnesses or expert witnesses. The arbitral tribunal is free to determine the manner in which witnesses or expert witnesses are examined.	6. Hearings shall be held *in camera* unless the parties agree otherwise. The arbitral tribunal may order ~~any witness or~~ witnesses or expert witnesses to retire during the testimony of other witnesses or expert witnesses. ~~The arbitral tribunal is free to determine the manner in which witnesses or expert witnesses are examined.~~
5. Evidence of witnesses or expert witnesses may also be presented in the form of written statements or reports signed by them.	~~5. Evidence of witnesses or expert witnesses may also be presented in the form of written statements or reports signed by them.~~
6. It shall not be improper for a party, its officers, employees, legal advisors or counsel to interview witnesses,	~~6. It shall not be improper for a party, its officers, employees, legal advisors or counsel to interview~~

Swiss Rules of International Arbitration Version 2004	**Swiss Rules of International Arbitration Revision 2012**
potential witnesses or expert witnesses.	~~witnesses, potential witnesses or expert witnesses.~~
7. The arbitral tribunal shall determine the admissibility, relevance, materiality and weight of the evidence offered.	~~7. The arbitral tribunal shall determine the admissibility, relevance, materiality and weight of the evidence offered.~~
INTERIM MEASURES OF PROTECTION **Article 26** 1. At the request of either party, the arbitral tribunal may take any interim measures it deems necessary or appropriate.	*INTERIM MEASURES OF PROTECTION* **Article 26** 1. At the request of a ~~either~~ party, the arbitral tribunal may grant any interim measures it deems necessary or appropriate. Upon the application of any party or, in exceptional circumstances and with prior notice to the parties, on its own initiative, the arbitral tribunal may also modify, suspend or terminate any interim measures granted.
2. Such interim measures may be established in the form of an interim award. The arbitral tribunal shall be entitled to order the provision of appropriate security.	2. Interim measures may be granted in the form of an interim award. The arbitral tribunal shall be entitled to order the provision of appropriate security.
	3. In exceptional circumstances, the arbitral tribunal may rule on a request for interim measures by way of a preliminary order before the request has been communicated to any other party, provided that such communication is made at the latest together with the preliminary order and that the other parties are immediately granted an opportunity to be heard.
	4. The arbitral tribunal may rule on claims for compensation for any damage caused by an unjustified interim measure or preliminary order.
	5. By submitting their dispute to

Swiss Rules of International Arbitration Version 2004	**Swiss Rules of International Arbitration Revision 2012**
3. A request for interim measures addressed by any party to a judicial authority shall not be deemed incompatible with the agreement to arbitrate, or as a waiver of that agreement.	arbitration under these Rules, the parties do not waive any right that they may have under the applicable laws to submit a request for interim measures to a judicial authority. A request for interim measures addressed by any party to a judicial authority shall not be deemed to be incompatible with the agreement to arbitrate, or to constitute a waiver of that agreement.
4. The arbitral tribunal shall have discretion to apportion the costs relating to a request for interim measures in the interim award or in the final award.	6. The arbitral tribunal shall have discretion to apportion the costs relating to a request for interim measures in an ~~the~~ interim award or in the final award.
TRIBUNAL-APPOINTED EXPERTS **Article 27** 1. The arbitral tribunal, after consulting with the parties, may appoint one or more experts to report to it, in writing, on specific issues to be determined by the tribunal. A copy of the expert's terms of reference, established by the arbitral tribunal, shall be communicated to the parties.	*TRIBUNAL-APPOINTED EXPERTS* **Article 27** 1. The arbitral tribunal, after consulting with the parties, may appoint one or more experts to report to it, in writing, on specific issues to be determined by the arbitral tribunal. A copy of the expert's terms of reference, established by the arbitral tribunal, shall be communicated to the parties.
2. The parties shall give the expert any relevant information or produce for his inspection any relevant documents or goods that he may require of them. Any dispute between a party and such expert as to the relevance of the required information or production shall be referred to the arbitral tribunal for decision.	2. The parties shall give the expert any relevant information or produce for the expert's inspection any relevant documents or goods that the expert may require of them. Any dispute between a party and the expert as to the relevance of the required information, documents or ~~production~~ goods shall be referred to the arbitral tribunal.
3. Upon receipt of the expert's report, the arbitral tribunal shall communicate a copy of the report to the parties who shall be given the opportunity to	3. Upon receipt of the expert's report, the arbitral tribunal shall communicate a copy of the report to the parties, which ~~who~~ shall be given

Swiss Rules of International Arbitration Version 2004	Swiss Rules of International Arbitration Revision 2012
express, in writing, their opinion on the report. A party shall be entitled to examine any document on which the expert has relied in his report.	the opportunity to express, in writing, their opinion on the report. A party shall be entitled to examine any document on which the expert has relied in the report.
4. At the request of either party the expert, after delivery of the report, may be heard at a hearing where the parties shall have the opportunity to be present and to interrogate the expert. At this hearing either party may present expert witnesses in order to testify on the points at issue. The provisions of Article 25 shall be applicable to such proceedings.	4. At the request of any ~~either~~ party, the expert, after delivery of the report, may be heard at a hearing during which the parties shall have the opportunity to be present and to examine the expert. At this hearing, any ~~either~~ party may present expert witnesses in order to testify on the points at issue. ~~The provisions of~~ Article 25 shall be applicable to such proceedings.
5. The provisions of Article 9 shall apply by analogy to any expert appointed by the arbitral tribunal.	5. ~~The provisions of~~ Articles 9 to 11 shall apply to any expert appointed by the arbitral tribunal.
DEFAULT **Article 28** 1. If, within the period of time set by the arbitral tribunal, the Claimant has failed to communicate its claim without showing sufficient cause for such failure, the arbitral tribunal shall issue an order for the termination of the arbitral proceedings. If, within the period of time set by the arbitral tribunal, the Respondent has failed to communicate its Statement of Defence without showing sufficient cause for such failure, the arbitral tribunal shall order that the proceedings continue.	*DEFAULT* **Article 28** 1. If, within the period of time set by the arbitral tribunal, the Claimant has failed to communicate its claim without showing sufficient cause for such failure, the arbitral tribunal shall issue an order for the termination of the arbitral proceedings. If, within the period of time set by the arbitral tribunal, the Respondent has failed to communicate its Statement of Defence without showing sufficient cause for such failure, the arbitral tribunal shall order that the proceedings continue.
2. If one of the parties, duly notified under these Rules, fails to appear at a hearing, without showing sufficient cause for such failure, the arbitral tribunal may proceed with the arbitration.	2. If one of the parties, duly notified under these Rules, fails to appear at a hearing, without showing sufficient cause for such failure, the arbitral tribunal may proceed with the arbitration.
3. If one of the parties, duly invited to produce documentary evidence, fails	3. If one of the parties, duly invited to produce documentary or other

Swiss Rules of International Arbitration Version 2004	**Swiss Rules of International Arbitration Revision 2012**
to do so within the established period of time, without showing sufficient cause for such failure, the arbitral tribunal may make the award on the evidence before it.	evidence, fails to do so within the period of time determined by the arbitral tribunal, without showing sufficient cause for such failure, the arbitral tribunal may make the award on the evidence before it.
CLOSURE OF PROCEEDINGS **Article 29** 1. The arbitral tribunal may inquire of the parties if they have any further proof to offer or witnesses to be heard or submissions to make and, if there are none, it may declare the proceedings closed.	*CLOSURE OF PROCEEDINGS* **Article 29** 1. ~~The arbitral tribunal may inquire of the parties if they have any further proof to offer or witnesses to be heard or submissions to make and, if there are none, it may declare the proceedings closed.~~ When it is satisfied that the parties have had a reasonable opportunity to present their respective cases on matters to be decided in an award, the arbitral tribunal may declare the proceedings closed with regard to such matters.
2. The arbitral tribunal may, if it considers it necessary owing to exceptional circumstances, decide, on its own motion or upon application of a party, to reopen the proceedings at any time before the award is made.	2. The arbitral tribunal may, if it considers it necessary owing to exceptional circumstances, decide, on its own initiative ~~motion~~ or upon the application of a party, to reopen the proceedings on the matters with regard to which the proceedings were closed pursuant to Article 29(1) at any time before the award on such matters is made.
WAIVER OF RULES **Article 30** A party who knows that any provision of, or requirement under, these Rules has not been complied with and yet proceeds with the arbitration without promptly stating its objection to such non-compliance, shall be deemed to have waived its right to object.	*WAIVER OF RULES* **Article 30** If a party ~~who~~ knows that any provision of, or requirement under, these Rules or any other applicable procedural rule has not been complied with and yet proceeds with the arbitration without promptly stating its objection to such non-compliance it shall be deemed to have waived its right to raise an objection.

Swiss Rules of International Arbitration Version 2004	**Swiss Rules of International Arbitration Revision 2012**
Section IV. The Award *DECISIONS* **Article 31** 1. When there are three arbitrators, any award or other decision of the arbitral tribunal shall be made by a majority of the arbitrators. If there is no majority, the award shall be made by the presiding arbitrator alone. 2. In the case of questions of procedure, when the arbitral tribunal so authorises, the presiding arbitrator may decide on his own, subject to revision, if any, by the arbitral tribunal. *FORM AND EFFECT OF THE AWARD* **Article 32** 1. In addition to making a final award, the arbitral tribunal shall be entitled to make interim, interlocutory, or partial awards. If appropriate, the arbitral tribunal may also award costs in awards that are not final. 2. The award shall be made in writing and shall be final and binding on the parties. The parties undertake to carry out the award without delay. 3. The arbitral tribunal shall state the reasons upon which the award is based, unless the parties have agreed that no reasons are to be given. 4. An award shall be signed by the arbitrators and it shall contain the date on which and the place where the award was made. Where there are three arbitrators and one or two of them fail(s) to sign, the award shall	**Section IV. The Award** *DECISIONS* **Article 31** 1. If the arbitral tribunal is composed of more than one arbitrator ~~are three arbitrators~~, any award or other decision of the arbitral tribunal shall be made by a majority of the arbitrators. If there is no majority, the award shall be made by the presiding arbitrator alone. 2. If authorized by the arbitral tribunal, the presiding arbitrator may decide on questions of procedure, subject to revision by the arbitral tribunal. *FORM AND EFFECT OF THE AWARD* **Article 32** 1. In addition to making a final award, the arbitral tribunal may make interim, interlocutory, or partial awards. If appropriate, the arbitral tribunal may also award costs in awards that are not final. 2. The award shall be made in writing and shall be final and binding on the parties. ~~The parties undertake to carry out the award without delay~~. 3. The arbitral tribunal shall state the reasons upon which the award is based, unless the parties have agreed that no reasons are to be given. 4. An award shall be signed by the arbitrators and it shall specify the seat of the arbitration and the date on which the award was made. Where the arbitral tribunal is composed of more than one

Swiss Rules of International Arbitration Version 2004	**Swiss Rules of International Arbitration Revision 2012**
state the reason for the absence of the signature(s).	arbitrator and any ~~one or two~~ of them fails~~(s)~~ to sign, the award shall state the reason for the absence of the signature~~(s).~~
5. Publication of the award is governed by Article 43.	5. The publication of the award is governed by Article 44.
6. Originals of the award signed by the arbitrators shall be communicated to the parties and to the Chambers by the arbitral tribunal. The Chambers shall retain a copy of the award.	6. Originals of the award signed by the arbitrators shall be communicated by the arbitral tribunal to the parties and to the Secretariat ~~by the arbitral tribunal~~. The Secretariat shall retain a copy of the award.
APPLICABLE LAW, AMIABLE COMPOSITEUR **Article 33** 1. The arbitral tribunal shall decide the case in accordance with the rules of law agreed upon by the parties or, in the absence of a choice of law, by applying the rules of law with which the dispute has the closest connection.	*APPLICABLE LAW, AMIABLE COMPOSITEUR* **Article 33** 1. The arbitral tribunal shall decide the case in accordance with the rules of law agreed upon by the parties or, in the absence of a choice of law, by applying the rules of law with which the dispute has the closest connection.
2. The arbitral tribunal shall decide as *amiable compositeur* or *ex aequo et bono* only if the parties have expressly authorised the arbitral tribunal to do so.	2. The arbitral tribunal shall decide as *amiable compositeur* or *ex aequo et bono* only if the parties have expressly authorised the arbitral tribunal to do so.
3. In all cases, the arbitral tribunal shall decide in accordance with the terms of the contract and shall take into account the usages of the trade applicable to the transaction.	3. In all cases, the arbitral tribunal shall decide in accordance with the terms of the contract and shall take into account the trade usages ~~of the trade~~ applicable to the transaction.
SETTLEMENT OR OTHER GROUNDS FOR TERMINATION **Article 34** 1. If, before the award is made, the parties agree on a settlement of the dispute, the arbitral tribunal shall	*SETTLEMENT OR OTHER GROUNDS FOR TERMINATION* **Article 34** 1. If, before the award is made, the parties agree on a settlement of the dispute, the arbitral tribunal shall

Swiss Rules of International Arbitration Version 2004	**Swiss Rules of International Arbitration Revision 2012**
either issue an order for the termination of the arbitral proceedings or, if requested by both parties and accepted by the tribunal, record the settlement in the form of an arbitral award on agreed terms. The arbitral tribunal is not obliged to give reasons for such an award.	either issue an order for the termination of the arbitral proceedings or, if requested by the parties and accepted by the arbitral tribunal, record the settlement in the form of an arbitral award on agreed terms. The arbitral tribunal is not obliged to give reasons for such an award.
2. If, before the award is made, the continuation of the arbitral proceedings becomes unnecessary or impossible for any reason not mentioned in paragraph 1, the arbitral tribunal shall inform the parties of its intention to issue an order for the termination of the proceedings. The arbitral tribunal shall have the power to issue such an order unless a party raises justifiable grounds for objection.	2. If, before the award is made, the continuation of the arbitral proceedings becomes unnecessary or impossible for any reason not mentioned in Article 34(1) ~~paragraph 1~~, the arbitral tribunal shall give advance notice to the parties that it may issue an order for the termination of the proceedings. The arbitral tribunal shall have the power to issue such an order, unless a party raises justifiable grounds for objection.
3. Copies of the order for termination of the arbitral proceedings or of the arbitral award on agreed terms, signed by the arbitrators, shall be communicated by the arbitral tribunal to the parties and to the Chambers. Where an arbitral award on agreed terms is made, the provisions of Article 32, paragraphs 2 and 4 to 6, shall apply.	3. Copies of the order for termination of the arbitral proceedings or of the arbitral award on agreed terms, signed by the arbitrators, shall be communicated by the arbitral tribunal to the parties and to the Secretariat. Where an arbitral award on agreed terms is made, ~~the provisions of~~ Articles 32(2) and (4) to (6) shall apply.
INTERPRETATION OF THE AWARD **Article 35** 1. Within thirty days after the receipt of the award, either party, with notice to the other party, may request that the arbitral tribunal give an interpretation of the award. The arbitral tribunal may set a time-limit, normally not exceeding thirty days, for the other party to comment on such request.	*INTERPRETATION OF THE AWARD* **Article 35** 1. Within thirty days after the receipt of the award, a party, with notice to the Secretariat and to the other parties, may request that the arbitral tribunal give an interpretation of the award. The arbitral tribunal may set a time-limit, as a rule not exceeding thirty days, for the other parties to comment on the request.

Swiss Rules of International Arbitration Version 2004	**Swiss Rules of International Arbitration Revision 2012**
2. The interpretation shall be given in writing within forty-five days after the receipt of the request. The interpretation shall form part of the award and the provisions of Article 32, paragraphs 2 to 6, shall apply.	2. The interpretation shall be given in writing within forty-five days after the receipt of the request. The Court may extend this time limit. The interpretation shall form part of the award and ~~the provisions of~~ Articles 32(2) to (6) shall apply.
CORRECTION OF THE AWARD **Article 36** 1. Within thirty days after the receipt of the award, either party, with notice to the other party, may request the arbitral tribunal to correct in the award any errors in computation, any clerical or typographical errors, or any errors of similar nature. The arbitral tribunal may set a time-limit, normally not exceeding thirty days, for the other party to comment on such request.	*CORRECTION OF THE AWARD* **Article 36** 1. Within thirty days after the receipt of the award, a party, with notice to the Secretariat and to the other parties, may request the arbitral tribunal to correct in the award any errors in computation, any clerical or typographical errors, or any errors of similar nature. The arbitral tribunal may set a time limit, as a rule not exceeding thirty days, for the other parties to comment on the request.
2. The arbitral tribunal may within thirty days after the communication of the award make such corrections on its own initiative.	2. The arbitral tribunal may within thirty days after the communication of the award make such corrections on its own initiative.
3. Such corrections shall be in writing, and the provisions of Article 32, paragraphs 2 to 6, shall apply.	3. Such corrections shall be in writing, and ~~the provisions of~~ Articles 32(2) to (6) shall apply.
ADDITIONAL AWARD **Article 37** 1. Within thirty days after the receipt of the award, either party, with notice to the other party, may request the arbitral tribunal to make an additional award as to claims presented in the arbitral proceedings but omitted from the award. The arbitral tribunal may set a time-limit, normally not exceeding thirty days, for the other party to comment on such request.	*ADDITIONAL AWARD* **Article 37** 1. Within thirty days after the receipt of the award, a party, with notice to the Secretariat and the other parties, may request the arbitral tribunal to make an additional award as to claims presented in the arbitral proceedings but omitted from the award. The arbitral tribunal may set a time-limit, as a rule not exceeding thirty days, for the other parties to comment on the request.

Swiss Rules of International Arbitration Version 2004	Swiss Rules of International Arbitration Revision 2012
2. If the arbitral tribunal considers the request for an additional award to be justified and considers that the omission can be rectified without any further hearings or evidence, it shall complete its award within sixty days after the receipt of the request.	2. If the arbitral tribunal considers the request for an additional award to be justified and considers that the omission can be rectified without any further hearings or evidence, it shall complete its award within sixty days after the receipt of the request. The Court may extend this time limit.
3. When an additional award is made, the provisions of Article 32, paragraphs 2 to 6, shall apply.	3. ~~When an additional award is made, the provisions of~~ Articles 32(2) to (6) shall apply to any additional award.
COSTS (Articles 38 to 40) **Article 38** The arbitral tribunal shall determine the costs of arbitration in its award. The term "costs" includes only:	*COSTS* ~~*(Articles 38 to 40)*~~ **Article 38** The ~~arbitral tribunal~~ award shall ~~determine~~ contain a determination of the costs of the arbitration ~~in its award~~. The term "costs" includes only:
(a) The fees of the arbitral tribunal to be stated separately as to each arbitrator and to be determined by the tribunal itself in accordance with Article 39;	*(a)* The fees of the arbitral tribunal to be stated separately as to each arbitrator and any secretary, and to be determined by the arbitral tribunal itself in accordance with Articles 39 and 40(3) to (5);
(b) The travel and other expenses incurred by the arbitrators;	*(b)* The travel and other expenses incurred by the arbitral tribunal and any secretary;
(c) The costs of expert advice and of other assistance required by the arbitral tribunal;	*(c)* The costs of expert advice and of other assistance required by the arbitral tribunal;
(d) The travel and other expenses of witnesses to the extent such expenses are approved by the arbitral tribunal;	*(d)* The travel and other expenses of witnesses, to the extent such expenses are approved by the arbitral tribunal;
(e) The costs for legal representation and assistance of the successful party if such costs were claimed during the	*(e)* The costs for legal representation and assistance, if such costs were claimed during the arbitral

Swiss Rules of International Arbitration Version 2004	**Swiss Rules of International Arbitration Revision 2012**
arbitral proceedings, and only to the extent that the arbitral tribunal determines that the amount of such costs is reasonable;	proceedings, and only to the extent that the arbitral tribunal determines that the amount of such costs is reasonable;
(f) The costs for the administration of the arbitration payable to the Chambers in accordance with Appendix B (Schedule of the Costs of Arbitration).	*(f)* The Registration Fee and the Administrative Costs in accordance with Appendix B (Schedule of ~~the~~ Costs ~~of Arbitration~~);
	(g) The Registration Fee, the fees and expenses of any emergency arbitrator, and the costs of expert advice and of other assistance required by such emergency arbitrator, determined in Accordance with Article 43(9).
Article 39 1. The fees of the arbitral tribunal shall be reasonable in amount, taking into account the amount in dispute, the complexity of the subject-matter, the time spent by the arbitrators and any other relevant circumstances of the case, including, but not limited to, the discontinuation of the arbitral proceedings in case of settlement or other reasons. In the event of such discontinuation, the fees of the arbitral tribunal may be less than the minimum amount resulting from Appendix B (Schedule of the Costs of Arbitration).	**Article 39** 1. The fees and expenses of the arbitral tribunal shall be reasonable in amount, taking into account the amount in dispute, the complexity of the subject-matter of the arbitration, the time spent ~~by the arbitrators~~ and any other relevant circumstances of the case, including, ~~but not limited to,~~ the discontinuation of the arbitral proceedings in case of settlement ~~or for other reasons~~. In the event of ~~such~~ a discontinuation of the arbitral proceedings, the fees of the arbitral tribunal may be less than the minimum amount resulting from Appendix B (Schedule of ~~the~~ Costs ~~of Arbitration~~).
2. The fees of the arbitral tribunal shall be determined in conformity with Appendix B (Schedule of the Costs of Arbitration).	2. The fees and expenses of the arbitral tribunal shall be determined in accordance with Appendix B (Schedule of ~~the~~ Costs ~~of Arbitration~~).

Swiss Rules of International Arbitration Version 2004	Swiss Rules of International Arbitration Revision 2012
3. The arbitral tribunal shall decide on the allocation of the fees among its members. As a rule, the Chairman shall receive between 40 % and 50 % and each co-arbitrator between 25 % and 30 % of the total fees, in view of the time and efforts spent by each arbitrator.	3. The arbitral tribunal shall decide on the allocation of ~~the~~ its fees among its members. As a rule, the presiding arbitrator ~~Chairman~~ shall receive between 40 % and 50 % and each co-arbitrator between 25 % and 30 % of the total fees, in view of the time and efforts spent by each arbitrator.
Article 40 1. Except as provided in paragraph 2, the costs of arbitration shall in principle be borne by the unsuccessful party. However, the arbitral tribunal may apportion each of such costs between the parties if it determines that apportionment is reasonable, taking into account the circumstances of the case.	**Article 40** 1. Except as provided in Article 40(2), the costs of the arbitration shall in principle be borne by the unsuccessful party. However, the arbitral tribunal may apportion any of the costs of the arbitration among the parties if it determines that such apportionment is reasonable, taking into account the circumstances of the case.
2. With respect to the costs of legal representation and assistance referred to in Article 38, paragraph (e), the arbitral tribunal, taking into account the circumstances of the case, shall be free to determine which party shall bear such costs or may apportion such costs between the parties if it determines that apportionment is reasonable.	2. With respect to the costs of legal representation and assistance referred to in Article 38(e), the arbitral tribunal, taking into account the circumstances of the case, shall be free to determine which party shall bear such costs or may apportion such costs among the parties if it determines that an apportionment is reasonable.
3. When the arbitral tribunal issues an order for the termination of the arbitral proceedings or makes an award on agreed terms, it shall determine the costs of arbitration referred to in Article 38 and Article 39, paragraph 1, in the text of that order or award.	3. If the arbitral tribunal issues an order for the termination of the arbitral proceedings or makes an award on agreed terms, it shall determine the costs of the arbitration referred to in Articles 38 and 39 ~~paragraph 1~~ in the order or award.
4. Before rendering the award, the arbitral tribunal shall submit its draft award to the Chambers for consultation on the decision as to the assessment and apportionment of the costs.	4. Before rendering an award, termination order, or decision on a request under Articles 35 to 37, the arbitral tribunal shall submit ~~its draft award~~ to the Secretariat a draft thereof for approval ~~consultation~~ or

Swiss Rules of International Arbitration Version 2004	**Swiss Rules of International Arbitration Revision 2012**
	adjustment by the Court of the determination on costs made pursuant ~~on the decision as~~ to Articles 38(a) to (c), and (f) and Article 39. ~~the assessment and apportionment of the costs.~~ Any such approval or adjustment shall be binding upon the arbitral tribunal.
5. No additional fees may be charged by an arbitral tribunal for interpretation or correction or completion of its award under Articles 35 to 37.	5. No additional costs ~~fees~~ may be charged by an arbitral tribunal for interpretation, correction, or completion of its award under Articles 35 to 37, unless they are justified by the circumstances.
DEPOSIT OF COSTS **Article 41** 1. The arbitral tribunal, on its establishment, shall request each party to deposit an equal amount as an advance for the costs referred to in Article 38, paragraphs (a), (b), (c) and (f). The arbitral tribunal shall provide a copy of such request for information to the Chambers.	*DEPOSIT OF COSTS* **Article 41** 1. The arbitral tribunal, once constituted, and after consulting with the Court, shall request each party to deposit an equal amount as an advance for the costs referred to in Articles 38(a) to (c) and the Administrative Costs referred to in Article 38(f). Any Provisional Deposit paid by a party in accordance with Appendix B (Schedule of Costs) shall be considered as a partial payment of its deposit. The arbitral tribunal shall provide a copy of such request to the Secretariat.
2. Where a Respondent submits a counterclaim, or it otherwise appears appropriate in the circumstances, the arbitral tribunal may in its discretion establish separate deposits.	2. Where a Respondent submits a counterclaim, or it otherwise appears appropriate in the circumstances, the arbitral tribunal may in its discretion establish separate deposits.
3. During the course of the arbitral proceedings the arbitral tribunal may request supplementary deposits from the parties. The arbitral tribunal shall provide a copy of such request for information to the Chambers.	3. During the course of the arbitral proceedings the arbitral tribunal may, after consulting with the Court, request supplementary deposits from the parties. The arbitral tribunal shall provide a copy of any such request to the Secretariat.

Swiss Rules of International Arbitration Version 2004	**Swiss Rules of International Arbitration Revision 2012**
4. If the required deposits are not paid in full within thirty days after the receipt of the request, the arbitral tribunal shall so inform the parties in order that one or another of them may make the required payment. If such payment is not made, the arbitral tribunal may order the suspension or termination of the arbitral proceedings.	4. If the required deposits are not paid in full within fifteen ~~thirty~~ days after the receipt of the request, the arbitral tribunal shall notify the parties in order that one or more of them may make the required payment. If such payment is not made, the arbitral tribunal may order the suspension or termination of the arbitral proceedings.
5. In its final award, the arbitral tribunal shall render an accounting to the parties of the deposits received. Any unexpended balance shall be returned to the parties.	5. In its final award, the arbitral tribunal shall issue to the parties a statement of account of the deposits received. Any unused amount shall be returned to the parties.
Section V. Expedited Procedure	**Section V. ~~Expedited Procedure~~ Other Provisions**
Article 42 1. If the parties so agree, or if the provisions of Article 42, paragraph 2 are applicable, the arbitral proceedings shall be conducted in accordance with an Expedited Procedure based upon the foregoing provisions of these Rules, subject to the following changes:	*EXPEDITED PROCEDURE* **Article 42** 1. If the parties so agree, or if ~~the provisions of~~ Article 42(2) ~~are~~ is applicable, the arbitral proceedings shall be conducted in accordance with an Expedited Procedure based upon the foregoing provisions of these Rules, subject to the following changes:
(a) The Chambers may shorten the time-limits for the appointment of arbitrators;	~~(a) The Swiss Chambers' Court may shorten the time-limits for the appointment of arbitrators;~~
	(a) The file shall be transmitted to the arbitral tribunal only upon payment of the Provisional Deposit, as required by Section 1.4 of Appendix B (Schedule of Costs);
(b) After the submission of the Answer to the Notice of Arbitration, the parties shall in principle be entitled to submit	(b) After the submission of the Answer to the Notice of Arbitration, the parties shall, as a rule, be entitled to submit

Swiss Rules of International Arbitration Version 2004	**Swiss Rules of International Arbitration Revision 2012**
one Statement of Claim and one Statement of Defence (and Counterclaim) and, where applicable, one Statement of Defence in reply to the Counterclaim;	only a Statement of Claim, a Statement of Defence (and counterclaim) and, where applicable, a Statement of Defence in reply to the counterclaim;
(c) Unless the parties agree that the dispute shall be decided on the basis of documentary evidence only, the arbitral tribunal shall hold a single hearing for the examination of the witnesses and expert witnesses as well as for oral argument;	(c) Unless the parties agree that the dispute shall be decided on the basis of documentary evidence only, the arbitral tribunal shall hold a single hearing for the examination of the witnesses and expert witnesses, as well as for oral argument;
(d) The award shall be made within six months from the date when the Chambers transmitted the file to the arbitral tribunal. In exceptional circumstances, the Chambers may extend this time-limit;	(d) The award shall be made within six months from the date on which the Secretariat transmitted the file to the arbitral tribunal. In exceptional circumstances, the Court may extend this time-limit;
(e) The arbitral tribunal shall state the reasons upon which the award is based in summary form, unless the parties have agreed that no reasons are to be given.	(e) The arbitral tribunal shall state the reasons upon which the award is based in summary form, unless the parties have agreed that no reasons are to be given.
2. The following provisions shall apply to all cases in which the amount in dispute representing the aggregate of the claim and the counterclaim (or any set-off defence) does not exceed CHF 1'000'000 (one million Swiss francs), unless the Chambers decide otherwise taking into account all relevant circumstances:	2. The following provisions shall apply to all cases in which the amount in dispute, representing the aggregate of the claim and the counterclaim (or any set-off defence), does not exceed CHF 1'000'000 (one million Swiss francs), unless the Court decides otherwise, taking into account all relevant circumstances:
(a) The arbitral proceedings shall be conducted in accordance with the Expedited Procedure set forth in Article 42,	(a) The arbitral proceedings shall be conducted in accordance with the Expedited Procedure set forth in Article 42(1);

Swiss Rules of International Arbitration Version 2004	**Swiss Rules of International Arbitration Revision 2012**
paragraph 1;	
(b) The case shall be referred to a sole arbitrator, unless the arbitration agreement provides for a three-member arbitral tribunal;	(b) The case shall be referred to a sole arbitrator, unless the arbitration agreement provides for more than one arbitrator;
(c) If the arbitration agreement provides for a three-member arbitral tribunal, the Chambers shall invite the parties to agree to refer the case to a sole arbitrator. If the parties do not agree to refer the case to a sole arbitrator, the fees of the three arbitrators shall be determined in accordance with Appendix B (Schedule of the Costs of Arbitration), but shall in no event be less than the fees resulting from the hourly rate of Section 2.8 of Appendix B.	(c) If the arbitration agreement provides for an arbitral tribunal composed of more than one arbitrator, the Secretariat shall invite the parties to agree to refer the case to a sole arbitrator. If the parties do not agree to refer the case to a sole arbitrator, the fees of the ~~three~~ arbitrators shall be determined in accordance with Appendix B (Schedule of ~~the~~ Costs ~~of Arbitration~~), but shall in no event be less than the fees resulting from the hourly rate set out in Section 2.8 of Appendix B.
	EMERGENCY RELIEF **Article 43** 1. Unless the parties have agreed otherwise, a party requiring urgent interim measures pursuant to Article 26 before the arbitral tribunal is constituted may submit to the Secretariat an application for emergency relief proceedings (hereinafter the "Application"). In addition to the particulars set out in Articles 3(3)(b) to (e), the Application shall include:
	(a) A statement of the measure(s) sought and the reasons therefor, in particular the reason for the purported urgency;

Swiss Rules of International Arbitration Version 2004	Swiss Rules of International Arbitration Revision 2012
	(b) Comments on the language, the seat of arbitration, and the applicable law; *(c)* Confirmation of payment by check or transfer to the relevant account listed in Appendix A of the Registration Fee and of the deposit for emergency relief proceedings as required by Section 1.6 of Appendix B (Schedule of Costs). 2. As soon as possible after receipt of the Application, the Registration Fee, and the deposit for emergency relief proceedings, the Court shall appoint and transmit the file to a sole emergency arbitrator, unless *(a)* there is manifestly no agreement to arbitrate referring to these Rules, or *(b)* it appears more appropriate to proceed with the constitution of the arbitral tribunal and refer the Application to it. 3. If the Application is submitted before the Notice of Arbitration, the Court shall terminate the emergency relief proceedings if the Notice of Arbitration is not submitted within ten days from the receipt of the Application. In exceptional circumstances, the Court may extend this time limit. 4. Articles 9 to 12 shall apply to the emergency arbitrator, except that the time-limits set out in Articles 11(1) and (2) are shortened to three days. 5. If the parties have not determined the seat of the arbitration, or if the

Swiss Rules of International Arbitration Version 2004	Swiss Rules of International Arbitration Revision 2012
	designation of the seat is unclear or incomplete, the seat of the arbitration for the emergency relief proceedings shall be determined by the Court without prejudice to the determination of the seat of the arbitration pursuant to Article 16(1). 6. The emergency arbitrator may conduct the emergency relief proceedings in such a manner as the emergency arbitrator considers appropriate, taking into account the urgency inherent in such proceedings and ensuring that each party has a reasonable opportunity to be heard on the Application. 7. The decision on the Application shall be made within fifteen days from the date on which the Secretariat transmitted the file to the emergency arbitrator. This period of time may be extended by agreement of the parties or, in appropriate circumstances, by the Court. The decision on the Application may be made even if in the meantime the file has been transmitted to the arbitral tribunal. 8. A decision of the emergency arbitrator shall have the same effects as a decision pursuant to Article 26. Any interim measure granted by the emergency arbitrator may be modified, suspended or terminated by the emergency arbitrator or, after transmission of the file to it, by the arbitral tribunal. 9. The decision on the Application shall include a determination of costs as referred to in Article 38(g). Before rendering the decision on the Application, the emergency arbitrator shall submit to the Secretariat a draft thereof for

Swiss Rules of International Arbitration Version 2004	Swiss Rules of International Arbitration Revision 2012
	approval or adjustment by the Court of the determination of costs. The costs shall be payable out of the deposit for emergency relief proceedings. The determination of costs pursuant to Article 38(d) and (e) and the apportionment of all costs among the parties shall be decided by the arbitral tribunal. If no arbitral tribunal is constituted, the determination of costs pursuant to Article 38(d) and (e) and the apportionment of all costs shall be decided by the emergency arbitrator in a separate award.
	10. Any measure granted by the emergency arbitrator ceases to be binding on the parties either upon the termination of the emergency relief proceedings pursuant to Article 43(3), upon the termination of the arbitral proceedings, or upon the rendering of a final award, unless the arbitral tribunal expressly decides otherwise in the final award.
	11. The emergency arbitrator may not serve as arbitrator in any arbitration relating to the dispute in respect of which the emergency arbitrator has acted, unless otherwise agreed by the parties.
	~~**Section VI. Confidentiality and exclusion of liability**~~
Section VI. Confidentiality and exclusion of liability	
Article 43 1. Unless the parties expressly agree in writing to the contrary, the parties undertake as a general principle to keep confidential all awards and orders as well as all materials submitted by another party in the	*CONFIDENTIALITY* **Article 44** 1. Unless the parties expressly agree in writing to the contrary, the parties undertake to keep confidential all awards and orders as well as all materials submitted by another party in the framework of

Swiss Rules of International Arbitration Version 2004	Swiss Rules of International Arbitration Revision 2012
framework of the arbitral proceedings not otherwise in the public domain, save and to the extent that a disclosure may be required of a party by a legal duty, to protect or pursue a legal right or to enforce or challenge an award in legal proceedings before a judicial authority. This undertaking also applies to the arbitrators, the tribunal-appointed experts, the secretary of the arbitral tribunal and the Chambers.	the arbitral proceedings not ~~otherwise~~ already in the public domain, except and to the extent that a disclosure may be required of a party by a legal duty, to protect or pursue a legal right, or to enforce or challenge an award in legal proceedings before a judicial authority. This undertaking also applies to the arbitrators, the tribunal-appointed experts, the secretary of the arbitral tribunal, the members of the board of directors of the Swiss Chambers' Arbitration Institution, the members of the Court and the Secretariat, and the staff of the individual Chambers.
2. The deliberations of the arbitral tribunal are confidential.	2. The deliberations of the arbitral tribunal are confidential.
3 An award may be published, whether in its entirety or in the form of excerpts or a summary, only under the following conditions:	3. An award or order may be published, whether in its entirety or in the form of excerpts or a summary, only under the following conditions:
(a) A request for publication is addressed to the Chambers;	*(a)* A request for publication is addressed to the Secretariat;
(b) All references to the parties' names are deleted; and	*(b)* All references to the parties' names are deleted; and
(c) No party objects to such publication within the time–limit fixed for that purpose by the Chambers.	*(c)* No party objects to such publication within the time-limit fixed for that purpose by the Secretariat.
Article 44 1. None of the Chambers or their staff, arbitrators, tribunal-appointed experts or the secretary of the arbitral tribunal shall be liable for any act or omission in connection with an arbitration conducted under these Rules, save where the act or omission is shown to constitute deliberate	*EXCLUSION OF LIABILITY* **Article 45** 1. Neither the members of the board of directors of the Swiss Chambers' Arbitration Institution, the members of the Court and the Secretariat, the individual Chambers or their staff, the arbitrators, the tribunal-appointed experts, nor the secretary of the arbitral tribunal shall be liable

Swiss Rules of International Arbitration Version 2004	**Swiss Rules of International Arbitration Revision 2012**
wrongdoing or extremely serious negligence. 2. After the award has been made and the possibilities of correction, interpretation and additional awards referred to in Articles 35 to 37 have lapsed or been exhausted, neither the Chambers nor the arbitrators, the tribunal-appointed experts or the secretary of the arbitral tribunal shall be under an obligation to make statements to any person about any matter concerning the arbitration, nor shall a party seek to make any of these persons a witness in any legal or other proceedings arising out of the arbitration.	for any act or omission in connection with an arbitration conducted under these Rules, except if the act or omission is shown to constitute intentional wrongdoing or gross negligence. 2. After the award or termination order has been made and the possibilities of correction, interpretation and additional awards referred to in Articles 35 to 37 have lapsed or have been exhausted, neither the members of the board of the Swiss Chambers' Arbitration Institution, the members of the Court and the Secretariat, the individual Chambers or their staff, the arbitrators, the tribunal-appointed experts, nor the secretary of the arbitral tribunal shall be under an obligation to make statements to any person about any matter concerning the arbitration. No party shall seek to make any of these persons a witness in any legal or other proceedings arising out of the arbitration.
Appendix B	**Appendix B**
APPENDIX B: Schedule of the Costs of Arbitration (All amounts in this Appendix B are in Swiss francs, hereinafter "CHF") **1. Registration Fee** 1.1 When submitting a Notice of Arbitration, the Claimant shall pay a Registration Fee of • CHF 4'500 for arbitrations where the amount in dispute does not exceed CHF 2'000'000; • CHF 6'000 for arbitrations where the amount in dispute is	**APPENDIX B: Schedule of ~~the~~ Costs ~~of Arbitration~~ (effective as of 1 June 2012)** (All amounts in this Appendix B are in Swiss francs, hereinafter "CHF") **1. Registration Fee and Deposits** 1.1 When submitting a Notice of Arbitration, the Claimant shall pay a non-refundable Registration Fee of • CHF 4'500 for arbitrations where the amount in dispute does not exceed CHF 2'000'000; • CHF 6'000 for arbitrations

Swiss Rules of International Arbitration Version 2004	**Swiss Rules of International Arbitration Revision 2012**
between CHF 2'000'001 and CHF 10'000'000; • CHF 8'000 for arbitrations where the amount in dispute exceeds CHF10'000'000.	where the amount in dispute is between CHF 2'000'001 and CHF 10'000'000; • CHF 8'000 for arbitrations where the amount in dispute exceeds CHF10'000'000.
1.2 If the amount in dispute is not quantified, the Claimant shall pay a Registration Fee of CHF 6'000.	1.2 If the amount in dispute is not quantified, the Claimant shall pay a non-refundable Registration Fee of CHF 6'000.
1.3 If the Claimant fails to pay the Registration Fee, the Chambers shall not proceed with the arbitration.	1.3 The above provisions shall apply to any counterclaim.
1.4 The Registration Fee is not refundable.	~~1.4 The Registration Fee is not refundable~~.
1.5 The above provisions shall apply to any counterclaim.	1.4 Under the Expedited Procedure, upon receipt of the Notice of Arbitration, the Court shall request the Claimant to pay a Provisional Deposit of CHF 5'000. 1.5 If the Registration Fee or any Provisional Deposit is not paid, the arbitration shall not proceed with respect to the related claim(s) or counterclaim(s).
	1.6 A party applying for Emergency Relief shall pay a non-refundable Registration Fee of CHF 4'500 and a deposit as an advance for the costs of the emergency relief proceedings of CHF 20'000 together with the Application. If the Registration Fee and the deposit are not paid, the Court shall not proceed with the emergency relief proceedings.
	1.7 In case of a request for the correction or interpretation of the award, or for an additional award made pursuant to Articles 35, 36 or 37, or where a judicial authority remits an award to the arbitral tribunal, the arbitral tribunal may

Swiss Rules of International Arbitration Version 2004	**Swiss Rules of International Arbitration Revision 2012**
	request a supplementary deposit with prior approval of the Court.
2. Arbitrators' fees and the Chambers' Administrative Costs 2.1 The arbitrators' fees (Article 38, paragraph a) shall cover the activities of the arbitral tribunal from the moment the file is transmitted until the last award.	**2. ~~Arbitrators' f~~Fees and Administrative Costs** 2.1 The ~~arbitrators'~~ fees referred to in Articles 38(a) and (g)) shall cover the activities of the arbitral tribunal and the emergency arbitrator, respectively, from the moment the file is transmitted until the final award, termination order, or decision in emergency relief proceedings.
2.2 Where the amount in dispute exceeds the threshold specified in Section 2.3 of this Appendix B, Administrative Costs shall be payable to the Chambers, in addition to the Registration Fee.	2.2 Where the amount in dispute exceeds the threshold specified in Section 6 of this Appendix B, Administrative Costs shall be payable to the Swiss Chambers' Arbitration Institution, in addition to the Registration Fee.
2.3 As a rule, the arbitrators' fees and the Chambers' Administrative Costs shall be computed on the basis of the following scale, taking into account the criteria of Article 39, paragraph 1:	2.3 As a rule, and except for emergency relief proceedings, the ~~arbitrators'~~ fees of the arbitral tribunal and the ~~Chambers'~~ Administrative Costs shall be computed on the basis of the ~~following~~ scale in Section 6 of this Appendix B, taking into account the criteria of Article 39(1).

Swiss Rules of International Arbitration Version 2004	**Swiss Rules of International Arbitration Revision 2012**

Swiss Rules of International Arbitration Version 2004

Amount in dispute (in Swiss francs)	Fee of Sole Arbitrator[4]		Fee of three-member arbitral tribunal		Administrative Costs fixed by the Chambers
	min.	max.	min.	max.	
up to CHF 300'000	4%	12%	10%	30%	---
CHF 300'001 to CHF 600'000	2%	8%	5%	20%	---
CHF 600'001 to CHF 1'000'000	1.5%	6%	3.75%	15%	---
CHF 1'000'001 to CHF 2'000'000	0.6%	3.6%	1.5%	9%	---
CHF 2'000'001 to CHF 10'000'000	0.38%	1.5%	0.95%	3.75 %	CHF 4'0 +0.2%
CHF 10'000'001 to CHF 20'000'000	0.3%	0.6%	0.75%	1.5%	0.1%
CHF 20'000'001 to CHF 50'000'000	0.1%	0.2%	0.25%	0.5%	0.05%
CHF 50'000'001 to CHF 100'000'000	0.06%	0.18%	0.15%	0.45 %	0.01%
CHF 100'000'001 to CHF 250'000'000	0.02%	0.1%	0.05%	0.25 %	CHF 50'00
over CHF 250'000'000	0.01%	0.06%	0.025 %	0.15 %	CHF 50'00

Swiss Rules of International Arbitration Revision 2012

~~Amount in dispute (in Swiss francs)~~	~~Fee of Sole Arbitrator~~[2]		~~Fee of three-member arbitral tribunal~~		~~Administrative Costs~~[3] ~~fixed by the Chambers~~
	~~min.~~	~~max.~~	~~min.~~	~~max.~~	
~~up to CHF 300'000~~	~~4%~~	~~12%~~	~~10%~~	~~30 %~~	~~---~~
~~CHF 300'001 to CHF 600'000~~	~~2%~~	~~8%~~	~~5%~~	~~20 %~~	~~---~~
~~CHF 600'001 to CHF 1'000'000~~	~~1.5%~~	~~6%~~	~~3.75%~~	~~15 %~~	~~---~~
~~CHF 1'000'001 to CHF 2'000'000~~	~~0.6%~~	~~3.6%~~	~~1.5%~~	~~9%~~	~~---~~
~~CHF 2'000'001 to CHF 10'000'000~~	~~0.38%~~	~~1.5%~~	~~0.95%~~	~~3.75%~~	~~CHF 4'000 +0.2%~~
~~CHF 10'000'001 to CHF 20'000'000~~	~~0.3%~~	~~0.6%~~	~~0.75%~~	~~1.5 %~~	~~0.1%~~
~~CHF 20'000'001 to CHF 50'000'000~~	~~0.1%~~	~~0.2%~~	~~0.25%~~	~~0.5 %~~	~~0.05%~~
~~CHF 50'000'001 to CHF 100'000'000~~	~~0.06%~~	~~0.18%~~	~~0.15%~~	~~0.45%~~	~~0.01%~~
~~CHF 100'000'001 to CHF 250'000'000~~	~~0.02%~~	~~0.1%~~	~~0.05%~~	~~0.25%~~	~~CHF 50'000~~
~~over CHF 250'000'000~~	~~0.01%~~	~~0.06%~~	~~0.025 %~~	~~0.15%~~	~~CHF 50'000~~

Version 2004	Revision 2012
The fees and administrative costs payable for each successive range in this chart are **added together**.	~~The fees and administrative costs payable for each successive range in this chart are **added together**.~~ The fees of the arbitral tribunal, the deposits requested pursuant to Article 41, as well as the ~~Chambers'~~ Administrative Costs may exceed the amounts set out in the scale ~~above~~ only in exceptional circumstances and with prior approval of the Court.
The arbitrators' fees and the Chambers' Administrative Costs may exceed the amounts set out in the scale above only in exceptional circumstances and with prior approval by the Chambers.	
2.4 Claims and counterclaims are added for the determination of the amount in dispute. The same rule	2.4 Claims and counterclaims are added for the determination of the amount in dispute. The same rule applies to set-off defences, unless

[4] ~~*The fees for a sole arbitrator represent 40% of the fees for a three-member arbitral tribunal.*~~

[5] *This is a contribution, in the maximum amount of CHF 50'000, to the Administrative Costs of the Swiss Chambers' Arbitration Institution, in addition to the Registration Fee. In the event of a discontinuation of the arbitral proceedings (Article 39(1)), the Swiss Chambers' Arbitration Institution may, in its discretion, decide not to charge ~~reimburse~~ all or part of the Administrative Costs.*

Swiss Rules of International Arbitration Version 2004	**Swiss Rules of International Arbitration Revision 2012**
applies to set-off defences, unless the arbitral tribunal, after consulting with the parties, concludes that such set-off claims will not require significant additional work.	the arbitral tribunal, after consulting with the parties, concludes that such set-off defences will not require significant additional work.
2.5 Interest claims shall not be taken into account for the calculation of the amount in dispute. However, when the interest claims exceed the amounts claimed in principal, the interest claims alone shall be considered in calculating the amount in dispute.	2.5 Interest claims shall not be taken into account for the calculation of the amount in dispute. However, when the interest claims exceed the amount claimed as principal, the interest claims alone shall be taken into account for the calculation of the amount in dispute.
2.6 Currencies other than the Swiss franc shall be converted into Swiss francs at the average rate of exchange between the date when the Notice of Arbitration is received by the Chambers and the date when the final award is made. For the purpose of determining the Registration Fee under Section 1 of this Appendix B, the rate of exchange shall be that of the date when the Notice of Arbitration is received by the Chambers.	2.6 Amounts in currencies other than the Swiss franc shall be converted into Swiss francs at the ~~average~~ rate of exchange ~~between the date~~ applicable at the time the Notice of Arbitration is received by the Secretariat ~~and the date when the final award is made. For the purpose of determining the Registration Fee under Section 1 of this Appendix B, the rate of exchange shall be that of the date when the Notice of Arbitration is received by the Swiss Chambers' Court~~ or at the time any new claim, counterclaim, set-off defence or amendment to a claim or defence is filed.
2.7 If the amount in dispute is not quantified, the Arbitrators' fees and the Chambers' Administrative costs shall be fixed by the arbitral tribunal, taking into account all relevant circumstances.	2.7 If the amount in dispute is not quantified, the ~~Arbitrators'~~ fees of the arbitral tribunal and the ~~Chambers'~~ Administrative Costs shall be determined ~~fixed~~ by the arbitral tribunal, taking into account all relevant circumstances.
2.8 Where the parties do not agree to refer the case to a Sole arbitrator as provided for by Article 42, paragraph 2 (Expedited Procedure), the fees of the three arbitrators shall be	2.8 Where the parties do not agree to refer the case to a sole arbitrator as provided for by Article 42(2) (Expedited Procedure), the fees of the ~~three~~ arbitrators shall be

Swiss Rules of International Arbitration Version 2004	**Swiss Rules of International Arbitration Revision 2012**
determined in accordance with the above Schedule of the Costs of Arbitration but shall in no event be less than the fees resulting from the application of an hourly rate of CHF 350 (three hundred fifty Swiss francs).	determined in accordance with the ~~above~~ scale in Section 6 of this Appendix B~~Schedule of the Costs of Arbitration~~, but shall ~~in no event~~ not be less than the fees resulting from the application of an hourly rate of CHF 350 (three hundred fifty Swiss francs) for the arbitrators. 2.9 The fees of the emergency arbitrator shall range from CHF 2'000 to CHF 20'000. They may exceed CHF 20'000 only in exceptional circumstances and with the approval of the Court.
3. Arbitrators' expenses The expenses of the arbitrators shall relate to the actual disbursements for the arbitration, such as expenses relating to: travel (first class airfare accepted only for distances exceeding 4000 kilometres), accommodation, meals (if in home city, only meals among arbitrators are taken into account), taxi, communications costs, and any other costs related to the conduct of the proceedings (including rental of hearing rooms, court reporting services, interpreters, etc.). The Chambers may issue general guidelines to the arbitrators for the accounting of their expenses.	**3. Expenses** The expenses of the arbitral tribunal and the emergency arbitrator shall cover ~~the actual~~ their reasonable disbursements for the arbitration, such as expenses for travel, ~~(first business class airfare or first class train fare; standard taxi fare for transport to and from airport and/or train station; flat rate of CHF 1.- for every kilometre driven by private car plus all necessary parking and toll charges incurred) accepted only for distances exceeding 4000 kilometres),~~ accommodation, meals, ~~(if in home city only meals among arbitrators are taken into account), taxi, communications costs,~~ and any other costs related to the conduct of the proceedings ~~(such as rental of hearing rooms, court reporting services, interpreters, etc.)~~. The Court shall issue general guidelines ~~to the arbitrators~~ for the accounting of such expenses.[6]

[6] The guidelines are available at www.swissarbitration.org

Swiss Rules of International Arbitration Version 2004	**Swiss Rules of International Arbitration Revision 2012**
4. Income earned on deposits made by the parties In consultation with the parties, the arbitral tribunal may invest the deposits made by the parties, taking into account market conditions and criteria of prudent and secure investment. When deciding whether to make such investments, the arbitral tribunal shall also have due regard to the possible need to make the deposited funds available immediately. Any income earned shall be included in the final computation of the costs of the arbitration in favour of the party or parties having made the deposit or deposits so invested.	**4. ~~Income earned on~~ Administration of Deposits ~~made by the parties~~** ~~In consultation with the parties, the arbitral tribunal may invest the deposits made by the parties, taking into account market conditions and criteria of prudent and secure investment. When deciding whether to make such investments, the arbitral tribunal shall also have due regard to the possible need to make the deposited funds available immediately. Any income earned shall be included in the final computation of the costs of the arbitration in favour of the party or parties having made the deposit or deposits so invested.~~ 4.1 The Secretariat, or, if so requested by the Secretariat, the arbitral tribunal, is to hold the deposits to be paid by the parties in a separate bank account, which is solely used for, and clearly identified as, relating to the arbitral proceedings in question. 4.2 With the approval of the Court, part of the deposits may from time to time be released to each member of the arbitral tribunal as an advance on costs, as the arbitration progresses. **5. Taxes and Charges Applicable to Fees** Amounts payable to the arbitral tribunal or emergency arbitrator do not include any possible value added taxes (VAT) or other taxes or charges that may be applicable to the fees of a member of the arbitral tribunal or emergency arbitrator.

Swiss Rules of International Arbitration Version 2004	Swiss Rules of International Arbitration Revision 2012
	Parties have a duty to pay any such taxes or charges. The recovery of any such taxes or charges is a matter solely between each member of the arbitral tribunal, or the emergency arbitrator, on the one hand, and the parties on the other.

6. Scale of Arbitrator's Fees and Administrative Costs

6.1 Sole Arbitrator

Amount in dispute (in Swiss francs)	**Administrative costs**	**Sole Arbitrator**	
		Minimum	Maximum
0 – 300'000	–	4% of amount	12% of amount
300'001 – 600'000	–	12'000 + 2% of amount over 300'000	36'000 + 8% of amount over 300'000
600'001 – 1'000'000	–	18'000 + 1.5% of amount over 600'000	60'000 + 6% of amount over 600'000
1'000'001 – 2'000'000	–	24'000 + 0.6% of amount over 1'000'000	84'000 + 3.6% of amount over 1'000'000
2'000'001 – 10'000'000	4'000 + 0.2% of amount over 2'000'000	30'000 + 0.38% of amount over 2'000'000	120'000 + 1.5% of amount over 2'000'000
10'000'001 – 20'000'000	20'000 + 0.1% of amount over 10'000'000	60'400 + 0.3% of amount over 10'000'000	240'000 + 0.6% of amount over 10'000'000
20'000'001 – 50'000'000	30'000 + 0.05% of amount over 20'000'000	90'400 + 0.1% of amount over 20'000'000	300'000 + 0.2% of amount over 20'000'000

50'000'001 – 100'000'000	45'000 + 0.01% of amount over 50'000'000	120'400 + 0.06% of amount over 50'000'000	360'000 + 0.18% of amount over 50'000'000
100'000'001 – 250'000'000	50'000	150'400 + 0.02% of amount over 100'000'000	450'000 + 0,1% of amount over 100'000'000
> 250'000'000	50'000	180'400 + 0.01% of amount over 250'000'000	600'000 + 0.06% of amount over 250'000'000

6.2 Three Arbitrators[7]

Amount in dispute (in Swiss francs)	**Administrative costs**	**Three-member arbitral tribunal**	
		Minimum	Maximum
0 – 300'000	–	10% of amount	30% of amount
300'001 – 600'000	–	30'000 + 5% of amount over 300'000	90'000 + 20% of amount over 300'000
600'001 – 1'000'000	–	45'000 + 3.75% of amount over 600'000	150'000 + 15% of amount over 600'000
1'000'001 – 2'000'000	–	60'000 + 1.5% of amount over 1'000'000	210'000 + 9% of amount over 1'000'000
2'000'001 – 10'000'000	4'000 + 0.2% of amount over 2'000'000	75'000 + 0.95% of amount over 2'000'000	300'000 + 3.75% of amount over 2'000'000
10'000'001 – 20'000'000	20'000 + 0.1% of amount over 10'000'000	151'000 + 0.75% of amount over 10'000'000	600'000 + 1.5% of amount over 10'000'000
20'000'001 – 50'000'000	30'000 + 0.05% of amount over 20'000'000	226'000 + 0.25% of amount over 20'000'000	750'000 + 0.5% of amount over 20'000'000

[7] The fees of an arbitral tribunal consisting of more than one arbitrator represent those of a sole arbitrator plus 75 % for each additional arbitrator, i.e. 250% of the fees of a sole arbitrator for a three-member tribunal.

50'000'001 – 100'000'000	45'000 + 0.01% of amount over 50'000'000	301'000 + 0.15% of amount over 50'000'000	900'000 + 0.45% of amount over 50'000'000
100'000'001 – 250'000'000	50'000	376'000 + 0.05% of amount over 100'000'000	1'125'000 + 0,25% of amount over 100'000'000
> 250'000'000	50'000	451'000 + 0.025% of amount over 250'000'000	1'500'000 + 0.15% of amount over 250'000'000

Appendix C:

Swiss Rules of International Arbitration (Swiss Rules)

Q1 Do you have practical experience with the SRIA?

Answered: 53 Skipped: 2

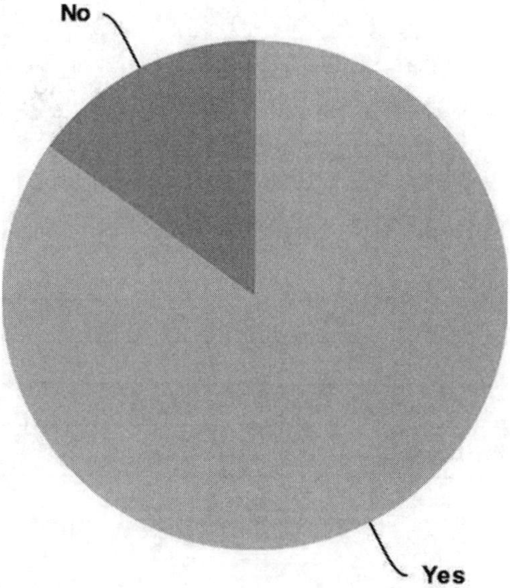

Answer Choices	Responses	
Yes	**84.91%**	45
No	**15.09%**	8
Total		**53**

Q2 In which role did you gain your experience with the SRIA?

Answered: 43 Skipped: 12

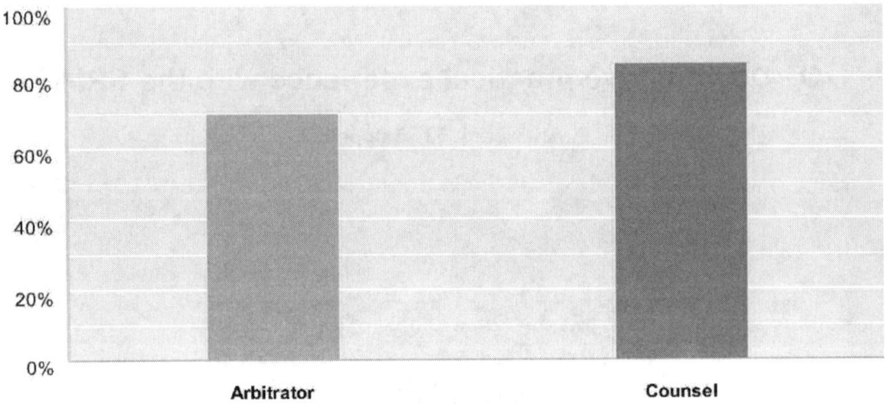

Answer Choices	Responses	
Arbitrator	**69.77%**	30
Counsel	**83.72%**	36
Total Respondents: 43		

#	other
1	Secretary to the Tribunal
2	Member of a local Arbitration committee
3	and also as advisor to major international companies when negotiating international agreements
4	Interpreter supplier
5	and as Secretary
6	Member of the Arbitration Court
7	Secretary
8	Secretary to Tribunal
9	admin secretary

Q3 In how many cases conducted under the SRIA were you involved either as arbitrator or as counsel?

Answered: 49 Skipped: 6

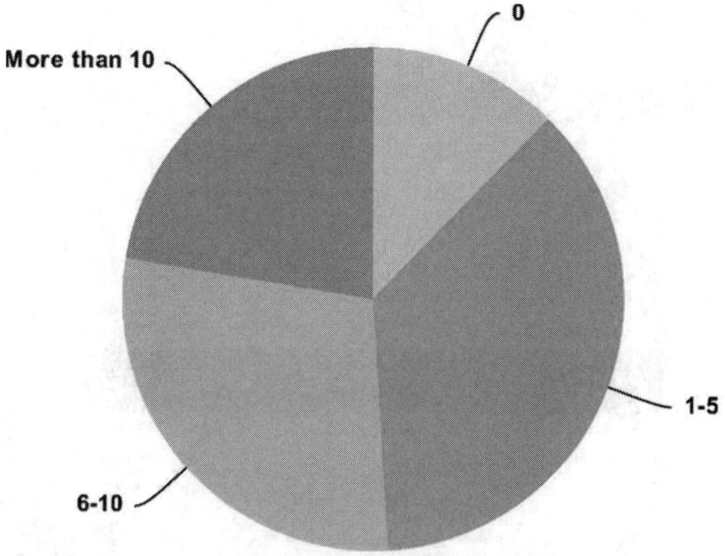

Answer Choices	Responses	
0	**12.24%**	6
1-5	**36.73%**	18
6-10	**28.57%**	14
More than 10	**22.45%**	11
Total		**49**

Q4 How did you learn about the SRIA?

Answered: 47 Skipped: 8

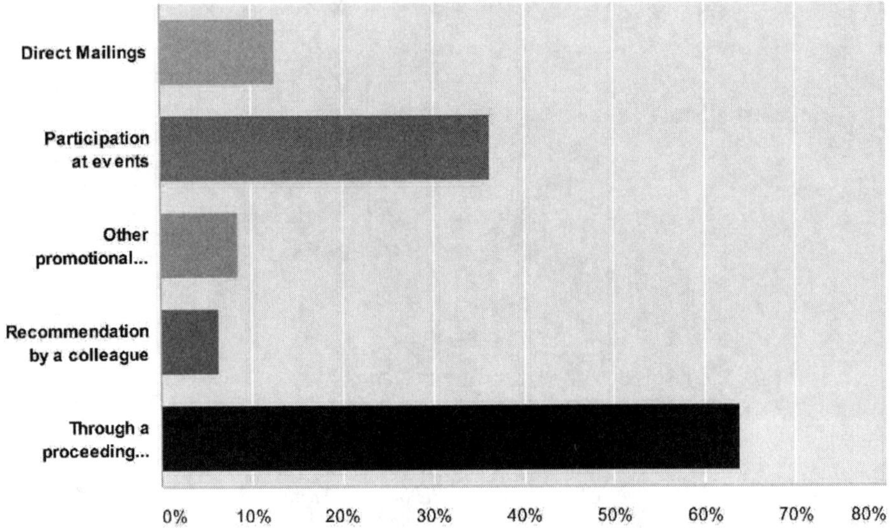

Answer Choices	Responses	
Direct Mailings	**12.77%**	6
Participation at events	**36.17%**	17
Other promotional activities	**8.51%**	4
Recommendation by a colleague	**6.38%**	3
Through a proceeding under the SRIA in which I was involved	**63.83%**	30
Total Respondents: 47		

Q5 In which of the following situations would you recommend the inclusion of the SRIA in an arbitration clause?

Answered: 43 Skipped: 12

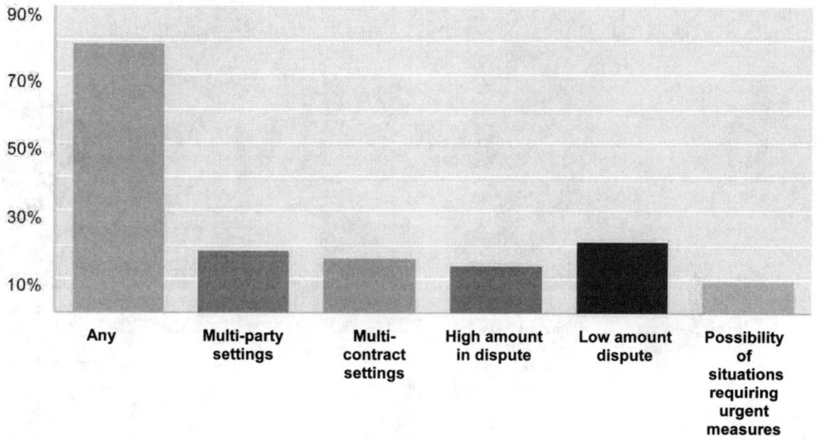

Answer Choices	Responses	
Any	**79.07%**	34
Multi-party settings	**18.60%**	8
Multi-contract settings	**16.28%**	7
High amount in dispute	**13.95%**	6
Low amount in dispute	**20.93%**	9
Possibility of situations requiring urgent measures	**9.30%**	4
Total Respondents: 43		

Q6 Which advantages distinguish the SRIA from other institutional rules?

Answered: 43 Skipped: 12

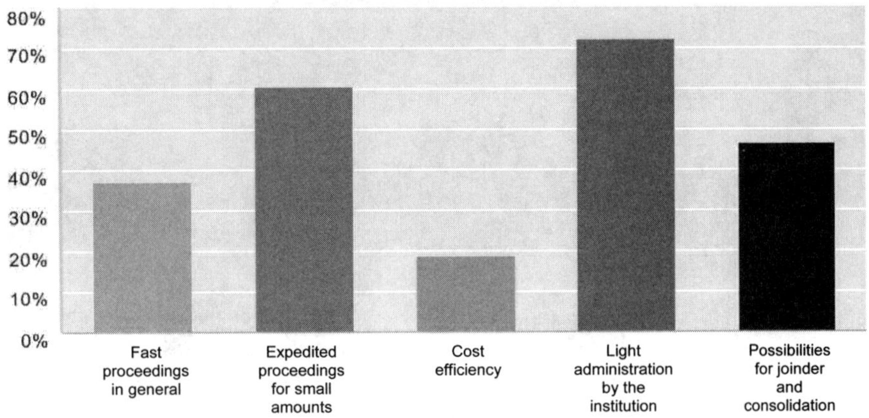

Answer Choices	Responses	
Fast proceedings in general	**37.21%**	16
Expedited proceedings for small amounts in dispute	**60.47%**	26
Cost efficiency	**18.60%**	8
"Light administration" by the institution	**72.09%**	31
Possibilities for joinder and consolidation in complex arbitrations	**46.51%**	20
Total Respondents: 43		

#	other
1	Default nominating procedure provides for co-arbitrators to nominate presiding arbitrator (contrary to ICC).

Q7 Do you see any disadvantages of the SRIA that might lead parties to choose another set of arbitration rules?

Answered: 23 Skipped: 32

#	Responses
1	In a dispute involving a Swiss and a non-Swiss party, the non-Swiss party may not want to elect the Swiss Rules because of the perceived Swiss link.
2	Lack of familiarity with SRIA - "local flavour" of Swiss Rules
3	Costs are higher than under other Rules. However, costs of other institutions are too low (for arbitrators)
4	high costs
5	Not really
6	Costs; 45 day deadline for submissions (for Respondents)
7	No.
8	In case of non-participating/recalcitrant parties, a more "heavy" administration can be helpful.
9	Some parties prefer the lower cost and higher level of scrutiny offered by the ICC; some prefer rules that specifically exclude discovery-like procedures.
10	The Swiss Rules are not sufficiently well-known. More promotion might be fruitful
11	No
12	Too light administration by the institution
13	Lack of brand recognition.
14	cost
15	Lack of centralised body; unclear institution No administration of funds by the institution
16	less supervision compared to ICC. Parties, counsel and arbitrators should be more experienced
17	Costs are cumbersome with interaction between arbitral tribunal and institution. Swiss banks make it difficult to administer advances by the arbitral tribunal. The institution does not administer advances.
18	Art. 21.5
19	No
20	May be considered as "local" rules as compared to ICC
21	"Swiss" in the name, i.e. not neutral when there is a Swiss party involved.
22	Costs
23	no

Q8 Which of the following "special features" of the Swiss Rules do you value most?

Answered: 44 Skipped: 11

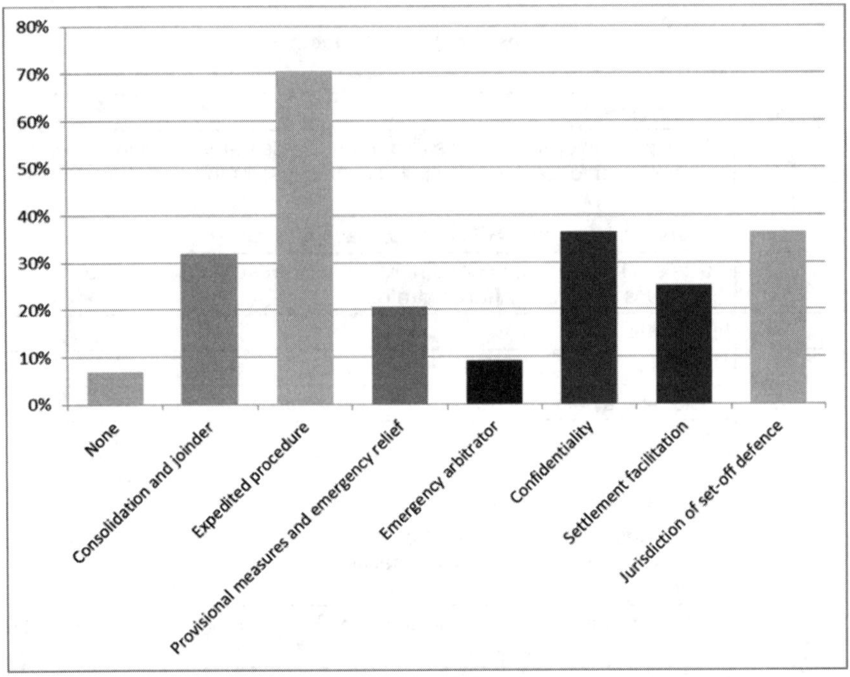

Answer Choices	Responses	
None	**6.82%**	3
Possibilities of consolidation and joinder in complex arbitration settings (Art. 4)	**31.82%**	14
Expedited procedure for small amounts in dispute (Art. 42)	**70.45%**	31
Possibilities to grant provisional measures and emergency relief (Art. 43)	**20.45%**	9
Possibility of appointment of an emergency arbitrator (Art. 43)	**9.09%**	4
Confidentiality of the proceedings (Art. 44)	**36.36%**	16
Possibility to opt for a settlement faciliation conducted by the arbitral tribunal (Art. 15.8)	**25.00%**	11
Jurisdiction of set-off defence (Art. 21.5)	**36.36%**	16
Total Respondents: 44		

Q9 Is the fee structure of the SRIA competitive compared to other arbitration rules?

Answered: 42 Skipped: 13

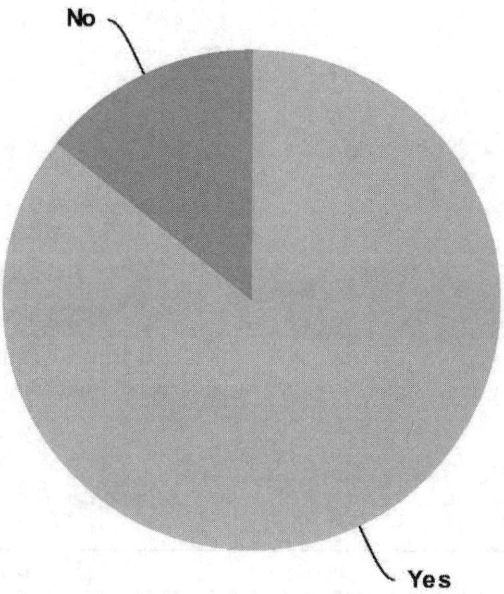

Answer Choices	Responses	
Yes	85.71%	36
No	14.29%	6
Total		42

Q10 How do you perceive the involvement of the Swiss Chambers' Arbitration Institution in proceedings under the SRIA?

Answered: 41 Skipped: 14

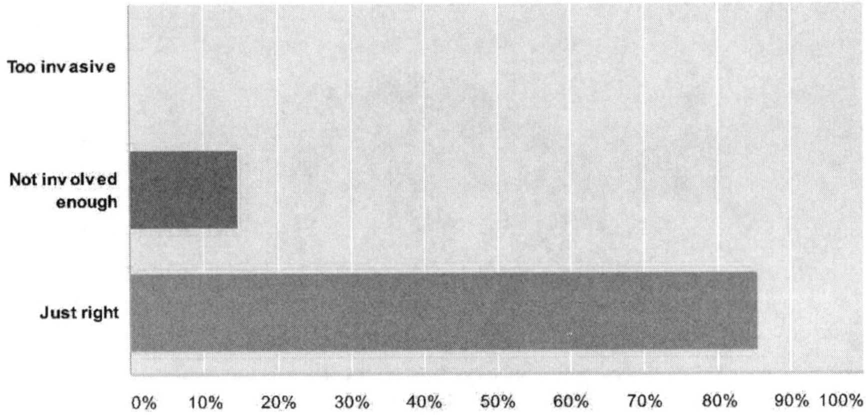

Answer Choices	Responses	
Too invasive	**0.00%**	0
Not involved enough	**14.63%**	6
Just right	**85.37%**	35
Total Respondents: 41		

Q11 Would you welcome published reasons by the Court of decisions on challenges to arbitrators?

Answered: 44 Skipped: 11

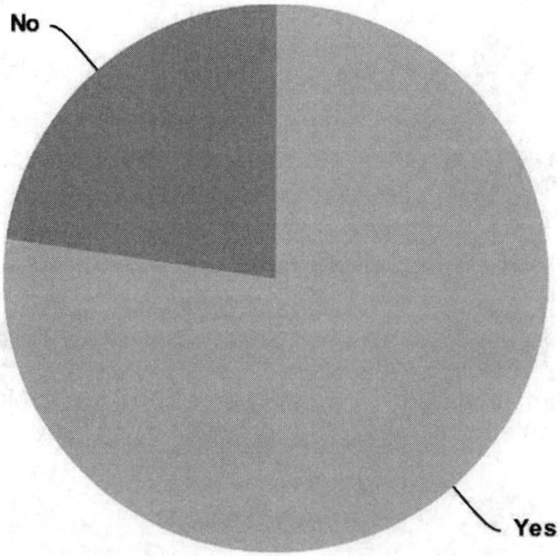

Answer Choices	Responses	
Yes	**77.27%**	34
No	**22.73%**	10
Total		**44**

Q12 Which of the following features should be considered to be included in a future revision of the SRIA?

Answered: 25 Skipped: 30

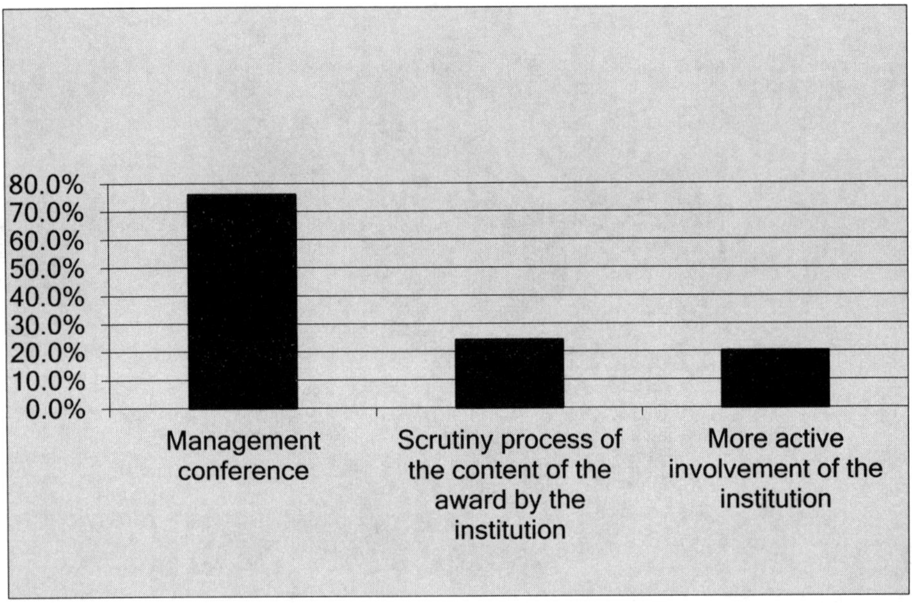

Answer Choices	Responses	
Management conference	**76.00%**	19
Scrutiny process of the content of the award by the institution	**24.00%**	6
More active involvement of the institution	**20.00%**	5
Total Respondents: 25		

#	other
1	None of them
2	administration of the funds by the institution (not the arbitrators)
3	see above on advances
4	Expedited proceedings for higher value disputes.
5	None of the above

Q13 Would you welcome more promotion and marketing efforts by the Swiss Chambers' Arbitration Institution?

Answered: 44 Skipped: 11

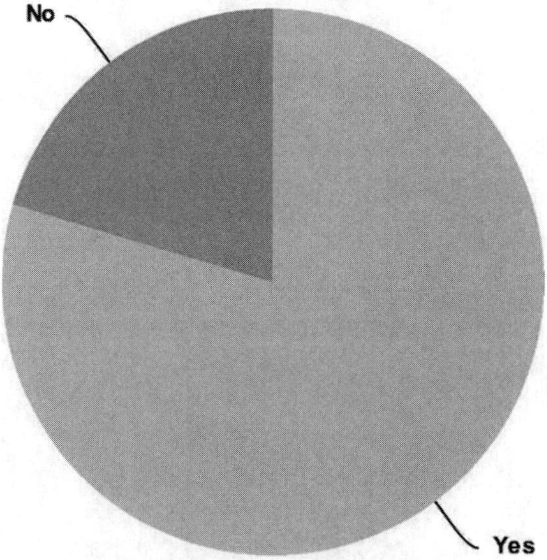

Answer Choices	Responses	
Yes	**79.55%**	35
No	**20.45%**	9
Total		**44**

Q14 Should the Swiss Chambers' Arbitration Institution also offer educational seminars, workshops and/or conferences?

Answered: 44 Skipped: 11

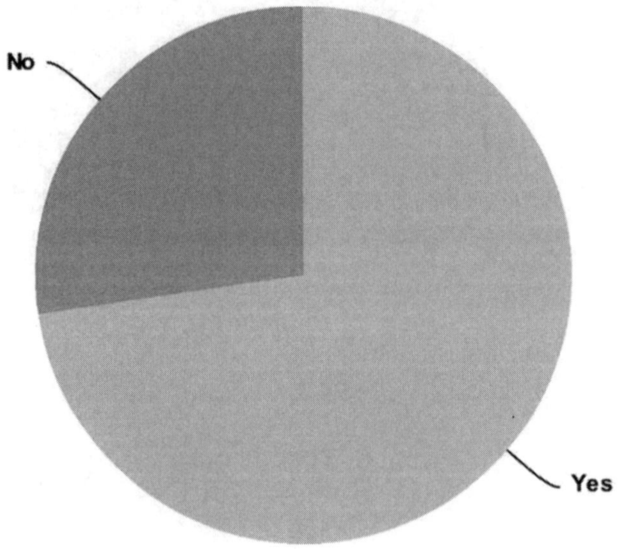

Answer Choices	Responses	
Yes	**72.73%**	32
No	**27.27%**	12
Total		**44**

Q15 How many such events would you consider to be needed?

Answered: 35 Skipped: 20

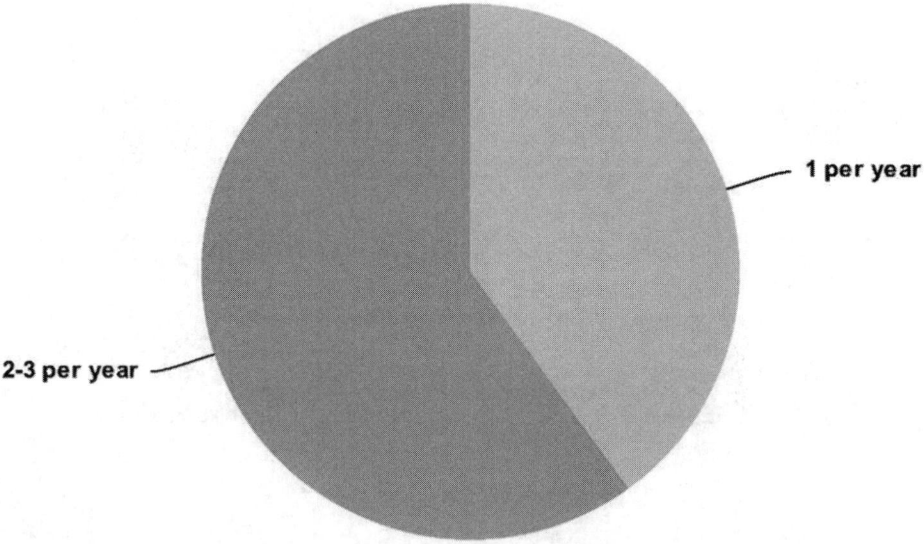

Answer Choices	Responses	
1 per year	**40.00%**	14
2-3 per year	**60.00%**	21
More than 3 per year	**0.00%**	0
Total		**35**

Q16 In which region should such events be organized?

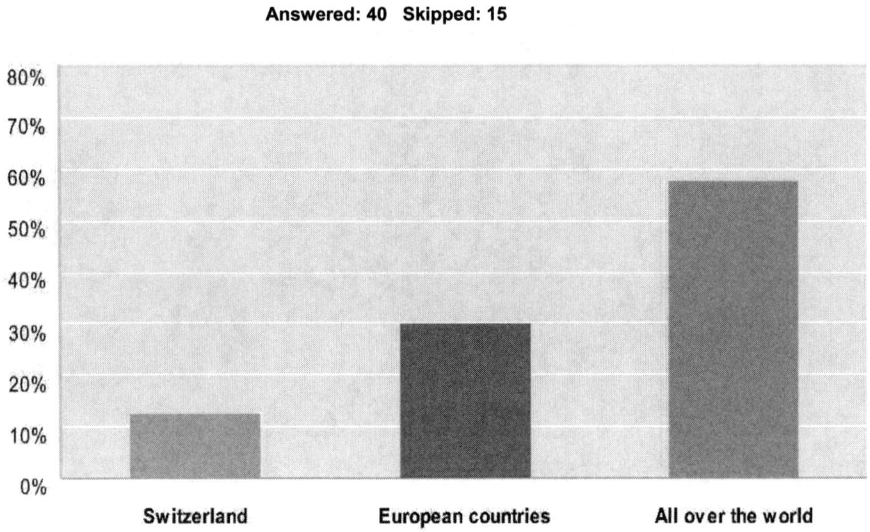

Answer Choices	Responses	
Switzerland	**12.50%**	5
European countries	**30.00%**	12
All over the world	**57.50%**	23
Total		**40**